The Pirates Unraveled

ALSO OF INTEREST

Edited by Angelo J. Louisa *and* David Cicotello:
*Mysteries from Baseball's Past: Investigations of
Nine Unsettled Questions* (McFarland, 2010)

Edited by David Cicotello *and* Angelo J. Louisa:
*Forbes Field: Essays and Memories of the Pirates'
Historic Ballpark, 1909–1971* (McFarland, 2007)

The Pirates Unraveled

Pittsburgh's 1926 Season

Angelo J. Louisa

Foreword by
David C. Ogden

McFarland & Company, Inc., Publishers
Jefferson, North Carolina

LIBRARY OF CONGRESS CATALOGUING-IN-PUBLICATION DATA [new form]

Names: Louisa, Angelo Joseph, author.
Title: The Pirates unraveled : Pittsburgh's 1926 season / Angelo J. Louisa ; foreword by David C. Ogden.
Description: Jefferson, North Carolina : McFarland & Company, Inc., Publishers, 2015. | Includes bibliographical references and index.
Identifiers: LCCN 2015043974 | ISBN 9780786470709 (softcover : acid free paper)
Subjects: LCSH: Pittsburgh Pirates (Baseball team)—History—20th century.
Classification: LCC GV875.P5 L68 2015 | DDC 796.357/640974886—dc23
LC record available at http://lccn.loc.gov/2015043974

BRITISH LIBRARY CATALOGUING DATA ARE AVAILABLE

ISBN (print) 978-0-7864-7070-9
ISBN (ebook) 978-1-4766-2254-5

© 2015 Angelo J. Louisa. All rights reserved

No part of this book may be reproduced or transmitted in any form or by any means, electronic or mechanical, including photocopying or recording, or by any information storage and retrieval system, without permission in writing from the publisher.

On the cover: Forbes Field, Pittsburgh, 1925 (Library of Congress); unraveled baseball (Erik Clegg/Thinkstock)

Printed in the United States of America

McFarland & Company, Inc., Publishers
 Box 611, Jefferson, North Carolina 28640
  www.mcfarlandpub.com

In memory of my favorite uncle,
William T. Gasper, who taught me to
always give credit where credit is due

Table of Contents

Foreword by David C. Ogden   1
Acknowledgments   3
Introduction: Setting the Record Straight   9

One. Colorful, Competitive and Consistently Falling Short   13
Two. The Return of Fred Clarke   46
Three. High Expectations, Disappointing Results   87
Four. The ABC Affair   123
Five. What Becomes of the Brokenhearted   163
Six. Making Sense of It All   207

Key to the Abbreviations Used in the Appendices   233
Appendix A: Biographical Information for the 1926 Pirates   234
Appendix B: Offensive Statistics   249
Appendix C: Pitching Statistics   254
Appendix D: Fielding Statistics   257
Chapter Notes   261
Bibliography   301
Index   313

Foreword

by David C. Ogden

Having been a lifelong Pittsburgh Pirate fan and, for the past 25 years, a serious baseball researcher, it is sometimes difficult for me to separate my scientific interest in the cultural nuances of baseball from my child-like wonder as a devout follower of the sport. As with others enthralled with the national pastime and a particular team, I find myself catching my breath in anticipation of what I will see in the box scores on any given morning (but especially on those mornings when I did not hear the results of the previous night's Pirate game).

Despite 20 consecutive losing seasons, the Bucs still claim a place in my heart and always will. To watch players like Andrew McCutchen, Starling Marte, and Josh Harrison become the nucleus of a winning team is pure joy. But what frames that joy and makes it even more profound is the rich heritage that the Pirates have. Roberto Clemente, Ralph Kiner, Paul and Lloyd Waner, and Honus Wagner forged a legacy throughout the decades that has been passed from one generation of fans to the next.

Angelo Louisa's book on the 1926 Buccos adds to that legacy not just by narrating the on-the-field accomplishments and failures of the players but also by focusing on the relationships among those players and their manager and coaches. Through his copiously documented study, Louisa shows that a baseball team is more than just the sum of its parts and is not isolated from its social and cultural surroundings.

Central to the account is the question of how a club that was the defending National League and World Series champion and was expected by the majority of preseason forecasters to dominate the senior circuit in 1926 could finish in third place. This book answers that question from two angles. First, by carefully examining countless articles and columns from the five mainstream Pittsburgh newspapers—not just those that have been digitized and are easily accessed online—as well as a plethora of other sources, Louisa dispels the traditional account that lays much of the blame on Fred Clarke and the ramifications of the ABC Affair and shows the effect that illnesses, injuries, scheduling, and weather had on the team's lack of success.

And second, Louisa uses statistics to define both the team and the season. His analysis of the Pirates' performance and that of the Cardinals and the Reds, the two clubs that finished ahead of the Bucs, offers some surprises and provides further insight into the team's fortunes.

But this book is not just a snapshot of one year in a baseball franchise's history. It is a detailed picture of the dynamics of a team struggling to live up to the expectations thrust upon it and the way the media influenced the lives of certain members of that team, a microcosm of what is often seen in the world of sports today.

Thus, *The Pirates Unraveled: Pittsburgh's 1926 Season* is a must read for any Pirate fan. It appeals to me as an ardent follower of the Pirates and it also appeals to me as a baseball scholar. Angelo Louisa is able to bridge those interests by writing a compelling account of a team that seemed slated for another World Series appearance but ended up breaking the hearts of its fans.

David C. Ogden is a professor in the School of Communication at the University of Nebraska–Omaha and a member of the Society for American Baseball Research. He is co-editor of three books on sports history, and he has published articles in *NINE: A Journal of Baseball History & Culture*, *Journal of Leisure Research*, *Journal of Black Studies*, and *Great Plains Research*.

Acknowledgments

Just as a manager needs a good team to win ballgames, an author needs a good team to produce a book. Fortunately for me, I was blessed with the following all-star team, a group of people who I cannot thank enough.

Jean Alicz, the registrar of Ottawa Township High School in Ottawa, Illinois, who examined the records of her school to see if Tom Sheehan had ever been a student there and who recommended that I talk with Susan MacDonald.

Kerri Bobish, the assistant EMIS coordinator for the Buckeye Local School District in Dillonvale, Ohio, who checked the available sources for all the schools in her district but could not find any mention of Jack Onslow.

Terri Bone, the assistant principal of Sheridan High School in Sheridan, Arkansas, who searched for evidence that Earl Smith had been a student at Sheridan and who forwarded my query about Smith to Roy L. Wilson.

Robert L. Bromfield, associate dean and registrar of the University of San Francisco in San Francisco, California, who sent my inquiry about Ray Kremer to Fr. Michael Kotlanger, SJ.

Margaret Donahoe Burroughs, Fred Clarke's granddaughter, who graciously entertained my wife and me while we interviewed her, showed us some of her grandfather's memorabilia, and shared with us her knowledge about the Clarke family.

Gabriel Chadwick, secretary in Student Services for the Cecil County Public Schools in Elkton, Maryland, who attempted to help me find out if Red Oldham had been educated at one of the public schools in her area.

Ralph Christian, the historian at the State Historical Society of Iowa in Des Moines, Iowa, who allowed me to read his paper on Ed Barrow and who patiently answered my questions about Fred Clarke.

David Cicotello, my good friend and editing partner, who not only proofread the draft of this book and offered a number of helpful suggestions, but who also was a supportive sounding board for my ideas about the 1926 Pirates and the ABC Affair and who assisted me in gathering information on Fred Clarke in the Winfield area of Kansas.

S. Kelly Cragg, the principal of Corry High School in Corry, Pennsylvania, who provided me with the correct name of his school when Carmen Hill had been a student there.

Carol Donache, the librarian of the Historical Society of Cecil County in Elkton, Maryland, who, while looking for evidence that Red Oldham had attended high school in Cecil County, discovered that he probably had gone to high school in Pennsylvania.

Daniel Donahoe, Fred Clarke's grandson, who answered my questions about his grandparents, encouraged me to write a book about his grandfather, and put me in touch with his sister, Margaret Donahoe Burroughs.

Peter Elwell, a librarian assistant in the Social Sciences Department of the Cleveland Public Library in Cleveland, Ohio, who made available for me Eugene C. Murdock's interviews of Carmen Hill and Eddie Moore.

T. S. Flynn, the great-great-nephew of Tom Sheehan, who provided information about his relative and who gave me a copy of an article that he had written about him.

Bill Francis, a library associate of and my guardian angel at the National Baseball Hall of Fame Library in Cooperstown, New York, who photocopied or had photocopied for me all but one of the player files used to write this book.

Jo Ann Gardner, a volunteer at the Historical Society of Cecil County in Elkton, Maryland, who assisted Carol Donache in looking for evidence about Red Oldham's education.

Jenny Gibson, the student data coordinator of the Harrison Hills City School District in Cadiz, Ohio, who discovered the correct name of Scio School in the early 1900s and that Jack Onslow had attended that school during the 1900–1901 and 1901–1902 academic years.

Audrey Glassman, the registrar of the Fordham University School of Law in New York, New York, who confirmed that Bud Culloton had received a law degree from Fordham.

Nancy Snell Griffith, the former Archives and Special Collections librarian at Presbyterian College in Clinton, South Carolina, who rechecked her files on Roy Mahaffey to see if she had any details on his schooling.

Kevin Hartley, the athletic director of Wichita High School East in Wichita, Kansas, who tried to help me determine if Fred Brickell had been a student at his school.

John Horne, Patricia Kelly's successor as the photograph archivist of the National Baseball Hall of Fame and Museum in Cooperstown, New York, who equalled his predecessor in the speedy delivery of the images that I had requested.

Dee Ann Horstman, the curator of the Scio Historical Museum in Scio, Ohio, who explained the Scio school system to me, made me aware of the existence of Jack Onslow's niece, Nancy Purviance, and sent me Ms. Purviance's telephone number.

Karen Hughes, the deputy register of deeds at the Cowley County Register of Deeds Office in Winfield, Kansas, who went above and beyond the call of duty to find the deeds for W. D. Clarke's property in Cowley County and two deeds for the Little Pirate Ranch.

Deborah Jayne, the director of membership and events for the Society for American Baseball Research (SABR) in Phoenix, Arizona, who provided me with reels of microfilm in a timely fashion and who handled all my requests in a courteous manner.

Kyle Jones, the assistant dean and dean of students of the University of Southern California (USC) Gould School of Law in Los Angeles, California, who informed me that the files in his office did not go back far enough to verify that Johnny Rawlings had attended law school at USC and who gave me Tom Tomlinson's e-mail address.

Patrice Kane, the head of Archives and Special Collections at Fordham University in New York, New York, who confirmed that Bud Culloton had received his undergraduate degree from Fordham.

Patricia Kelly, the photograph archivist of the National Baseball Hall of Fame and Museum in Cooperstown, New York, who assisted me in obtaining images from baseball's pantheon.

Kathleen Kist, the principal of North East High School in North East, Maryland, who found out that Red Oldham had not been a student at her school.

Fr. Michael Kotlanger, SJ, the archivist for the University of San Francisco in San Francisco, California, who discovered evidence of Ray Kremer's enrollment at St. Ignatius College.

Anna M. Louisa, my beloved mother, who sparked my interest in baseball when I was four years old and who, despite being in her 90s and having memory problems, allowed me to bore her with my reading of various sections of the book.

Pamela A. Louisa, my wife, lover, best friend, research assistant, secretary, computer expert, cook, financial benefactor, psychiatrist, travel companion, and co-caregiver, who helped me to track down valuable details, proofread and formatted multiple drafts of the book, and lifted my spirits when I got frustrated or depressed.

Susan MacDonald, the secretary to the superintendent of Ottawa Township High School in Ottawa, Illinois, who searched the files of her school to see if Tom Sheehan had attended it and who put me in touch with Carole Nagle.

David Mathis, the superintendent of Grand Ridge Elementary School in

Grand Ridge, Illinois, who discussed Tom Sheehan's schooling with me and who made me aware of the school system in the Grand Ridge area.

Patricia Miller, the director of the Scottdale Public Library in Scottdale, Pennsylvania, who attempted to help me find out if Jack Onslow had gone to school in the Scottdale area.

Beth Moore, a volunteer at the Historical Society of Cecil County in Elkton, Maryland, who assisted Carol Donache in looking for evidence about Red Oldham's education.

Anne Elise Morris, the president of the Wilkinsburg Historical Society in Pittsburgh, Pennsylvania, who provided me with information on Bill McKechnie.

Carole Nagle, the great-niece-in-law of Tom Sheehan, who discussed her relative with me and who recommended that I talk with her nephew, T. S. Flynn.

Marisa Novotney, secretary to the principal/athletic director of Streator Township High School in Streator, Illinois, who searched in vain for evidence that Tom Sheehan had attended her school.

Kip P. Nygren, the president of Wyoming Seminary Prep School in Kingston, Pennsylvania, who forwarded my query about Adam Comorosky to John H. Shafer.

David C. Ogden, professor of communication at the University of Nebraska Omaha in Omaha, Nebraska, and the co-editor of three books on baseball history, who took time from his busy schedule to read the manuscript of this book and to write the foreword for it.

Jacob Pomrenke, the web content editor/producer for SABR in Phoenix, Arizona, who sent me the interviews of Charlie Grimm, Art McKennan, and Jimmy Zinn that were conducted by members of SABR's Oral History Research Committee.

David L. Porter, Louis Tuttle Shangle Professor of History at William Penn University in Oskaloosa, Iowa, who responded to my questions about Fred Clarke's education.

Nancy Purviance, the niece of Jack Onslow and the daughter of Jack's brother Eddie, another major leaguer, who told me which school her uncle had attended and who regaled me with some fascinating stories about her interactions with Bill McKechnie, Kenesaw Mountain Landis, and other baseball personages.

Carol Quinn, my wife's and my dear friend, who sacrificed a lot of her time to watch my mother on multiple evenings so that my wife and I could escape to a quiet place to proofread the final draft of the book.

Diane M. Rebar, the information services coordinator for the Hoyt Library in Kingston, Pennsylvania, who looked for information on Adam Comorosky's father.

Beverly and Scott Reiter, the owners of the Little Pirate Ranch near Winfield, Kansas, who gave David Cicotello and me a tour of Winfield and what used to be Fred Clarke's property and who entertained us with stories about Clarke and his family.

Liz Robbins, the executive director of the Garland County Historical Society in Hot Springs, Arkansas, who found an article showing that Earl Smith had been a student at Jones School.

Lauren Ellis Romer, assistant registrar of Farmingdale State College in Farmingdale, New York, who confirmed that Chet Nichols had attended the New York State School of Agriculture on Long Island.

John Roush, Jr., the principal of Elkton High School in Elkton, Maryland, who recommended that I contact the Historical Society of Cecil County, Maryland, to see if Carol Donache could tell me where Red Oldham had gone to high school.

Brent Ruswick, assistant professor of history at West Chester University in West Chester, Pennsylvania, and my friend and former student, who supported my writing of this book and who listened attentively to my attempts at explaining the complexities of the ABC Affair while we ate Mexican food at Fernando's on Pacific in Omaha, Nebraska.

Bill Santin, registrar services associate at Columbia University in New York, New York, who confirmed that Bud Culloton had been a student at Columbia College but did not graduate from Columbia University.

Melissa Scott, assistant to the registrar of the University of Mount Union in Alliance, Ohio, who verified that the Scio College records did not contain any mention of Jack Onslow.

John H. Shafer, the vice president of advancement at Wyoming Seminary Prep School in Kingston, Pennsylvania, who found no evidence in his school's academic records and yearbooks that Adam Comorosky had attended Wyoming Seminary between the mid–1910s and the mid–1920s.

Dana Snider, the superintendent of the Harrison Hills City School District in Cadiz, Ohio, who forwarded my questions regarding Jack Onslow and Scio School to Jenny Gibson.

Rosie Springer, library associate for the State Historical Society of Iowa Library in Des Moines, Iowa, who mailed me a photocopy of a page from the *Iowa State Register*.

Lindsey Stanton, the director of the Grant County Museum in Sheridan, Arkansas, who sent me a photocopy of Jase Goins' article on Earl Smith.

Steve Steinberg, baseball historian and award-winning author, who graciously answered my questions about Monitor and the *New York World* and who enthusiastically reacted to the news that I had received a contract to publish this book.

Tom Tomlinson, a former employee of and the current unofficial historian for the University of Southern California Gould School of Law in Los Angeles, California, who discovered that Johnny Rawlings had been a student at USC's law school for two consecutive academic years: 1912–1913 and 1913–1914.

An unnamed employee in the Scottdale Public Library in Scottdale, Pennsylvania, who assisted me in trying to determine if Jack Onslow had gone to school in the Scottdale area.

Doug Upshaw, the director of human resources and communication for the Hot Springs School District in Hot Springs, Arkansas, who recommended that I contact the Garland County Historical Society to find information about Earl Smith's education.

Mark Walters, the coordinator of the Interlibrary Loan department of Criss Library at the University of Nebraska–Omaha in Omaha, Nebraska, who made my research much easier by acquiring for me a number of books and reels of microfilm, some of which were quite difficult to obtain.

Brian J. Williams, the superintendent of the Buckeye Local Schools in Medina, Ohio, who alerted me to the fact that there are five Buckeye school districts in Ohio and who gave me the e-mail address for the district that includes Mt. Pleasant, Ohio.

Rodney Williams, the principal of Sheridan High School in Sheridan, Arkansas, who forwarded my question about Earl Smith to Terri Bone.

Roy L. Wilson, the author of *Sheridan and Grant County*, a volume in Arcadia's Images of America series, and the GT/AP coordinator of the Sheridan School District in Sheridan, Arkansas, who found the names and some details on various Smiths affiliated with Sheridan High School and who recommended several sources for possible information on Earl Smith.

Jasminn L. Winters of the Customer Service Section of the Office of Business Enterprises at the Library of Congress (LOC) in Washington, District of Columbia, who assisted me in procuring images from the national library of the United States.

Gregory Wolf, professor of German at North Central College in Naperville, Illinois, who shared with me his findings on Ray Kremer's year of birth and schooling and who expressed support for my writing of this book.

Michelle Wright of the Customer Service Section of the Office of Business Enterprises at the LOC in Washington, District of Columbia, and Kenneth Johnson of Duplication Services of the Digital Department at the LOC in Washington, District of Columbia, who worked together to quickly provide a late addition to the images used in this book.

Introduction

Setting the Record Straight

"[A] simple story, however inaccurate or misleading, is preferred to a complicated explanation, however true. Perhaps it's a general human characteristic. But it certainly applies to baseball."

—Leonard Koppett, 1998

On August 7, 1926, the three players with the most seniority on the defending World Series champion Pittsburgh Pirates—Charles "Babe" Adams, Carson "Skeeter" Bigbee, and team captain Max "Scoops" Carey—approached manager Bill McKechnie and told him that they wanted to call a players' meeting to discuss stopping the vice president, head of scouting, and assistant to the manager, Fred Clarke, from continuing to sit on the bench during games.[1] The exact reason or reasons the trio desired to have this meeting will be explored in detail in this book, but at first glance, it appears to have been a knee-jerk reaction to a comment that Clarke had made to McKechnie earlier that day. League-leading Pittsburgh, considered by the majority of preseason prognosticators to be the favorite to capture the National League (NL) pennant for the second year in a row, had dropped a doubleheader to lowly Boston by identical scores of 2–0, and in between the first and second games, Clarke, the great player-manager of the Pirates from 1900 through 1915, suggested that McKechnie remove the slumping Carey and replace him with anyone else he could find. Carey did not hear the remark, but allegedly his good friend Bigbee did and told him.[2] The two then went to Adams, the oldest player on the team and the member with the most seasons in a Pirate uniform, and asked for his opinion of the matter. Although sources differ as to his exact words, Adams is said to have uttered something to the effect that there should be only one manager on the team.[3]

And, thus, the three men disclosed their plan to McKechnie, a plan that, according to them, McKechnie had initially favored. He later changed his mind and cancelled the meeting.

What followed was a series of events that became known as the notorious ABC Affair, so called because of the first letter in each of the last names of Adams, Bigbee, and Carey. Adams and Bigbee were unconditionally released, and neither was picked up by another major league club; Carey was put on waivers and claimed by the Brooklyn Robins; the Pirates finished in third place, four and a half games behind the St. Louis Cardinals; McKechnie saw his contract go unrenewed; and Clarke resigned his positions

Charles "Babe" Adams (Library of Congress, National Photo Company Collection, LC-DIG-npcc–14193).

Carson "Skeeter" Bigbee (National Baseball Hall of Fame Library, Cooperstown, New York).

with the Pirate organization and returned to his ranch near Winfield, Kansas.

The matter should have ended there, but it did not. Once the season was over, Adams, Bigbee, and Carey came forth with a self-serving article published by the *Pittsburgh Press* on September 30, saying that Clarke was the source of dissension on the Pirate team and that his presence had created problems as far back as mid–June of 1925, shortly after he had been rehired to help the team acquire the mental toughness that it had lacked.⁴ Clarke emphatically denied the accusations in a news conference held that evening, the most complete version of which was published by the *Pittsburgh Post* the next morning,⁵ but some writers—both at the time and in the future—apparently taking what the banished players had to say at face value and ignoring Clarke's rebuttal, placed the blame for the Pirates' reversal of fortune squarely on the former player-manager. The usual argument was and still is that Clarke should not have been sitting on the bench in the first place, or that even if his presence was somehow justified, he should not have been offering suggestions or advice to McKechnie. Furthermore, it was said that Clarke's criticisms were oftentimes put forth in a rough fashion that offended the players and that his comment about Carey was the catalyst that brought about the ruination of a team that could have dominated the National League for at least a few more years. Two relatively recent writers have even branded Clarke "a nuisance, a know-it-all who had little regard for McKechnie's authority" and have argued that "[t]he power struggle between [Clarke and McKechnie] ... would explode and destroy everything around it in 1926."⁶

Max "Scoops" Carey (Library of Congress, George Grantham Bain Collection, LC-DIG-ggbain-36176).

That "everything" was a team about which one unknown scribe wrote before the '26 season began, "Everywhere one hears the refrain that the Pittsburgh club is the greatest club of modern days—probably the greatest since the Athletics['] juggernaut of the period of Bender, Plank, Baker, Collins, McInnis, Barry and Strunk."⁷ It was a team said to have "no weakness."⁸ A team with virtually the same personnel—manager, coaching staff, scouts, and players—that had stopped the New York Giants' mini-dynasty and had won both the National League pennant and the World Series the previous season. A team that further strengthened itself by adding two minor league stars. A team with five future Hall of Famers on it—seven if the manager and the assistant to the manager are counted. And a team that Fred Clarke himself believed was capable of not only winning the pennant that season but also of winning pennants for several seasons thereafter.[9]

A close examination of the situation, however, shows that the blame attributed to Clarke has been largely misplaced and that the causes of both the ABC Affair and the reasons for the Bucs failing to win the pennant in 1926 were far more complex than has been presented in the usual retellings of the incident and its ramifications. But to fully understand those causes and reasons, the ABC Affair must be placed within the larger picture of Pirate baseball during the 1920s, and a study of the composition of and the challenges faced by the 1926 team, as well as the environment out of which that team emerged, must be undertaken.

It is the purpose of this book to present the results of such a study to disclose what really happened to the 1926 Pirates. And we begin not on Opening Day 1926 but rather on January 23, 1921.

One

Colorful, Competitive and Consistently Falling Short

> It takes 'guts' to win a pennant, and your club here [Pittsburgh] lacks just that one thing. They thought they had the rag sewed up three years ago, but they blew up at a critical stage, and they will blow up again this season.
> —Hughie Jennings, 1924

Barney Dreyfuss, the owner of the Pittsburgh Pirates, had to be feeling good on January 23, 1921. He had just pulled off a multiplayer trade in which he gave outfielders Fred Nicholson and Billy Southworth, third baseman Walter Barbare, and $15,000 to the Boston Braves to acquire the services of defensive standout Walter "Rabbit" Maranville. True, Maranville was known to be a drinker and a prankster—not the type of player a no-nonsense businessman like Dreyfuss should have been attracted to—and the Pittsburgh magnate had certainly paid a high price to get him. Nicholson had batted .360 in 99 games for the Pirates during the 1920 season; Southworth was a decent hitter and the Bucs' starting right fielder; and Barbare was a useful utility infielder. But Maranville, despite his reputation for alcohol and frivolity, was one of the best fielding shortstops in the majors and the person who Dreyfuss viewed as being an integral piece in his efforts to build a pennant-winning team.

The previous season saw the Pirates, under first-year manager George Gibson, using a nice mix of veterans and youngsters to come in fourth with a 79–75–1 record. The average age of the team as a whole—those members playing in one or more major league games in a Pirate uniform—was 26.97, while that of the nonpitchers with at least 300 at bats and the pitchers with a minimum of 100 innings pitched was 28.69.[1] And with established stars like Max Carey, Walter Schmidt, Babe Adams, and Wilbur Cooper being joined by relative newcomers like Charlie Grimm and Johnny "Jughandle" Morrison, the future looked very promising. Carey, a defensive whiz in center field and an outstanding base stealer, Schmidt, who as late as 1969 was still being considered by Pirate fans as the best catcher that the Bucs had ever had,[2] and Adams and Cooper, arguably two of the four greatest moundsmen to wear Pirate uniforms, had been mainstays for the Pittsburgh club for a number of years. At the other end of the age spectrum, Grimm, a smooth-fielding first baseman, and Morrison, a pitcher whose curveball may have been the best since that of Mordecai "Three Finger" Brown,[3] were part of a talented group of neophytes who were ready to make names for themselves in the big leagues. Admittedly, there was no traditional cleanup hitter on the team—or for that matter, no dominant hitter, period—but if pitching and defense win ballgames, the Pirates were ready to capture their first pennant since 1909. As Ralph Davis, the sports editor of the *Pittsburgh Press* and the Pittsburgh correspondent to *The Sporting News*, wrote a week and a day after the trade for Maranville, "The Pirates are well equipped with pitchers, and their admirers are of the opinion that they are better prepared for a real pennant battle this year than they have been for a long time."[4]

For Barney Dreyfuss to have his franchise back atop the senior circuit would have been a dream come true. A German immigrant who had traveled to the United States to work in his cousins' bourbon distillery in Paducah, Kentucky, and to escape military service in his native land, Dreyfuss was a self-taught student of the game of baseball and had served as an executive with the Louisville Colonels during the 1890s, eventually becoming the club's president in 1899. Then, when the National League magnates decided to get rid of Louisville and three other franchises after the '99 season was over, Dreyfuss shrewdly acquired partial ownership of the Pittsburgh club before the contraction had taken place and traded the best Louisville players—including

A German immigrant who rose to become the owner of the Pirates, Barney Dreyfuss was trying to return his club to the winner's circle in 1921 (National Baseball Hall of Fame Library, Cooperstown, New York).

fiery player-manager Fred Clarke and the legendary Honus Wagner—to the Steel City franchise.

What followed was the transformation of the Pirates into one of the premier clubs in the majors. From 1900 through 1913, Pittsburgh, under the leadership of Dreyfuss, who became sole owner of the Bucs in 1901, and Clarke, who excelled as a hitter, base runner, and defender, as well as the skipper of the Pirate craft, finished in the first division 14 seasons in a row, captured four pennants, and defeated Detroit in the 1909 World Series. Furthermore, during those years, the Bucs had the best regular-season won-lost percentage (.614) and averaged the highest final-standings placement (2.2; 1.0 would equal coming in first every year) of all the National League clubs (see Table 1). In fact, even though it can be argued that the comparison is apples to oranges because the teams did not play each other throughout the course of the regular season, Pittsburgh's figures topped those of all eight American League (AL) franchises as well.[5]

Table 1: National League Franchises, 1900–1913[6]

Name of the Franchise	Won-Lost Record	Won-Lost Percentage	Average Placement in the Standings
Boston	805–1267	.389	6.4
Brooklyn	900–1164	.436	5.3
Chicago	1254–828	.602	2.8
Cincinnati	989–1098	.474	5.3
New York	1217–861	.586	3.1
Philadelphia	1027–1042	.496	4.4
Pittsburgh	1280–803	.614	2.2
St. Louis	832–1241	.401	6.4

But Dreyfuss' luck and that of the Pirate organization changed considerably between 1914 and 1917. Trades that did not pan out and the loss of players to the Federal League caused the club to plummet to the second division in 1914, and there it stayed for the next three seasons.

Finally, in 1918 and 1919, a resurrection took place under college football-basketball-baseball coach turned major league baseball manager Hugo Bezdek, as Pittsburgh recorded back-to-back winning records and fourth-place finishes. And although Bezdek left the Pirates after the 1919 season to concentrate on coaching football and baseball at Penn State and to be the school's athletic director and, for one season, its interim basketball coach, the foundation had been laid for his successor, George Gibson.[7]

Gibson, who had served as Fred Clarke's first-string catcher for nine of the 10 seasons from 1906 through 1915[8] and who had a reputation for helping to develop young pitchers, was a player's manager: supportive of his troops to outsiders and no disciplinarian. Because of this, most of the Pirates enjoyed playing for him, though a handful, including Max Carey and Walter Schmidt, who was never fond of his catching predecessor, criticized some of his strategical moves.[9] But despite these criticisms, Pittsburgh repeated as a winning fourth-place team in 1920, and with the acquisition of Maranville, the club looked to be a pennant contender for several years to come.

However, unfortunately for both Dreyfuss and the Pittsburgh fans, the next four seasons proved to be a series of frustrations, with the Pirates fielding colorful, competitive teams, but ones that consistently ended up in second or third place. In 1921, based on games behind, the Bucs were either leading their league or tied for the lead 142 out of 173 days, and as late as August 23, they were seven and a half games ahead of New York, with just 37 games left.[10] Spirits were high in the Steel City, as Ralph Davis wrote:

> Each fleeting day is brightening the pennant hopes of George Gibson's Buccaneers and their followers.... It may be some time before the Pirates will have the gonfalon mathematically cinched, but even now they are practically sure of the flag. The only thing that can prevent them from winning will be such a slump as would amount to almost a calamity.[11]

And James Isaminger, the Philadelphia correspondent to *The Sporting News*, added, "George Gibson ... discourages pennant talk, but if the Pirates don't win the championship this year[,] what other team can?"[12]

But then, the "almost a calamity" happened. After traveling to New York for a five-game series, Gibson's men were swept by the Giants and went into a tailspin, losing 17 of their remaining 32 games and finishing second to their Manhattan rivals.[13]

In 1922, the details were different, but the results were equally disappointing. This time, the Pirates survived a mediocre first two-thirds of the season, including a June swoon which contributed to Gibson's resignation, to make a strong comeback under new manager Bill McKechnie. And amazingly, by the end of the day on September 21, the Bucs were trailing the league-leading Giants by a mere three and a half games and were poised to redeem themselves for their collapse during the previous season. But such was not to be the case as they then proceeded to lose seven out of their remaining nine games—four of them to second-division teams—and came in tied for third.[14]

Nineteen twenty-three was similar to 1922 in that after the dust had settled on September 15, the Pirates were tied for second, four games out of first, but went on to drop 10 out of their last 16 contests to wind up in third place, eight

One. *Colorful, Competitive and Consistently Falling Short*

and half games behind the champion Giants. This particular late-season decline was especially galling because it contained three consecutive losses at home to New York.[15]

And finally, in 1924, Pittsburgh got off to a slow start, but played .654 ball between July 1 and September 20 to get to within a game and a half of the front-running New Yorkers, who were attempting to four-peat as National League pennant winners. But immediately thereafter, the demons of '22 and '23 returned to haunt the Bucs and caused them to lose four games in a row— one to Brooklyn and three to New York—and to land yet again in third place, this time with the Giants and the Robins ahead of them.[16]

So, between 1921 and 1924, there were no pennants for Pittsburgh, and the big question is why.

Years later, Charlie Grimm would say that the answer is simple: The '21-'24 Pirates had the misfortune to be playing at the same time as the '21-'24 Giants, who in Grimm's words were "the National League's greatest dynasty."[17] And on face value alone, it is hard to argue with Grimm's assessment. No NL franchise to date has equaled New York's feat of capturing four successive flags, and the Giants went further to add two World Series championships to their list of honors during that period. For that matter, the New York franchise would finish in first or second place for nine straight years beginning in 1917 and continuing through 1925.

But this does not explain why the Pirates were not able to dethrone the Giants for at least one season or why the 1921 team folded down the stretch. Nor does it explain why Cincinnati in 1922 and 1923 and Brooklyn in 1924 finished with better records than Pittsburgh or why the '22–'24 Pirates could get close to overtaking the Giants but were not able to do so. Were the Giants more talented than the Pirates? And what

Part of the nucleus of the 1921–1924 Pirates, Johnny "Jughandle" Morrison got his nickname because he threw a high overhand quick curveball that jumped down (National Baseball Hall of Fame Library, Cooperstown, New York).

about the '22 and '23 Reds and the '24 Robins? Were the Pirates underachievers? And if so, why? Or were there other factors involved?

In an attempt to answer these questions, both statistical information and narrative accounts will be examined, but before either of these is looked at, one factor that can be eliminated is extremism on the part of Barney Dreyfuss. As much as it pained Dreyfuss to see his teams continually falling short of capturing a pennant, he did not overreact by having a garage sale to clean house, but he did not stand pat either. Instead, each season, he made purchases and trades in an attempt to strengthen what he had already established. Thus, the nucleus of the 1921–1924 teams—players who had at least 300 at bats or 100 innings pitched—consisted of 24 men: the aforementioned Maranville, Carey, Schmidt, Adams, Cooper, Grimm, and Morrison plus seven more pitchers and 10 more nonpitchers.[18]

Of those 24 men, four were future Hall of Famers: Maranville, Carey, run-producing third baseman Harold "Pie" Traynor, who would take over the hot corner beginning in 1922, and the fleet-footed, hard-hitting Hazen "Kiki" Cuyler, who could play all three outfield positions and who would earn a starting berth in 1924. And 13 of them made Pittsburgh baseball historians David Finoli and Bill Ranier's list of the top 100 Pirate players.[19] These numbers become even more significant when it is learned that the 1900–1903 Pirates, who won three pennants and came in second once, had only three Hall of Famers and nine members on Finoli and Ranier's list. So, the talent was not lacking, but how did that talent perform?

Perhaps the best way to answer that question is to compare the statistics of the 1921–1924 Pirate teams with each other and then to compare them with the teams that finished ahead of them in the yearly standings. Tables 2, 3, and 4 contain the first comparison, with each table showing three to six key trends.

Table 2

- The Pirates played very well at home. The average home-field won-lost percentage in the National League between 1921 and 1924 was .533.[20] But the '21-'24 Bucs had home won-lost percentages ranging from .577 to .636 and even led the league one season in that category.

- Nor were the Pirates slouches on the road. If the average home-field won-lost percentage in the NL during the '21-'24 period was .533, then the average away won-lost percentage was .467, but the Bucs were winning on the road between 51.9 and 58.4 percent of the time.

- With the exception of the 1923 team, the Pirates held their own in one-run games and won nearly 60 percent of them in 1924.

- The Bucs struggled against the better teams in the National League in 1921 and 1922, but had winning records against them in 1923 and 1924.

- The Pirates feasted on the weaker teams in the league in 1921 and had impressive records against them during the following three seasons.

- And finally, two of the more respected methods of determining what a team's regular-season won-lost record should have been disagree somewhat, with the projected won-lost record being consistently lower than the expected won-lost record. This is especially noticeable with the '24 team. However, both methods agree that the '21 and '23 teams overachieved and that the '22 team underachieved. With the '24 Pirates, one system has them underachieving by a game, while the other system has them overachieving by more than three games.

Table 3

- Each Pirate team won more seasonal series than it lost against its opponents, going 5–2 in 1921, 3–1–3 in 1922, 4–1–2 in 1923, and 5–2 in 1924.

- But the Bucs had a difficult time beating the champion Giants, winning only one seasonal series and tying another.

- And surprisingly, Pittsburgh struggled against Wilbert Robinson's Brooklyn Robins, despite the fact that Brooklyn had just one first-division team during those four years.

Table 4

- Pitching, fielding, and base stealing were the Pirates' strengths—hitting was not. With the exception of the 1922 team, the Bucs were not winning many games with their bats. Of course, after they got on base, they became an offensive threat, but as Barney Dreyfuss supposedly told Max Carey when Carey was asking for a higher salary, "You can't steal first base."[23]

- If the traditional baseball wisdom that pitching and defense win ballgames is true, Pittsburgh should have won the pennant in 1921. And this raises the question of how much did the lack of a powerful hitting attack impede the Pirates.

Table 2: The Won-Lost Records of the 1921–1924 Pittsburgh Pirates[21]

Team	Won-Lost Record	Home Won-Lost Record	Away Won-Lost Record	Won-Lost Record in One-Run Games	Won-Lost Record Against Teams That Were .500 or Better	Won-Lost Record Against Teams That Were Under .500	Expected Won-Lost Record*	Projected Won-Lost Record**
1921	90–63	45–31	45–32	28–23	41–46	49–17	87–66	84.2–68.8
1922	85–69	45–33	40–36	17–17	43–45	42–24	88–66	85.7–68.3
1923	87–67	**47–30**	40–37	18–26	46–42	41–25	86–68	83.0–71.0
1924	90–63	49–28	41–35	31–21	47–41	43–22	91–62	86.9–66.1

Or if these numbers were converted to percentages, the results would be as follows:

Team	Won-Lost Percentage	Home Won-Lost Percentage	Away Won-Lost Percentage	Won-Lost Percentage in One-Run Games	Won-Lost Percentage Against Teams That Were .500 or Better	Won-Lost Percentage Against Teams That Were Under .500	Expected Won-Lost Percentage	Projected Won-Lost Percentage
1921	.588	.592	**.584**	.549	.471	.742	.569	.550
1922	.552	.577	.526	.500	.489	.636	.571	.556
1923	.565	**.610**	.519	.409	.523	.621	.558	.539
1924	.588	.636	.539	.596	.534	.662	.595	.568

*Expected Won-Lost Record or Pythagorean Won-Lost Record. The won-lost record based on the number of runs scored and the number of runs allowed by the team. For example, the 1922 Pirates won 85 games, but they were expected to win 88 games. So, they underachieved by three wins. **Projected Won-Lost Record or Differential. The won-lost record based on the team's batting, pitching, fielding, and base stealing. For example, the 1923 Pirates won 87 games, but they were projected to win 83 games. So, they overachieved by four wins. League leaders are in boldface.

- Just based on runs scored and runs allowed—perhaps the two most telling statistics for baseball teams—the contrast between the 1921 and 1922 Pirates is startling. The '22 Bucs scored 173 more runs than their '21 counterparts, but they gave up 141 more as well.

- Again just based on runs scored and runs allowed, the most balanced of the four teams was that of 1924. However, based on the other statistics found in this table, the 1922 and 1923 teams were the most balanced.

If tables 2, 3, and 4 provide a statistical view of the 1921–1924 Pirates, then tables 5–16, show how those teams matched up against their senior circuit rivals who won more games than they did. And here, it is best to look at the tables in groups of three.

First baseman Charlie Grimm. His glovework was one of the major reasons why the Pirates fielded strong defensive teams during the 1921–1924 seasons (Library of Congress, George Grantham Bain Collection, LC-DIG-ggbain-36177).

Thus, in won-lost records for the 1921 season (Table 5), the Giants topped the Pirates in five of the eight categories, but the two that stand out the most are home won-lost percentage and won-lost percentage against teams that were .500 or above. Pittsburgh was the best National League team when playing on the road, but New York was extremely difficult to beat in the Polo Grounds. In fact, no Pirate team between 1921 and 1924 would come close to the '21 Giants' .671 home won-lost percentage. And the same can be said about the Giants' record against the stronger teams in the league. No Pittsburgh team during this period would win more than 53.4 percent of its games against opponents that were at least .500.

Turning to their interclub records for 1921 (Table 6), New York and Pittsburgh were remarkably similar. Each team played well against Boston, Chicago, Cincinnati, and Philadelphia and each team struggled with Brooklyn and St. Louis, with the Pirates actually winning six more games than the Giants: 84 to

Table 3: The Won-Lost Records of the 1921–1924 Pittsburgh Pirates Versus the Other Teams in the National League[22]

Team	Boston	Brooklyn	Chicago	Cincinnati	New York	Philadelphia	St. Louis
1921	13–9	12–10	17–5	14–8	6–16	18–4	10–11
1922	12–10	11–11	12–10	11–11	11–11	19–3	9–13
1923	17–5	11–11	11–11	14–8	9–13	13–9	12–10
1924	15–7	9–13	15–7	10–12	13–9	13–8	15–7

Table 4: Team Statistics for the 1921–1924 Pittsburgh Pirates[24]

Team	Runs Scored	Runs Allowed	AOPS*	AERA**	Batting Wins+	Pitching Wins++	Fielding Wins#	Base-Stealing Wins##	Number of Positive Categories That the Team Led the League In
1921	692	**595**	93	**121**	-5.6	**10.2**	2.3	0.9	18
1922	**865**	736	106	102	4.2	1.3	**1.5**	1.7	13
1923	786	696	102	103	0.6	1.8	2.3	1.4	8
1924	724	586	100	117	-0.4	8.7	0.5	1.6	10

*Adjusted On-Base Percentage Plus Slugging Average. "On-base percentage and slugging average are added and normalized for the context of the offensive level of the league and the team's home park(s) and then converted to a scale in which 100 is average. **Adjusted Earned Run Average. "Calculated by normalizing ERA for the context of the offensive level of the league and the team's home park(s) and converting to a scale in which 100 is average." +Batting Wins. "Total number of wins the team achieved through its hitting compared to the average team in the context of the offensive level of the league and the team's home park(s)." 0.0 is average. ++Pitching Wins. "Total number of wins the team achieved through its pitching compared to the average team in the context of the offensive level of the league and the team's home park(s)." 0.0 is average. #Fielding Wins. "Total number of wins the team achieved through its fielding compared to the average team in the context of the offensive level of the league and the team's home park(s)." 0.0 is average. ##Base-Stealing Wins. "Total number of wins the team achieved through its [base stealing] compared to the average team in the context of the offensive level of the league and the team's home park(s)." 0.0 is average. League leaders are in boldface.

the New Yorkers' 78. What hurt the Bucs was their inability to beat the Manhattanites in head-to-head meetings, losing 16 out of 22 times.

In team statistics (Table 7), Pittsburgh was clearly the better club in pitching, fielding, base stealing, and leading the league in positive categories, but New York's big advantage was run differential. Although the Pirates gave up only 595 runs, they scored just 97 more. The Giants, on the other hand, gave up 637 runs, but they scored 203 more.

During the 1922 season, the Pirate hitting attack came to life, with five starting players batting .329 or higher, four scoring 89 or more runs, of which three scored over 100, and six driving in 70 or more runs. Leading this attack were second baseman James "Cotton" Tierney and left fielder Carson Bigbee, each of whom was having a career year with the bat, and Max Carey, who had personal bests with 51 stolen bases out of 53 attempts and 140 runs scored.[28] But sadly for the Bucs, as tables 8, 9, and 10 indicate, they dropped to third place, finishing behind both the Giants and the Cincinnati Reds.

When the tables for 1922 are studied, it is easy to see why New York won the National League pennant and beat out Pittsburgh in the process. In the 17 categories covered by tables 8 and 10, the Giants led the Pirates in 14. The Bucs outscored the Giants by 13 runs and were slightly better fielders as well as much better base stealers, but the Giants more than compensated for these minor setbacks with impressive records at home and against opponents who were at least .500 and with a nicely balanced combination of hitting and pitching. And though it is true that Pittsburgh was able to hold its own in head-to-head games with New York (see Table 9), the Pirates had a hard time defeating three second-division teams—Boston, Brooklyn, and Chicago—and had a losing record against St. Louis, a team that tied Pittsburgh for third place. Conversely, the Giants edged Cincinnati and clearly triumphed over the remaining clubs.

However, what is not so easy to see from the tables is why Pittsburgh ended up trailing Cincinnati in the standings. As Table 10 shows, with the exception of pitching, Pittsburgh was the superior team. This assessment is further supported by most of the results found in Table 8, including both expected won-lost records and projected won-lost records. But the Reds played the Pirates even in head-to-head meetings and won four more games than the Pirates did against the weaker teams in the league. Therefore, it appears that the combination of those two factors secured second place for the team from Ohio.

Table 5: The Won-Lost Records of the 1921 New York Giants and Pittsburgh Pirates[25]

Team	Won-Lost Record	Home Won-Lost Record	Away Won-Lost Record	Won-Lost Record in One-Run Games	Won-Lost Record Against Teams That Were .500 or Better	Won-Lost Record Against Teams That Were Under .500	Expected Won-Lost Record	Projected Won-Lost Record
New York	94–59	53–26	41–33	22–25	50–37	44–22	95–58	89.0–64.0
Pittsburgh	90–63	45–31	45–32	28–23	41–46	49–17	87–66	84.2–68.8

Or if these numbers were converted to percentages, the results would be as follows:

Team	Won-Lost Percentage	Home Won-Lost Percentage	Away Won-Lost Percentage	Won-Lost Percentage in One-Run Games	Won-Lost Percentage Against Teams That Were .500 or Better	Won-Lost Percentage Against Teams That Were Under .500	Expected Won-Lost Percentage	Projected Won-Lost Percentage
New York	.614	.671	.554	.468	.575	.667	.621	.582
Pittsburgh	.588	.592	.584	.549	.471	.742	.569	.550

League leaders are in boldface.

One. *Colorful, Competitive and Consistently Falling Short* 25

Table 6: The Won-Lost Records of the
1921 New York Giants and Pittsburgh Pirates
Versus the Other Teams in the National League[26]

Team	Boston	Brooklyn	Chicago	Cincinnati	New York	Philadelphia	Pittsburgh	St. Louis
New York	13–8	10–12	14–8	14–8		16–6	16–6	11–11
Pittsburgh	13–9	12–10	17–5	14–8	6–16	18–4		10–11

Table 7: Team Statistics for the
1921 New York Giants and Pittsburgh Pirates[27]

Team	Runs Scored	Runs Allowed	AOPS	AERA	Batting Wins	Pitching Wins	Fielding Wins	Base-Stealing Wins	Number of Positive Categories That the Team Led the League In
New York	840	637	112	103	9.4	1.7	1.3	0.2	8
Pittsburgh	692	595	93	121	–5.6	10.2	2.3	0.9	18

League leaders are in boldface.

Table 8: The Won-Lost Records of the 1922 New York Giants, Cincinnati Reds, and Pittsburgh Pirates[29]

Team	Won-Lost Record	Home Won-Lost Record	Away Won-Lost Record	Won-Lost Record in One-Run Games	Won-Lost Record Against Teams That Were .500 or Better	Won-Lost Record Against Teams That Were Under .500	Expected Won-Lost Record	Projected Won-Lost Record
New York	93-61	51-27	42-34	30-23	50-38	43-23	95-59	93.2-60.8
Cincinnati	86-68	48-29	38-39	23-26	40-48	46-20	86-68	84.9-69.1
Pittsburgh	85-69	45-33	40-36	17-17	43-45	42-24	88-66	85.7-68.3

Or if these numbers were converted to percentages, the results would be as follows:

Team	Won-Lost Percentage	Home Won-Lost Percentage	Away Won-Lost Percentage	Won-Lost Percentage in One-Run Games	Won-Lost Percentage Against Teams That Were .500 or Better	Won-Lost Percentage Against Teams That Were Under .500	Expected Won-Lost Percentage	Projected Won-Lost Percentage
New York	.604	.654	.553	.566	.568	.652	.617	.605
Cincinnati	.558	.623	.494	.469	.455	.697	.558	.551
Pittsburgh	.552	.577	.526	.500	.489	.636	.571	.556

League leaders are in boldface.

For the 1923 season, the numbers were different, but the results were the same: New York won the pennant, Cincinnati came in second, and Pittsburgh finished third. In addition, the Giants again dominated the won-lost and team statistics, leading the league in 11 of the 17 categories contained in tables 11 and 13.

But these tables also highlight a few chinks in the New Yorkers' armor that were not present in 1922. First, the expected won-lost record, which is based on run differential, and the projected won-lost record, which is based on hitting, pitching, fielding, and base stealing, both show fewer victories for the Giant team than its actual won-lost record (see Table 11). This decline is particularly evident in the projected wins and losses, where the Giants' offensive and defensive production on the field should have given them a little over 86 wins and put them in the runner-up spot in the standings behind Cincinnati. And second, New York's pitching dropped precipitously from topping the senior circuit in both adjusted earned run average and pitching wins in '22 to being below average in both categories in '23 (see Table 13).

However, the Pirates were unable to take full advantage of these chinks, being outplayed by the Giants in seven of eight categories found in Table 11 and six of nine in Table 13 and losing 13 of 22 games to the Manhattanites (see Table 12). Like New York, Pittsburgh's expected and projected wins were less than those of 1922 and less than its actual wins in 1923. But if the Giants overachieved by three to almost nine games, depending on the determining system, the Pirates overachieved by just one to four games, thus suggesting that the Giants possessed certain intangibles that the Pirates lacked. Perhaps it was the inspirational leadership of John McGraw, New York's passionate, never-say-die manager, who had already won eight pennants and three World Series titles going into 1923. Or perhaps it was the on-the-field leadership of Frankie Frisch and the other Giant veterans, who were confident in their ability to capture pennants. Or perhaps both.

But whatever the reason or reasons, the '23 Bucs were able to win only two more games than their '22 predecessors, despite improving their pitching and fielding and giving up 40 less runs than they did the previous year. Of course, the '23 team's inability to squeak out one-run games and their drop-off in hitting and run production did nothing to help their cause.

As for finishing behind the Reds, the key statistics appear to be the difference in one-run victories (see Table 11), Pittsburgh's failure to have better records against Brooklyn, Chicago, New York, and Philadelphia (see Table 12), and Cincinnati's outstanding pitching staff (see Table 13). None of these factors alone may have been responsible for the Bucs ending up in third rather than second, but taken together they helped to negate whatever advantage the Bucs had gained by decisively clinching their intraleague series with the Reds and by outperforming Cincinnati in fielding and base stealing.

Table 9: The Won-Lost Records of the 1922 New York Giants, Cincinnati Reds, and Pittsburgh Pirates Versus the Other Teams in the National League[30]

Team	Boston	Brooklyn	Chicago	Cincinnati	New York	Philadelphia	Pittsburgh	St. Louis
New York	14–8	14–8	14–8	12–10		15–7	11–11	13–9
Cincinnati	17–5	14–8	11–11		10–12	15–7	11–11	8–14
Pittsburgh	12–10	11–11	12–10	11–11	11–11	19–3		9–13

Table 10: Team Statistics for the 1922 New York Giants, Cincinnati Reds, and Pittsburgh Pirates[31]

Team	Runs Scored	Runs Allowed	AOPS	AERA	Batting Wins	Pitching Wins	Fielding Wins	Base-Stealing Wins	Number of Positive Categories That the Team Led the League In
New York	852	658	109	116	6.8	8.0	1.1	0.3	14
Cincinnati	766	677	102	113	2.0	6.7	0.4	-1.1	6
Pittsburgh	**865**	736	106	102	4.2	1.3	1.5	1.7	13

League leaders are in boldface.

Table 11: The Won-Lost Records of the 1923 New York Giants, Cincinnati Reds, and Pittsburgh Pirates[32]

Team	Won-Lost Record	Home Won-Lost Record	Away Won-Lost Record	Won-Lost Record in One-Run Games	Won-Lost Record Against Teams That Were .500 or Better	Won-Lost Record Against Teams That Were Under .500	Expected Won-Lost Record	Projected Won-Lost Record
New York	95–58	47–30	48–28	28–17	49–38	46–20	92–61	86.1–66.9
Cincinnati	91–63	46–32	45–31	31–19	43–45	48–18	85–69	88.0–66.0
Pittsburgh	87–67	47–30	40–37	18–26	46–42	41–25	86–68	83.0–71.0

Or if these numbers were converted to percentages, the results would be as follows:

Team	Won-Lost Percentage	Home Won-Lost Percentage	Away Won-Lost Percentage	Won-Lost Percentage in One-Run Games	Won-Lost Percentage Against Teams That Were .500 or Better	Won-Lost Percentage Against Teams That Were Under .500	Expected Won-Lost Percentage	Projected Won-Lost Percentage
New York	.621	.610	.632	.622	.563	.697	.601	.563
Cincinnati	.591	.590	.592	.620	.489	.727	.552	.571
Pittsburgh	.565	.610	.519	.409	.523	.621	.558	.539

League leaders are in boldface.

Table 12: The Won Lost Records of the 1923 New York Giants, Cincinnati Reds, and Pittsburgh Pirates Versus the Other Teams in the National League[33]

Team	Boston	Brooklyn	Chicago	Cincinnati	New York	Philadelphia	Pittsburgh	St. Louis
New York	16–6	11–11	12–10	10–12		19–3	13–9	14–7
Cincinnati	15–7	14–8	13–9		12–10	19–3	8–14	10–12
Pittsburgh	17–5	11–11	11–11	14–8	9–13	13–9		12–10

Table 13: Team Statistics for the 1923 New York Giants, Cincinnati Reds, and Pittsburgh Pirates[34]

Team	Runs Scored	Runs Allowed	AOPS	AERA	Batting Wins	Pitching Wins	Fielding Wins	Base-Stealing Wins	Number of Positive Categories That the Team Led the League In
New York	**854**	679	**110**	98	**8.1**	-1.3	**2.4**	0.5	**18**
Cincinnati	708	**629**	102	**120**	1.3	**9.8**	0.9	-1.0	11
Pittsburgh	786	696	102	103	0.6	1.8	2.3	**1.4**	8

League leaders are in boldface.

The 1924 season saw New York and Pittsburgh remaining first and third and Brooklyn, a second-division team the previous three years, surprisingly taking over Cincinnati's place in second. All three teams won 90 or more games; all three teams played well home and away; all three teams had winning records against clubs that were at least .500; and all three teams dominated the losing clubs (see Table 14).

In head-to-head series, the trio beat each other in circular fashion, with New York defeating Brooklyn, Brooklyn defeating Pittsburgh, and Pittsburgh defeating New York (see Table 15). And New York and Brooklyn won all their five remaining intraleague series, while Pittsburgh went 4–1, being edged by Cincinnati, 12 victories to 10 (see Table 15).

However, that's where the similarities end. As Table 16 points out, New York was a powerful hitting team with slightly above average pitching, fielding, and base stealing. Brooklyn had decent hitting and pitching, but was a little below average in fielding and base stealing. And Pittsburgh had the best pitching and base stealing of the three to go along with fielding that was similar to New York's, but its Achilles' heel was its hitting.

Furthermore, New York led its two rivals and the rest of the National League in nine of the 17 categories represented in tables 14 and 16. The best that Brooklyn and Pittsburgh could do was to attain three and one league leaderships, respectively, with Pittsburgh leading New York and Brooklyn but not the league in the remaining four categories.

So, as in 1921 and to lesser extent 1923, Pirate pitching could not prevent Giant hitting from taking the pennant. Nor could the Pirates' beating the Giants 13 out of 22 times or the Giants' poor record in one-run games derail the McGraw Express. In fact, the Bucs' on-the-field performances show that they should have finished anywhere from five (expected won-lost record) to over six (projected won-lost record) games behind the New Yorkers.

But when comparing the Bucs to the Robins, the picture is different. As can be seen from Table 14, the Pirates finished a game and a half behind the Robins, but they should have finished between 10 and a half (expected won-lost record) and four and a half (projected won-lost record) games ahead of them.

With the exception of hitting, the Pirates were without question the superior team (see Table 16). Yet, Brooklyn outplayed Pittsburgh on the road and against the weaker teams in the league, had a slightly higher won-lost percentage in one-run contests, and captured the head-to-head series, thus raising further questions about the Pirates' lack of success.

◆ ◆ ◆

Table 14: The Won-Lost Records of the 1924 New York Giants, Brooklyn Robins, and Pittsburgh Pirates[35]

Team	Won-Lost Record	Home Won-Lost Record	Away Won-Lost Record	Won-Lost Record in One-Run Games	Won-Lost Record Against Teams That Were .500 or Better	Won-Lost Record Against Teams That Were Under .500	Expected Won-Lost Record	Projected Won-Lost Record
New York	93–60	51–26	42–34	18–19	49–39	44–21	96–57	93.3–59.7
Brooklyn	92–62	46–31	46–31	29–19	45–43	47–19	81–73	82.9–71.1
Pittsburgh	90–63	49–28	41–35	31–21	47–41	43–22	91–62	86.9–66.1

Or if these numbers were converted to percentages, the results would be as follows:

Team	Won-Lost Percentage	Home Won-Lost Percentage	Away Won-Lost Percentage	Won-Lost Percentage in One-Run Games	Won-Lost Percentage Against Teams That Were .500 or Better	Won-Lost Percentage Against Teams That Were Under .500	Expected Won-Lost Percentage	Projected Won-Lost Percentage
New York	.608	.662	.553	.486	.557	.677	.627	.610
Brooklyn	.597	.597	.597	.604	.511	.712	.526	.538
Pittsburgh	.588	.636	.539	.596	.534	.662	.595	.568

League leaders are in boldface.

Table 15: The Won-Lost Records of the
1924 New York Giants, Brooklyn Robins, and Pittsburgh Pirates Versus the Other Teams in the National League[36]

Team	Boston	Brooklyn	Chicago	Cincinnati	New York	Philadelphia	Pittsburgh	St. Louis
New York	17–5	14–8	13–9	13–9		14–7	9–13	13–9
Brooklyn	15–7		12–10	12–10	8–14	17–5	13–9	15–7
Pittsburgh	15–7	9–13	15–7	10–12	13–9	13–8		15–7

Table 16: Team Statistics for the
1924 New York Giants, Brooklyn Robins, and Pittsburgh Pirates[37]

Team	Runs Scored	Runs Allowed	AOPS	AERA	Batting Wins	Pitching Wins	Fielding Wins	Base-Stealing Wins	Number of Positive Categories That the Team Led the League In
New York	857	641	120	101	15.0	0.7	0.4	0.7	13*
Brooklyn	717	679	105	103	4.5	1.7	-0.2	-0.0	2
Pittsburgh	724	586	100	117	-0.4	8.7	0.5	1.6	10

League leaders are in boldface. *Tied with Cincinnati

In 1983, Toby Harrah, then the third baseman for the Cleveland Indians, was reported to have said, "Statistics are like a girl in a bikini. They show a lot, but not everything."[38] And so it is with tables 2–16. The tables are great for identifying the strengths and weaknesses of the on-the-field play of the Pirates and for highlighting how the Pirates compared to those teams who finished ahead of them in the standings. But they do not explain the why behind the how. For example, a team may be seen as overachieving one season and underachieving the next, but why did this happen? Were the players fired up during the first season but not putting out during the second, or were there other factors involved? Or a team's pitching may rise one year and fall the next, but why was this so? Were certain pitchers injured? Was there a new catcher to handle them? Or did something else happen? To answer these questions, an examination of the narrative accounts is necessary, for if the statistical information serves as the skeleton for understanding the Pirates' inability to win a pennant between 1921 and 1924, the narrative accounts provide the flesh for that skeleton.

And all the narrative accounts agree that the 1921–1924 Pirates were a loose, fun-loving team. As Pie Traynor's biographers James Forr and David Proctor have written:

> Lots of clubs hazed and ostracized young players as a rite of passage, but most of the veterans on the Pirates were too busy laughing and causing mayhem to deliberately make someone else's life miserable. Art McKennan, the team's batboy, likened the clubhouse atmosphere to that of a circus. "There was not much serious play with that crowd." McKennan said things got quiet after losses, but after a victory he would find the players in the shower whacking each other with brooms.[39]

If the atmosphere was indeed like a circus, then the head clown was the hard-drinking, party-loving Rabbit Maranville, a small man who enjoyed pulling pranks both on and off the field. Glenn Wright, who as a rookie in 1924, played next to Maranville as part of the Bucs' middle infield combination, recalled that he

The Pirate "circus" had its share of characters, but the wackiest one was The Rascally Rabbit: Walter James Vincent Maranville (National Baseball Hall of Fame Library, Cooperstown, New York).

once fielded a grounder and threw it to Maranville to start a double play, but Maranville promptly threw it back to him and told him, "Don't throw them so hard."[40] And that was during a regular-season game. Off the field, the diminutive mischief maker was even more creative. According to Bill Veeck, the former owner of the Cleveland Indians, St. Louis Browns, and Chicago White Sox, whose father was the president of the Chicago Cubs, the club that Maranville played for in 1925:

> A few days after [Maranville] reported [to the Cubs' spring training site on Catalina Island], he disappeared onto the mainland overnight ... and returned to the island on the excursion boat. Upon debarking, he snatched up a coal scuttle full of ashes, for he had learned that it was Ash Wednesday. Stationing himself at the entrance of the huge dining room of the St. Catherine Hotel, he dabbed ashes onto the foreheads of all the incoming guests. Regrettably, he was so loaded that he couldn't tell their foreheads from their elbows and he was flinging the ashes all over the place. The management had to serve more than 100 meals over again.[41]

But perhaps Maranville's most famous prank is one that he and his drinking buddy and roommate, pitcher Mose YellowHorse,[42] a full-blooded Pawnee, played on Bill McKechnie after McKechnie had replaced George Gibson as manager of the Bucs. As Babe Adams recounted in 1960:

> Barney Dreyfuss told [McKechnie] to keep a look out for Maranville and YellowHorse. I heard that Dreyfuss [had] called 'em both wild Indians, and he wanted to make sure they stayed in line. So Deacon [one of McKechnie's nicknames] decided to bunk with Rabbit and the Chief [what YellowHorse was called by his teammates] when the team's on the road....
> It became known as "The Pigeon Affair of 1922." And it was in New York. What happened was that the Chief and Rabbit made a bet to see who could catch the most pigeons bare-handed. To make it fun, they decided to do their pigeon catching from a sixteenth-story ledge at the hotel where we were staying....
> [Meanwhile, McKechnie] was out having dinner with John McGraw. He didn't know what [Maranville and YellowHorse] were up to. When he got back to the hotel room around ten o'clock, he was surprised and happy to find both of 'em sleeping. He figured he [had] caught a break since he didn't have to go looking for them, like usual. Then he opened his closet door to hang up his coat. Started reaching for a hanger. But he got a face full of pigeons [instead]. They were flying right for his head, and he ducked. Rabbit told me that the Deacon hit the floor so loud it must've startled God.[43]

Of course, Maranville and YellowHorse were not the only performers in the circus. Others included Charlie Grimm, Cotton Tierney, and George "Possum" Whitted. In fact, Maranville, Grimm, Tierney, and Whitted even formed their own quartet—with Tierney singing lead, Maranville singing tenor, Whitted singing baritone, and Grimm playing the banjo and singing bass[44]—and used it to entertain the fans prior to games.[45] The foursome also amused the fans with comedic routines,[46] sometimes doing them while a game was in progress. For example, according to Bill James:

> One time in 1922, Pirate first baseman Charlie Grimm fielded a hard hit ground ball by a slow runner, no one on base. Instead of going over to touch first, he fired the ball to second baseman Cotton Tierney, singing out loud enough to be heard in the bleachers, "Have we got him, Mr. Tierney?" Tierney sang back, "Absolutely, Mr. Grimm"—an echo of a famous vaudeville routine by Gallagher and Sheen. The runner was out at first, 3–4–3.[47]

Whitted's sale to Brooklyn in March of 1922 put an end to what had become known as the "Peerless Quartet," but it did not cause the music to stop. Instead, it gave way to a slightly larger vocal-instrumental group, which, according to the *Pittsburgh Post*, initially had Max Carey on ukulele, Clyde Barnhart and Johnny Morrison on mandolins, Johnny Mokan on trombone—until he was purchased by Philadelphia in mid–July of '22—and Grimm continuing to play banjo and sing.[48] In 1926, *Pittsburgh Post* sportswriter Edward Balinger would praise the 1924 version of the group by penning, "Two years ago the Pirates possessed a glee club and string band that was unexcelled in the baseball world, with the possible exception of Chicago, where the Cubs maintained a jazz orchestra of about a dozen pieces."[49]

And when it came to imbibing alcohol, Maranville and YellowHorse, both of whom preferred hard liquor, may have again been the leaders of the pack, but they were not without their followers. Johnny Morrison also had a reputation for being a heavy drinker,[50] and one who would guzzle any "brand of moonshine or bootleg [that] happened to be handy."[51] Ralph Davis called Morrison "his own enemy" and went further to say, "He is of a careless nature, and does not take his baseball seriously. Many tales are being told of his escapades."[52] Glenn Wright, no teetotaler himself,[53] remembered Pie Traynor carrying a gallon of wine with him on road trips and drinking a lot of beer,[54] while sportswriter Fred Lieb said that Grimm and Whitted "sang best when they sprinkled their tonsils with lager."[55]

But whatever their drink of choice, not all the Pirates confined their carousing to after hours. In his autobiography, Charlie Grimm described an on-the-field incident that happened in either 1921 or 1922:

> One hot day in St. Louis[,] Yellowhorse [*sic*] was called on in a late inning to snuff out a Cardinal rally. When he ignored the catcher's signal, [George] Gibson told me to go over and see what was the matter. The Chief just muttered. Maranville and Tierney and the catcher joined me at the mound. "I'll not throw a ball until I get a shot of booze," said Yellowhorse [*sic*].
> "Not a bad idea," said Maranville. "Let's all gather around the Chief."
> Perhaps that was the first and only time a baseball mound has doubled as a

cocktail lounge. Maranville just happened to have the wherewithal to satisfy Yellowhorse's [*sic*] thirst.

After the inning was over, Gibson demanded an explanation.

"Chief's supporter was binding him," said the Rabbit. "He didn't know what to do about it in front of all those people!"[56]

As for off-the-field activities, Jimmy Zinn, a pitcher who was not a partier himself, estimated that two-thirds of the members of the '21 and '22 clubs were.[57] Zinn preferred to "romance a little bit,"[58] but that is another matter.

Whether the clowning around, drinking, and partying were responsible for the Pirates not winning one or more pennants during the 1921–1924 period is a subject open to debate. Many years later, Grimm would say, "Despite the cut-ups on the club, including myself, we were serious when the action started."[59] Glenn Wright felt that the antics "made those clubs more of a family."[60] Walter Schmidt in commenting about the 1921 season said, "The boys all played their heads off and a fifth [place] club finished second just because they hustled."[61] And George Gibson, looking back on his two stints as a Pirate manager—1920–1922 and 1932–1934—would tell Lawrence Ritter:

> Didn't win any pennants but we came close a few times. Always seemed to fade in the stretch. I have a sneaking suspicion we'd have won those pennants if I only could have gotten my pitchers into a little better shape.[62]

Gibson's last statement may have been said tongue-in-cheek because the former catcher was known to get his pitchers in shape by having them chase fly balls that he hit just out of their reach.[63] But leaving aside Gibson's facetiousness, none of those men suggested that the frivolity and penchant for alcohol displayed by some of the Pittsburgh players had anything to do with the club coming home empty-handed in the pennant hunt.

Furthermore, it could be argued that based on where Pittsburgh was predicted to end up each season, the questionable behavior of the Bucs had little or no affect on the team's final position in the standings. According to Lyle Spatz and Steve Steinberg, the authors of the definitive work on the 1921 season, most of the preseason prognosticators for '21 were picking New York to capture the National League flag, with Brooklyn coming in second and Pittsburgh third.[64] Even Ralph Davis gave the Giants the edge for winning the pennant, though he put the Pirates second.[65]

In 1922, the Bucs were expected to finish second, third, or fourth, depending on the source,[66] while in 1923, the *Los Angeles Times* reported that "close followers of baseball pick the Pirates as a 'one, two, three' team"[67]—meaning that they could end up first, second, or third. Other selectors placed the team at least third or as a toss-up for fourth or fifth.[68] And 1924 saw the eccentric sportswriter and Renaissance man W.A. Phelon, an associate editor of *Baseball Magazine* at the time, forecasting that either Pittsburgh or Cincinnati would take the pennant,[69] but rival prognosticators had the Corsairs coming in somewhere between second and fourth.[70]

Then there is the question of what effect did Walter Schmidt's holding out for the first two-thirds of the '22 season and Carson Bigbee's sinus problems have on hurting the Bucs' pennant chances. Schmidt, considered by F.C. Lane, editor in chief of *Baseball Magazine*, to be the best catcher in the National League and the second best in the majors for 1921,[71] refused to play because he was supposedly dissatisfied with the contract that Barney Dreyfuss had offered him. It was rumored that the Pirate veteran had received a one-year contract for $9,000—the equivalent of $708,000 in 2013[72]—but turned it down because he wanted a two-year contract for $10,000 per year, something that Dreyfuss was not willing to provide.[73] Although this may be true, it appears that Schmidt's reluctance to rejoin the Pirates may have been based as much on his dislike of George Gibson as on the amount of money that Dreyfuss was willing to pay him—Schmidt's statements to the contrary notwithstanding.[74]

The owner of multiple farms in California and a shrewd businessman who had purchased his own release from the San Francisco Seals in 1915, Schmidt did not need Dreyfuss' money or baseball to make a living, and yet, he held out until Opening Day for a two-year contract in 1920.[75] And while the 1921 season was in progress, he was believed to have been one of three players guilty of insubordination towards Gibson—the other two being Possum Whitted and Davis "Dave" or, as he was referred to in Pittsburgh, "Davy" Robertson, a slugging outfielder who the Pirates had acquired in a trade with the Cubs for curveballer Elmer Ponder on July 1 of that year.[76] The following January, Schmidt sent a letter to *Pittsburgh Gazette Times* sportswriter Charles "Chilly" Doyle in which he said, among other things, that "[i]f Gibby starts to fight his players[,] it will be a bad condition," that he and his teammates "absolutely can't see why certain players should be blamed [for losing the pennant]," and that "[n]othing would suit me better than to be traded, as our club won't have much chance under present methods."[77] So, even though Schmidt had rhetorically asked in a telegram sent to the *Pittsburgh Post* on April 23, 1922, "Why should I join the Pirates at the salary offered me?" it appears that there was more to his holdout than just his wanting a larger sum of money.[78] In fact, Dreyfuss himself was "reported to have said [that same month] that bringing Schmidt into line [had] never been a question of money, ... [but rather] a matter of discipline."[79] However, once Gibson had resigned, Bill McKechnie was able to get Dreyfuss and Schmidt to reconcile and to have Schmidt return to the team during the week of July 16.[80]

But whatever the reason or reasons for Schmidt's holdout, without the veteran catcher to handle them, the Pirate pitchers floundered. Their collective ERA ballooned to 4.86 and their WHIP soared to 1.55, compared to their ERA of 3.51 and their WHIP of 1.26 once Schmidt was back in a Pirate uniform.[81]

As for Bigbee, he had two excellent seasons in 1921 and 1922, in which he finished in the top 10 in his league in positive offensive categories 23 times[82] and in the top 10 in positive defensive categories for a left fielder 10 times.[83] F.C. Lane ranked him as one of the best outfielders in the senior circuit for both years,[84] while John McGraw and Dave Bancroft, McGraw's shortstop and team captain, each placed him on his respective National League all-star team for the latter season.[85] And in June of 1922, George Gibson said of him:

Independently minded, financially shrewd, and a skillful handler of pitchers, Walter Schmidt did not need the Pirates as much as they needed him (National Baseball Hall of Fame Library, Cooperstown, New York).

> Carson Bigbee has no equal in the National League as an outfielder, when one considers his intelligence, his ground-covering ability, his batting and his base running. He is the equal of Tris Speaker when it comes to patrolling the outfield.[86]

But the following year, Bigbee began suffering sinus problems that gave him headaches and affected his eyesight, and though he would remain with the Pirates until August 13 of 1926, he was never the same player.

So, maybe the clowning around and drinking had nothing to do with Pittsburgh consistently falling short of first place, and the real reason was that the Pirates, as talented as they may have been, were just not talented enough to win the pennant.

However, not all narrative accounts agree with this assessment. After the Bucs collapsed in 1921, Ralph Davis wrote in his weekly column for *The Sporting News*:

> Walter Maranville was a real hero when he reported in the spring, but the feeling toward him has changed apparently, and many fans are yelling now for his scalp. Scores who laughed at his clownish actions in the spring now declare themselves disgusted with them.

The much-touted "Pirate Quartet" was popular for a time, but its melodies later failed to soothe the angered fans, and the charge has been made that the Buccaneers have done too much singing and too little real ball playing. It has been suggested that Dreyfuss insert an anti-singing clause in the 1922 contracts.

In fact, few members of the team have escaped a panning, and Manager Gibson has not been exempt. He has been accused of making numerous mistakes in the handling of his pitchers, and of allowing his players too much freedom off the field.

Probably no set of players in either big league had as few restrictions placed upon them as the Pirates. The players were permitted to govern themselves when not in uniform, and it is hinted that some of them went a bit too far in the matter of personal liberty, and at times were not in condition to do themselves justice when game-time rolled around.[87]

Nor was Davis alone in his criticism. Speaking in early 1927 about the Pirates getting swept by the Giants in August of '21, Barney Dreyfuss said, "It is generally understood that some of the Pittsburgh players broke training rules at that time, and their actions in a large part were blamed for the collapse of the team and the loss of the pennant."[88] The *Pittsburgh Post* was more damning when it reported in its May 5, 1922, issue that "it was stated a few days ago that [Possum] Whitted was the alleged leader of a gang which threw away last year's pennant chances."[89] And after the 1922 season was over, W.A. Phelon stated that one of the reasons for Pittsburgh not capturing the pennant that year was "the failure of the men to work whole-heartedly for George Gibson."[90]

But the situation did not change when Gibson stepped down. Maranville's drinking appears to have gotten worse[91] and his pranks seem to have become more dangerous. For example, Glenn Wright remembered a time in New York when he saw Maranville throwing laundry sacks full of water on cars from a 14th- or 15th-story hotel window.[92] Now, it is not inconceivable that the devilish Rabbit may have pulled this prank on occasions before Wright witnessed it, but his practical jokes certainly did not get any less dangerous.

Other players continued to overimbibe, too, and even as late as March of 1925, McKechnie, who admitted that when it came to his previous teams, he had "winked at violations of the Volstead [A]ct" and had protected the guilty parties, threatened to suspend any of his men who were caught drinking hard liquor.[93] Presumably, though, beer and wine were still permissible.

Moreover, the charges against the Bucs went further than just too much booze and too many shenanigans. By 1924, the Pirates were viewed as not having the perseverance, class, and mental toughness to go all the way. Frank Smith of the *Chicago Daily Tribune* wrote shortly before the 1924 season began, "The makeup of the Pirates lacks the stamina required for the grueling battle scheduled for the parent organization,"[94] while an unidentified writer for the *New York Times* commented that the Bucs "have not in three years shown that indefinable thing called class."⁹⁵ W.A. Phelon was more detailed in his analysis when, in comparing the 1924 Reds to the 1924 Pirates, he stated:

> [The Pirates] can outhit and outrun the Reds. Yes—but this much seems freely admitted by the men of the six other teams—the Reds possess, in a greater degree than the Pirates, the quality vulgarly known as "guts." Three years in succession, when topmost honors seemed surely in their grasp, the Pirates have failed to show the nerve and steadfast determination that a champion club must have.⁹⁶

And later that season, Phelon added to his appraisal:

> "I don't see why that Pirate team isn't up ahead." Almost every player in the National League has made that remark after tackling the Pittsburgh club. On all-around form, the Pirates should be up there, ahead of the Giants, beating all competitors, and yet it [sic] isn't, and only a miraculous dash to the front can give it [sic] final victory.⁹⁷

But such comments were not limited just to the sportswriters. Hughie Jennings, the former Detroit Tiger skipper who served as John McGraw's coach between 1921 and 1926, concurred with Phelon's remark about the Pirates not possessing intestinal fortitude when he said about the '24 team, "It takes 'guts' to win a pennant, and your club here [Pittsburgh] lacks just that one thing. They thought they had the rag sewed up three years ago, but they blew up at a critical stage, and they will blow up again this season."⁹⁸

Perhaps, though, it was Zach Wheat, the captain and star leftfielder of the Brooklyn Robins, who best expressed what was wrong with the Bucs when he told F. C. Lane:

> Where the Giants have it on the Pirates is this. They can go out with a big lead against them and score three or four runs. The Pirates look like a million dollars when they are ahead, but when things start going bad, they don't seem to have the punch.⁹⁹

However, despite their inability to overcome adversity, the Corsairs were also viewed as being cocky. As Noel Hynd, the author of *The Giants of the Polo Grounds: The Glorious Times of Baseball's New York Giants*, described the attitude of the Pirates prior to the first game of their ill-fated series against McGraw's men in August of 1921:

> On the field, the Pirates, chipper and confident, laughed their way through batting and fielding practice. In the Pirate dugout, Charlie Grimm strummed his ukulele.¹⁰⁰ Pittsburgh looked like a team of college kids at their end-of-term softball outing. Then they all assembled, right there at the Polo Grounds, and had their team picture taken for the upcoming World Series program.¹⁰¹

Maranville, realizing that the taking of the photograph would jinx the team, claimed that he had protested against having it done.¹⁰² But over 39 years later,

Babe Adams said that he had heard that Maranville had been boasting to the newspaper people about what the Pirates were going to do to the Giants and that this had helped to motivate the Giants to sweep the Bucs and begin the process that would put an end to Pittsburgh's pennant hopes for that season.[103]

But even losing a doubleheader to the Giants on the day that they had posed for the program photo did not stop the Pirates from entertaining the New York media with more photos the next day.[104] As Chicago sportswriter Irving Vaughan would later write, "The boys figured the pennant was a cinch and started to spend the [W]orld [S]eries pot before it was earned."[105]

It might have been because of this cockiness that the hatred for the Pirates in Brooklyn during the 1921 season was so extreme that during the August 28 game between the Bucs and the Robins, the Brooklyn fans cheered when the scoreboard showed that the Giants had taken the lead against the Cubs.[106] New York at that time was only two and a half games behind Pittsburgh and apparently the Brooklyn rooters would have rather seen their age-old enemy win the pennant than the upstarts from the Steel City.

Added to these charges were after-the-fact player complaints about both Gibson and McKechnie. While being interviewed in 1989, Jimmy Zinn criticized Gibson for not communicating properly and for not having any suggestions for his players, especially him.[107] According to Zinn, Gibson's idea of strategy was to shout, "Let's go, let's go" and "fight it out."[108] And Eddie Moore, a substitute infielder-outfielder on the '24 Pirates and later the starting second baseman for the '25 team, told Eugene Murdock in 1975 that he thought McKechnie was "sometimes ... a little too much of a gentleman—too easy in spots."[109]

Of course, Moore's statement was no startling revelation. McKechnie's reputation for being a bright, likeable manager, but "too easy in spots" was well known in the 1920s. For example, in his column in the October 18, 1923, issue of *The Sporting News,* Ralph Davis had written, "Perhaps [McKechnie's] one weakness is a tendency to be too easy on his charges," and "that a very good friend of [the manager] ... [had] advised him to put on a bit sterner front in the future in dealing with certain of his men."[110] What is more, McKechnie himself admitted in early March of 1925, "I have never fined nor suspended a player since I became manager of the Pittsburgh club"[111]—an amazing statement considering some of the characters he had been managing during that time.

It may have been in part because of McKechnie's permissive nature that in July of 1922, not long after the popular Wilkinsburg, Pennsylvania, native assumed command of the Pirate ship, Barney Dreyfuss attempted to hire Honus Wagner to be the club's assistant manager.[112] Wagner, who enjoyed drinking beer as much as anyone on the Pirate team, was certainly no disciplinarian, but perhaps Dreyfuss felt that because the Pirate players held the former superstar in such great respect, "The Flying Dutchman" could teach them how to play the game with the same seriousness that he had played it. Nothing came of the idea because Wagner turned down the offer to continue running the sporting goods business that he had established,[113] but Dreyfuss did not forget about the concept of having an assistant manager to aid McKechnie and would resurrect that concept in a somewhat different form three years later.

It may also have been in part because of McKechnie's permissive nature that Ralph Davis accused the Pirate skipper of not getting enough out of his men. In early August of 1923, Davis wrote in one of his columns in *The Sporting News*:

> There is little to choose between the Pirates, Reds and Giants in baseball ability. The three outfits seem to be very evenly matched, and it may be, in the last analysis, that morale and generalship will be the deciding factors.
> [John] McGraw is a great fellow to get the last ounce out of his men. [Pat] Moran[, the Cincinnati manager,] is not so successful, and neither is McKechnie. There have been rumors floating about recently that two or three of the Buccaneers have been kicking over the traces [i.e., rebelling against authority].[114]

And if these criticisms were not enough, Davis reported the previous summer that there had been factionalism on the Pirate teams during Gibson's tenure and that this factionalism had remained even after McKechnie had taken charge.[115] Elaborating on what the *Pittsburgh Post* had brought forth about Possum Whitted two months earlier, Davis went on to say:

> It has been charged that the passing of Gibson is due largely to a "player conspiracy." This is more or less true. There are men still on the roster who not did give Gibson their best efforts. In fact, one or two of them defied him....
> Cooperation among the Corsairs has been sadly lacking.[116]

As disturbing as Davis' statements are, what makes them even more disturbing is that they were published after alleged troublemakers Whitted and Davy Robertson and complainer Jimmy Zinn had left the Pirates and before Walter Schmidt had rejoined the club.

A final problem which allegedly contributed to the disfunctionality of the club was a somewhat humorous one: wives and children traveling with the team. According to an article in the May 13, 1923, issue of the *Boston Daily Globe*:

> There have been rumors from time to time of the wives of the Pirate players precipitating trouble between the men, and it is known that two pitchers on the team broke their friendship several years ago by reason of some indiscreet remarks by one of the women. A few years ago a well-known player was traded to another club, although his value to the local club was ace high, and one of the officials of the club was overheard to say that he was glad the trade was made because of the objectionable things brought up from time to time by the wife of the traded player.[117]

Whether or not these rumors were true, Dreyfuss outlawed the practice of bringing wives and children on road trips in 1923—a practice that had begun after George Gibson became manager. His arguments for doing so were that family members distracted the players from mentally preparing for games, that they were a burden for the business manager because they all wanted lower berths on trains and it was difficult to find enough hotel rooms for them, and that in their presence, the players could not relax on the trains by removing their outer clothing.[118]

Thus, the consensus answer of the narrative accounts to the question of why the 1921–1924 Pirates did not win at least one pennant appears to echo the words of Ed Balinger, who wrote in February of 1922: "The average baseball enthusiast is willing to give the Giants some credit for their performance, but he prefers to place most of the blame on the home fellows."[119] Balinger, of course, was referring to the way baseball fans viewed the pennant race of 1921, but his astute observation can be applied to the way many observers perceived the 1922–1924 races as well.

For Barney Dreyfuss, the 1921–1924 seasons were ones of missed opportunities and disappointment, and he had had enough. The future that had looked so promising in 1921 had turned into a forgettable past. The nice mix of veterans and youngsters failed to materialize in the way that Dreyfuss had hoped, and the trades, purchases, and other moves that he had made during this period had not gotten him the pennant that he had so desperately desired.

To make matters worse for the Pirate owner, the pennants his teams had not captured had been seized by teams led by his hated nemesis, John McGraw. Dreyfuss' animosity for McGraw was long-standing, going back to at least 1905 when McGraw had humiliated Dreyfuss at a Pirate-Giant game at the Polo Grounds on May 20. According to Dreyfuss:

> On Saturday, May 20, I was standing in the main entrance of the Polo Grounds, talking quietly to some friends, when McGraw, who had been put off the grounds for using foul language, appeared on the balcony of the clubhouse and shouted: "Hey[,] Barney!"
> I did not answer that too familiar greeting and did not respond to any of his several attempts to attract my attention. Then he urged me to make a wager. He was very insistent[,] but I had nothing to say to him. He also made remarks about me controlling umpires and other false and malicious statements.[120]

Then, to add injury to insult, New York repeated as National League champions that year and won eight more pennants by the end of the '24 season, while Pittsburgh won only one. For that matter, since the time McGraw had re-entered the senior circuit in July of 1902,[121] the Giants had racked up 10 pennants and three out of nine World Series titles to the Pirates' three pennants and one out of two Series titles.

Because of all this frustration, Dreyfuss became determined—some might say obsessed—to reverse his misfortune, but to do this, he had to figure out what was causing his teams to fall short and then remedy the situation. He knew that he had talented players and an equally talented though lenient manager, so in his mind—a mind that admired order and discipline—the problem was that his men were not playing up to their potential because of their continued drinking and clowning around and their lack of mental toughness. And these were matters that he intended to change.

Two

The Return of Fred Clarke

> With the possible exception of Cobb and John McGraw, baseball never knew a sturdier competitor than Clarke. As a player and manager, he gave the fans and his employer, Barney Dreyfuss, everything he had every hour of the day.
>
> —Fred Lieb, 1960

Dreyfuss did not waste much time in implementing his renovation plans. On October 27, 1924—less than a month after the season had ended—the Pittsburgh owner pulled off his biggest trade since he had acquired Rabbit Maranville. This time Maranville and Charlie Grimm—one-half of the Pirates' infield—as well as ace pitcher Wilbur Cooper were dealt to the Chicago Cubs in return for curveballer Vic Aldridge, good hit, no field second sacker George Grantham, and rookie first baseman Al Niehaus.

However, as might be expected, the trade was viewed with mixed feelings by the Pittsburgh fans, though it delighted Cub supporters and made at least one sportswriter question Dreyfuss' sanity.[1] And understandably so. During the '24 season, the Pirate infield was arguably the best defensive quartet in the National League if not the majors. The fancy-fielding Grimm was either first or second among major league first basemen in putouts (first), double plays (first), range factor (second), and fielding percentage (first). Maranville, who had been moved to second base to make room for the young Glenn Wright, led all major league keystoners in assists and double plays, was second in range factor, and third in fielding percentage, though first in the senior circuit in the last category. Wright, only a rookie that season, topped major league shortstops in assists, double plays, and range factor and was third in his league in putouts for his position. And Pie Traynor came in first among NL third basemen in double plays, second in putouts, range factor, and fielding percentage, and tied for third in assists, which for major league third basemen, placed him tied for first, third, fourth, third, and tied for fourth, respectively, in those categories.[2]

Nor do current defensive measurements lessen the effectiveness of some of the members of the foursome. Pete Palmer's linear weights ranks Wright as the fourth best defensive infielder in the National League for 1924, while Baseball-Reference.com's updated version of Sean Smith's defensive Wins Above Replacement (WAR) for nonpitchers places Wright as the top defensive player in the majors and has Maranville finishing third for that season.[3]

Furthermore, eyewitness accounts support the statistics. F. C. Lane, in commenting about the October 27 trade, wrote, "the most striking feature of the deal was not the fact that Barney Dreyfuss apparently gave up more strength than he received, but rather that he deliberately disrupted what was probably the greatest defensive infield on the diamond."[4] Jack Hendricks, the manager of Cincinnati at that time, remarked, "I think the Pirates have the smoothest working infield I ever looked at."[5] Jim Bottomley, St. Louis' run-producing first baseman, added, "The Pirates have the greatest infield in the National League,"[6] while Carl Mays, the former Boston Red Sox and New York Yankee ace who was then pitching for Cincinnati, topped Bottomley's assessment by saying, "They have the best infield I ever saw from a defensive standpoint."[7] And when Lane asked 15 NL managers, coaches, and players to compare the Pirate infield to the highly publicized pennant-winning Giant infield of George Kelly, Frankie Frisch, Travis Jackson, and Heinie Groh, almost all of them chose the Pirates or tied the two units.[8]

What makes these assessments even more impressive is that neither Wright nor Traynor had accurate throwing arms. Both were exceptional fielders and had strong arms and quick releases, but there was no telling how close to first base the ball would land after they threw it, which underscores the importance of Charlie Grimm. Or as *Pittsburgh Gazette Times* sports editor Chester "Chet" Smith wrote:

> [Wright and Traynor] [e]ach possesses a throwing arm like a steel spring and each is imbued with the idea that he is there to cover the whole infield and as much of the outfield as he can reach.... [However,] [n]either has yet learned that a second of time used to "set" himself after fielding a particular difficult ground ball is often the means of saving a wild throw....
>
> To cope with this pair of untamed youths[,] Lefty [one of Grimm's nicknames] has perfected two modes of defense. [The first] has been dubbed the "Grimm nose dive" and is effective when the ball is some five or six feet wide of the bag and low. The idea is simple. Lefty merely hooks one toe around the sack and falls head first into the dirt, meanwhile poking his mitt in the line of the pellet's flight. The second—"the Grimm scooper"[—] can be imitated only by scraping up a handful of snow from a spot where the beautiful is not more than an inch or two

deep. Of the two, the former is the more spectacular, but the latter infinitely harder and more dangerous to the front teeth.⁹

But if getting rid of the right half of Pittsburgh's vaunted infield was not painful enough for the Pirate faithful, Dreyfuss also traded away the finest left-handed pitcher in the history of the Buc's franchise to date: Wilbur Cooper. Debuting with the Pirates on August 29, 1912, Cooper had used what he described as "an easy motion, a sneaky fast ball [sic], a sharp curve, a change of pace and wonderful control for a lefthander [sic]"¹⁰ to compile a 2.74 ERA, a 1.199 WHIP, and 202 victories while a Corsair.¹¹ By 1914, he had established himself as one the Pirate starters, and between then and when he left Pittsburgh, he finished in the top 10 in his league in positive pitching categories 98 times and led the league six of those times.¹² Also, he was no slouch with the bat, pounding out 269 hits and driving in 93 runs during his 13-year career in the Steel City, which, when combined with his pitching prowess, put him in the first six in NL WAR for all positions for six seasons.¹³ Finoli and Ranier have placed him 13th on their list of the top 100 Pirate players through 2002,¹⁴ and in 1969, Pittsburgh fans chose him as the franchise's best southpaw.¹⁵

So, in one fell swoop, Dreyfuss had removed three of the mainstays of the 1921–1924 teams, but what had he gotten in return? Well, in October of '24, Vic Aldridge appeared to be the most promising of the trio of newcomers. Known for his hard, sharp-breaking curveball, Aldridge had pitched for three clubs during two seasons in the minors before getting his first big league start with the Cubs in 1917. He remained with Chicago through 1918, spent three more years in the minors, and then resurfaced with the Cubs in 1922 to provide them with three solidly good seasons. The knock on Aldridge was not his pitching—some considered his curveball to be second only to that of Johnny Morrison¹⁶—but his age: he was 31 when he arrived in Pittsburgh.

Although unsteady in the field, George Grantham was one of the best fastball hitters that Glenn Wright had ever seen (National Baseball Hall of Fame Library, Cooperstown, New York).

George Grantham was different story. Since he was just 24 at the time of the trade, his age was not a factor, but his fielding was. Grantham had been a minor league shortstop-third baseman who the Cubs moved to second, but no matter what position he was stationed at, he had trouble with his defensive play. As Glenn Wright would later say, Grantham "never was sure of himself" in the field,[17] and this lack of confidence apparently affected the way he performed, though to his credit, he led all major league second basemen in assists, as well as in errors, in 1923.[18] But what Grantham did not bring with his glove he made up for with his bat. An outstanding fastball hitter,[19] he had finished tied for second in the National League in doubles in 1923 and eighth in on-base percentage in 1924.[20] His only weakness at the plate was that he struck out a lot for the era in which he played, coming in second in the majors in K's in both '23 and '24.[21]

As for Al Niehaus, he was a 25-year-old first baseman who had distinguished himself with his hitting in the minors, but who had yet to play a game in the majors. This made him the unknown quantity in the trade, but interestingly enough, in late 1924, he was projected to be the Pirates' replacement for Grimm.[22]

Thus, on paper, the swap appeared to favor the Cubs, but this did not faze Dreyfuss, who told Fred Lieb not long after the exchange took place, "I got rid of my banjo players"[23]—implying those players who he viewed as carefree carousing clowns. Actually, though, Dreyfuss' statement was only partially true for three reasons. First, he had already gotten rid of three members of the Grimm-Maranville faction before 1924. Possum Whitted, who was rumored to have been insubordinate during the 1921 season[24] and was one of three Pirates allegedly arrested in a nightclub raid in New York that same season,[25] had been sold to Brooklyn in March of 1922 after holding out for more money. Mose YellowHorse, a one-time fan favorite who gradually fell out of favor, was part of a multi-player swap with Sacramento approximately nine months later.[26] And Cotton Tierney, one of Whitted's crooning buddies, was sent to Philadelphia along with starting right-hander Charles "Whitey" Glazner and $50,000 of Dreyfuss' money for veteran second-baseman-shortstop Johnny Rawlings and sidearm curveballer Lee "Specs" Meadows on May 23, 1923. Tierney, who batted .345 and drove in 86 runs during the previous season, was not a heavy drinker,[27] but he had limited range at second base and was perceived by Dreyfuss as not being a serious player.

Second, Cooper was not part of the Grimm-Maranville faction. If anything, he was just the opposite. A perfectionist on the field, he would yell at his teammates if they made mistakes behind him, which did nothing to help his popularity and which may have prompted Dreyfuss to toss him into the package that he was offering the Cubs. As Ralph Davis wrote, "Despite [Cooper's] great native ability, he has never been universally popular here, on account of a peculiar moodiness, which causes him to show plainly his dissatisfaction, when matters are going against him in a game."[28]

And finally, a few "banjo players" remained, such as Johnny Morrison, who not only played the banjo but also the mandolin and fiddle,[29] and who could more than hold his own when it came to imbibing alcohol.

Added to these departures, Dreyfuss released another Corsair who he had once viewed as a malcontent: Cooper's battery mate, Walter Schmidt. At 37 years of age, the former outspoken catcher who had been so important to the success of the Pirate pitching staffs during the first half of the '20s was found to be expendable after Dreyfuss had purchased Earl Smith from the Boston Braves in the middle of the previous season. Although Schmidt's attitude had changed 180 degrees in a positive direction since McKechnie had replaced Gibson,[30] his age and his $12,000 salary—a large amount of money in 1924 for a defensive specialist—hurt his chances of staying with the Bucs. Also, it is possible that Schmidt's holdouts, his complaints in the letter that he had sent to Chilly Doyle in January of 1922—a letter that had been printed in the *Pittsburgh Gazette Times*—and his feuding with Gibson had made him a marked man in Dreyfuss' eyes and that the Pirate magnate was just waiting to find an adequate replacement for him before letting him go.[31]

Other changes of a lesser note occurred, but with the passing of Grimm, Maranville, Cooper, and Schmidt, only 13 of the 24 core players for the 1921–1924 teams were left. Of those 13, three—Carson Bigbee, Johnny Rawlings, and catcher Johnny Gooch, who had filled in for Schmidt when the older signal caller was absent or hurt—were relegated to backup status. The remaining 10 consisted of longtime veterans Babe Adams, Max Carey, and Lee Meadows, the first 20th-century major leaguer to wear glasses while playing[32]; newer veterans Johnny Morrison, Pie Traynor, and Clyde "Pooch" Barnhart, who had debuted with Pittsburgh in 1920 as a third baseman, but who had since been converted to playing right field; second-year men Glenn Wright and pitchers Remy "Ray" Kremer and Emil Yde; and Kiki Cuyler, who had first put on a Pirate uniform in 1921, but who had spent most of his time in the minors until becoming the starting left fielder for the Bucs in 1924. Adams and Carey had been with Pittsburgh since 1909 and 1910, respectively. The nearsighted Meadows, as mentioned earlier, had joined the club in 1923, but he had been pitching in the majors since 1915. The other men, similar to Barnhart and Cuyler, had begun their big league careers between 1920 and 1924, all with the Pirates.

Joining this core as proposed starters were 1924 utility man Eddie Moore, now designated to take Maranville's place at second, Vic Aldridge and Al

Niehaus, two of the trio obtained from the Cubs, and Schmidt's replacement, Earl Smith, a rough-and-tumble backstop who had mastered the art of one-handed catching.[33] The rest of the team was made up of George Grantham, the third former Cub, who was initially designated as a reserve outfielder, rookies Bernard "Bud" Culloton, Lou Koupal, and Roy Spencer, and virtual rookie—he had appeared in four games in 1924—Don Songer. Culloton, Koupal, and Songer were pitchers; Spencer was the third-string catcher.[34] Other young players, such as shortstop Joe Cronin, would make Pittsburgh's expanded roster—from 1923 through 1931 and again in 1944, teams were permitted to increase the number of players on their rosters from 25 to 40 before June 15 and after August 31[35]—but none of them would see any major league action that season.

Supporting this group in a limited capacity was player-coach Jewel Ens, who had held that split position for several years. Ens was neither fish nor fowl, being listed as a member of the playing roster, but actually being more valuable by helping McKechnie on the sidelines.

Also helping McKechnie on the sidelines was new coach Jack Onslow. A former catcher who had spent most of his playing career in the minors, Onslow was hired as the pitching coach to replace Grover Land, who had requested and received "permission to seek another position which promised to give him more opportunity to advance."[36] Although Onslow did not have any major league coaching experience, he had established a reputation as a fighter and "a clever handler of young players" while successfully managing the semiprofessional Allegheny Steel club for several years and winning a pennant with the Richmond Colts of the Virginia League the preceding season.[37]

So, heading into their opener with the Cubs, the reconstructed Pirates heralded the end of one era in Pittsburgh baseball—1921–1924—and the start of another, though there were some parallels between the two eras. Both periods began with blockbuster trades: the former with one that had seen Rabbit Maranville coming to the Steel City; the latter with one that saw Maranville leaving the Steel City. Both periods began with teams that were a nice mix of veterans and less experienced men. And both periods began as a breath of fresh air for Pittsburgh fans.

However, the teams of the first era had toyed with the emotions of their loyal followers, teasing them by coming close to winning a pennant each year only to break their hearts by having defeat snatched from the jaws of victory. Would the teams of the second era do the same?

That was a key question on the minds of the preseason prognosticators as they made their annual predictions. On one hand, some of them were impressed with the talent that the Pirates possessed and with the youthful enthusiasm of the team as a whole. In particular, they liked what Chet Smith called "the greatest assemblage of young blood ever corralled in one big league park"[38]—five "sophomores": Kiki Cuyler, Glenn Wright, Eddie Moore, Emil Yde, and Ray Kremer.

A member of Chet Smith's "Fab Five" sophomores of 1925, Hazen "Kiki" Cuyler was arguably the best offensive player on the 1924 team (National Baseball Hall of Fame Library, Cooperstown, New York).

Cuyler, who had debuted with the Bucs on September 29, 1921, but who had only 49 plate appearances prior to 1924, and Wright, whose defensive excellence was highlighted earlier in this chapter, were the leading run producers for the team. In addition, Cuyler was fourth in the National League in batting average (.354), sixth in on-base percentage (.402), and fourth in slugging average (.539).[39]

Moore did not see as much playing time as either Cuyler or Wright, but he still hit the ball at a .359 clip while compiling an on-base percentage of .437 and a slugging average of .464.[40] And Yde and Kremer each finished in the top ten in his league in wins (tied for sixth and fifth, respectively), winning percentage (first and eighth), adjusted ERA (fifth and ninth), WHIP (fifth and eighth), and shutouts (each tied for first).[41]

The ages of the first four as of Opening Day 1925 ranged from 24 to 26, while Kremer was the elder statesman of the group, having started the '25 season not long after he had turned 30 or 32, depending on the source.[42] But as McKechnie said when he was being teased for recommending that the Pirates sign such an "old" rookie in late 1923, "If he's 60, he's still a good pitcher."[43] This assessment, no doubt, was at least partially influenced by Kremer's four-pitch repertoire—a fastball, a changeup that would become praised as the best in the National League, a curve, and a screwball—and the hurler's ability to deliver his pitches in two ways: overhand and low sidearm.[44]

When combined with such established regulars as Carey, Morrison, Traynor, and Meadows, it is easy to see why the Bucs were an appealing choice to win it all in the senior loop. Wilbert Robinson, Brooklyn's avuncular manager, called them "the best balanced ball club [sic] on the circuit,"[45] and an unknown scribe writing for the *New York Times* declared that they "have the best young team in either league."[46]

On the other hand, there were still questions about the club's mental toughness. The 1921–1924 Pirates had been labeled as underachievers, a group of physically talented individuals who were unable to go all the way because they lacked discipline, focus, determination, and the ability to overcome adversity. The 1925 Pirates, fairly or unfairly, were put on the spot to prove that they were not cut from the same cloth, and they were considered guilty until proven innocent. W. A. Phelon nicely summed up this line of thinking when, after discussing how Pittsburgh would miss the play of Cooper, Schmidt, Grimm, and Maranville, he wrote, "Add to this the fact that the Pirates, for several successive seasons, have seemed to get footsore and disheartened when the going got tough, and it can be seen why I don't hand them any pennant. It's a club that OUGHT [Phelon's emphasis] to win, but it doesn't do it."[47]

Also, the inexperience of the '25 Bucs was held against them. The same scribe who christened them "the best young team in either league" was quick to follow his statement with a disclaimer saying that "unfortunately, however, the Buccaneers may be a little too young for practical purposes.... [I]t is a question if Barney Dreyfuss and Bill McKechnie, in their rush to sign impetuous youth, have not gone to extremes."[48]

This tension between what ought to be and what has been and between known and unknown quantities was perhaps best reflected in the results of the preseason picks. For an article for *Baseball Magazine*, Phelon took a survey of the publication's editorial staff and some of its regular contributors as to their forecast for the upcoming season, and the results showed the Pirates being chosen first twice, first or second once, second once, third twice, fourth once, and fourth or fifth once, with the composite prediction putting them second.[49] The consensus of another group of sportswriters put them fourth, with New York, Brooklyn, and Chicago ahead of them, in that order.[50] Other baseball pundits had the Bucs finishing anywhere from first to fourth or battling it out with the Giants and the Robins and possibly the Cardinals or the Cubs for the top spot.[51] In the words of the mystery scribe from the *New York Times*, "The Pirates [were] the big gamble of the 1925 season."[52]

As for Barney Dreyfuss, he seemed pleased with the changes that had been made. As early as December of 1924, he had publicly said:

> I believe that trade which we made with the Chicago Cubs helped us in more ways than one. It gives us a better hitting team, a better stealing combination, and I believe there will be more harmony, and a greater respect for discipline and the rules.

> We won't have so many clowns on the team, but I imagine we can get along very well without the comedy stuff. Baseball is a serious business, and we have sought to get players who will so take it.[53]

In support of Dreyfuss' emphasis on discipline, rules, and seriousness, and in an attempt to change his image as "Mr. Nice Guy" or "Mr. Look-the-Other-Way," McKechnie gave a tough-talking speech to his troops the first day of spring training at Paso Robles, California. In it, he forbade the drinking of whisky and the playing of high-stake card games,[54] threatened to suspend any player caught "boozing"—whether McKechnie meant drinking alcohol in general, drinking alcohol in large quantities, or just drinking whiskey is not clear—and came forth with the following confession:

> In the past three or four years, our chances have been hurt by such actions [boozing] on the part of some of the players. During that time[,] I have shielded them. I have never fined nor suspended a player since I became manager of the Pittsburgh club. But I am through covering up the faults of others. It has got me nowhere in the past and I fail to see where it will obtain better results in the future.[55]

Furthermore, to underscore that he meant business, McKechnie let it be known that he would enforce his rule about drinking even if he had to "break up [his] entire club."[56]

But behind the public display of confidence and the rhetoric, Dreyfuss probably could not help but wonder if he had done enough to prevent the 1925 Pirates from being nothing more than an updated version of the four previous teams. This concern may have been especially true when a series of problems struck his club during the first two months of the new season.

First, Vic Aldridge, one-third of the package from Chicago, held out until almost Opening Day. No one is sure if he did this because he was dissatisfied with his contract or because he detested spring training or both, but what is certain is that he was in no shape to help the team when he did arrive and his performances showed it. Throughout April and May, Aldridge pitched in only six games, starting three and compiling an ERA of 5.46 and a WHIP of 1.66.[57]

Next, Al Niehaus, another third of the Chi-Town package, suffered a leg injury during a preseason exhibition game,[58] reinjured the same leg during a regular-season game,[59] and by May 30, had appeared in just 17 games, hitting a miserable .219 and making six errors.[60]

Then, in part because of Aldridge and Niehaus, but also in part because of ineffective pitching—probably due to the absence of Walter Schmidt—and sloppy defense, the team got off to a slow start. By the end of April, it was playing .385 ball and was tied for sixth place. By May 24, it had moved up to fifth place, but its winning percentage was still under .500. And to make matters worse, the hated Giants were winning at a .750 clip and were already six games ahead of the pack.

But if those setbacks were not enough, on May 14, starting catcher Earl Smith got himself in trouble for going into the stands at Boston to punch a fan who had been heckling him. Smith, a former Boston player, was ejected from the game by umpire crew chief Charles "Cy" Rigler, suspended indefinitely by National League president John Heydler, and charged with assault by the fan who he struck.[61] Then, to add injury to insult, another Boston fan threw a chair which hit Smith in the head.[62] Fortunately, though, for both Smith and the Pirates, Rigler defended the hardboiled backstop in his umpires' report to Heydler, which got Smith reinstated four days after his suspension,[63] and the heckler, Walter J. Lewis, who did not show up three times for the hearing, eventually asked that the charges be dropped.[64] Maybe Lewis came to the realization of what Rigler had written in his report: that Smith had been receiving a lot of abuse from the Boston fans "and when he went after [a] foul ball that landed in the stand[,] something was said about his [m]other and that is when Smith hit the [s]pectator. From what I saw and Smith[']s general conduct[,] I would not [f]ine or [s]uspend him. The general impression around the [b]ox where this man sat is that he got what he deserved."[65]

Hard-nosed, hard-drinking Earl Smith showed his lack of appreciation for hecklers when he attacked a Boston fan who had verbally abused him (Library of Congress, George Grantham Bain Collection, LC-DIG-ggbain–38574).

As the month of May began to wind down, the Pirates began to come to life, and from the 25th through the 31st, they went 7–1, raising their won-lost percentage to .553 and getting them to within five and a half games of the Giants and one game of the second-place Robins. It was during this time that Dreyfuss made two more strategic moves. First, he picked up veteran first baseman John "Stuffy" McInnis, who had been released by Boston on April 13. And second, he traded the struggling Al Niehaus to Cincinnati for pitcher Tom Sheehan.

Although neither McInnis nor Sheehan were spring chickens—McInnis would turn 35 that September and Sheehan was already 31—each had something to offer the Bucs. McInnis, a member of Connie Mack's legendary "$100,000 infield" as well as a starter for three other franchises, had played on five pennant winners, four of which had also won the World Series. So, he knew what it took to be a champion and he had the experience to help stabilize Pittsburgh's young infield.

Sheehan, a very good minor league pitcher with several years of major league service, was picked up to bolster the Corsairs' relief corps. He had a reputation for "a world of speed and a fast curve" and for being "willing to work often and out of turn, if necessary."[66]

As with the trade of Grimm, Maranville, and Cooper and the release of Schmidt, the acquisition of McInnis and Sheehan raises the question of how much influence did McKechnie have in creating the new-look Pirates. Just using the swap with Chicago as an example to get to the heart of this matter, the process appears to have been for Dreyfuss and McKechnie to work hand in hand to arrange any deal with any team, much in the same way that Dreyfuss had worked with former Pirate skipper Fred Clarke.[67]

Ronald Waldo, the author of a book on the 1925 Bucs, has written that "McKechnie was the one who initiated and finalized the trade with Chicago,"[68] but this is an overstatement. As *Pittsburgh Post* sportswriter Edward Balinger reported:

> The negotiations for this transaction were opened ... when President William L. Veeck and Manager William J. Killefer of the Cubs reached [Pittsburgh for a dinner held in honor of Barney Dreyfuss]....
> They asked Dreyfuss if he was willing to listen to a proposition along lines of swapping. He replied that he never would turn a deaf ear to anything that might tend to benefit his club, but nothing would be done without the full approval of McKechnie.
> Accordingly, Veeck, Dreyfuss, Killefer and McKechnie agreed to meet at the same time and endeavor to talk turkey. The Chicago magnates were determined to have three players. Killefer said he would part with Grantham ... provided that he could obtain in return a star second baseman of the highest magnitude. The Pirates had only one who would fill the bill, Maranville. The Cub leader also was willing to trade Aldridge, one of his most effective right-handed hurlers, for a moundsman who delivered from the left side. No second-rater would be accepted under any circumstances.
> First base was the next problem in the argument. Charley Grimm was looked upon with favor by the Cubs, but they had no seasoned performer to offer. However, they hold [*sic*] title to the services of a youngster named Albert Niehaus....
> McKechnie, after looking at the proposition from every angle, ... announced that he was perfectly willing to close the deal. Dreyfuss ... without a moment's

hesitation, declared he would back up the pilot to the letter. He could have traded Emil Yde instead of Cooper. The name of Don Songer also was mentioned, but McKechnie decided that of the three southpaws, it would seem the wisest policy to part with the one who had seen the longest service.[69]

Thus, it was Veeck and Killefer who initiated the trade and McKechnie and Dreyfuss who jointly finalized it.

In Waldo's defense, he elaborates on his statement by adding, "Of course, Dreyfuss agreed with his manager ... and stood by his manager's decision to trade Grimm, Cooper and Maranville.... Dreyfuss had the final word in all things involving the Pittsburgh organization."[70] That Dreyfuss was so quick to support McKechnie's willingness to part with three standouts was probably because he had already decided in his own mind that they had to go, though he wanted quality players in return for them. As Ralph Davis explained in his column in the November 6, 1924, issue of *The Sporting News*:

> Maranville lost his hold on Dreyfuss by his conduct off the field during the campaigns of 1922 and 1923. During the past season he behaved himself much better, but his fate had already been sealed. It is an open secret that he would have been disposed of a year ago, had any decent offer been made for him.
>
> As for Grimm, he had a serious run-in with his manager last summer, following his attempt to secure more salary in the spring.[71]

Beyond his obvious dissatisfaction with Maranville, Dreyfuss had no time for holdouts and would have seen Grimm's quarrel with McKechnie as a form of insubordination, something that he was no longer willing to put up with. The same could be said about Cooper, whose interpersonal perfectionism on the field, as discussed earlier in this chapter, may have made Dreyfuss view him as a disruptive force. However, it is interesting to note that Grimm was quoted as "denying that there were any differences between the Pirate management and himself that might be said to have led to the making of the big trade with the Cubs" and that he was "surprised at the suddenness of the deal."[72]

But whatever the exact dynamics were of the Dreyfuss-McKechnie relationship, the acquiring of McInnis and Sheehan was followed by another move that would eventually be considered Dreyfuss' most controversial decision of the season: the hiring of Fred Clarke as Dreyfuss' personal assistant, assistant to the manager, and head of scouting.

For most students of baseball history, Clarke is best known as the fiery player-manager of the Louisville Colonels and Pittsburgh Pirates, who is perhaps the only man who could have been elected to the National Baseball Hall of Fame as both a player and a manager. As a player, Clarke was an excellent hitter, an aggressive base runner—an earlier version of Ty Cobb—a daring defender, and a fierce competitor. And as a manager, his statistics speak for themselves. Competing against the likes of Ned Hanlon, Frank Selee, John McGraw, Frank Chance, and George Stallings, Clarke won four pennants and one World Series championship, led his teams to 14 first-division finishes out of 18 and a half seasons, and compiled a .576 winning percentage—most of which was accomplished while he was also playing.

But Clarke was much more than just a baseball star. The ninth of 12 children of a blacksmith-farmer and his homemaker wife, and possessing no more than an eighth-grade education, he rose to become a creative inventor, a prosperous landowner, an expert trapshooter, an accomplished rider, hunter, and fisherman, a community leader in Winfield, Kansas, and a multimillionaire. In short, Fred Clarke was the Horatio Alger myth personified.

And the transformation was brought about by three factors: Clarke's belief in fate, his love for the land, and his passion for playing baseball. The first of these three served to shape Clarke's world view and to give Clarke the optimistic demeanor that helped him to overcome or bounce back from the disappointments and setbacks that he encountered during his earthly odyssey. As Clarke said in a candid and surprisingly detailed interview (Clarke was not known for his loquaciousness) in the March 5, 1911, issue of the *New York Herald*, "I attribute my success to fate.... Life is a funny game, and a little thing, almost a trifle, may make a splash in your affairs so big that the ripples from it will be felt as long as you live."[73] The interview later disclosed that Clarke was referring to a specific incident that had occurred in the 1890s, but a close examination of Clarke's life certainly furnishes believers in fate with enough evidence to reinforce their beliefs. Of course, whether fate actually played a role in shaping Clarke's life is something that can be neither proved nor disproved, but the fact that Clarke thought that it did provided him with the impetus to be highly successful in a variety of undertakings.

However, if fate was the guiding force in Clarke's life, the driving forces were land and baseball. Land brought Clarke stability and wealth; baseball brought him fame; and combined they gave him influence and power. In fact, in certain ways, land and baseball would be Clarke's "mistresses." This is not to say that Clarke would not become a happily married man, which he would, but rather that land would be his other love and baseball would be his other passion. And like two jealous paramours, land and baseball would not only vie with Clarke's family for Clarke's attention, but they also would compete with each other, pulling Clarke in different directions.

The love of the land would make its appearance first, being planted in Clarke's genes by his ancestors, or was it by fate? Fred's paternal great-great-great-grandfather was Joshua Clarke or Clark,[74] a Maryland planter, and though Fred's paternal great-great-grandfather, another Joshua, was a merchant by profession, he held 4,280 acres of land in Maryland's Caroline, Talbot, and Queen Anne's counties at the time of his death.[75] Fred's maternal grandfather's side, the Cutlers—a family originally from Sprowston, England, a suburban village that borders Norwich in Norfolk County—arrived at Hingham, Massachusetts, in 1637, where the patriarch of the family, John Cutler, Sr., received land.[76]

As for Fred himself, he was born on a farm near Winterset in Madison County, Iowa, on October 3, 1872, and given the names Fred—not Frederick—Clifford. His father, William Dickinson Clarke, a native of Caroline County, Maryland, and the son of yet another Joshua Clarke (as can be seen, Joshua was a popular name in the Clarke family) and Sarah Ann Elizabeth Dickinson,[77] was a blacksmith by trade, but one who yearned to own his own land.[78] By the time of Fred's birth, William had traveled from his home state to Carthage, Illinois, where he married Lucy Cutler, and then to various places in Illinois and Iowa before finally going to the Winterset area, presumably in search of land.[79]

Because no deed for property in William's name has been found in the Madison County Recorder's office, Fred's father may have been a tenant farmer or a sharecropper who was providing his skills as a blacksmith to a farm owner when Fred was born.[80] But William's desire to own property was so overwhelming that, on May 13, 1874, he bought about 160 acres of land north of Winfield, Kansas, and then proceeded to move his family there by covered wagon.[81]

It was during this first stay in the Sunflower State that the young Fred fell in love with the soil in general and the Winfield region in particular, a place to which he would return beginning in 1899 and gradually buy sections of land to create his Little Pirate Ranch. And it would be on the Little Pirate Ranch that oil would eventually be discovered, making Clarke a multimillionaire and a force to be reckoned with.

But if Clarke gained stability and wealth in Kansas, it was in Iowa where he became exposed to his passion: baseball. Sometime between the second half of 1880 and July of 1881, and probably for financial reasons, the Clarke family returned to Iowa and settled in the city of Des Moines.[82] It was here that the young Fred watched the local ball teams competing and was bitten by the bug, becoming a player himself. This led to his rising in the ranks from the amateur to the semi-professional to the minor league levels and finally to a major league career that culminated with his induction into the National Baseball Hall of Fame in 1945.[83]

And it appears that fate may have lent a hand in this ascent at least a half dozen times. First, if the Clarke family had remained in southern Kansas, there is a strong possibility that Clarke would have followed in his father's footsteps as a farmer and never have gotten involved with professional baseball. But Des Moines in the late 1880s was a hotbed for baseball activity. As historian Ralph Christian has written:

Baseball fever hit the city with a vengeance in 1887 when the Des Moines Hawkeyes, the city's entry in the Northwestern League and first avowedly professional team, took the field, causing one commentator to note: "Base ball [sic] is all the rage at present. All other sport is laid in the shade." ... Baseball mania reached an even greater pitch in 1888. The Des Moines team, re-christened the "Colts" and competing in the new Western Association, handily won the league pennant, and topped their season off by defeating [Cap] Anson and his White Stockings in late October as the latter team embarked on one of its world wide [sic] exhibition tours.[84]

One of the people infected by this baseball fever was an impressionable teenager by the name of Fred Clifford Clarke, who launched his baseball career by playing on a Des Moines amateur team that had been organized and developed by Ed Barrow, the same Ed Barrow who is best known for turning the New York Yankees into a powerhouse.[85]

Another example of fate's perceived role in Clarke's life occurred in 1893 when the future Hall of Famer, perhaps tired of being an itinerant minor leaguer whose leagues kept shutting down prematurely,[86] attempted to stake a claim in the Cherokee Strip, a section of land in what is now Oklahoma.[87] If he had been successful, the land mistress may have triumphed and Clarke may have given up on ever becoming a major leaguer. But he failed, which, in turn, pushed him to return to Organized Baseball the following year. As Clarke would later say, that failure was "[o]ne of my real lucky breaks."[88]

Fate in the form of failure showed up again in 1894. This time, Savannah, the minor league team that Clarke was then playing for, folded, and Clarke was all set to go to Milwaukee to play for yet another minor league team, when the major league franchise of Louisville expressed an interest in him and sent him transportation money before Milwaukee's arrived.[89] Thus, Clarke received the opportunity that he had been waiting for, and once he got to Louisville, he took advantage of this opportunity by having one of the most impressive debuts in major league history. Using a small bat and facing veteran pitcher Gus Weyhing, Clarke went five for five, hitting four singles and a triple.

Nor does it seem that fate deserted Clarke after getting him to the big league (the National League was the only major league from 1892 through 1899). Instead, it took a new form: that of Barney Dreyfuss. Over seven years older than Clarke and one of the owners and executives of the Louisville club when Clarke arrived in the Derby City, Dreyfuss would exert immense influence on Clarke's life for most of the next 32 years. This influence was particularly evident on three occasions between 1894 and 1900:

> 1. After Clarke had established himself as a member of the Colonels—the nickname of the Louisville team—he attempted to imitate the

lifestyles of the veteran players, lifestyles that consisted of a lot of carousing and womanizing. Keep in mind that Clarke was only 21 years of age when he joined the Colonels and still impressionable, despite the previous experiences that he had had. Well, Clarke continued these dissolute ways, even though they were hurting his on-field performances, until one day Dreyfuss called him into his office and asked him:

> Are you fair with yourself?
> You can be a top notcher [*sic*] or you can remain what you are—a very ordinary player. You will live in the major league a few years only if you continue to dim your batting eye and weaken your physical self by carousing around. Then you will go back to the minors and be swallowed up, and you never will have been any one [*sic*]. It's up to you. Think it over.[90]

Fred Clarke: The Hall of Fame player-manager as a Louisville Colonel. It was at Louisville that Clarke first demonstrated his leadership qualities (National Baseball Hall of Fame Library, Cooperstown, New York).

Clarke did think it over, cleaned up his act, and became the star of his team, hitting the ball at a .334 clip, with an on-base percentage of .398 and 966 runs produced during the five and a half years that he played for Louisville. But Clarke was more than just an offensive threat. Defensively while in a Colonel uniform, his range factor far exceeded the league average for outfielders, and three times he finished in the top five in putouts for fly chasers.[91] Clarke's one weakness as a defender was going back for fly balls, but he compensated for this problem by playing a relatively deep left field and then using his speed and agility to help him make diving catches.

2. Recognizing Clarke's leadership qualities—possibly even before Clarke himself recognized them—Dreyfuss was instrumental in having Clarke named the Colonels' manager in June of 1897.[92] A by-product of this promotion was Clarke receiving the nickname of "Cap" because managers in the 1890s were often referred to as captains.

3. When Dreyfuss became partial owner of the Pirates and engineered his famous trade with Louisville in which he sent Clarke and the other good Colonel players to the Steel City franchise, the move ushered Clarke onto the stage where he would achieve his greatest fame.

After arriving in Pittsburgh, Clarke made the most of the cards that fate had dealt him. From 1900 through 1911, he not only patrolled left field and hit in the upper third of the batting order for the Bucs, usually second or third, but he also managed the Pirates from the field. Then between 1912 and 1915, he benched himself for all but a dozen games and led the team from the dugout.

It was during the first phase—1900–1911—that Clarke led the National League eight times in positive offensive categories, finished in the league's top 10 in positive offensive categories 121 times, and hit for the cycle twice.[93] In the 1909 World Series, Clarke's clutch performances at the plate contributed to each of the Pirate victories. On the base paths, Clarke continued to play in the style that he had developed at Louisville, using his arms and legs to jar balls loose from fielders, breaking up double plays with reckless abandon, and holding his own in fights with Cupid Childs, Fred Tenney, and others. Even while still at the plate, he showed his will to win by trying to hit the catcher with the backswing of his bat or by throwing his bat back at the catcher on a close play at third or home.

In addition, Clarke excelled defensively, leading outfielders in the National League twice in fielding percentage and once in putouts,[94] finishing in the league's top five in positive defensive categories for an outfielder 13 times,[95] recording four assists in a game in 1910, and making 10 putouts in a game in 1911.[96] And according to Baseball-Reference.com, his overall play—offensive plus defensive—placed him in the senior loop's top 10 in WAR for position players seven of the 12 seasons for this phase.[97]

It was during both phases, in particular the first, that Clarke showed his acumen as a manager, piloting his club to 1422 victories for a winning percentage of .595, leading his teams to nine first- or second-place finishes, and not having a losing season until 1914. His last two years were disappointing, but his entire body of managerial work was quite impressive, and he still holds the Pirate records for most victories, highest won-lost percentage, most pennants, most winning seasons, and most first-division finishes.

For Clarke, the secrets to being a successful manager were the same as the secrets to being a successful businessman. As he explained to H. Perry Lewis for an article that was published in the May 23, 1915, issue of the *Philadelphia Public Ledger*:

> The business man [*sic*] aims first to surround himself with capable men. Then he strives to get the maximum results from these men. To do the first[,] he must understand his business so thoroughly that he intuitively knows when a man will fit into his way of doing things. To accomplish the second[,] he must do a lot of things.[98]

Applied to the baseball world, these words, according to Clarke, meant that the successful manager had to have the "baseball knowledge, shrewdness, cheek, information ... and money" to get the best players that he could.[99] Then he had to shape those players into "a big, happy whole, both on and off the field."[100]

And how was the successful manager to do the latter? Well, to Clarke's way of thinking, there were a number of things that he could do. First, he had to maintain a positive attitude no matter what happened. As Clarke put it, "[the manager] must learn to smile, smile all the time; smile harder when things go wrong than when they go right. If a team believes that the manager is worried and discouraged[,] they are going to become worried and discouraged. That's disastrous."[101] For Clarke, smiling was not difficult. A supreme optimist buoyed by his belief in fate and his faith in the Roman Catholic religion, the former Pirate skipper was not one to let setbacks keep him down. His attitude in this regard might be summed up best by a story that Margaret Donahoe Burroughs, one of Clarke's granddaughters, told the author:

> I was my grandfather's favorite grandchild. He bought me a shotgun and a pony, but unfortunately, the pony was the nastiest, most ornery horse that I ever came across. His name was Billy and he would throw me, bite me, and lay down in the middle of a creek when I was trying to ride across it. When I first got on him, he threw me, and I was lying on the ground crying, when my grandfather came up and said, "Stop crying and get back on him."[102]

"Stop crying and get back on him"—that was how Clarke approached managing and life.

Second, the successful manager had to lead by example. In Clarke's case, this meant that he wanted his players to be as combative as he was on the field—no quarter asked and no quarter given—but he expected them to behave like gentlemen off the field, a dichotomy that he could easily make.

Third, the successful manager had to use his knowledge of baseball to get his players to understand what their strengths and weaknesses were and then to play accordingly. Clarke was not going to ask one of his players to do something that he felt that the player was incapable of doing. Nor would he give into a player's whim to allow the player to do something that the player thought that he could do but that went against Clarke's better judgment. The bottom line here was that the manager was in charge. As Clarke said to Lewis, "To the men must come the realization that the manager knows more [about baseball] than they do, otherwise the cogs will never work well."[103]

Fourth, the successful manager had to be willing to take chances. Clarke demonstrated this time and time again during his managerial career. Whether it was moving Claude Ritchey from shortstop to second base, turning Honus Wagner into a full-time shortstop, or starting rookie pitcher Babe Adams in the first game of the 1909 World Series and then starting him twice more later in the Series, Clarke was willing to take chances to win ballgames.

Fifth, the successful manager should not tolerate mental mistakes. Clarke understood that much of the game of baseball is played above the neck, so he would not put up with bonehead plays, even castigating himself if he was guilty of committing one.[104]

And finally, the successful manager should not suffer unruly players lightly. This is why Clarke convinced Barney Dreyfuss to sell Rube Waddell in 1901. It was not that Clarke did not recognize Waddell's greatness as a pitcher, but rather that he saw Waddell as a disruptive force. Many years later, when Clarke chose his all-time all-star team, he selected Waddell as the best left-handed pitcher he had ever seen.[105] Similarly, when he was asked to submit an all-star team of the top major leaguers that he had played with or against, he had Waddell as part of his starting pitching staff.[106] But Clarke viewed Waddell's antics as disturbing to the harmony of the rest of the team, so the eccentric moundsman had to go. Thus, in Clarke's eyes, a troublesome or troublemaking player who was not willing to change his ways had to be gotten rid of, no matter how good he was on the field.[107]

These were traits that had worked well for Clarke during his managerial years from 1897 through 1915 and ones that he would bring with him when he returned to the Pirates in June of 1925. But whether they would continue to work on a new generation of players was yet to be seen.

Along the way of his life's journey, Clarke became even more versatile as he developed a penchant for outdoor activities such as horseback riding, hunting, and fishing—all, no doubt, an extension of his love for the land—and became fascinated with mechanical items, leading to his creation of a variety of baseball-related inventions. Among these inventions were flip-down sunglasses, a sliding pad, an additional rubber strip placed in front of the pitching rubber to help prevent pitchers from slipping, a small equipment bag, and a mechanical way of handling the tarpaulin.[108] Thus, over the years, Clarke had become the outdoorsy version of a Renaissance man.

After retiring from Organized Baseball in 1915, Clarke went back to the Little Pirate Ranch, which would encompass 1,320 acres at its peak, to give year-round attention to his land paramour, as well as to indulge in his hobbies

Two. *The Return of Fred Clarke* 65

of hunting, fishing, and trapshooting. Then, the following year, oil was discovered on his land, and by 1917 Clarke's financial worth soared to $1,000,000—the equivalent of $90,900,000 in 2013.[109] At this point in his life, Clarke could have remained the prosperous rancher that he had become. He was happily married with two teenage daughters. In addition to his large ranch, he had made a fortune from lucrative coal, oil, and milling interests. And he was developing into a power in the Winfield area. Between his first departure from the Pirates and his second coming, he was instrumental in the establishment of a new St. Mary's Hospital in Winfield (ironically, the place where he would die in 1960); he helped to rebuild Winfield's Holy Name Catholic Church after the house of worship had been destroyed by fire in 1921; he was one of the founding fathers of the Winfield Rotary Club and the Winfield Country Club; and he had stood up to the Ku Klux Klan.[110] But his other mistress, baseball, kept tugging at his sleeve and Clarke could not resist pleasing her.

Although no longer residing in Pittsburgh for part of the year, Clarke maintained his relationship with Dreyfuss and attended special events held in the Steel City, like a birthday dinner for Honus Wagner in February of 1917,[111] where he advocated for more aggressive play on the diamond.[112] Between 1916 and 1919, he was rumored to be part of a syndicate (in 1916), part of a partnership (in 1918), or independently (in 1919) desiring to buy the Pirates.[113] Nothing came of these rumors even if they were true, but in 1921, George Gibson invited his former manager to attend the Bucs' spring training as an advisor. As Ralph Davis wrote in his March 24, 1921, column for *The Sporting News*: "Fred Clarke ... is giving Gibson some valuable assistance. No one is better able to judge ball players [sic] than Clarke.... He has taken several [rookies] under his wing, and is giving them the benefit of his experience."[114] It was during this time that Clarke helped turn Charlie Grimm from a .227 hitter into a .274 hitter and set him on the road to develop into the .290 career hitter that he eventually became.[115] Grimm had not forgotten what Clarke had done for him, and in 1925, he told Ralph Davis:

> I was a very poor hitter when I first broke in.... The credit for whatever improvement I have made belongs not to me but to Fred Clarke.
> Fred used to meet up ... at the training camp at Hot Springs ... and for some reason or other[,] he took an interest in me. He saw at a glance what my batting faults were and set out to correct them....
> ... he spotted [my faults] and worked patiently with me until I had got [sic] rid of most of them.[116]

Returning to spring training the following year before missing it in 1923,[117] Clarke was given the responsibility of finding a new spring site for the club in 1924. The Bucs had trained at Hot Springs, Arkansas, from 1901 through 1916, and then again from 1920 through 1923,[118] but because of a possible shortage of rooms due to a fire destroying one of the two hotels in the area, Dreyfuss wanted a change of scenery, so he asked Clarke if he could find a new place in California.[119] Clarke, who was familiar with the Golden State through his sojourns there to visit relatives, participate in trapshooting contests, and give speeches,[120] gladly obliged and selected Paso Robles, the site where the Pirates would continue to train through 1934.[121]

During the latter part of the 1922 season, when Clarke and his family were vacationing in Atlantic City, they visited friends in Pittsburgh, and while there, Bill McKechnie invited his former skipper to put on a uniform and "make himself perfectly at home in the big Dreyfuss stadium [Forbes Field] and clubhouse which had been the scene of [Clarke's] many triumphs."[122] Clarke not only accepted but also practiced with the Pirates before several games, accompanied the team when it "completed [its] last swing around the eastern end of the circuit," and "was in uniform before the closing clash with the Chicago Cubs" at home.[123] So, if there was any enmity between McKechnie and Clarke, it certainly was not apparent in 1922.

In addition to his work with the Pirates, Clarke covered the 1922 World Series for the *Pittsburgh Post*, writing each article himself.[124] As *Post* sportswriter Edward Balinger explained:

> Fred Clarke has signed up to write a special series of articles exclusively for [t]he *Pittsburgh Post*, covering the world's championship baseball games between the two major league teams of New York City, to be played on the Polo Grounds....
> Every word that will appear under the signature of Fred C. Clarke will be written by him. It will not be interviews hashed up by someone else, nor will it be a series of stories ground out by another person with Clarke's name printed above it. All the articles will be from the pen of the former skipper and outfield star of the Buccaneers. He will leave the general story of the games to the able corps of experts who have been specially engaged to detail the contests in the sporting columns of [t]he *Post*.
> Clarke has been requested to pick out such plays and such incidents as he may deem of special interest to the baseball public, and give his personal views of what happened. He will commend or criticize as occasion may demand, according to his judgment.[125]

Also in 1922, the *Los Angeles Times* broke a story in late December that Clarke was seriously considering becoming the Pirate manager for the 1923 season and that Barney Dreyfuss "is resorting to every means, persuasive and financial, to bring this about."[126] The *Times* added, "That these developments should first become known here in Los Angeles, instead of the East, is ... due to the presence here temporarily of an acquaintance of Dreyfuss and Clarke familiar with the negotiations which have been conducted secretly."[127] Was this just another rumor, or was Dreyfuss seriously considering removing McKechnie after the '22 season? As with the stories of Clarke buying the Pirates, nothing came of this story either, so the answer may never be known.

More stories of Clarke's permanent return to Organized Baseball came forth in both 1923 and 1924. During the former year, Clarke's name was suggested as a candidate for the position of president of the Pacific Coast League,[128] while during the latter year, Clarke was said to be interested in purchasing a minor league club, purchasing the Philadelphia Phillies, managing the Phillies, or purchasing some eastern major league club (which, of course, included Philadelphia).[129] And later it was learned that Miller Huggins, the skipper of the New York Yankees, had asked Clarke in 1924 to assist him in managing his team, an offer that Clarke laughed off.[130] But whatever specific plans Clarke may have had, by October 29, 1924, he certainly contemplated rejoining the ranks of Organized Baseball when he met with its commissioner, Kenesaw Mountain Landis, to check on "his standing in baseball."[131]

Besides being the subject of sports gossip, Clarke visited the spring training sites of several other teams in 1924.[132] It was as if he was familiarizing himself with both the National and American League players to ease his transition back to "The Show."

When Clarke rejoined the Pirate club on June 12 of 1925, he was already a legend in his own time. Lauded by the *Pittsburgh Post* as "baseball's grand old man," Clarke had been chosen by his rival John McGraw in 1922 as the best National League left fielder of the previous 20 years. "'The greatest of all,' pronounced McGraw. 'He had everything a winning ball player [sic] needs. It is too bad that Fred couldn't turn over his stuff when he retired.'"[133] Two years later, sportswriter W. B. Hanna topped McGraw's assessment when he wrote an article singling out Clarke as one of the top 25 major leaguers of all time.[134] In 1922, the University of Kansas had invited him to assist in coaching their baseball players during spring training,[135] and when he returned to Pittsburgh to play in an exhibition game honoring the Bucs' 1901 pennant winners, he was feted by the East End Republican Club and was one of the guests of honor at an informal dinner held by A. A. Maass in the East Liberty neighborhood of the Steel City.[136]

So, not surprisingly, Dreyfuss' announcement that he had rehired Clarke was warmly received by the Pirate faithful. The *Pittsburgh Press* wrote:

> The appointment of Clarke finds favor with Pittsburgh fans. The fiery leader of the Buccos from past years has always held a warm place in the hearts of fans in this section, not merely because of his diamond exploits but because he is a man in every respect. As an assistant to Manager Bill McKechnie[,] he should be a great help for he is known as a diplomat[,] and working with the pilot[,] greater things may fall the way of Pittsburgh teams of the future.[137]

Ralph Davis in his "Sport Chat" column in the *Press* added, "Fred Clarke's return to major league baseball ... is being hailed with delight among the fans, as it should be,"[138] while the *Pittsburgh Post* declared, "The value of Clarke to the Pirates at this particular stage cannot be underestimated."[139]

But despite the warm welcome that Clarke received from Pittsburgh fans and sportswriters alike, throughout the years there has been a certain amount of confusion over Clarke's new titles with the Pirates, his responsibilities, and the reasons as to why Dreyfuss hired him back in the first place—confusion that has added to the eventual misunderstanding surrounding the 1926 Pirates in general and the ABC Affair in particular.

To begin with, contrary to what some baseball historians have written, Clarke was not initially re-signed to be the Pirates' vice president. Also, though he was later referred to as a coach or assistant manager, the correct titles of his positions were "assistant to President Barney Dreyfuss, assistant to Manager Bill McKechnie, and ... chief of all the scouts ... on the Pirate payroll."[140] His responsibilities naturally followed from those titles and were described by the *Pittsburgh Post*:

> Familiar with duties connected with the promotion of a major league ball club [*sic*], Clarke will act in an advisory capacity with President Dreyfuss; rated as one of the greatest managers in the game, the former pilot, before the game can talk things over with McKechnie and on the field can be called upon for advice during an emergency. Off the field, with direct supervision over the scouts [one of whom was his brother-in-law, Charles 'Chick' Fraser], Clarke will likely be the last word in the purchase or drafting of suitable minor league material.[141]

The *Post* went further to say that

> never before has [Dreyfuss] divided his tasks and given anyone the authority for actions such as Clarke will have in his new regime. It shows the faith Dreyfuss has in the ability of Clarke.... [However,] [w]hile Clarke will have much to do with the business and playing duties of the Pirates in his new position, he will not have a financial interest in the club at this time and his plans along those lines for the future are indefinite.[142]

The last point was contradicted by Ralph Davis in his June 18, 1925, column in *The Sporting News* when he wrote that "it was stated that Dreyfuss permitted Clarke to purchase an interest in the club in order to work out the new arrangement,"[143] though the exact date of the investment was not specified. In all likelihood, Davis was correct. Clarke certainly bought stock in the Pirates after the 1925 season, and it would have made sense for Dreyfuss to try to sweeten the pot and also give Clarke an increased vested interest in the franchise by allowing him to acquire Pirate stock sometime during his tenure with the club. Furthermore, Clarke was a shrewd businessman with more than his share of money to spend, and if he intended to get back into major league baseball for the long haul, he may have felt comfortable investing in a product that he was familiar with and one that was considered financially worthwhile.[144] For that matter, Clarke himself more or less said as much when, without giving away any details, he told New York sportswriter Daniel Daniel, "I am interested in the Pittsburgh [c]lub financially. That was the only basis on which I would consent to return."[145]

Regarding Clarke's purchasing stock in the Pirates, it is interesting to note that during Clarke's player-manager days, he refused to get involved in such a practice because he felt that he "couldn't do himself or his club justice if he had an investment in the club which employed him."[146] Thus, his recent change of heart implied that even though he would have managerial advisory duties, he was viewing himself as part of the front office, a distinction that needs to be kept in mind when looking at his relationship with the Pirate players. As Clarke later explained to Dan Daniel, "My duties have to do with the business office as much as with the team on the field."[147]

And this leads to the question of why did Dreyfuss rehire Clarke. According to Dreyfuss himself when he announced Clarke's appointment, "he was getting old and needed some one [sic] who understood the business to aid him."[148] But this statement is rather odd considering that Dreyfuss was grooming his son, Samuel, or as he was better known in baseball circles, Sam, to be his successor. Sam, who was 28 years old when Clarke was brought back, was a 1919 Princeton graduate and had been working for his father shortly after earning his degree, becoming the treasurer of the Pirate organization in 1921.[149] He would receive the office of vice president of the club in 1929 while maintaining his position of treasurer, and at the time of his death in 1931, the *New York Times* wrote, "He was considered one of the best informed executives in the baseball world."[150] No, Dreyfuss already had "someone who understood the business to aid him"—his heir apparent to the throne.

Nor does it appear that Clarke was rehired to eventually buy the Pittsburgh club or to replace Bill McKechnie as manager. Concerning the former possibility, there was a rumor in October of 1925 that Clarke was part of another syndicate that was going to purchase the Pirates.[151] But as with previous rumors of this sort, nothing materialized, and nothing materialized because Dreyfuss wanted to turn the franchise over to his son once he retired. As the *Pittsburgh Press* wrote the day after Sam died in 1931:

> The owner of the Pirates cherished an ambition that his son should some day [sic] succeed him as the owner of the Pittsburgh team since Samuel Dreyfuss was a small boy....
> The Pirate owner was known to have received attractive offers for his club in

the last 10 years.... Each time he refused to sell. The general belief was that the prime reason why he wanted to retain ownership of the team was so that his son might some day [sic] have it.[152]

Concerning the latter possibility, if Dreyfuss had wanted to get rid of McKechnie, he would have done it sooner than mid- or even late 1925—perhaps after the 1922 season when the story broke that Dreyfuss was attempting to bring back Clarke as field manager. But by 1925, Dreyfuss had come to respect McKechnie's knowledge of the game and desired to keep him as the team's skipper.

So why then invite Clarke to rejoin the Pirate family? The most logical answer is to have him provide what Dreyfuss perceived the club had been lacking during the previous four years: discipline and mental toughness. McKechnie was a brilliant strategist, but he was no disciplinarian, and as was seen in the previous chapter, the 1921–1924 Pirates had been castigated for not being serious enough about their jobs, not handling adversity well, and not having the tenacity to win a pennant.

Added to these criticisms were Ralph Davis' specific comments about the failings of the '24 Bucs, in which he said, among other things, that the carousing of Johnny Morrison and "a few other members of the club, notably older men, who should have set the youngsters a good example, instead of violating all rules of discipline" had hurt the team and that "[a] stern disciplinarian is apparently one of the Pirates' greatest needs."[153] Dreyfuss could not have said it better himself, and this is why Clarke was rehired.

Although several heavy drinkers like Morrison remained, Dreyfuss had gotten rid of his "banjo players" and others who had been or were thought to be disruptive forces. He knew that he had bona fide stars in Carey, Traynor, Cuyler, Wright, and Kremer, and a skilled manager to lead them. On talent alone, he realized that his team could finish second or third again, and Dreyfuss was no slouch in assessing talent—"Branch Rickey once called [him] 'the best judge of players' that he had ever seen."[154] But one piece of the elusive solution to coming in first was still missing, and Clarke was brought back to supply that piece.

And the timing was ideal. The day that Clarke was hired, the Pirates were beginning a four-game series at Forbes Field against their hated rivals: the league leading Giants, who were playing .673 ball to the Bucs' winning percentage of .543. If fiery play and mental toughness were ever needed, this would have been the time for them.

Of course, Dreyfuss was taking a chance that Clarke's demographical makeup would mesh with the collective demographical makeup of the team and not cause more problems. When it came to baseball knowledge, there was no question that the '25 Pirates could benefit from Clarke's presence, but would

Clarke's personality—a personality formed from his regional origins, generational type, social background, and education or lack thereof—clash with the group personality of the men that he was over?

Clarke was Midwestern born and raised, the member of an idealist generation, the son of a farmer-laborer, and educated only through the eighth grade,[155] while the team was both similar and different in its makeup. As can be seen from Table 17, the plurality of Pirate players also came from the Midwest,[156] and 26 percent grew up in households where the heads were farmers,[157] whereas the household heads of another 13 percent were members of the working class.[158] In addition, 39 percent had started in one class but ended up in another one. But what Table 17 does not show is that in all the multiple-class cases, the household heads had been part of the farming and/or working class at one time. No problems there. Despite traveling around the United States, Clarke was still a Midwesterner at heart, and even though he had become a multimillionaire, he had not forgotten his roots.

The other two categories, however, could be sticky. In their provocative and well-researched books, *Generations: The History of America's Future, 1584 to 2069* and *The Fourth Turning: An American Prophecy*, William Strauss and Neil Howe discuss the common traits inherent in each American generation from the late 16th century through the middle of the 21st century and the trends that exist between types of generations.[159] Among their conclusions are:

- There are four basic types of generations: idealist, reactive, civic, and adaptive. Within each of these generations are leaders, followers, and nonconformists—those who do not fit the common traits of their generational type. However, in general, idealists have a positive reputation of being principled, resolute, and creative, with the driving forces in their lives being vision, values, and religion, and a negative reputation of being narcissistic, presumptuous, and ruthless. Reactives have a positive reputation of being savvy, practical, and perceptive, with the driving forces in their lives being liberty, survival, and honor, and a negative reputation of being unfeeling, uncultured, and amoral. Civics have a positive reputation of being selfless, rational, and competent, with the driving forces in their lives being community, affluence, and technology, and a negative reputation of being unreflective, mechanistic, and overbold. And adaptives have a positive reputation of being caring, open-minded, and experts at what they do, with the driving forces in their lives being pluralism, expertise, and due process, and a negative reputation of being sentimental, complicating, and indecisive.[160]

- The four types have, with one notable exception, repeated themselves in cyclical fashion throughout American history in periods ranging from 18 to 30 years.[161]

- Within each type, there are individual generations, each of which the authors label with a descriptive title to identify it (e.g., the Silent Generation for those adaptives born between 1925 and 1942), and each of those individual generations experienced or, in some cases, are still experiencing different specific issues depending on the particular time in history when the members of the generation were born. But the general characteristics of the type will remain the same. For example, the Glorious Generation, people born between 1648 and 1673, and the Republican Generation, people born between 1742 and 1766, both were civic types, so the pattern of their lives and their general behavior towards issues and events were similar, despite each generation facing dissimilar specific challenges.[162]

Obviously, genes, birth order, and environmental factors can modify the thoughts and actions of individuals within a generation, and Strauss and Howe's findings are not to be taken to underestimate the personal experiences of each generational member, but as depicters of generation types, they are quite useful.

Well, Clarke, as mentioned earlier, came from an idealist type—the Missionary Generation—but 91 percent of the Pirate players came from a reactive type—the Lost Generation—and unlike civics, who relate well to idealist leadership, reactives do not. So, would the generational divide lead to dissension on the team?

The formative effects of education could be problematic, too. When Clarke had managed the Pirates from 1900 through 1915, he had had some college men on his teams, but the majority of his players had gone only as far as elementary school or high school. However, now he would be dealing with a team where, based on the information found by the author, 52 percent of the players had at least attended some postsecondary institution,[163] while 35 percent had attended high school. Of the remaining three players, two (nine percent) had eighth-grade educations and the other one, who definitely had been an elementary school student, may have gone to high school for two years, but whether he did could not be confirmed by the author.[164] So, would such a group of better-educated men relate well to Clarke's old school ways of dispensing advice, which included, in addition to positive reinforcement, the use of profanity, vulgarity, and sarcasm whenever Clarke deemed it necessary? Clarke was an optimist, but he also did not mince words, and as mentioned earlier in this chapter, he did not tolerate mental mistakes or what he perceived to be disruptive forces. Although it is true that McKechnie's father was a laborer and the Pirate skipper did not attend college either, his nature was different than that of Clarke's, being low key and viewed as fatherly by his players.

As for the staff that Clarke would be working with, the demographical material for player-coach Jewel Ens has been added to that of the players and is reflected in the results found in Table 17. Bill McKechnie was born and raised in Wilkinsburg, Pennsylvania, came from a working-class family[165] and the Lost Generation, and, if the story told by his youngest child, Carol McKechnie Montgomery, is to be believed, "got kicked out of school in the fifth grade when he brought a snake to school ..., [thus ending] his formal education."[166] But according to Anne Elise Morris of the Wilkinsburg Historical Society, McKechnie had attended Wilkinsburg High School to play baseball for the school's team, though he never graduated.[167] As Morris told the author:

> The story is that he was dating the sister of [one of the other boys on the high school team] and McKechnie wanted to play, get noticed by the minor leagues and please his girlfriend's brother by helping the Wilkinsburg High team to do well. At that time, 1905, Wilkinsburg had high school courses held in various rooms within the six elementary schools in the district. The actual building for a high school did not exist until 1911. Therefore, the sports program was rather loosely organized and it would have been easy for a ballplayer to "sneak" into the sports program, while only attending a few academic classes but not officially [be] part of a class. As far as I can tell, the year of 1905 was the only year that he played for Wilkinsburg High School.[168]

McKechnie himself said that he had an eighth-grade education.[169]

The highest level of education for Jack Onslow and scout Bill Hinchman have not been found by the author,[170] but both men were from Pennsylvania[171] and the Lost Generation, and while Onslow's father was the superintendent of an oil company,[172] the occupation of Hinchman's father was not found by the author. On the other hand, scout Chick Fraser, Clarke's brother-in-law, differed from the rest of the staff by having been born in Chicago, coming from the Missionary Generation, and being educated at a business college, though like McKechnie, his social background was working class.[173]

Thus, there were differences that needed to be overcome. But at least for 1925, those differences did not prove to be troublesome. Fired up by Clarke's contributions—inspirational, strategical, and in dispensing advice on batting—the Bucs swept the Giants in their June series to get to within two and a half games of McGraw's men. They then captured first place on June 29 and, with the exception of five days, held on to it, winning the pennant by eight and half games over their hated New York rivals. Rather than collapsing during the

Table 17: Demographic Makeup of the Pittsburgh Pirate Active Roster on June 12, 1925[174]

Regional Origin[175]		Generational Type		Social Background[176]		Highest Level of Education by 1925	
Northeast	17%	Idealist	4%	Upper Class	0%	Seminary	4%
Southeast	26%	Reactive	91%	Middle Class	22%	College or University	35%
Midwest	39%	Civic	4%	Working Class	13%	Normal School	13%
Southwest	0%	Adaptive	0%	Farming Class	26%	High School	35%
West Coast	9%			Multiple	39%	Eighth Grade	9%
Multiple	9%					Elementary School	4%

Only players who could definitely be identified as being members of Pittsburgh's 25-man roster were included. Three other players would join the Pirates and see playing time after June 12, but their demographic information does not significantly change the general trends presented in this table, and two of the three would not be with the Pirates in 1926.[177]

Percentages have been rounded and may not equal 100%.

second half of the season or coming close only to fade away before the season was over, Pittsburgh went 38–21 in August and September and had during that time two winning streaks of nine games apiece and one stretch when they ran up 18 victories out of 22 games.[178] But perhaps the Pirates' most impressive accomplishment and one that proved that they had exorcised the demons of the previous four seasons was going into the Polo Grounds in late August with only a three-game lead over the Giants and taking four out of five games from the New Yorkers. The *Boston Globe* called the matchup the "little World's Series" and added, "Not alone were the Giants outplayed in the field, but they were outfought in the way of strategy."[179]

The Pirates' dominance over the Giants and the rest of the National League is best shown in tables 18, 19, and 20. From these tables, the following can be seen:

- The Pirates led the senior circuit in five of the six won-lost categories and even won two to four games more than their statistics reflected.

- The Giants were better in one-run games and won seven or eight games more than the results of their play on the field would indicate—possibly because of McGraw's leadership—but that was about it. Nineteen twenty-five was clearly the Pirates' year.

- Unlike previous seasons where the Pirates could best league rivals five times at most in head-to-head series, the 1925 crew came within two games of going 7–0. Ironically, the one series that the Bucs lost came at the hands of the Cubs, who had finished dead last despite having early on been considered the benefactors of the Grimm-Maranville-Cooper trade. But Pittsburgh edged the Giants and decisively beat third-place Cincinnati and fourth-place St. Louis. And three of the losses to the Giants were throwaway games, played after the Bucs had clinched the pennant.

- In team statistics, as presented by Table 20, the Bucs led the Giants in seven out of nine categories and the league in five out of nine. What the table does not show is that in adjusted ERA and pitching wins, Pittsburgh finished second to Cincinnati's powerful mound crew, and in run differential, it topped the league.

- The lone weakness of the team based on Table 20's stats was fielding, where it was a tad below average, but as will be discussed a little later in this chapter, that -0.9 rating may be a statistical illusion.

- Finally, the team showed a nice balance between offense (batting wins plus base-stealing wins) and defense (pitching wins plus fielding wins), though it is best remembered for its offensive attack.

Table 18: The Won-Lost Records of the 1925 Pittsburgh Pirates and New York Giants[180]

Team	Won-Lost Record	Home Won-Lost Record	Away Won-Lost Record	Won-Lost Record in One-Run Games	Won-Lost Record Against Teams That Were .500 or Better	Won-Lost Record Against Teams That Were Under .500	Expected Won-Lost Record	Projected Won-Lost Record
Pittsburgh	95–58	52–25	43–33	27–20	39–26	56–32	93–60	90.9–72.1
New York	86–66	47–29	39–37	28–16	35–30	51–36	79–73	78.4–73.6

Or if these numbers were converted to percentages, the results would be as follows:

Team	Won-Lost Percentage	Home Won-Lost Percentage	Away Won-Lost Percentage	Won-Lost Percentage in One-Run Games	Won-Lost Percentage Against Teams That Were .500 or Better	Won-Lost Percentage Against Teams That Were Under .500	Expected Won-Lost Percentage	Projected Won-Lost Percentage
Pittsburgh	.621	.675	.566	.574	.600	.636	.608	.594
New York	.566	.618	.513	.636	.538	.586	.520	.516

League leaders are in boldface.

Table 19: The Won-Lost Records of the 1925 Pittsburgh Pirates and New York Giants Versus the Other Teams in the National League[181]

Team	Boston	Brooklyn	Chicago	Cincinnati	New York	Philadelphia	Pittsburgh	St. Louis
Pittsburgh	15–7	17–5	10–12	13–8	12–10	14–8		14–8
New York	11–11	12–10	15–7	13–9		13–8	10–12	12–9

Table 20: Team Statistics for the 1925 Pittsburgh Pirates and New York Giants[182]

Team	Runs Scored	Runs Allowed	AOPS	AERA	Batting Wins	Pitching Wins	Fielding Wins	Base-Stealing Wins	Number of Positive Categories That the Team Led the League In
Pittsburgh	**912**	715	108	115	5.8	7.9	-0.9	1.6	21
New York	736	702	101	102	0.3	1.7	0.5	-0.0	2

League leaders are in boldface.

In fact, so strong was the Pittsburgh offensive attack that seven out of eight starters hit over .300, and the lone exception, Eddie Moore, batted .298. True, the entire National League averaged .292, but no other starting eight could match that of the Buccos, whose entire team averaged .307. Five men scored 97 or more runs, while four drove in 102 or more. Spearheading this attack were

- the multitalented Kiki Cuyler, who had a career year by batting .357 (fourth in the NL), with an on-base percentage of .423 (fifth), a slugging average of .598 (second), 228 runs produced (second), and 41 stolen bases (second) in 54 attempts;

- the 35-year-old team captain, Max Carey, who despite his age, hit .343 (seventh in the senior loop), got on base almost 42 percent of the time (sixth), stole 46 bases (first) in 57 attempts, and scored 109 runs (sixth); and

- the run-producing twins: Pie Traynor, who drove in 106 runs and scored 114, mostly from the fifth slot in the batting order, and Glenn Wright, who usually batted immediately after Traynor and who topped him with 121 RBI, while scoring 97.[183]

But the pitching was no slouch either. Among National League leaders, Vic Aldridge, Lee Meadows, and Ray Kremer finished eighth, ninth, and 10th, respectively, in adjusted ERA; Aldridge and Meadows came in fifth and tied for sixth, respectively, in strikeouts; Kremer was sixth in the fewest walks given up per nine innings pitched and ninth in WHIP; Johnny Morrison tied for

Harold "Pie" Traynor, Pittsburgh's star third baseman. He was an outstanding fielder, but Traynor's weakness as a defensive player was an inaccurate throwing arm. To compensate for it, he would release the ball as soon as he caught it so that the first baseman would have enough time to leave the bag, catch the ball, and return to the bag to record the out (National Baseball Hall of Fame Library, Cooperstown, New York).

first in saves; and all five of the Pirates' regular starters—Aldridge, Meadows, Kremer, Morrison, and Emil Yde—were part of the top 10 in wins.[184]

Defensively, contrary to what might be expected based on Pittsburgh's rating in fielding wins in Table 20, a number of Pirates finished in the top three in the NL at their particular positions. Earl Smith came in third in assists for catchers; Moore was third in putouts for second basemen; Wright ended up second in putouts, first in assists and double plays, and third in range factor for shortstops; Traynor finished first in putouts, assists, double plays, range factor, and fielding percentage for third basemen; Barnhart came in second in putouts and fielding percentage and third in assists (tied with one other) and range factor for left fielders; Carey was second in putouts, first in assists, and third in double plays (tied with five others) and range factor for center fielders; and Cuyler rounded out the group by ending up first in putouts, third in assists (tied with one other) and double plays (tied with two others), and second in range factor for right fielders.[185]

So, how did such good performances amount to a below average score in fielding wins based on linear weights? It could be because the average fielding percentage of all teams in the National League was .966, while that of the Pirates was .964, and that both Moore and Carey led their positions in errors. But fielding percentage is one of the weakest statistics to determine the greatness of a fielder and oftentimes better defensive players will make more errors because they get to balls that lesser fielders would not. A prime example of this on the '25 team was Barnhart and Carey. Barnhart, who fielded his position well, had a .962 fielding average for 318 total chances. Carey had a .950 average for 403 total chances. Barnhart's contributions were important to the Pirates' success, but no one ever confused Barnhart with Carey as a fielder.[186]

Regarding the results of the big trade with the Cubs, the title of Jim Steinman's love song, "Two Out of Three Ain't Bad,"[187] would be apropos. Niehaus was gone, but Grantham became the starting first baseman and had a potent season with the bat, lowering his strikeout total to just 29, hitting .326, and finishing eighth in his league in on-base percentage with a .413 average. And Aldridge, after a slow start, came on strong to post a 3.63 ERA (as mentioned above, eighth in his league when adjusted), 88 strikeouts (fifth), and a 15–7 record (ninth in wins; fourth in won-lost percentage). In contrast, only Charlie Grimm did well with Chicago. Maranville broke his leg and had a lousy season, and Cooper had one of the worst years of his career.[188]

The acquisition of Stuffy McInnis also reaped dividends as the veteran first sacker batted .368 in 175 plate appearances, with an on-base percentage of .437, and made only three errors in 404 chances.[189]

Another key pickup was John "Red" Oldham, who the Pirates acquired from Des Moines on August 10. A left-handed starter-reliever, Oldham's regular-season stats were modest—11 appearances, 53 innings pitched, three wins out of five decisions, and one unofficial save[190]—however, for one brief and shining moment in the upcoming World Series, he would cement a fond spot for himself in the hearts of all Pirate fans. But more on that later.

As might be expected, postseason awards and praise were plentiful for the Corsair crew. Carey, Cuyler, Traynor, and Wright made *The Sporting News'* Major League All-Star Team, with the last three also being chosen for *Baseball Magazine's* Major League All-America Club, while all four of them and Smith were selected to *Baseball Magazine's* National League All-Star Club.[191] Cuyler finished second in the voting for his league's most valuable player award, and Wright, Traynor, Carey, and Aldridge came in fourth, eighth, 11th, and 21st, respectively.[192] And in a poll of the National League players conducted by the *Pittsburgh Gazette Times*, Wright, Traynor, and Cuyler were chosen as their league's best at their particular positions,[193] and Carey was voted the NL's most dangerous base runner.[194]

Recognition also came in the form of a variety of articles written about members of the team by *Baseball Magazine*. In the November 1925 issue alone, an issue that went to print before the season had ended, there were pieces on Adams, Barnhart, Cuyler, and Wright.[195] The December issue had features on Aldridge, Carey, and Meadows, and the March 1926 issue had a story that in part discussed Wright and Traynor.[196]

Clarke received his share of accolades, too. As early as June 22, Ralph Davis reported:

> Perhaps the presence of Fred Clarke in the dugout has had something to do with the new spirit that is apparent on all sides...
> Clarke is of the type that never knows when it is beaten, a type that has been far too scarce on Pittsburg[h] rosters of modern times. Perhaps Fred has imbued the 1925 Buccaneers with some of his old-time enthusiasm and grit.[197]

Less than two weeks later, Jack Gallagher of the *Los Angeles Times* was more emphatic when he wrote:

> A month ago[,] the 1925 [National League] pennant was conceded to Muggsy [*sic*] McGraw. At that time[,] the Corsairs were endeavoring to climb out of seventh place and Bill McKechnie was having a hard time trying to co-ordinate [*sic*] his hard-hitting machine.
> About that time[,] McGraw's old baseball enemy, Fred Clarke, stepped into the picture again as adviser to the Pirate team ... and, after that, the baseball world witnessed the boys from Pittsburgh literally smash their way to the top of the parent [league]....
> No one has learned just what prompted Barney Dreyfuss, owner of the Pirates, to bring his former manager back into active service. The logical conclusion is

that after the Pirates missed three or four pennants that seemed to be within their grasp, Dreyfuss decided that something was lacking and that Clarke could supply that particular something. He did.[198]

And on that same day, an unknown scribe for the *Washington Post* added:

> The deeds of the Pittsburghers since Clarke moved in speak for themselves.... Clarke undoubtedly will instill in the Pirates a spirit that seems to have been lacking.... You can be sure of one thing and that is that he'll have the Pirates fighting harder than they've fought in several seasons.[199]

But the greatest compliments for Clarke came from Dan Daniel, who contributed a detailed article to *Baseball Magazine,* lauding Clarke for being the team psychologist who got the Pirates over their collective inferiority complex and for serving as "the spiritual adviser and the father confessor of the players," as well as "the strategical aid of McKechnie."[200] Daniel pointed out how Clarke's mantra was "Don't under-rate [sic] yourself and over-rate [sic] your opposition."[201] And when it came to McGraw, Clarke repeatedly told the team:

> This man McGraw is no god. You can beat him....
> Play your natural way.... If you press[,] you will act in a strained way and you will lose your chances. Take every game in its natural course. The Giants are no greater than any other team in the league. Do not make any special effort when you meet them.
> Don't worry over your games. But keep fighting....[202]

Clarke, in turn, had nothing but praise for McKechnie, telling Daniel that "Bill McKechnie deserves a world of credit for bringing [the team] along the way he did after that poor start in the spring."[203] Daniel himself added, "McKechnie ... was [the] manager in fact as well as in name. There is no truth in the report that from time to time Clarke took over the managerial reins."[204]

Others echoed Clarke's sentiments toward the Pirate skipper. Ralph Davis applauded McKechnie for his "rare, shrewd judgment,"[205] and many years later, Ronald Waldo would sum up the local adulation for McKechnie by writing, "[Pittsburgh] [f]ans and scribes had proclaimed McKechnie a hero for leading his troops to first place."[206]

The players, for their part, extolled the leadership qualities of both Clarke and McKechnie. According to the *New York Times,* once the team had clinched the pennant, the members "crowded about Bill McKechnie ... and Fred Clarke, singing the praise of the men who led them to victory."[207]

McKechnie reciprocated by making "a speech, in which he thanked his men for what they had accomplished," and John Heydler, who had watched the flag-winning game from the press box, went into the clubhouse and personally congratulated Clarke, McKechnie, and the rest of the battling Bucs.[208]

The Pirates' biggest challenge, however, was yet to come: facing the defending American League and World Series champion Washington Senators in the October classic. The Senators possessed a talented team and one that, at least on paper, was stronger offensively than their '24 contingent. Led by 28-year-old player-manager Stanley "Bucky" Harris, Washington boasted a hitting attack centered around star outfielders Leon "Goose" Goslin (first in triples, third in total bases, and fourth in both runs scored and RBI in the AL) and Edgar "Sam" Rice (second in hits, tied for fourth in triples, and sixth in total bases), first baseman-outfielder Joe Harris (seventh in on-base percentage and slugging average), and first sacker Joe Judge, a line drive hitter who was not among the offensive leaders, but who had batted .314, with an on-base average of .406. The Senator defense featured third baseman Ossie Bluege and shortstop Roger Peckinpaugh, the junior circuit MVP, who have been rated second and tied for fourth, respectively, in defensive WAR for position players in the American League. Other defensive standouts were Goslin, who led AL left fielders in putouts, assists (tied with two others), range factor, and fielding percentage; Rice, who was first in assists and range factor and second in putouts and fielding percentage for his league's right fielders; Muddy Ruel, who was first in putouts, assists, range factor, and double plays for AL catchers; and Bucky Harris himself, who finished second in putouts, assists, and fielding percentage, and third in range factor among second basemen in the junior circuit. But the team's biggest luminary was the outstanding right-handed pitcher, Walter Johnson, arguably the best major league moundsman of all time. Johnson was 37 years old when the World Series began, but he still finished fourth in the American League in ERA, fifth in WHIP, second in strikeouts, first in strikeouts to walks ratio, and tied for third in wins. Behind Johnson were Stanley Coveleski, another oldie but goodie at 36 years of age, who was first in ERA, third in WHIP, and tied for third in wins; 18-game winner Walter "Dutch" Ruether; and ace reliever Frederick "Firpo" Marberry, whose 16 unofficial saves led the junior loop.[209]

A poll of the major league baseball writers taken by *The Sporting News* on the eve of the World Series gave Pittsburgh the edge.[210] However, in a more telling article written before the '25 season ended, but one that was published in the November 1925 issue of *Baseball Magazine*, W. B. Hanna compared the various units—pitchers, catchers, infielders, and outfielders—of the Pirates, Giants, Senators, and Philadelphia Athletics, and concluded that Washington had a better catching pair and a better infield than the Bucs, but Pittsburgh had a better outfield.[211] The pitching was considered even, "barring the fact that Marberry is the best relief man on any of the four teams, and therefore, an asset of utmost importance."[212] And, of course, Harris' men had the advantage of having already played in and won a World Series.

Thus, the Senators could have been the force that, to use a cliché, rained on the Pirates' parade, but instead, to use another cliché, they proved to be the icing on the cake. Down three games to one and facing elimination, the Bucs showed the fire that they had exhibited since sweeping the Giants in mid–June and rallied to win the remaining games to become the first team in major league history to capture the World Series championship after trailing by such a margin. And although the Series is best remembered for Roger Peckinpaugh's eight errors, Sam Rice's controversial catch of a near home run hit by Earl Smith, and Kiki Cuyler's clutch double in the rain in the seventh game, a number of Pirates acquitted themselves well. Vic Aldridge had strong pitching performances to help win the second and fifth games. Glenn Wright and Cuyler had key home runs in Aldridge's first outing to secure a narrow 3–2 victory. Those two were joined in Aldridge's second outing by the entire Pittsburgh offensive attack, which pounded out 13 hits to win, 6–3. In the sixth game, Ray Kremer threw a six-hitter, Eddie Moore provided the decisive run with a solo homer, and the Pirates rallied from being down 2–0 to take a 3–2 squeaker. As for the seventh game, much has been written about the rain, the way Pittsburgh won after spotting Washington and Walter Johnson a four-run lead, Peckinpaugh's errors, and Cuyler's two-out double in the bottom half of the eighth that drove in what proved to be the winning runs, but other highlights include:

- A tremendous performance by team captain Max Carey, who went 4-for-5, with three doubles, three runs scored, two runs driven in, and a stolen base. Carey's feat was even more remarkable considering that he had fractured a rib and torn some ligaments loose in a collision with Bucky Harris in Game Five.[213] Showing the gutsiness of the old Deadball Era veteran that he was, the ace center fielder not only refused to sit out the remainder of the Series but also continued to play well, finishing with a .458 batting average, a .552 on-base percentage, and a .625 slugging average.

- RBI by Moore, Barnhart, and Traynor.

- Carson Bigbee's pressure-filled pinch hit in the eighth to drive in the tying run and put himself in the position to eventually score the game- and series-winning run when Cuyler would later double. Two decades later, Barney Dreyfuss' widow, Florence, would tell Pittsburgh sportswriter Les Biederman that "I always regard Carson Bigbee's hit that tied the game as the one that gave me the biggest thrill. Some say Kiki Cuyler's hit that won was the thrill, but after all, you have to tie before you can win. And we were behind when Bigbee made that hit."[214]

- Kremer coming into the game as a reliever on just one-day's rest and pitching four innings of one-hit, one-run ball.

- And finally, Red Oldham, the August pickup, facing Sam Rice, Bucky Harris, and Goose Goslin in the top of the ninth inning and retiring the side in order by striking out Rice, getting Harris to line out to Moore, and fanning Goslin. It took Oldham only 12 pitches to put the final nail in Washington's coffin: five fastballs to Rice, three more to Harris, and four slow curves to Goslin.[215]

Throughout the Series, both McKechnie and Clarke also acquitted themselves well. McKechnie was credited with outmanaging Harris, and the praise was certainly deserved. On multiple occasions, he followed Clarke's rule about taking chances to win, and he did so because he knew his players and what they were capable of. For example, in the top of the fifth inning in the second game, with the scored tied 1–1, the Senators loaded the bases with no one out and Rice, Harris, and Goslin coming to bat. But rather than lifting Aldridge and/or ordering his infielders to play at double-play depth, McKechnie had his infielders play in and the results could not have been better for the Bucs. Rice hit a grounder to Aldridge, which led to a force out at home of the runner on third. Harris hit a grounder to Wright, which led to a force out at home of the next runner on third. And Goslin hit a grounder to George Grantham, the first baseman, who retired him unassisted. Aldridge got into another tight spot in the top of the ninth when, with the Pirates leading 3–1, the Senators again loaded the bases with no one out. But as before, McKechnie showed the faith that he had in his pitcher by sticking with him, and Aldridge responded by getting pinch-hitter Bobby Veach to hit a sacrifice fly, pinch-hitter Dutch Ruether—a good hitting pitcher—to strike out, and Rice to ground out. McKechnie would later say, "Aldridge is that kind of pitcher. He is a good man who goes best when he is in a jam of one kind or another."[216] Or how about bringing in Red Oldham in the top half of the ninth inning of the seventh game? McKechnie knew that Oldham had not only faced Rice, Harris, and Goslin a number of times in the American League, but that he had also pitched well against them, holding Rice to a .211 batting average, Harris to .162, and Goslin to .222.

Nor was McKechnie averse to taking advice from other people as well as from Clarke. After the fourth game, a 4–0 loss that put Pittsburgh on the brink of defeat, the Pirates' old nemesis, John McGraw, suggested to McKechnie that he replace Grantham with Stuffy McInnis.[217] McGraw may have hated Barney Dreyfuss, but he hated American League president Byron "Ban" Johnson even more, and he liked McKechnie, who had played under him for part of 1916. Besides, he probably was still smarting from having lost to Bucky Harris and his team in the previous World Series and did not want to see them go all the way again. So, he felt that Pittsburgh had a better chance of making a comeback if the youngster Grantham, who had batted only .143 in the first four games, was benched in favor of World Series veteran McInnis. To McGraw's way of thinking, McInnis' experience and his reputation as a good defensive player would steady the Pirate infield—as mentioned earlier in this chapter, Grantham was not sure of himself in the field—and his bat would be an added plus. McKechnie accepted the advice, made the change, and McInnis hit .308 for the last three games and fielded 33 chances without an error. For that matter, the entire Pirate infield made just one error in those games.

As for Clarke, he continued to be the team psychologist—the dispenser of mental toughness and confidence—and McKechnie's right-hand man. The words of wisdom that he used during the pennant race were now repeated with a greater sense of urgency: "Don't under-rate [sic] yourself and over-rate [sic] your opposition. Don't press, don't become over-anxious [sic], for it's just as fatal in baseball as in golf or business. Don't worry. The other fellows are worrying and you've got something they haven't got."[218] Before the first game, Clarke could be found "everywhere ... chatting to the overly nervous members of the Pirates" in an attempt to steady them for what they were about to experience.[219] After the disastrous Game Four, when the Buccos were shut out by Walter Johnson and had had just 26 hits in 127 at bats for the first four contests, Clarke, the eternal optimist, told "the members of the team that they [were] bound to hit in the fifth game, and that only a few basehits [sic] [were] needed to put them back in the running."[220] Or as Dan Daniel wrote, "Clarke went before the players at a meeting in a Washington hotel and insisted that they would begin to hit [the next] day and eventually take the championship."[221] When Ray Kremer was warming up prior to the sixth game, it was Clarke who talked with him

Fred Clarke and Bill McKechnie: Two parts of the winning formula for the '25 Pirates (National Baseball Hall of Fame Library, Cooperstown, New York).

to calm his nerves, and throughout the Series, Clarke worked with McKechnie and scout Chick Fraser to analyze the weaknesses of the Senators.[222]

The contributions of Fraser and fellow scout Bill Hinchman may have gone unnoticed by most sportswriters and fans, but McKechnie certainly appreciated them. In a speech given at the Craft Club in Crafton, Pennsylvania, on February 20, 1926, the Pirate skipper sang the praises of his scouts by saying:

> As soon as it looked to me as if we were certain to win the pennant, I figured that we would have to meet either Washington or Philadelphia in the [World Series.] So, when these two teams met in their last series in Philadelphia, I sent Hinchman and Fraser over there to watch them play. They kept their eyes and ears open throughout that series and got much valuable information. They detailed it to me upon their return, and in that way[,] we got many pointers that were of much help to us when the fall classic rolled around.
>
> You don't hear Hinchman and Fraser much spoken about in connection with the [S]eries, but I call them the silent heroes of the [S]eries, for they did their work well in advance.[223]

Thus, all the pieces of Barney Dreyfuss' mosaic had come together to work in harmony. A formula for success had finally been ascertained: McKechnie plus Clarke plus astute scouts plus a group of serious-minded, talented veterans and younger players equals a pennant and a World Series championship. It was a formula that promised future success for the Pirates and one that caused Fred Clarke to emphatically respond to Dan Daniel's question of will the Pirates win again in 1926: "Will the Pirates win again in 1926? What a question! That ball club [sic] is good for three more pennants. We'll tie McGraw's record and then we will beat it."[224] But such would not to be the case.

Three

High Expectations, Disappointing Results

With even more talent on the way, the 1925 title could've been just the beginning.
—Mitchell Conrad Stinson, 2012

During the speech to his players after the Pirates had clinched the National League pennant in 1925, Bill McKechnie was said to have "thanked his men for the cooperation displayed and the harmonious spirit that was a big factor in bringing the flag to Forbes [F]ield."[1] Yet, two later stories alleged that there were signs of dissension while the World Series was in progress and shortly after it ended.

The first was a rumor that McKechnie and Clarke "had had a verbal encounter during one of the games, and that they had almost come to blows."[2] But as Ralph Davis reported, it was "[a] silly tale" that "was vehemently denied by Clarke, and McKechnie also entered a denial, adding that it was too silly to dignify by any extended statement."[3] In actuality, McKechnie had already issued an extended statement over a month before Davis' column was printed when he had told Ed Balinger:

> There has been no such a thing as friction in the Pirate family this year....
> I cannot understand how the reports originated about a disagreement between Fred Clarke and myself. We got along without any hitch from the moment he came to Pittsburgh until he left for a business trip to Kansas City after the [W]orld [S]eries. To show how much I think of Fred, I will state that we were together for more than two hours just before he boarded his train for the [W]est last month.[4]

End of rumor.

The second story, however, has been used by certain future writers as the first overt indication that Clarke and at least some of the Pirate players were not getting along, so it needs to be explored further. When the Pittsburgh team received the winning percentage of the World Series money, McKechnie set up a four-player committee consisting of Babe Adams, Max Carey, Earl Smith, and Pie Traynor to propose how the money should be divided, with the team then voting on the proposals.[5] The total amount was split into 35 not-all-equal sums, with McKechnie, Jack Onslow, player-coach Jewel Ens, club secretary Sam Watters, and 21 players each receiving $5,332.71.[6] The rest of the money was apportioned in the following fashion:

- $2,055.14 to Red Oldham
- $1,777.57 to George "Chauff" Aston, the trainer
- $1,000 apiece to Clarke, Chick Fraser, Bill Hinchman, and Lafayette Fresco "Tommy" Thompson, a rookie second baseman who joined the team in early September and played in 14 games
- $500 each to Jack Fogarty, the Forbes Field groundskeeper, and George "Mule" Haas, a rookie outfielder who joined the team in mid–August and played in four games
- And $250 apiece to Caleb "Socko" McCarey, the clubhouse boy, and Joe Devine, Pittsburgh's West Coast scout. Devine was the man who signed Ray Kremer to a Pirate contract and who would make a name for himself by signing or recommending Joe Cronin, Paul Waner, Lloyd Waner, and Gus Suhr, while Devine was with the Pirates; Frank Crosetti, Joe DiMaggio, and Billy Martin, while Devine was with the Yankees; and many other successful major leaguers.[7]

That was that and nothing more was said at the time. But approximately 11 months later, in their self-serving, tell-all article that was published in the *Pittsburgh Press* on September 30, 1926, Babe Adams, Carson Bigbee, and Max Carey claimed:

> The committee suggested [a] one-half share for Clarke. After a discussion, a final vote was taken by ballot, and passed, to give Clarke nothing. Capt. Carey did not vote on this ballot, as his vote was not necessary.
> However, he suggested giving Clarke something, inasmuch as the secretary, the trainer, the clubhouse boy and the groundkeeper [sic] had all been voted a portion of the [W]orld's [S]eries money. One thousand dollars was suggested and passed for Clarke by one vote.
> When Clarke learned this, he went to Mr. Dreyfuss and said he didn't think he was wanted here. Mr. Dreyfuss called in McKechnie and wanted to know what the trouble was, and if there wasn't "enough honor and glory for everyone." McKechnie then saw Clarke, and had some warm words with him.

Three. *High Expectations, Disappointing Results*   89

> Later[,] Clarke returned his [S]eries check of one thousand dollars to Mr. Dreyfuss with a letter, indicating ill-feeling, requesting him to present it to Mr. McKechnie with his compliments. Mr. Dreyfuss, however, later on prevailed upon Clarke accepting it.[8]

The trio went further to say that they were bringing up the matter at such a late date to show that there was disharmony on the Pirate club between Clarke and the players and between Clarke and McKechnie dating back to the previous season.

And unfortunately for Clarke, most later writers and baseball historians who have dealt with the 1926 Pirates have taken what the trio said at face value and castigated the future Hall of Famer for his behavior. But when the threesome's words are examined closely, several problems arise. First, if the incident did indeed happen, would not the details have gone public sooner than late September of the next year? Ralph Davis, as the sports editor of the *Press* and the Pittsburgh correspondent for *The Sporting News*, had a variety of sources and was quick to pick up on any gossip or innuendos involving the Pirates, and yet he wrote nothing about the incident until the Adams-Bigbee-Carey article was published. Nor did any other Pittsburgh sportswriter, except for Havey Boyle, the sports editor of the *Pittsburgh Chronicle Telegraph*, who apparently through an inside connection found out that Clarke would be sending back the check he had received, but whose account of the incident varies significantly from that of Adams, Bigbee, and Carey. Included in his column of October 29, 1925, Boyle reported:

> As public acknowledgment of his fine assistance, the Pirates voted $1,000 of their [s]eries pot to Fred Clarke. This pleased the old warrior, but because he likely felt he could do without it[,] he is going to return the check it is learned.[9]

There is no mention of any grumbling or hurt feelings, only that Clarke was appreciative of what the players had presented to him, but since he did not need the money, he decided to turn down his share. Also, it should be noted that, as will be seen later, Boyle would not pass up or cover up a scoop if he came across it.

Second, unless Dreyfuss, Clarke, and/or McKechnie told the trio about what was said in Dreyfuss' office—and it is unlikely that any of them did—how did the threesome know what was discussed? The same can be said about the contents of Clarke's letter. Did Dreyfuss show the letter to Adams, Bigbee, and Carey or disclose to them why Clarke returned the check? That would be highly doubtful. Furthermore, in defending himself at a press conference the evening of September 30, Clarke told the Pittsburgh sportswriters:

> A ball club [*sic*] that wins a [W]orld [S]eries is entitled to all the glory and every cent of the money derived from it. I wasn't a player, I wasn't a scout, I played no

vital part in the winning of the pennant or the taking of the [S]eries. For that reason and that reason only I refused to take the $1,000 check tendered me as my share and sent it back to McKechnie [not Dreyfuss] with words to that effect. There was no harshness in the letter, but the plain statement of fact that the money belonged to the players, and as I was not one, I had no right to it. Had it been a full share, half share or 30 cents[,] I would have done the same thing.... [T]hankfully, I have reached the point where money does not mean as much as it used to.[10]

Clarke's critics may fault him for false modesty, but leaving aside the obvious fact that Clarke did indeed play a "vital part in the winning of the pennant [and] the taking of the Series," the rest of his explanation makes a lot of sense. In short, money was no longer an object in Clarke's life.

Third, the comment that "McKechnie then saw Clarke, and had some warm words with him" seems out of character for McKechnie, who did not readily show his anger publicly.

And finally, notice how Carey made himself to be the hero of the situation, coming forth to convince his fellow players to give Clarke at least $1,000. What better way to win sympathy from the Pittsburgh fans: the poor Max Carey being ousted in 1926 by the man who he had helped the previous season?

Clarke would later say that he wondered if Adams, Bigbee, and Carey had actually written the article, implying that perhaps someone working for the *Press* or some other outsider had been the real author,[11] but even if the trio had written the article and even if the story about the vote was true, it still does not necessarily show any dissension on the '25 team. The players knew that Clarke was a millionaire and that he did not need any of the World Series spoils and that may have influenced their decision not to give him any. Or they may have just been greedy or ungrateful. Or they may have been exercising some of the traits of reactive types, being practical—we need the money more than he does—and unfeeling at the same time. It was one thing to publically praise Clarke after they won the pennant, as was mentioned in the previous chapter, but quite another thing to part with money that they wanted.

Whatever the truth may be behind the story, Dreyfuss must have been satisfied with Clarke's performance because during the 1925–1926 offseason, he appointed Clarke vice president of the club and allowed him to buy some stock in the franchise, thus making him one of the directors of the Pittsburgh Athletic Company, as the Pirate organization was formally titled.[12] As discussed in the last chapter, the stock purchases may have been part of the deal that Ralph Davis mentioned when Clarke joined the Bucs in June of 1925.

But Clarke's good fortune was not the only Pirate news after the '25 season had ended. Amidst ludicrous rumors that Clarke was (a) leaving the Pittsburgh club to become the partial owner and manager of the Brooklyn Robins or (b) interested in a syndicate that was going to buy the Pirates from the Dreyfuss family—rumors that were denied by both Clarke and Dreyfuss and pooh-poohed by Ralph Davis[13]— the Pirate front office, management, and scouts began to strengthen the team for the next season even as the World Series was in progress. On October 13, Pittsburgh acquired Paul Waner and Harold "Hal" Rhyne from the San Francisco Seals of the Pacific Coast League (PCL). Only 22 years of age at the time, Waner was a left-handed line-drive hitting outfielder with great eye-hand coordination. Glenn Wright would later tell Walter Langford:

He would become known as "Big Poison," but in 1926, Paul Waner was a highly touted rookie from Oklahoma who had batted .401 for San Francisco of the Pacific Coast League in 1925 (National Baseball Hall of Fame Library, Cooperstown, New York).

> I helped Paul sign his first contract. I used to hunt with Fred Clarke.... I would go to Kansas and hunt with him in quail season and he'd come to Missouri to hunt with me....
>
> Anyway ... Paul wanted me to help him with his first contract in 1926. So I invited him over to Fred's place, with Fred's permission, of course....
>
> Well, we got out in the field the next day and the dogs found a bird. I said, "Paul, this is your bird." And he said, "All right." So we kicked the bird out and Paul up and shot and he didn't have his gun anywhere near his shoulder. Just shot from the hip, you know. But the bird fell deader than a doornail....
>
> The dogs found another bird and I said, "Paul you take this one too." But he said, "No, this is yours or Mr. Clarke's." So I told him, "Well, to tell you the truth, we think that first shot was an accident." "Oh," he said, "all right."
>
> "We kicked the bird out and the same thing—gun still down by his hip but the bird didn't even flutter after it fell. He didn't miss a bird all day."[14]

Waner demonstrated that kind of coordination on the baseball diamond, too, leading the PCL in batting with a .401 average and in doubles with 75.[15] Rhyne, a native of Paso Robles, where the Pirates held spring training, and another Joe Devine discovery (if anyone deserved more money from the Pirates, it was Devine), was a 26-year-old shortstop who covered a lot of ground and who could also play second base. Although not possessing much power, he had pounded out 965 hits in five minor league seasons for a .300 average and had "been considered a star in Coast League circles since the day he broke in, almost."[16] San Francisco won the PCL pennant in '25 as well as a postseason series against Louisville, the American Association champion, and both Waner and Rhyne were chosen by Daniel E. Dugdale, the former president of the Seattle club of the defunct Northwestern League, as first-team PCL all-stars.[17] And it is interesting to note that Dugdale selected Rhyne as his starting shortstop over future Yankee great Tony Lazzeri, who had led the Pacific Coast League in home runs with 60, runs scored with 202, runs driven in with 222, and total bases with 512.[18]

What made the acquisition more interesting was that it was provisional, meaning that Pittsburgh could pay cash for the duo or it could give the Seals a combination of cash and players, and no decision was necessary until December 15, 1926.[19]

To make room for the two PCL celebrities, Pittsburgh got rid of Fresco Thompson, who is better known for his middle name than either his first name or his nickname, and Mule Haas. Thompson was sold to Buffalo of the International League in December of '25,[20] while Haas was released outright to Atlanta of the Southern Association in February of '26.[21] As mentioned earlier in this chapter, both Thompson and Haas had joined the 1925 Pirate team during the second half of the season and saw limited action. Specifically, Thompson had been under option with Kansas City in the American Association when Pittsburgh brought him up to the majors, and Haas had similarly been with Birmingham in the Southern Association when he received word to join the Bucs. Both had seen their last days with the Pirates, but it was a blessing in disguise for each of them, as they made names for themselves elsewhere. Thompson would play second base for several National League clubs before becoming a minor league manager and then an executive in the Brooklyn–Los Angeles Dodger organization, whereas Haas would go on to play center field for Connie Mack's great 1929–1931 Philadelphia Athletic teams and then spend seven more seasons in the American League with Philadelphia and Chicago.

But with the exception of Thompson and Haas, the entire 1925 World Series championship team was returning, though player-coach Jewel Ens stopped playing to concentrate solely on his coaching. Other returnees included coach Jack Onslow and scouts Chick Fraser and Bill Hinchman, so there was continuity across the board, leading the Pirate faithful to have high expectations for the upcoming season. It was as if the formula for success that had been developed in 1925 had remained in place or had even been upgraded with the addition of Waner and Rhyne.

Nor were there any serious problems with contract negotiations. Although it had been speculated that Aldridge, Cuyler, and Wright would be difficult to re-sign, such talk did not faze the wily Barney Dreyfuss. Instead, he used the occasion of the National League's golden jubilee dinner in February to invite his players to attend the festivities and then to meet with them individually to discuss their contracts for the upcoming season. Many accepted and all of them went away pleased. As Ralph Davis reported, "One by one they visited their boss in his rooms at the Waldorf. And each one came from the rooms with a broad smile, and apparently happy."[22] As for the potential holdouts, "Cuyler was one of the easiest to satisfy.... Aldridge [was] another Buccaneer who [was] delighted over the manner in which he has been treated.... [And] Wright was just as easily satisfied."[23] By mid–February, all but two players had been signed[24]; by February 23, everyone had agreed to the terms that they were offered.[25] Thus, if there was any dissension or disgruntlement on the 1925 team as Adams, Bigbee, and Carey would later claim, it was either forgotten or well disguised by the time training camp began at Paso Robles on February 26.

Clarke did not show any hints of ill-feeling either. As the subheading of a *Pittsburgh Post* article on Clarke agreeing to stay with the Pirates for the '26 season stated, "Veteran Enthusiastically Renews Verbal Agreement." The article went on to say that "Fred declared that no contract was necessary, as Barney's word always had been as good as gold.... [And] he is more than delighted to be associated with Dreyfuss, McKechnie and company."[26] Furthermore, on March 16, Clarke let it be known that he would treat the spring training squad to dinner at the Little Pirate Ranch and introduce them to the prominent citizens of Winfield when the Pirates stopped in Wichita to play two exhibition games as they proceeded eastward from their California base.[27]

Of those players who would eventually report to Paso Robles, it appears that 18 were pitchers, four were catchers, 10 were infielders, and six were outfielders. Ralph Davis mentioned in his column for the February 25, 1926, issue of *The Sporting News* that the Pirate roster as of February 22 contained 35 men: 17 pitchers, three catchers, nine infielders, and six outfielders.[28] But Davis apparently meant men under written contract because a close reading of the Pittsburgh newspapers shows three more players working out with team. More specifically, the cast of characters included everyone who had seen action during the regular season for the 1925 Pirates—minus the aforementioned Thompson and Haas and, of course, the traded Al Niehaus—and 14 who had not. Among the latter were Waner and Rhyne as well as pitchers Eddie Brower, Joe Brown, John Cook, Alvin Crowder, George Kissinger, Phil Morrison, and Bill Pierson; catcher Romuald "Romey" McDonald; infielders Joe Cronin, Eddie Hock, and Arthur Traynor; and outfielder Phil Voyles. Some of these men had been part of Pittsburgh's 40-man roster the previous year, most were trying to make the 25-man roster for the upcoming season, but a few, like McDonald, were just hoping to perform well enough to receive a minor league contract. As Ed Balinger reported for the *Pittsburgh Post*:

> McDonald, who is 24 years old, has been a member of the Oakland club in the Pacific Coast League for three years, but he did a great deal of bench warming with that team. He took part in about 50 games last summer, but most of his work was done in the capacity of pinch hitter [sic] or relief catcher. He was released outright last fall and was glad of the opportunity to join a big league training squad. This ambitious young Scotchman [sic] is aware that he is only under a verbal agreement to help out in warming up the pitchers, but he believes he can give McKechnie such a favorable impression that he will be aided in hooking up with some good minor league club.[29]

Two of the yannigans, as rookies were then called, were brothers of established regulars on the team: Johnny Morrison's older sibling, Phil, and Pie Traynor's younger sibling, Arthur. Like McDonald, both were there only under verbal agreements and not expected to make the team. The elder Morrison, who several years earlier was "said to possess a curve ball [sic] that [was] quite as good as Johnny's"[30] and to have "the best assortment of curves [in the Southern League] since Dazzy Vance showed his stuff,"[31] had made a brief appearance with the '21 Pirates but never was able to earn a lasting spot on a major league team. This anomaly causes one to wonder if Phil had the same drinking habits as Johnny but was less able to control their effects on his pitching. Or perhaps the rheumatism that kept him out of Organized Baseball for the 1924 and 1925 seasons was already beginning to impair his performance at an earlier date, though by 1926, he was supposed to have been over his ailment.[32] Who knows? Without more information on Phil's lifestyle and health, the best that can be said is that the natural ability was there, but something else was missing.[33]

As for Arthur Traynor, James Forr and David Proctor found him to be "a fun, life-of-the-party kind of guy"[34] with a "profound lack of talent," who "didn't take baseball too seriously" or "much of anything too seriously."[35] Forr and Proctor surmise that Art was in camp only because of his relationship to Pie, who probably "pulled some strings to wrangle an invitation for his brother."[36] Some of the Pittsburgh sportswriters at the time disagreed with Forr and Proctor's assessment of the younger Traynor, saying that he had "displayed many earmarks of coming greatness,"[37] that "[h]e owns a good throwing arm, and, like Harold [Pie], goes after everything that comes his way,"[38] and that he made "a favorable impression."[39] But perhaps the fairest evaluation of Art's skills came from *Pittsburgh Press* sport staff correspondent Lou Wollen, who, after watching Art in spring training, stated, "He showed some skill as a third baseman, but it will require a great deal of polish to fit him for service in the higher classifications of professional baseball."[40]

Whatever the case, neither Phil nor Art would be in the majors during the '26 season or any season thereafter, with Phil signing with Indianapolis of the American Association on April 6[41] and Art being found a spot with Columbia of the South Atlantic League less than a week later.[42]

Another recruit not meant for the majors was Eddie Brower, a semipro hurler from Lexington, Tennessee, who had been recommended by Dreyfuss' and Clarke's friend John McCloskey, the former Louisville Colonel and St. Louis Cardinal manager and longtime minor league player-manager. Brower was said to "[possess] ability, but he did not seem to have the hustling qualities required of a young man aspiring to be a big leaguer"[43] and, like Art Traynor, or at least Forr and Proctor's view of him, he "did not seem to take baseball very seriously."[44] However, unlike Art Traynor, he was accused of petty larceny after being the first player cut by the Bucs. Lou Wollen wrote of the incident from Paso Robles:

> Brower, the youth who was brought back here from Los Angeles [after being released by the Pirates] to answer to a charge of pilfering a watch and rifle, left for his home in Lexington, Tenn., yesterday. A hearing was to have been held yesterday morning, but it failed to materialize when the proprietor of the sporting goods store, owner of the firearm, agreed to withdraw as prosecutor in the case at the behest of the Pittsburgh club management.[45]

Ed Balinger's account differed somewhat, not mentioning the watch and saying that "[a] rifle, alleged to have been taken, was returned and when the case came up for hearing this morning, it was dismissed."[46] But no matter what the correct details are, Brower was gone.

Of the remaining 10 "new men," only Crowder, Cronin, Rhyne, and Waner would be with the Pirates when they opened their season at St. Louis on April 13, though it was understood that Cronin would "be carried for a time, before he is shipped out for further seasoning."[47] As for the others, Eddie Hock, a onetime outfielder who had played shortstop for Oklahoma City of the Western League in 1925, was released outright to his former club on March 31 and became a career minor leaguer.[48] Bill Pierson, a southpaw from Atlantic City, New Jersey, was told to go home on April 2 and await assignment to a minor league franchise,[49] something that he did until he was picked up by the same Columbia, South Carolina, club that Art Traynor had received a spot on.[50] George Kissinger, a 6-foot-4 right-hander with a good fastball, and Phil Voyles, a fleet-footed outfielder, were optioned to Columbia on April 3.[51] Joe Brown, better known as "Sawmill Joe," another right-hander and one who some of the Pittsburgh sportswriters had spoken highly of,[52] was optioned to Kansas City

Table 21: Players in a Pirate Uniform on Opening Day, April 13, 1926

Name	Number of Seasons in the Majors Prior to 1926*	Number of Seasons with the Pirates Prior to 1926*	Member of the 1925 Pirate Team	Position/Positions Played with the Pirates during the 1925 Season	Comments
Babe Adams	18	17	Yes	Pitcher	
Vic Aldridge	6	1	Yes	Pitcher	Was one of the five main starting pitchers for the 1925 Pirates
Clyde Barnhart	6	6	Yes	Left Fielder	Was the starting left fielder for the 1925 Pirates
Carson Bigbee	10	10	Yes	Left Fielder, Right Fielder, Center Fielder	
Max Carey	16	16	Yes	Center Fielder	Was the starting center fielder for the 1925 Pirates
Joe Cronin	0	0	No	Not Applicable	Was a rookie in 1926
Alvin Crowder	0	0	No	Not Applicable	Was a rookie in 1926
Bud Culloton	1	1	Yes	Pitcher	
Kiki Cuyler	5	5	Yes	Right Fielder, Center Fielder	Was the starting right fielder for the 1925 Pirates
Johnny Gooch	5	5	Yes	Catcher	
George Grantham	4	1	Yes	First Baseman	Was the starting first baseman for the 1925 Pirates
Ray Kremer	2	2	Yes	Pitcher	Was one of the five main starting pitchers for the 1925 Pirates

Name	Number of Seasons in the Majors Prior to 1926*	Number of Seasons with the Pirates Prior to 1926*	Member of the 1925 Pirate Team	Position/Positions Played with the Pirates during the 1925 Season	Comments
Stuffy McInnis	17	1	Yes	First Baseman	Was signed as a free agent by Pittsburgh on May 29, 1925
Lee Meadows	11	3	Yes	Pitcher	Was one of the five main starting pitchers for the 1925 Pirates
Eddie Moore	3	3	Yes	Second Baseman, Right Fielder, Third Baseman	Was the starting second baseman for the 1925 Pirates
Johnny Morrison	6	6	Yes	Pitcher	Was one of the five main starting pitchers for the 1925 Pirates
Red Oldham	6	1	Yes	Pitcher	Purchased from Des Moines of the Western League on August 10, 1925
Johnny Rawlings	11	3	Yes	Second Baseman	
Hal Rhyne	0	0	No	Not Applicable	Was a rookie in 1926
Tom Sheehan	5	1	Yes	Pitcher	Acquired from Cincinnati in a trade for Al Niehaus on May 30, 1925
Earl Smith	7	2	Yes	Catcher	Was the starting catcher for the 1925 Pirates

Table 21: Players in a Pirate Uniform on Opening Day, April 13, 1926

Name	Number of Seasons in the Majors Prior to 1926*	Number of Seasons with the Pirates Prior to 1926*	Member of the 1925 Pirate Team	Position/Positions Played with the Pirates during the 1925 Season	Comments
Don Songer	2	2	Yes	Pitcher	Optioned to Oklahoma City of the Western League on June 10, 1925; considered a rookie in 1926
Roy Spencer	1	1	Yes	Catcher	
Pie Traynor	6	6	Yes	Third Baseman, Shortstop	Was the starting third baseman for the 1925 Pirates
Paul Waner	0	0	No	Not Applicable	Was a rookie in 1926
Glenn Wright	2	2	Yes	Shortstop, Third Baseman	Was the starting shortstop for the 1925 Pirates
Emil Yde	2	2	Yes	Pitcher	Was one of the five main starting pitchers for the 1925 Pirates

*For purposes of this table, a season is defined as playing in at least one game.

of the American Association on April 7.[53] And four days later, Brown's fellow Arkansan—they both lived in the Little Rock area[54]—and right-handed pitcher, John "Doc" Cook, was released to join several of the other Pirate rookies on the Columbia team,[55] which was quickly becoming a haven for Pirate wannabes.

In addition to these cuts, Lou Koupal, who had pitched nine innings in six games for the '25 Bucs, but who was still considered a rookie, was optioned to Buffalo of the International League on April 8.[56] However, Don Songer, another pitcher who had seen limited service with the '25 team—in his case, 11 2/3 innings spread over eight games—and who was also viewed as a rookie, was kept by Pittsburgh.

This meant that of the 27 men in a Pirate uniform by Opening Day, 23 had contributed to varying degrees to the 1925 championship team, and 19 of the 23 had been on that championship team from start to finish (see Table 21). These numbers attest to the talent level of the '26 team, a level so high that only several newbies could earn a spot on the team's roster. In fact, as mentioned in the introduction of this book, one unknown scribe wrote as early as March 30, "Everywhere one hears the refrain that the Pittsburgh club is the greatest club of modern days—probably the greatest since the Athletics['] juggernaut of the period of Bender, Plank, Baker, Collins, McInnis, Barry and Strunk."[57] The scribe went further to quote from an anonymous source referred to only as "one of the wisest old heads in the National League":

> [The team] positively has no weakness.... It can slug and it is fast and can beat 'em out. It is a fast[-]fielding and a fast base running [sic] club. And though the pitching staff is not remarkable[,] it is extremely well balanced and efficient. It holds up its share.[58]

But if there was no shortage of talent for the Pirates during spring training, there was also no shortage of illnesses and injuries, something that would continue to plague the Bucs throughout the '26 season. To begin with, as mentioned in the previous chapter, Max Carey had suffered a chest injury in the fifth game of the World Series, which, combined with his playing in the rain during the seventh game, may have led to more serious lung problems than was originally thought. Nine days after the Series ended, Carey entered Mercy Hospital in Pittsburgh to have his fractured rib and torn ligaments repaired and to receive treatment for pleurisy.[59] Fortunately for the aging center fielder, the illness was caught in time before it developed into pneumonia, but while traveling on the train to Paso Robles, he again became ill and was admitted to Deaconess Hospital in St. Louis with "a deep cold," "a slight fever," and "threatened pneumonia."[60] The result was a wasted spring training for Carey, who lost time recovering from his illness and then from its ramifications. Even after he had been released from the hospital and rejoined the rest of the team, he was troubled by respiratory problems. In an article published on March 23, Ed Balinger reported that as of March 22:

> The Pirate captain is slowly recuperating from his recent illness and it is feared he is a long way from being restored to health. His ailment is believed to have developed into sinus trouble and he complains of pains in the ears....[61]

And as late as April 3, Lou Wollen wrote in an article that was published the following day:

> It is a virtual certainty that Max Carey will not have recovered from his illness sufficiently by next week to take his place in center field. As long as the Pirates basked in the hot sunshine of the Pacific Coast, Carey appeared to be making great strides in the direction of [a] normal condition. As soon as the cooler climate of the middle-west [sic] was encountered, however, he seemed to lose much of his pop and just now great care must be taken to prevent him from suffering a backset.[62]

To these accounts, Ralph Davis added in his column for the April 15 issue of *The Sporting News*, a column that had been written on April 12, only a day before the Pirates began regular-season play, "Even if Max does play at the start of the season, he has had so little practice to date that he is likely to be far from his best for some time to come."[63]

However, Carey was not alone. Besides the usual assortment of aches and pains associated with spring training, a number of Bucs were handicapped by "real" ailments and injuries. For example:

- Lou Koupal had been stricken with a bout of influenza during the previous winter, which weakened him and hindered his efforts to compete for a spot on the team's roster.[64]

- Just before leaving Flint, Michigan, to join his teammates in California, Kiki Cuyler slipped on the ice and sprained his ankle, though the swelling, if not the pain, had subsided by the time he reached Paso Robles.[65]

- On the train trip to Paso Robles, Joe Brown came down with what was then called the grippe—a catchall term for any influenza-like illness—and was taken to a hospital in Dalhart, Texas.[66] He rejoined his teammates only three days later, but when he arrived in camp, "he appeared to be in a weakened condition" and "complained of slight dizziness."[67]

- Also on the way to California, George Grantham experienced "severe muscle pains in his right shoulder," which made him stop in Los Angeles to see a doctor. But the visit only increased his woes when a shot he received to immunize him against colds and the flu may have caused neuritis in his left shoulder.⁶⁸

The aches and pains continued in camp:

- Pie Traynor lined a drive off Babe Adams' ankle, which temporarily bruised and hobbled the veteran hurler but caused no serious damage.⁶⁹
- Traynor, in turn, wrenched a tendon in one of his own ankles, preventing him from seeing any action—with the exception of one pinch-hinting appearance—for over three weeks.⁷⁰ And the day after he returned to action, he crashed into Alvin Crowder shagging fly balls and reinjured his ankle.⁷¹
- Traynor's brother, Art, had a sore throwing arm,⁷² followed by "signs of lameness" after being bothered by tight leg tendons,⁷³ and later "was laid up with a bad ankle."⁷⁴
- Eddie Moore arrived in camp with a heavy cold,⁷⁵ got over it, but then twisted his ankle during an intrasquad game.⁷⁶ Moore would later claim that the injury was actually a broken bone in the part of his foot near his ankle, though no one including Moore himself knew it at the time. As the former second sacker described to Eugene Murdock in 1975:

    I stepped around catcher Roy Spencer, while we were having an intra-squad [sic] game and somehow I busted this bone down by my ankle. We didn't x-ray it, we just taped it up and I went on playing. I went into the season and tried to play, but I couldn't. It took quite awhile [sic] for that thing to heal. Then in 1931 when I was with Oakland out on the coast[,] I broke the bone again. The doctor x-rayed my foot this time and told me that it had been cracked sometime before. He showed me the x-ray and I could see where I had banged it up back in 1926.⁷⁷

- Like Moore, Stuffy McInnis arrived in camp with a malady—in his case, "a touch of stomach trouble"⁷⁸—recovered from it, but then was spiked on his right instep by Cuyler during another intrasquad game.⁷⁹
- Hal Rhyne hurt his knee in a pregame warmup.⁸⁰
- Red Oldham was hindered by a wrenched side.⁸¹
- Johnny Gooch was hampered by a sore back⁸² and a weight loss.⁸³
- Clyde Barnhart was struck so hard on the right elbow by one of Phil Morrison's pitches that initially it was believed that his arm had been broken. But luckily for both him and the Pirates, x-rays showed no fracture, though

the arm was "bruised and swollen"[84] and may have been the cause of Barnhart's poor offensive performance during the regular season.

Eddie Moore's plight was representative of what was happening to the team in general. After having a career year in 1925, Moore suffered a broken bone in his foot, which would greatly affect his play in 1926 (National Baseball Hall of Fame Library, Cooperstown, New York).

- Cuyler injured his thumb trying to grab a fly ball that he had been chasing.[85]
- Paul Waner was hit in the face by a foul ball that somehow got through the netting around the batting cage he was standing behind and he needed 11 stitches to close the wound.[86]

Even coach Jewel Ens and Joshua Clarke, Fred's younger brother who was visiting the training camp, were not immune to the curse. Ens was struck in the face by a batted ball and suffered a gash over one of his eyes that took five stitches to repair,[87] while Clarke was tossed over the head of a horse that he was riding at a Pirate outing on an off day when rookie John Cook startled the beast by shooting at a bird that was flying by.[88] Clarke ended up with "just" a sprained back, but he very easily could have broken his neck,[89] and Cook's carelessness probably did nothing to help his chances of winning a place on the team.

In addition to the plethora of maladies and mishaps costing various Pirates valuable playing time, the weather in Kansas cost even the healthy members of the team a number of exhibition games. When the spring training squad arrived in Wichita at the end of March, they found that the area had been hit with a blizzard, which led them to cancel two games with the local minor league club and six games with the minor league franchise in Kansas City.[90] Another casualty of the snow was the feast at the Little Pirate Ranch that Fred Clarke had planned for the staff and players.[91] However, the quick thinking of McKechnie and Sam Dreyfuss, who was with the team at that time, partially made up for the lost exhibitions by changing the club's itinerary so that the squad detoured to Hot Springs, Arkansas, to play three games against Indianapolis of the American Association. But games scheduled at Terre Haute, Little Rock, and Louisville had to be called off because of wet grounds (Terra Haute) or rain (Little Rock and Louisville).[92]

On a positive note, both McKechnie and Clarke lectured the pitchers, catchers, and rookies as a group early on during spring training, letting them know what would be expected of them. During his talk, McKechnie spelled out his rules and warned his troops that "[t]here will be no gambling on this club for excessive stakes, and anybody that thinks he can break this rule will find himself out of a job" and that "[d]ice are absolutely taboo," though he made no mention of drinking alcohol.[93] For his part, Clarke "gave the batterymen a fine talk," cautioned "the youngsters about starting out with too much vigor," and "touched on the serious business side of the game."[94]

And perhaps because of these lectures, there was only one disciplinary problem throughout all of spring training and it was nothing more than a minor offense. Several players violated McKechnie's "rule of early to bed and early to rise," were reprimanded for doing so, and that was that.[95] As Ralph Davis wrote, "There is no tendency on the part of any of the players to question the rules that have been laid down, and, so far as can be learned, the same harmony which made possible the glorious achievements of 1925, still pervades the club."[96] A very interesting assessment, especially considering what would occur later.

While spring training was still in progress, the preseason prognosticators came forth with their predictions, and to no one's surprise, the Pirates were one of the favorites. Though, in part because of the maladies and mishaps they had experienced during the preseason and Carey's uncertain future, and in part because their pitching was viewed by some forecasters as not being good enough to help carry them to another pennant, they were not unanimous favorites.

In early March, New York sportswriter John B. Foster sang the Corsairs' praises, saying that no eastern National League team would beat them and that they could "expect a battle from only one club—St. Louis."[97] Similarly, a little more than a month later, Chicago sportswriter Irving Vaughan wrote:

> Counting the Giants and Cardinals as having a chance with the world's champion Pirates is giving the former the benefit of the doubt. It also is an allowance for the possibility that the Pirates might not live up to the last year's form. However, the possibility is not a probability because the Pirates constitute a real ball team, and real ball teams usually reign for two or three successive seasons at least.[98]

Vaughan went further to qualify his assessment by adding that the only thing that could derail the Pirates would be a collapse of their pitching staff, but that he did not foresee the five major Pittsburgh starters—Aldridge, Kremer, Meadows, Morrison, and Yde—all self-destructing at the same time.[99] Nor did he think that the New York and St. Louis staffs were as good as Pittsburgh's, "so that makes the winning of the pennant dependent on other factors, and nobody is going to dispute the ability of the Pirates to collect runs, to show speed on the bases, and to hold their own in fielding."[100]

Fred Lieb, the baseball editor of the *New York Telegram*, and Hugh Fullerton, then writing for *Liberty*, one of the best weekly general-interest magazines of its day, also selected the Bucs to repeat, putting them ahead of the Giants, the Cardinals, and the Reds, in that order.[101] Davis J. Walsh of the International News Service concurred with them, adding "One can point out that [the Pirate] pitchers are not as good as they seem to be and that the right side of the infield lacks real class[,] but when those young men start hitting[,] they make any defensive fault look like a virtue."[102] And the *St. Louis Post-Dispatch's* poll of eight baseball scribes, each from a different major league city, had as its consensus picks Pittsburgh first, New York second, St. Louis third, and Cincinnati fourth.[103]

But these strong endorsements were modified by rival analysts. For example, the Associated Press (AP) contributed several articles on the subject, in which the Bucs went from John McGraw's choice as the team to beat to "their rating as favorites remains unchanged among the experts," but "observers are convinced that at least four and probably five clubs will be in the thick of [the] pennant hunt" to not being "conceded more than [an] even chance of again setting the pace."[104] By April 10, the AP felt that New York, St. Louis, and Cincinnati were the biggest threats to seize Pittsburgh's crown, with Boston being a dark horse.[105]

Some prognosticators saw the Pirates and Giants as co-favorites, with one or more of the remaining teams as legitimate contenders. The *Los Angeles Times* printed an article by an unknown scribe a few days before the season began which stated that "the National League race this year is expected to be a two-club battle between the Pirates and Giants, with the Cardinals having possibly an outside chance."[106] And the *New York Times'* Richards Vidmer wrote an article for his newspaper on April 11, in which he was more generous with the number of contenders that the two front-runners would have to fight off. Vidmer believed that "[a]lthough the Giants and Pirates are generally considered the teams between whom ultimate victory lies, ... every team [has] a chance," except for possibly the Cubs and the Phillies.[107]

St. Louis sportswriter James Gould also picked the Pirates to be co-favorites, but with the Cardinals rather than the Giants. After claiming to have "consulted many of the leading authorities of the game," Gould's NL standings had Pittsburgh and St. Louis as either first and second or second and first, New York third, and Cincinnati fourth,[108] though his comments implied that he was giving the edge to the Redbirds. For Gould, St. Louis had "[a] fast young team, just coming into the realization that it is a great aggregation ... [t]he Mound City's best team in many, many moons,"[109] whereas the Pirate pitching was suspect. "Critics believe [McKechnie's] hurlers cannot stand the strain of a second successful season, if it be hard-fought [sic] from start to finish, as it probably will be."[110] Gould went further to add a metaphysical dimension to the possibility of St. Louis success by discussing the baseball superstition of a new ballpark attracting a pennant, and although Sportsman's Park in St. Louis—the home of the Cardinals—was not newly erected, it had been extensively remodeled prior to the 1926 season to increase its seating capacity.[111]

For still other forecasters, the Bucs were not even co-favorites. In an article written by George Daley, under his pseudonym, Monitor, for the *New York World* News Service and published in the April 11 issue of the *Pittsburgh Post*, the Giants were dubbed the favorites and the Pirates were predicted to come in second, with the Cards and Reds rounding out the first division. Daley defended his picks by arguing that the Giants had the best pitching staff in the senior circuit, an improved hitting attack and defense from the previous season, and the right combination of veterans and youngsters. The Pirates, on the other hand, had strong hitting and defense, but they lacked the pitching necessary to surpass their New York rivals.[112]

Daley's views were supported by the oddsmakers on Wall Street, who had the Giants as 7 to 5 favorites on March 25 and 8 to 5 on April 3 and 13, compared to the Pirates, who were 8 to 5 on the 25th, 9 to 5 on the 3rd, and 2 to 1 on the 13th.[113] Thus, among the gambling crowd, New York carried a slight lead into its opener against Brooklyn.

The Pirate faithful, of course, were not buying the arguments of the doubters. Both the *Pittsburgh Post* and its rival, the *Pittsburgh Press*, expressed the sentiments of the majority of Pittsburghers, who had high hopes for their team. In a lengthy article with no byline but probably written by Ed Balinger or Regis Welsh, the sports editor of the *Post*, the author enthusiastically declared:

> Even the skeptical [fans] will pay no heed to the Giants, the Reds, the Cards and the Braves, all of whom have been touted to furnish the opposition which will take away the title of champions from the first Pittsburgh club to win it in 16 years....
>
> The hard luck streaks of the training camp will fade into insignificance as the season grows on [because]....
>
> The Pirates look like the great team which breezed in last year and then fought heroically to stave impending defeat in the final game and rose to [the] greatest heights....
>
> [In addition,] McKechnie ... will be more matured, better able to diagnose, better acquainted with the ins and outs of his material than he ever has been.... [and]

[h]e will have Ens and Onslow to help and Clarke to confide in when things don't go right, all of which makes as well balanced a combination on the bench as in the field.[114]

To this ringing endorsement of the home team, Ralph Davis added his own in his April 13 column for the *Press*:

> In spite of all the hardships that [the team has] been through this spring ... McKechnie's men on paper look like the best bet in the National League....
> The Pirates have the punch—they have the speed—they are fine defensive workers—they have the self-confidence—they have the pitchers....
> So far as Pittsburgh is concerned, the outlook is more roseate than it has been in many years, and it will surely be a distinct disappointment to Buccaneer followers if the team falls down.[115]

McKechnie himself did nothing to dampen the hype when he confidently told L. J. O'Conner of the International News Service, "The Pirates will repeat.... [They] look 25 per cent [*sic*] better now than they did this time last year."[116]

So, it was with these lofty expectations that the Bucs opened their season at Sportsmen's Park in St. Louis on a clear sunny day. But unfortunately for them and their followers, the weather that day was virtually the only thing that was sunny during the month of April. After dropping three out of four games to the Cardinals, the Pirate ship sailed to Cincinnati and duplicated the "feat" against the Reds. This was followed by the Corsairs losing their home opener in 10 innings to the pesky Cards and then playing slightly better than .500 ball for the remainder of the month. Thus, by the close of play on April 30, the defending World Series champs were 7–10 and in seventh place, three and a half games behind the league-leading Brooklyn Robins (see Table 23).[117]

However, pinpointing the cause of the slow start is more difficult than it first appears. Superficially, it looks as if the Pittsburgh hitting attack had not come out of hibernation, and certainly the Bucs' collective batting average (.233), on-base percentage (.304), and slugging average (.298) were abysmal and dead last in the National League. And yet, the Pirates managed to score 4.71 runs per game, the fourth highest among NL teams, which indicates that they were probably getting the most runs possible out of their dismal batting stats. Nor was the pitching staff entirely to blame. The team's ERA was 3.72—not great, but good enough for fifth place—and Morrison and Aldridge were pitching well. No, the two major culprits appear to have been giving up almost as many runs they scored—77 to 80—in part because of erratic fielding, and dropping five games by a single run and another one in extra innings.[118]

Compounding the Pirates' April problems were two other matters: the continual presence of the illness and injury bug and a baffling transaction that would later haunt the club. Regarding the former matter, Carey was still struggling as the month closed. Making his first appearance against the Reds on April 18, he played in 12 games, hit a miserable .152, got on base only 22 percent of the time, and committed three errors. As Lou Wollen reported:

> [Carey] apparently has not recovered from his recent illness. That he is not right is reflected in his general play and spirit. He goes about his tasks as a player who feels he must do his bit, not as one who is eager for the battle.[119]

The rest of the walking wounded consisted of Tom Sheehan, who had been hit in the chest with a line drive in batting practice and then caught cold; Eddie Moore, who continued to be bothered by the ankle he had hurt in spring training; Glenn Wright, who was spiked on the hand during a game in Cincinnati; Pie Traynor, who suffered a spiked foot and smashed toe against St. Louis; and George Grantham, who received a stone bruise on his throwing hand.[120] Sheehan's, Wright's, and Traynor's injuries, as well as Sheehan's congestion, were not considered serious, but there was concern about the slow recovery of Carey and Moore, and Grantham was replaced at first by Stuffy McInnis.

Carey's lackluster play, Moore's nagging ankle problem, and the mishaps to four more members of the team were frustrating though not surprising, considering the jinx that the team had been battling since spring training had begun. But the shocker was the outright release of talented rookie Alvin Crowder to the Birmingham Barons of the Southern Association on April 14.[121] Whether it was Ed Balinger: "He looks better every time he gets into a game"; or Ralph Davis: "He looked mighty good in the training camp"; or Chilly Doyle: "He showed a rare fast ball [sic] and a dandy curve"; or Lou Wollen: "[He] looked like a real find during the training season," Crowder received nothing but praise.[122] Balinger even likened Crowder's pitching style to that of one of the aging Pirate heroes of yesteryear, who just so happened to still be on the team, when he wrote:

> Alvin Crowder's actions upon the mound are very similar to those of Babe Adams. The youngster leans gracefully back and brings his hands up above his head, then suddenly cuts loose with a short, snappy throw.[123]

And later, an anonymous *Pittsburgh Post* scribe, in all likelihood Balinger or Regis Welsh, added, "[Crowder] was regarded as one of the most promising youngsters taken to California, his greatest asset being the ability to pitch without a warm-up."[124]

So what happened? Why was Crowder's stay with the Bucs abruptly cut short? Perhaps the best answer was supplied by Ralph Davis:

> [Pittsburgh] bought [Crowder] on option. That is, it paid so much outright, and was to pay so much additional if he were retained after May 1, 1926. However,

it is claimed that the Birmingham [c]lub tried to raise the ante, when it seemed certain that the twirler would stick, and [Dreyfuss] called the bluff by shipping the young man back, without any strings attached.

It doubtless is a pity, so far as Crowder is concerned, that the incident occurred, and it remains to be seen whether Dreyfuss cut off his own nose, or some other person's.[125]

It was a pity, but not for Crowder. He was purchased by Washington in July and went on to perform well for three American League teams during an 11-season major league career which saw him playing for three pennant winners and one World Series champion.[126] The Pirates, however, received nothing in return for his departure and definitely could have used his arm as the season progressed.

But despite the Pirates' early struggles and the loss of Crowder, the team's fan base remained loyal, as evidenced by the 31,000 who turned out to witness the home opener on April 22. And the crowd was a real cross-section of life. Among those in attendance were politicians, including Pennsylvania Governor Gifford Pinchot, judges, prohibition agents, bootleggers, policemen, gamblers, old and new box seat holders, disabled war veterans from one of the area hospitals, sports celebrities, such as Honus Wagner, and common men, women, and children, and all present were treated to quite a show.[127]

> About five minutes before game time [the game was scheduled to begin at 3:00 p.m.] the [East Liberty American Legion] band ... lined up at the plate. Regular army soldiers bearing the colors stood at attention. The players of both teams, with the exception [of the starting pitchers and the men warming them up], fell in behind. Bringing up the rear flank ... came [National League president John] Heydler and [Barney] Dreyfuss, [Pennsylvania senator] George Wharton Pepper and [former Pennsylvania governor] John K. Tener, himself once a player who had never enjoyed the thrill of being a champion....
>
> Out over the field the column marched, the band splitting the air with a stirring march. Down to the fence and then—the untying of the huge bundle, the raising and unfurling of the [United States flag] and the [National League] pennant.... Then the march back ... and then ... [John] Tener[, the former governor of Pennsylvania,] making a perfect throw of the first ball.[128]

The results were disappointing—in part because of some costly fielding errors and Pittsburgh's failure to manufacture any runs after the second inning—but not for lack of support or enthusiasm on the part of the Pirate faithful.

Nor was Opening Day an exception to the rule. In a National League that would average 615,050 spectators per franchise, the '26 Pirates would draw 798,542, the second highest total among the eight clubs. This would be just the third time since league attendance records were kept that Pittsburgh had finished first or second, with the other seasons being 1921 (second) and 1925 (first). And while it is true that average attendance per game would be slightly below that of 1925 (10,108 to 10,446), that average would remain the third best in Pirate history until 1947.[129]

Even when the Pirates were on the road, fan interest was so great that a number of people would attend the Moose Temple on Penn Avenue in Pittsburgh "to watch on the big electronic scoreboard the reproduction" of away games.[130]

But attendance and fan interest, though appreciated, were not McKechnie's concerns in April—winning was. So, in an attempt to jumpstart the Bucs' hitting attack and to counter the absences of his temporarily missing regulars, Deacon Bill toyed with his batting order. Opening the season with Moore at second, Bigbee in left, Cuyler in center, Wright at short, Traynor at third, Barnhart in right, Grantham at first, and Smith behind the plate, he made small changes with his starting eight during the time that the team was on the road against St. Louis and Cincinnati. Waner was used in left and batted second, then first. Rhyne replaced Moore at second, but batted seventh. Carey resumed his center field spot and second slot in the order. And Gooch subbed twice for Smith and batted eighth.

Another highly touted rookie, Hal Rhyne made his major league debut on April 18 in Cincinnati (National Baseball Hall of Fame Library, Cooperstown, New York).

However, once the Pirates returned to Pittsburgh, McKechnie switched to his World Series batting order of Moore at second, Carey in center, Cuyler in right, Barnhart in left, Traynor at third, Wright at short, McInnis at first, and Smith doing the catching. This alignment would remain almost intact until May 7, with three exceptions, one of them notable:

- Rhyne replaced Wright for two games at shortstop and batted sixth when Wright was slightly hurt.

- As would be expected, Gooch and third-string catcher Roy Spencer occasionally relieved Smith.

- And on April 27, Rhyne took over as the starting second baseman and lead-off hitter after Moore reinjured his ankle in a game against Chicago the previous day.[131] Moore would not start again until June 9, though he would see action as a pinch-hitter or a pinch-runner in six games (see Table 22).[132]

Table 22: Select Pirate Batting Orders, April 13-May 6, 1926

April 13	April 22-May 6
Moore, 2B	Moore, 2B (April 27-May 6: Rhyne, 2B)
Bigbee, LF	Carey, CF
Cuyler, CF	Cuyler, RF
Wright, SS	Barnhart, LF
Traynor, 3B	Traynor, 3B
Barnhart, RF	Wright, SS (April 24-April 25: Rhyne, SS)
Grantham, 1B	McInnis, 1B
Smith, C	Smith/Spencer/Gooch, C

As for results, the World Series batting order plus Rhyne began to pump life into the team, as Pittsburgh finished the month by winning four of its last five games while pounding out 58 hits (11.6 per game) and scoring 41 runs (8.2 per game).

Table 23: National League Standings at the End of the Day on April 30, 1926[133]

Team	Wins	Losses	Ties	Winning Percentage	Games Back	Runs Scored	Runs Allowed
Brooklyn	9	5	0	.643	—	58	68
New York	9	6	0	.600	0.5	76	59
Cincinnati	8	6	1	.571	1.0	61	81
Chicago	8	7	1	.533	1.5	92	72
St. Louis	8	8	0	.500	2.0	69	72
Philadelphia	7	9	0	.438	3.0	81	69
Pittsburgh	7	10	0	.412	3.5	80	77
Boston	5	10	0	.333	4.5	55	74

May proved to be a mixed bag for McKechnie's men. On the positive side, the big bats that had started to awaken towards the end of April continued to hit. The team's batting average (.312), on-base percentage (.368), and slugging average (.462) all rose considerably as 137 runs were scored in 26 games. This offensive explosion was helped by more tinkering with the batting order by McKechnie, possibly with input from Clarke and the coaches. After making some minor changes earlier in the month, on the 19th, McKechnie moved Carey to the leadoff spot and lowered Rhyne to the second slot; kept Cuyler batting third but placed him in left field; removed the slumping Barnhart from the lineup completely; put Waner in right field and had him bat sixth; and brought in Grantham to replace the tired McInnis, whose batting average, on-base percentage, and slugging average had plummeted from .378, .410, and .432 on April 30 to .305, .345, and .390 on May 18. Like McInnis, Grantham would play first base and bat seventh. With the exception of catching changes—and the catcher, whether Smith, Gooch, or Spencer, always batted eighth—this alignment would remain intact until June 3.[134]

Table 24: Pirate Batting Orders, May 7-June 2, 1926

May 7-May 18	May 19-June 2
Rhyne, 2B	Carey, CF
Bigbee, LF (May 11: Carey, CF; May 12-May 18: Waner, RF)	Rhyne, 2B
Cuyler, CF (May 11: RF)	Cuyler, LF
Wright, SS	Wright, SS
Traynor, 3B	Traynor, 3B
Barnhart, RF (May 11-May 18: LF)	Waner, RF
McInnis, 1B	Grantham, 1B
Smith/Gooch/Spencer, C	Smith/Gooch, C

The pitching improved as well, with the staff's collective ERA dropping to 3.64, the third best in the senior circuit, while the pitching and defense combined gave up 112 runs, leading to a run differential of +25, second only to that of Cincinnati. The result of these improvements was a 16–8–2 record for the month, again second to only the red-hot Reds, who went 21–10.[135]

And when it came to individual play, the offensive leaders were Wright (a .346 batting average, .375 on-base percentage, and .570 slugging average, with 37 runs produced); Traynor (.429, .467, .551, and 38); Cuyler (.415, .451, .708, and 37); and Waner (.342, .398, .671, and 33), while Earl Smith, who did not produce many runs, held his own in the other three categories with averages of .419, .468, and .512.[136] Defensively, newcomer Hal Rhyne, who had taken over at second for the hobbling Eddie Moore, received a lot of praise for his outstanding play. Handling 168 total chances—95 of them assists—with only four errors, he had a terrific per-game range factor of 6.3,[137] which caused Ralph Davis to write:

> Now, it looks as if Moore will have difficulty in regaining his position, for Rhyne has been setting the field afire with his spectacular defensive stunts....
> Rhyne is one of those loose-jointed lads, seemingly able to throw from any position, no matter how badly his arms and legs may seem to be twisted up with each other. He is a real ball hawk, and pounces readily on everything driven in his direction. He gets the ball away from him without the loss of a fraction of a second, and his throwing has been speedy and accurate. He is a heady fellow, seems to know exactly what to do with the ball, and his work to date has stamped him as one of the classiest infield recruits the Pirates have had in a long time.[138]

In fact, Rhyne was playing so well that McKechnie felt comfortable optioning the young Joe Cronin to New Haven on May 11, though with the provision that he could be recalled with five days notice.[139]

As for pitchers, Meadows, with a 2.41 ERA and a 1.22 WHIP, and Kremer, 2.57 and 1.32, put up the best numbers as starters, and Don Songer, 1.83 and 1.17, was the top reliever. But the workhorse of the staff was Johnny Morrison, who started seven games, relieved in three others, pitched 59 innings, and was credited with five victories, though his ERA (3.20) and WHIP (1.42) were higher than those of Meadows, Kremer, and Songer. Then, in a move foreshadowing more mound changes to come, Songer was switched to a starting role on the 31st and did not pitch badly, surrendering three earned runs in eight innings.[140]

Two additional positive happenings occurred before the month was over, though neither of them had an effect on the pennant race. On May 19, before the Giant-Pirate game began, Jack Onslow and Giant outfielder Al Tyson were honored by the citizens of Tarentum, a borough 22 miles northeast of the downtown center of Pittsburgh, for their accomplishments while with the Allegheny Steel baseball club, which had a reputation for fielding some of the best semipro baseball teams in western Pennsylvania, if not the entire country.[141] Onslow received an easy chair, while Tyson was given a chest of silverware.[142] This was followed on May 27, when, prior to the Cub-Pirate game, the World Series championship flag was raised at Forbes Field and baseball commissioner Kenesaw Mountain Landis presented each member of the championship team with a diamond-studded medallion. Also in attendance that day were National League president John Heydler, Cub president William Veeck, and various Pittsburgh and Allegheny County officials.[143]

On the negative side, Carey continued to struggle. Playing in 20 of the Bucs' 26 games, he hit .250, with an on-base percentage of .325 and no stolen bases, and he committed five errors.[144] Similarly, the defense as a whole still left something to be desired, making 39 errors, tied for the third highest total in the league.[145] As Lou Wollen lamented, "Thumbs seem to be predominant on Pirate mitts by the way they have gummed up offerings in the field."[146] Then, the mishap and malady jinx struck again. Eddie Moore came down with influenza[147]; Ray Kremer and Vic Aldridge developed arm problems; and Lee Meadows had trouble with his sinuses.[148] Both Kremer and Aldridge were hurting enough to be sent to John "Bonesetter" Reese, the famous Welsh-born muscle, ligament, and joint manipulator who lived in Youngstown, Ohio.[149] What Reese practiced was similar to osteopathy and he made a name for himself treating everyone from mill workers to celebrities, including a number of major leaguers. In fact, in 1903, the Pirates had invited Reese to become their team physician, but he turned them down.[150] And finally, despite their strong won-lost record, a record that pushed the team into third place, the Bucs found themselves half a game further behind the league leaders—this time, the Reds—than they were at the end of April (see Table 25).

Table 25: National League Standings at the End of the Day on May 31, 1926[151]

Team	Wins	Losses	Ties	Winning Percentage	Games Back	Runs Scored	Runs Allowed
Cincinnati	29	16	1	.644	—	238	205
Chicago	23	17	1	.575	3.5	230	191
Pittsburgh	23	18	2	.561	4.0	217	189
Brooklyn	21	19	2	.525	5.5	156	174
St. Louis	23	24	0	.489	7.0	232	231
New York	20	22	0	.476	7.5	207	176
Philadelphia	16	24	0	.400	10.5	178	219
Boston	12	27	0	.308	14.0	154	227

But if May was a combination of good and bad fortune, June would be downright frustrating, though not before teasing the Pirate faithful with a certain amount of success. Maintaining its momentum from the previous month, the team continued playing well for the most part through June 22. During that time, the Pirates went 11–5, with eight of the victories coming on the road, beat the hated Giants three out of four times at the Polo Grounds, and scored over six runs per game. True, they lost a pair of slugfests to tailender Philadelphia on June 10 and 11 and a squeaker to seventh place Boston on the 14th, all of which caused some of the Pittsburgh sportswriters to gnash their teeth, but on the 9th, they charged into first place and then stayed first or second until the 22nd, when they were only a half game behind the league-leading Reds.[152]

One of the keys to the Bucs' success was the pitching of Don Songer. Between June 8 and June 18, the Kansas native started three games, relieved in a fourth one, and gave up only four earned runs in 26 innings, while recording three victories.[153]

Another key was more tinkering with the batting order. With Carey suffering sinus problems at the beginning of June, McKechnie moved Cuyler to center and brought in Carson Bigbee to play left and bat leadoff. This order remained the same until June 12, with the exception of the usual catching changes and with Eddie Moore replacing Rhyne for three games when the rookie sprained his left wrist playing against Brooklyn on the 8th, and produced a 4–3 record. At that point, Carey was returned to center field and the leadoff spot, Rhyne was returned to second base and the number two slot, and Cuyler was moved back to left field, and the team went 2–1. Then, on June 17, as Pittsburgh prepared to take on New York for a four-game series, McKechnie dropped Rhyne to the seventh spot, vaulted Waner to the second slot, and had Grantham batting sixth. This alignment probably would have remained intact indefinitely if Traynor had not injured his knee in the first game against McGraw's men and was replaced by Moore, who hit fifth as well as playing third. But with or without the Pie Man, the Bucs proceeded to go 5–1 in the six games that they played from the 17th through the 22nd and again began to look like the defending World Series champions.[154]

Table 26: Pirate Batting Orders, June 3–June 22, 1926

June 3–June 11	June 12–June 16	June 17–June 22
Bigbee, LF	Carey, CF	Carey, CF
Rhyne, 2B		
(June 9–June 11: Moore, 2B)	Rhyne, 2B	Waner, RF
Cuyler, CF	Cuyler, LF	Cuyler, LF
Wright, SS	Wright, SS	Wright, SS
Traynor, 3B	Traynor, 3B	Traynor, 3B
		(June 18–June 22: Moore, 3B)
Waner, RF	Waner, RF	Grantham, 1B
Grantham, 1B	Grantham, 1B	Rhyne, 2B
Gooch/Smith, C	Gooch/Smith, C	Smith/Gooch, C

None of this, of course, was frustrating, but also during this period in June, the Pirate leadership attempted to bolster the team's pitching corps, and that is when the frustrations began. Although Kremer, Aldridge, and Meadows all claimed to be feeling much better by June 4,[155] Kremer's arm would not be ready for starting duty until the 19th, and Aldridge, who returned as a starter on the 6th, experienced further arm trouble after pitching a four-hitter against Brooklyn, which he lost, 3–0.[156] Then to make matters worse, Aldridge's next start, on the 11th versus the Phillies in their Baker Bowl bandbox, was a complete disaster, in which he gave up seven hits and six earned runs in one and a third innings pitched.[157] However, fortunately for the Bucs, the former Indiana schoolmaster would redeem himself on the 16th and the 20th when he would toss complete-game victories against Boston in Beantown and then against New York before 40,000 fans at the Polo Grounds.[158] But as Aldridge appeared to regain his pitching prowess, Johnny Morrison lost his. Not long after going the distance in a nine-inning win over the Reds on May 31, Jughandle Johnny came down with what was being called "an ailment ... of a grippy nature."[159] This was followed by his complaining about having a sore arm, an arm so sore that he found it "painful to heave the ball even for short distances."[160] Sadly, though Morrison's respiratory malady may have been unexpected, the latter problem should have come as no surprise to anyone, considering how often the curveballer had been used during the previous month.

So, McKechnie and Clarke began to make some pitching moves. But in this endeavor, they were without the services of Barney Dreyfuss, who decided that it was time to take a break from his usual workaholic schedule and visit Europe with his wife. The vacation would begin on June 10 with a trip across the Atlantic on the steamer *Columbus*, continue with stops in Germany, Switzerland, France, and Belgium, and eventually end with a return to the states in September.[161] Now, readers may question the time of Dreyfuss' departure—leaving when the season was not even one-third over—and considering what would happen during his absence, Dreyfuss himself may have later second-guessed his own sense of timing. But on June 10, 1926, there was no indicator that he would regret temporarily getting away from a business that he had been obsessed with for decades. His team had righted itself, winning 12 of its last 16 games, and on the day before Dreyfuss left, it had recaptured first place by seven percentage points over Cincinnati.[162] In McKechnie, Clarke, and his son, Sam, Dreyfuss had capable subordinates to delegate authority to, and it was this trio that he chose to run the club while he was gone. And in spite of the various injuries and ailments that had plagued the Bucs, the spirit of the players as a whole was sky high, as evidenced by the farewell message that the team sent to Dreyfuss as he prepared to embark:

> Every good wish for a refreshing and comfortable voyage and a safe return to find us leading the league by a pennant-winning margin. Appreciating the confidence you repose in us during your absence, we, by our personal signatures to this mes-

sage, mutually pledge to each other and to you the very best that is in us to bring another pennant and world's championship to Pittsburg[h]. We can win, and we will.[163]

Then, with the exception of Sam Watters, who used S. E. Watters, each man signed the message with his nickname (e.g., Pie) or the name that the rest of the team called him (e.g., Gooch).[164]

However, even before Dreyfuss left, the remodeling plans began. On June 5, Tom Sheehan was released outright to Kansas City of the American Association. Sheehan had been inconsistent in his first few outings, but by the end of May, his ERA had ballooned to 5.84, and despite receiving a high level of run support (5.5 runs per outing), he was unable to win or save any games.[165] Could the injury that he had sustained in April been more serious than even he realized? Possibly. As mentioned earlier in this chapter, Sheehan had been struck by a line drive while pitching batting practice. Well, that mishap occurred on April 19, and though he pitched two innings of relief the next day and did not allow any earned runs, he did surrender three hits, walked a man, and hurt his own cause by committing an error.[166] And after that, he made one appearance as a starter and five as a reliever and proceeded to give up 20 earned runs in 24 and a third innings.[167] Of course, since Sheehan did not say more about his injury, the issue has to be left unresolved.

The next step was to acquire one or more new arms, and here McKechnie and Clarke coveted Doug McWeeny and Bob McGraw of Brooklyn and were willing to trade Eddie Moore and another outfielder—no doubt, Barnhart or Bigbee—for one of them. Clarke even went to New York to discuss the trade in person, but nothing came of it and the trading deadline of June 15 passed before Pittsburgh could pick up anyone else.[168] The Pirate leaders then turned in another direction and tried to get Grover Cleveland Alexander, who had been placed on waivers by the Chicago Cubs on June 22.

Alexander was one of the greatest pitchers to have ever put on a major league uniform, but by June of 1926, he was also an epileptic and an unreformable alcoholic who had run afoul of the new Cub skipper, Joe McCarthy. According to Alexander's wife, Aimee, McCarthy, a my-way-or-the-highway type of leader, "was the only manager Alex [as Alexander was called] ever had trouble with."[169] The problem was that the natures of the two men were just too different for the odd-couple relationship to last long.

Alexander was a legend in his own time: a brilliant pitcher, possessing a lot of baseball savvy as well as a good sinking fastball, an even better sharp-breaking curve (probably an early form of a slider), an underrated changeup, and pinpoint control. Although age, drinking, and the ravages of having experienced combat in the First World War had eroded his skills, he was still a very good moundsman, as evidenced by the 2.51 ERA and the 1.02 WHIP that he recorded for his first five pitching appearances during the '26 season.[170] Conversely, he was severely dependent on alcohol and had little regard for training rules, leading Bill McKechnie biographer Mitchell Conrad Stinson to write, "At his worst, [Alexander] was a staggering drunk who couldn't be counted on by bosses or teammates—at his best, a high-functioning alcoholic."[171]

Joe McCarthy was a rookie manager and a quiet though strict disciplinarian who was trying to assert his will on a veteran team that had a reputation for being undisciplined. Never having played in the majors, McCarthy may have felt it necessary to show his troops that he was in command by making an example out of anyone who dared to violate his regulations, even if that the person was a flawed superstar.

So, McCarthy tolerated Alexander's presence throughout April and May, but as John Skipper, one of Alexander's biographers writes:

> When the Cubs made an eastern road trip in early June, Alex stayed behind, missing games in Pittsburgh, Brooklyn, New York and Boston. When he joined the team in Philadelphia, he was in no condition to pitch. He had broken training rules by his excessive drinking....
> [McCarthy] saw Alex's antics as insubordination and a way of testing the leadership and guts of a rookie manager.[172]

Did Barney Dreyfuss make a mistake by visiting Europe during the 1926 season (National Baseball Hall of Fame Library, Cooperstown, New York)?

The result was that Alexander was suspended indefinitely without pay on June 15 and put on waivers seven days later. And here is when the Pirates entered the picture. Going into their respective games on June 22, Cincinnati, Pittsburgh, and St. Louis all claimed Alexander, with Cincinnati being in first place at the time; Pittsburgh being in second, a half game behind the Reds; and St. Louis in third, a game behind the Bucs. Now, the waiver period ended at the close of play on the 22nd, and since the lowest team in the standings that made a claim would get the wayward right-hander, the games played that day were extremely important. Well, it just so happened that Pittsburgh was playing St. Louis at Sportsman's Park, while Cincinnati entertained the Cubs at Redland Field, which meant that the loser of the game between the Pirates and the Cardinals would win Alexander. This would be the equivalent of losing a battle with the hope that the ramifications of it would help win the war. But even here the Pirates got stymied. Despite being on foreign turf, Lee Meadows pitched a six-hitter, the Bucs won, 3–1, and the Cards received Alexander.[173]

After failing to procure a frontline major league starter, the Pirate brain trust turned to the minor leagues and purchased Chester "Chet" Nichols from the New Haven Profs of the Eastern League on June 25. In addition to the allegedly generous sum of money paid for Nichols' pitching skills, Pittsburgh optioned Bud Culloton to the Profs, leaving open the possibility of recalling him later in the season.[174] Unfortunately, though, for the Pirates and their fans, Nichols may have been a hot prospect, but he was no big league star and would be used sparingly.

Besides acquiring Nichols, Pittsburgh attempted to regain Lou Koupal from the Buffalo Bisons, the club that he had been sent to on April 8, but the Buffalo powers refused to let him go at that time. As Ed Balinger explained:

> Fred Clarke, upon his return from Buffalo, where he made an effort to obtain [p]itcher Louis Koupal, announced that while the Bisons at present declined to give him up, they had promised to do all they could to help [the] champions out of their predicament. Koupal is subject to recall under an optional agreement, but the hitch comes from the fact that Buffalo is right at the heels of the leading Baltimore club and as Louie has been the most consistent winner on the team, it would be a tough blow to give him up just now.[175]

Further frustration followed the Bucs' inability to get Alexander—this time in the form of the team going into a tailspin. Beginning on June 23 and continuing through June 30, the Corsairs lost seven out of eight games, tied the game that they did not lose, and dropped to third place, six games behind the league-leading Reds (see Table 27). During that stretch, the vaunted Pirate hitting attack had a collective batting average of .233 and scored only 20 runs, 2.5 per game, while the not-yet-remodeled pitching corps gave up 47 earned runs and a combination of 122 hits and walks in 68 innings pitched for a collective 6.22 ERA and a 1.79 WHIP. Poor fielding—14 errors—contributed to a total of 61 runs being given up or an average of 7.6 per game.[176] Fingers could be pointed in a variety of directions, but the bottom line is that the collapse was a team effort. And what made that collapse even more frustrating was that on June 22, the Bucs were poised to wrest away the top spot in the league from the Reds and their fate was in their own hands. The remaining games for the month were against St. Louis and Cincinnati, the teams immediately above and below them, so they were not dependent on other teams to help them advance. But instead of taking the great leap forward, they took the great fall backward.

Table 27: National League Standings at the End of the Day on June 30, 1926[177]

Team	Wins	Losses	Ties	Winning Percentage	Games Back	Runs Scored	Runs Allowed
Cincinnati	43	27	1	.614	—	387	324
St. Louis	39	30	1	.565	3.5	359	319
Pittsburgh	34	30	3	.531	6.0	335	323
Brooklyn	35	31	2	.530	6.0	287	304
Chicago	34	34	1	.500	8.0	357	345
New York	34	35	0	.493	8.5	331	308
Philadelphia	26	41	0	.388	15.5	331	407
Boston	25	42	0	.373	16.5	303	360

Compounding matters were two other forms of frustration: the inability to improve defensively and the ever-present injury and illness bug. Whether winning or losing, the Pirates' fielding left much to be desired, causing Lou Wollen to complain after a 9–1 loss to Cincinnati in which the Bucs made four errors:

> They throw the ball around in fearful fashion and when they weren't gumming up rollers, they were heaving balls wide of the mark at which they were aimed. Two wild and woolly flings by Eddie Moore aided the Reds considerably in scoring four of their runs; another bit of inaccurate pegging by Traynor provided them with two more, and Carey's fumble was of much assistance in the scoring of another.[178]

Obviously, Wollen was referring to just one game, but the gist of his comments could apply to other games as well. Pittsburgh led the National League in errors per game in June, averaging 1.83, with over 61 percent of those errors contributing to opposing runs being scored. At the other extreme was St. Louis with only .78 errors per game.[179]

As for the injury and illness bug, the Pirates' roster again took on the appearance of a hospital register. Besides the aforementioned problems suffered by Kremer, Aldridge, Meadows, Morrison, and Traynor, Kiki Cuyler had been playing with a bone bruise on his foot since at least June 12; Hal Rhyne, who earlier in the month had missed three games with a sprained wrist, experienced soreness in his right arm and shoulder sometime before the 23rd, soreness caused by a problem with his elbow; Glenn Wright, who had been nursing a cut toe that he had received when he was spiked during a game with Brooklyn on June 6, came down with a heavy cold which led to an attack of the grippe and slight congestion in one of his lungs on the 25th; Johnny Gooch was stricken with a painful toothache and an infected throat during the latter part of the month; and newcomer Chet Nichols arrived with an injured foot.[180] This last piece of misfortune prompted one Pittsburgh scribe to sarcastically remark, "The Pirates went out and bought a fellow on crutches, and a minor leaguer at that. All they need now is a wheelchair and a couple of divans for those fellows who think they are entitled to be on a real club."[181]

Kremer's, Morrison's, and Rhyne's problems were serious enough that when the team traveled from St. Louis to Pittsburgh on June 24 and 25, they were dropped off in Youngstown to see Bonesetter Reese. Reese's diagnosis was that Kremer had rheumatism in the muscles of his throwing arm and that he needed to stop pitching for a short period of time, but that Morrison's and Rhyne's aches could be eliminated that day. In Morrison's case, Reese straightened out a kink in Jughandle Johnny's shoulder and then told the curveballer that he would be able to pitch again in a day or two, while for Rhyne, the "miracle manipulator" snapped something in his elbow, which permitted the rookie to start the Pirates' game against Cincinnati on the 26th.[182]

Unfortunately, though, for the Bucs, Reese may have been a miracle manipulator, but he was not perfect. The rest that Kremer took might have backfired on him, as he was knocked out of the box after pitching only three and a third innings against the Reds on the 29th. Morrison made a brief appearance in a 16–0 shellacking that the Pirates received, also at the hands of the Reds, two days earlier, missed the plate with four straight pitches, and then left the game with more arm problems. And Rhyne's elbow began to swell up so much in that same game that the second sacker had to be replaced by Johnny Rawlings.[183]

Even the coaching staff was not immune to bumps and bruises. On June 20 before the start of the Pirate-Giant game, Jack Onslow was confronted by a group of McGraw's men, fully attired in their New York uniforms and cleated baseball shoes, who proceeded to tell him that they did not appreciate his bench jockeying during the previous games between the two teams that season. When Onslow, who was in street clothes and noncleated shoes, replied by taking a swing at and missing Frank "Pancho" Snyder, the Giant catcher, Snyder reciprocated by knocking him to the ground with a hard right to the chin, and after he got up, Snyder decked him again with another right. Onslow, however, would not be deterred as he came up swinging a second time, only to be held back by the other New York players who were present.[184] The results were a black eye and a loss of pride for Onslow, who could usually more than hold his own in a fist fight; "a couple of fractured maulers" for Snyder, who would not see action

Three. *High Expectations, Disappointing Results* 121

again until August 3; and a challenge issued to the Giants by the embarrassed Pirate coach, Earl Smith, Eddie Moore, Vic Aldridge, "and a few more of the recognized bruisers on the [Pirate] club ... to resume hostilities" whenever the Giants were ready to do so.[185]

As might be expected with a losing streak, rumors began to spread of dissension and dissipation on the team. But the reports of dissension had nothing to do with Fred Clarke, who was not even with the team for part of the month. Because Clarke wore three different hats—that of vice president of the club, assistant to the manager, and head of scouting—he was not able to be on the bench or even in the ballpark for every game. For example, probably in May, he had traveled to Columbia, South Carolina, to watch the players from the spring training roster who Pittsburgh had sent there before the season had started.[186] Such activities increased in June when the team desperately needed pitching help, which led Clarke to go to New York, Buffalo, and other places where the team was not playing to try to secure some new arms. Thus, contrary to the picture that Adams, Bigbee, and Carey would paint later that year, there were no stories at this time about players complaining about Clarke or about Clarke's alleged attempts to contradict and/or usurp power from McKechnie. Instead, the dissension rumors centered around players fighting with each. Aldridge supposedly had had a fist fight with Wright, the results of which were said to be the real reason that Wright had missed several games between June 26 and 29. Also, Smith and Yde were specifically mentioned as being involved in some form of fisticuffs.

As for the dissipation, it was the usual recycled claims that had been haunting the Bucs since 1921. A certain player had been seen having one too many in a bar in a certain town or another player had been seen partying too much in another town.

But as Ralph Davis, Regis Welsh, and some other Pittsburgh scribes argued, these rumors were nothing more than totally unfounded or exaggerated stories that had been created or embellished by disgruntled fans with overactive imaginations and/or by the gambling element that had been hit hard by the team's slump. The unattributed column titled "Playing the Game with the Pirates" found in the June 29 issue of the *Pittsburgh Press* and probably written by Lou Wollen reported:

> The old booze gag didn't go over so big so trouble-shooters skirted arund [*sic*] the ends and located another cause for the Pirates' present predicament. Fist fights galore were staged between members of the team in clubhouse, alley and barroom, to hear them tell it.
> Glenn Wright, Vic Aldridge, Earl Smith and Emil Yde were those said to have been mixed up in riotous doings[,] but prompt denials by officials of the club and

players and lack of evidence of encounters seem to make it plain that nothing of the sort happened.

The fact is that nothing but the best of feeling exists among the world's champions. They are one happy family on and off the ball field and while slight signs of irritability may crop out at times—natural enough when matters are breaking badly—no idea is held that ragged play is intentional.[187]

To this, Davis added in his June 30 column in the *Press*, "Some of the tales told about the Buccaneers are silly in the extreme, and probably the silliest is that about the alleged fight between Glenn Wright and Vic Aldridge, both of whom are sensible fellows—and good friends."[188] Davis went further to say in his column published in the July 8 issue of *The Sporting News*: "There were also rumors of other clubhouse fights, in which half the team was said to be embroiled. There was not a single basis, in fact, for any of these rumors, but that did not prevent their wide circulation."[189]

As for where the tales of carousing may have come from, Davis wrote:

> There is no doubt that some of the stories about dissipation have been exaggerated, although there is partial foundation for some of them. Ball players are public characters, and everything that they do is closely watched. So long as they are winning, nothing is said, but let them lose a few games, and tongues begin to wag. Some of the players have taken an occasional drink. One or two of have gone further than that, but the Pittsburgh team is not an aggregation of drunkards and roués.[190]

The consensus of the Pittsburgh sportswriting community was that the real reasons for the Pirates' slump were the plague of mishaps and maladies and the inability to execute well enough on the playing field to win games. Of course, this diagnosis did not lessen the frustration for the Pirate management, who believed that some changes were necessary to remedy both matters.

Four

The ABC Affair

> Life is a funny game, and a little thing, almost a trifle, may make a splash in your affairs so big that the ripples from it will be felt as long as you live.
> —Fred Clarke, 1911

Not wanting to waste any time in getting the team back to its winning ways, the Pirate leaders made the first of their changes shortly before the month of June ended. During the debacle in Cincinnati—a five-game series in which the Bucs got swept by a combined score of 46 to 13—Sam Dreyfuss and Bill McKechnie contacted free agent pitcher Leslie "Bullet Joe" Bush and asked him if he would like to come aboard the Pirate ship. Bush jumped at the invitation and, after meeting with Dreyfuss and McKechnie in Pittsburgh prior to the Pirate-Cardinal game on June 30, signed a contract to be a Bucco that evening.[1] Although Bush would turn 34 in November of '26 and had been released by Washington a week before joining Pittsburgh, he had had a long and distinguished career in the American League. Playing in the junior circuit for over 14 seasons, he had pitched for five pennant winners, been among the top 10 yearly leaders in wins, earned run average, strikeouts, and other positive pitching categories a number of times, and in 1922, came in fourth in the balloting for the American League's new award to honor "the baseball player who is of the greatest all-around service to his club and credit to the sport during each season."[2] Because of the rules that were in place at that time, Bush was not allowed to see action with the Pirates for 10 days from the time of his release by the Senators, but still, his acquisition was considered a needed addition to a pitching staff that was hurting.[3]

What followed was a month of contradictions, as the team's fortunes on the field soared, but at the same time, a series of personnel problems emerged. The irony of the situation was that when the Bucs were mired in their June swoon, the club was reported to be "one happy family on and off the ball field," but apparently the pressures of winning affected some players in an adverse fashion.

Immediately after acquiring Bush, Pittsburgh broke the losing spell it had been under by winning three games in a row and then continued to play championship ball for the remainder of the month. Losing streaks were held to no more than a pair of two-gamers, while five times the team reeled off three consecutive wins. Just as impressively, all of this was done while encountering a brutal schedule of 31 games in 31 days, including five doubleheaders.[4]

During this period, the vaunted Pirate hitting attack scored 178 runs for 5.74 runs per game, edging St. Louis for the best in the league, while collectively batting .306, with a .368 on-base percentage and a .434 slugging average. The troubled pitching staff rebounded to lower its ERA to 3.89 for the month, and the much maligned defense reduced its average number of errors per game from 1.83 during the previous month to 1.16 and its percentage of errors that led to runs from 61.4 to 47.2. The combination of better pitching and an improved defense led to 135 runs being given up, which when subtracted from the offensive output, produced a run differential of +43, by far the top monthly mark in the league. In comparison, the Cubs were second in run differential with a +16 and four of the teams had minus differentials. The results were a 21–10 record and the recapturing of first place, a spot that Pittsburgh held by being two games ahead of Cincinnati at the end of play on July 31 (see Table 28).[5]

Table 28: National League Standings at the End of the Day on July 31, 1926[6]

Team	Wins	Losses	Ties	Winning Percentage	Games Back	Runs Scored	Runs Allowed
Pittsburgh	55	40	3	.579	—	513	458
Cincinnati	56	45	1	.554	2.0	509	458
St. Louis	53	46	1	.535	4.0	531	491
Chicago	50	48	1	.510	6.5	464	436
Brooklyn	51	49	2	.510	6.5	439	447
New York	48	49	0	.495	8.0	453	439
Boston	40	57	0	.412	16.0	437	515
Philadelphia	38	57	0	.400	17.0	462	564

The team's turnaround from June can be attributed to several factors. First and foremost was McKechnie's juggling of his lineup and batting order. Whether he received help with this matter from Clarke and/or the two coaches is unknown, but the adjustments righted the Pirate ship as it started to flounder. After making 10 lineup changes—not including rotating the catchers—and using five different batting orders during the first 18 games, a time that saw the team going 11–7, Deacon Bill went with the same lineup and batting order for the last 13 games, which led to 10 wins. An almost ideal starting eight or nine on paper, provided that all the men were healthy, the July 19–July 31 batting order consisted of Carey, CF; Waner, RF; Cuyler, LF; Wright, SS; Traynor, 3B; Grantham, 1B; Rawlings, 2B; and Gooch/Smith, C, and produced 75 runs, while the lineup, steadied by the presence of the veteran Rawlings, provided better defense.[7] As the anonymous writer of "The Post" column in the *Pittsburgh Post* remarked after an earlier game in which Rawlings subbed for Rhyne and Moore, "Johnny didn't do much with the stick, but ... [he] is still a ball hawk."[8]

Second, throughout the month, the hot bats of Waner, Cuyler, Traynor, Grantham, Smith, and Gooch were instrumental in propelling the team to success. As can be seen from Table 29, all six men hit over .300, five had on-base percentages of .375 or above, and four had slugging averages of .500 or higher. The two catchers, playing in less games than the other four men and batting in the eighth slot, had fewer runs scored or driven in, but averaged nearly a run produced for each game in which they saw action.

Table 29: Pittsburgh's Top Hitters for the Month of July[9]

Name	G	BA	OBP	SLG	R	RBI
Waner	31	.357	.463	.589	31	22
Cuyler	31	.303	.357	.412	24	20
Traynor	31	.376	.460	.560	20	19
Grantham	31	.393	.447	.634	19	26
Smith	19	.318	.375	.500	8	10
Gooch	17	.327	.397	.423	6	11

Third, although the pitching staff did not have as many standout performers as the nonpitchers, Ray Kremer, Don Songer, and, to a lesser degree, Emil Yde posted good numbers. Kremer recovered nicely from the ailment that had lessened his effectiveness in May and June to start six games, finish three others, pitch a shutout, record a 2.62 ERA, and be credited with five wins and two saves. As Lou Wollen commented, "Kremer showed that rheumatism can't last forever."[10] Songer put up almost identical stats, with six starts, three finishes, one shutout, a 2.79 ERA, four wins, and two saves. And Yde, who started five games and finished two, had no shutouts or saves and a 3.40 ERA, but he did have three strong outings, two for wins, and chalked up three victories. As for the new oldster, Joe Bush, he was up and down, though in three of his appearances—two starts and a virtual start—he gave up a total of seven earned runs in 26 innings but was saddled with two losses and a no-decision, in part because his teammates could score only three times for him.[11]

Fourth, the ability of McKechnie, Clarke, and the coaches to work around the continuing injury-illness curse and get the best men possible on the field of play cannot be underestimated. Throughout the course of the month, Bush was struck with a mild bout of ptomaine poisoning; Wright, who had been playing despite suffering from an attack of grippe, missed four games with a stone bruise on his hip; Rhyne, who had played in seven games during the first 15 days of the month, reinjured his wrist on the 16th and saw action in only one more game until August 3; the cause of Nichols' ankle injury proved to be "a small particle of bone [that] had been chipped away from the main bone," which kept the hurler from making his major league debut until the 30th; after four starts, Aldridge came down with another sore arm—or more specifically another sore elbow—was removed in the first inning of a game against Brooklyn on the 21st, and did not pitch again until August 4; and Morrison, who had been ailing since early June, underwent surgery to have his tonsils removed, an operation that was supposed to cure all his ills.[12] It was later reported that "after X-ray examination ... [Nichols'] injury [was] not so severe as was at first thought,"[13] but he still was not able to help the team for most of the month.

And finally, McKechnie, taking a page from the Fred Clarke book of managing and in all likelihood influenced or at least supported by Clarke, jumped on the personnel problems as they arose and attempted to stamp them out before they infected the rest of the team. These problems began with lackadaisical play on the part of Emil Yde and Eddie Moore during the first half of a doubleheader loss to New York on July 14. Yde had come in as a long reliever in the fourth inning and had given up four hits, five walks, and three earned runs in six innings. Moore had hit well, as did Yde for that matter, but his fielding left much to be desired. However, far more serious than just not performing to the level that they were capable of, neither man appeared to be trying to win. At best, it seemed that both Yde and Moore, for whatever reason or reasons, were not concentrating on what they were doing; at worst, it looked as if they were throwing the game, though no Pittsburgh sportswriter ever accused them of doing so. But according to the Pirate management, both men "were warned repeatedly ... that lack of conscientious effort would bring salty doses," so neither culprit was a first-time offender.[14] And this raises the question of why were Yde and Moore behaving in such a manner. Was it just a reactive generation response to authority? Or was there more to this matter than meets the eye?

Four. *The ABC Affair*

For Yde, it may have been a case of letting his frustrations get the best of him. Going into the July 14 game, he had been an inconsistent starter and an ineffective reliever, and to make matters worse, in the five starts in which he did pitch well, three of them resulted in losses because he did not receive much run support. His detractors had labeled his pitching performances for the first half of the season as "terrible"[15] and said that "[h]is record [was] really much better looking on the books than on the ball field,"[16] which only intensified his feelings of dissatisfaction and led to a noncaring attitude. So, based on what Ralph Davis gathered from Yde's friends, the fastball-throwing southpaw "had become discouraged ... and had permitted himself to assume a frame of mind that was not conducive to his best work."[17] Or as Havey Boyle wrote, "[Yde had come] to the conclusion that the whole world was against him, and that it really did him little good to 'bear down,' as he always [had done] in the past."[18]

Moore's situation, however, was different. If Yde had become disheartened, Moore had become disgruntled. The starting second baseman for the 1925 Pirates, Moore had finished among the National League leaders in sacrifice hits (fourth), walks (third), stolen bases (seventh), and runs scored (seventh) during the '25 season, and his clutch home run in the sixth game of the World Series helped to defeat the Senators and keep the Bucs' championship hopes alive. Defensively for NL second sackers, he led the league in errors, though it was not for want of trying, as he finished in the top five for his position in putouts (third), assists (fifth), double plays (fourth), and range factor (fourth).[19]

But 1926 was not 1925. As described in the previous chapter, Moore had been injured during spring training—an injury that at the time was diagnosed as a twisted ankle but very well may have been a broken bone in Moore's foot—had been reinjured in the same spot during the regular season, and then had come down with influenza, which Moore would later recall as really being

Along with Eddie Moore, Emil Yde was fined for indifferent play (Library of Congress, George Grantham Bain Collection, LC-DIG-ggbain-38579).

pneumonia.[20] He had lost his starting position to Hal Rhyne and, after Rhyne hurt his wrist again, to Johnny Rawlings. When he did get a chance to play, his mobility was limited because of his ankle/foot problem, perhaps making it appear that he was not trying. Tennis star Pancho Segura had told the young Jimmy Connors: "If you're injured, don't play; if you play, you're not injured."[21] But in major league baseball during the 1920s, if you did not play, there was a good chance that someone else would take your job. So, Moore played, but not often well. And because of this, he was booed by the fans, castigated by some of the Pittsburgh sportswriters, and made the subject of trade and waiver rumors, which led to a no-win situation in his mind. Ralph Davis captured this mood best when he wrote, "[Moore] knows, doubtless, that he is simply being tolerated here by the owners, and that the only reason he is still on the payroll is because no suitable deal could be made for his transfer."[22]

To make matters worse, as Moore freely admitted to Eugene Murdock nearly 50 years later, he "didn't take very good care of [him]self," "did funny things at night," and "didn't follow the rules very closely."[23] He also admitted that "some of [his] antics got on Barney Dreyfuss' nerves" and that off the field, the Pirate authorities "could never tell what [he] was going to do."[24] Apparently, as long as Moore's performance on the field was not noticeably affected by them, such antics were tolerated, but once Moore's level of play dropped, those antics were no longer winked at by the authorities, which may have added to Moore's disgruntlement. Ralph Davis summarized the situation nicely when he wrote, "Eddie's experiences in Pittsburg [*sic*] [during the 1926 season] have been none too pleasant."[25]

But no matter what the reason or reasons for Yde's and Moore's behavior, McKechnie did not hesitate to act. Charging both men with "indifferent play," Deacon Bill decided to make examples out of them.[26] Yde was fined $50, while Moore received the brunt of the Pirate skipper's penalties, being fined $100, benched indefinitely, and put on waivers several days later, from where he was picked up by the Boston Braves.[27]

The extent of Moore's punishment—especially in comparison to that of Yde's—has raised the question of whether the second sacker was a marked man for a specific offense that he might have committed prior to or during the '26 season. Ralph Davis speculated at the time of Moore's demise that "it seems that Eddie did something last [f]all, either during or following the World's Series, which angered President Barney Dreyfuss."[28] This thought was echoed in an article in the *Pittsburgh Press* that lacked a byline but may have been written by Lou Wollen.[29] If so, Wollen would later change his tune when he wrote, under his byline, that Moore was released because "he criticized the McKechnie system of strategl [*sic*]."[30] And later still, Adams, Bigbee, and Carey would say that Moore was released because he "was outspoken enough to tell Clarke to 'get off the bench.'"³¹

However, in defending himself the evening of the day Adams, Bigbee, and Carey's comments were published, Clarke, "a big booster for Moore" in 1923,³² "emphatically denied [the trio's version of the story] and branded [it] as a deliberate falsehood" while telling members of the Pittsburgh media:

> When the fans were riding Eddie every time he walked on the field and he was retorting to them in his natural way, I said[,] "Don't pay any attention to them. Just get out there and hustle; keep your head up and everything will be all right." Moore had a peculiar temperament and although never had [sic] to handle, was figured to be better off with another club. It was Moore's own fault that he was let go and the fact that he and I are still friendly, even though he is with another club now, might be proved by the fact that several times since he left here[,] I have seen Eddie and talked with him about many things.³³

Also in Clarke's defense, though it was true that Moore "often concealed his disappointment under a smile,"³⁴ ironically it may have been a tactic that he had learned from Clarke himself—to stay positive even when things go wrong—and, therefore, Clarke would have been unlikely to have yelled at him for smiling after making a mistake on the field. This is not to say that Clarke would have condoned indifferent play or a lack of hustle on Moore's part, and he certainly would have gotten rid of Moore if he thought that the delinquent infielder was disgruntled, especially to keep him from becoming a disruptive force on the team, but the story put forth by Carey, Bigbee, Adams, and their *Pittsburgh Press* supporters sounds contrived.

Interestingly enough, as the anti–Clarke and pro–Clarke forces brought forth their arguments once the season was over, apparently no one bothered to ask Moore for his side of the story until Eugene Murdock interviewed the controversial player almost 49 years after he left the Pirates. What Moore told Murdock had nothing to do with Clarke or even indifferent play but rather with a falling out with Barney Dreyfuss that Moore had had when he had become ill in May of 1926. As Murdock wrote in his book, *Baseball Players in Their Times: Oral Histories of the Game, 1920–1940*:

> [Moore] contracted pneumonia. About this time the Pirates departed on a road trip and left Moore behind. While the team was away and without owner Barney Dreyfuss' knowledge, Moore visited a doctor in Conneaut, Ohio, who had been recommended to him. When Moore got back to Pittsburgh[,] he told Dreyfuss that he had visited a doctor in Conneaut. Dreyfuss blew up, saying that he was Moore's doctor and that he wasn't going to pay a nickel of the doctor's bill. Moore shouted back that Dreyfuss was not his doctor "when my health is concerned." Dreyfuss shouted back, "I'll send you so far away that you'll never come back!" Moore called

Dreyfuss a liar and stormed out of the office slamming the door as he went. In fact, he slammed the door so hard he broke all the glass in it.³⁵

Thus, if Moore's memory is to be believed, his fate was sealed once he had angered Dreyfuss—something that certain Pittsburgh sportswriters had previously alluded to, though they had misdiagnosed the specific cause of the anger—and it was only a matter of time before he would no longer be wearing a Pirate uniform. As for when that time should have come, there was no consensus among the local scribes, with some writers thinking that it would have been better for the Bucs to have hung on to Moore and used him as part of a trade during the offseason.³⁶ But it was highly unlikely that in the midst of a pennant race, the Pirate powers were going to keep a discontented .227 hitter who "didn't follow the rules very closely" and who had incurred the wrath of Barney Dreyfuss. At the opposite extreme, Regis Welsh criticized the powers for "waiting until this time [meaning until after the trading deadline had passed] to let a player go by waiver when this player, ... and a few of the other almost useless ones, might have gotten the club a pitcher and a catcher not so long ago."³⁷ On the surface, Welsh's point appears to be well taken. The Pirates definitely needed a pitcher, though not necessarily a catcher, and if his memory is correct about the timing of events, Moore's confrontation with Dreyfuss probably took place towards the end of May, over two weeks before the trading deadline. However, what Welsh forgets is that the Pirates, as shown in the previous chapter, did attempt to trade Moore as part of a package to get a pitcher in early June, but they were unsuccessful.

An antiauthority attitude, a misdiagnosed broken bone in his foot, and an argument with Barney Dreyfuss, not Fred Clarke, led to the end of Eddie Moore's tenure with the Pirates (Library of Congress, George Grantham Bain Collection, LC-DIG-ggbain–38565).

Shortly after Moore's departure, another personnel issue occurred. Vic Aldridge, who as a former school teacher should have known something about obeying rules, violated one of McKechnie's regulations and ended up being fined $50. As petty as it may seem to some people, McKechnie required each of his players to check in with him before leaving the clubhouse. But after a poor brief outing against Brooklyn in the second game of a doubleheader on July 21, Aldridge was in no mood to abide by what he may have perceived as a meaningless dictate, so he hurriedly dressed and left the ballpark without receiving anyone's consent. And McKechnie quickly responded by hitting the struggling curveballer with the before-mentioned fine.

In Aldridge's defense, his behavior may have been caused by the frustrations that he had been experiencing that season, and especially by being used in the game in question against the Robins after telling McKechnie and Clarke that they should not pitch him. As Clarke explained to the author of "The Post" column:

> Vic had a bad arm early in the season. He is an elbow pitcher and sore arms are part of their trade. He started off well enough and was used a lot. In Cincinnati early in the year, he complained of elbow trouble. The club trainer and Vic himself did everything to relieve the trouble. Then came the dearth of pitching material and he just had to be used. He was worked a lot, but said that the soreness was still there. Yesterday[,] he complained of not being right, but there was no other hurler really available and we tried to get by with him. You and everyone else saw what happened. The soreness will have to be worked out, that's the only way. Until it is, Vic may not be any better pitcher than he was yesterday.[38]

Thus, like Eddie Moore, Aldridge had been placed in a no-win situation. Pitching with a sore elbow because of the shortage of effective starters, he had been booed by the fans, criticized by certain sportswriters such as "The Post" columnist who constantly lambasted him with comments like "[Aldridge] won't exert himself warming up; he won't try when he is in there" and "why not plaster a [large fine] on [him], [so that he] might be forced to take his work seriously,"[39] and fined when he let his frustrations get the best of him. Lou Wollen may have accurately summed up the Indiana schoolmaster's predicament when he wrote about Aldridge's performance on the 21st:

> Vic Aldridge failed again. His mound tenure in the second game of the twin bill was short and not so sweet. Three men faced him and all of them got on base. That was enough and he was yanked without delay. Boos of fans greeted him as he strode to the bench. Possibly they were deserved[,] but an ailing arm, used when it shouldn't have been, may be the trouble rather than lack of effort as some fans seem to believe.[40]

Of course, Aldridge may have been the cause of his own misfortune when he altered his pitching style to accommodate his move from Wrigley Field to Forbes Field. After the '25 season, Aldridge explained in an article in *Baseball Magazine*:

> I used to depend principally upon my curve ball [sic]. I had practiced with a curve until I could control it absolutely. I really felt safer using a curve than a fast ball [sic]. But that was at Chicago. Pitching is sometimes a matter of geography. In the Cubs relatively small field with encroaching bleacher seats, the pitcher had to guard particularly against a fluky home run. A curve is less likely to be changed into a homer than a fast ball [sic]. When I came to Pittsburgh, however, with a larger field in which to navigate, I found it advisable to depend more upon my fast ball [sic]. This changed policy of mine seemed to unsettle my control for I have had more difficulty in getting the ball over the plate this year than I have experienced since I was an amateur.[41]

Because of this, the put-upon right-hander may have overcompensated for his lack of control by throwing more curveballs in 1926, after his arm had gotten used to throwing less of them, and, in the process, hurt his elbow.

Whatever the source of Aldridge's pain, the details concerning his, Yde's, and Moore's infractions pale in comparison to the Johnny Morrison saga. As previously mentioned, Morrison was having a good season through the end of May. Starting 10 games and finishing two more, he had posted a 2.59 ERA with two shutouts and was credited with six wins. In fact, Chilly Doyle thought so well of Jughandle Johnny that he wrote on May 16, "Morrison has pitched better ball than a majority of flingers in the two major leagues ... [and] is offering a fine example to other Pirate pitchers, especially to the first string flingers."[42]

But then the hard-drinking hurler began having a series of problems. After coming down with a vague respiratory ailment in early June, Morrison started experiencing pain in his throwing arm, which, with the exception of facing one batter on June 27, incapacitated him for an extended length of time. This was followed by him having his tonsils removed in early July because some physician had convinced him that the procedure would be the panacea for his troubles. But rather than returning to the Pirate pitching staff once he had recovered from his operation, Morrison quietly slipped out of Pittsburgh and went back to his hometown of Owensboro, Kentucky. And apparently, he was so quiet about his departure that Lou Wollen wrote, "Morrison was 'off the premises' for three days before his absence was discovered by the management."[43] Morrison's departure also caused Wollen to criticize the Pirate management for being penny wise and dollar foolish: fining Aldridge for not telling McKechnie that he was leaving the clubhouse, but not caring enough about Morrison to realize that he had disappeared until 72 hours after he had vanished.

Once the Pirate authorities did notice that Morrison was missing, they attempted to coax him into returning, even allowing him a three-day grace period that was expanded to four to come back with no penalties attached.[44] But Morrison would not budge, sending the authorities a letter by special delivery in which he told them "that he was not ready to go to work."[45] The author-

Four. *The ABC Affair* 133

ities, in turn, responded by suspending the wayward pitcher indefinitely, to which Morrison replied, "I just got tired of staying around Pittsburg [*sic*] and not being able to do anything for the team, [so] I came on home. When my arm gets well[,] I hope to be of service to the Pirates."[46]

Jughandle Johnny's missive was followed by a report from Dr. O. W. Rash, a physician in Owensboro, which stated that the real reason for Morrison's misery was a fracture near the moundsman's elbow, something Rash had seen while looking at an X-ray of Morrison's arm.[47] But as might be expected, Rash's report was not well received by the Pirate authorities, who said that if the doctor was correct, Morrison must have broken his arm after traveling to Owensboro because there was no fracture before he left.[48]

The ball was back in Morrison's court and he responded on July 29 with a telegram to McKechnie telling the Pirate skipper "that his arm [was] not broken, and that he [would be able to] rejoin the team as soon as possible."[49] Morrison's message was confirmed, oddly enough, by Dr. Rash, who shortly after the arrival of the telegram, came forth and corrected himself by saying that it was really an X-ray of Phil Morrison's arm that he had looked at.[50]

The entire Morrison episode was bizarre from start to finish, leaving one to wonder how much Jughandle Johnny's alcoholism was to blame for it. But whatever the cause of yet another hurdle in the Pirates' quest to repeat as pennant winners, Morrison was reinstated on August 17.[51]

Although the disciplinary issues served as a distraction to the Pirates in general and to McKechnie in particular, several positive things resulted from them:

- First, after being fined, Emil Yde turned his season around and had seven strong starts and a handful of effective relief appearances. His post–July 14

The alcoholic Johnny Morrison went AWOL in July, adding to the team's woes (Library of Congress, George Grantham Bain Collection, LC-DIG-ggbain-38576).

ERA and WHIP were 2.88 and 1.32 as opposed to the 4.47 and 1.49 that he had through the 14th, and he was credited with six wins.[52] A prime example of this change for the better was his July 22 performance against Brooklyn. As the *Pittsburgh Sun* reported:

> Emil Yde, starting his first game since a fine of $50 was tacked on him on July 14 for alleged indifferent work, showed a vast improvement in pitching form. He worked like the proverbial beaver from start to finish and with such good effect that he had the visitors at his mercy practically all the way.[53]

- Second, the Aldridge incident may have convinced the Pirate officials that the Indiana curveballer needed serious medical attention. So, on July 27, Aldridge was sent to Rochester, New York, to see Dr. Harry Knight, a physician who had a reputation for "[making] new ball players out of old."[54] Apparently, Knight was as good as his press clippings because on the 29th Ed Balinger revealed to his readers that the good doctor had told the club authorities that after applying a special treatment to Aldridge's arm, "most of the soreness ... [had] faded away"—to use Balinger's words—and that the pitcher would be able to return to the team in a few more days.[55] This Aldridge did on August 1.[56]

- McKechnie sent out a message that slovenly play and/or defiance of his rules would not be tolerated, and the Pittsburgh sportswriters in general supported his actions. Whether it was Ralph Davis ("[McKechnie] has been entirely justified in the steps he has taken thus far to restore morale, [sic] and bring his athletes out of their trance. And if further steps are necessary[,] he will be fully justified in taking them")[57]; Chilly Doyle ("The management struck at the listless play by fining two members of the club.... This procedure should have beneficial results")[58]; Lou Wollen ("Whatever may be the facts in Morrison's case, it seems that he is wholly in the wrong. No player has the right, no matter what his physical condition may be, to absent himself without permission")[59]; or Mr. Post Clock ("Slapping it on where it hurts, and that is in the pocketbook, may be just the means of whipping [delinquent players] into shape"),[60] some of the most read Steel City columnists were backing the Pirate skipper and the other two members of the decision-making triumvirate: Clarke and Sam Dreyfuss.[61] True, as described earlier in this chapter, there was a difference of opinion on how and when Moore should have been disposed of, and Lou Wollen thought that the initial treatment of Morrison was not consistent with the way that Aldridge had been treated, but the consensus among the Pittsburgh scribes was that the Pirate authorities were correct with their disciplinary tactics.

Four. *The ABC Affair*   135

Of course, despite newspaper support, there were rumors that the incidents involving Yde, Moore, Aldridge, and Morrison were the prodromal signs of what would occur the following month. As one fan wrote in a letter to Ralph Davis:

> I venture to say that 90 per cent [*sic*] of the rumors floating around are true. If there is dissension on the team, I suggest getting rid of those who are to blame.
> Players like Moore, Yde, Aldridge, Smith [who had been criticized for not hustling while catching, though he continued to be an offensive threat][,] and Morrison should be gotten rid of and Crowder, Koupal, Cronin[,] and others brought in.[62]

McKechnie was quick to dismiss such talk as the work of gamblers,[63] and the details of the cases involving the penalized Pirates were all different enough to dispel any theories of unified opposition to McKechnie and/or Clarke.

But if the month of July was one of contradictions, it was also a month of change. Not only had Moore been waived and Morrison suspended, but Joe Cronin was recalled from New Haven on the 14th and joined the Bucs on the 19th, and Red Oldham, one of the 1925 World Series heroes, was released to Kansas City the day Cronin arrived to make room for the young shortstop.[64] In addition, on July 24, the club bought Fred Brickell, a fleet-footed 19-year-old outfielder who had been a three-sport star in high school and who had been playing that season for the Wichita Izzies of the Western League.[65] Considered by scout Chick Fraser as "the best-looking young ball player he ever recommended," Brickell had been hitting .361 with 12 homers in 79 games when he was purchased.[66] So, in return for his services either that fall or the next spring, the Pirates reportedly agreed to pay the Izzies $15,000 and send them two players under option after spring training of the following year.[67] However, as fate would have it, Brickell would join the Corsairs in August, making his major league debut on the 19th of the month.[68]

August would prove to be a month of turmoil for the Bucs—turmoil that most sportswriters and baseball historians who have dealt with the subject would later say caused the sinking of the Pirate ship. But as will be argued in the next two chapters, a close study of what transpired that month and during the first half of September shows that though the sinking started in late August, factors beyond the turmoil ultimately brought about the ship's demise.

The month began with an 8–3 loss to the cross-state rival Phillies, who took advantage of four Pirate errors to score four unearned runs, as well as getting 12 hits off Songer, Nichols, and Adams to score four earned runs. But then the Bucs rebounded nicely to win four out of the next five games, a 14–2 pounding of Philadelphia and three tough victories over Boston. Those wins, combined with the Reds going 2–2 during the same four-day stretch, gave Pittsburgh a three-game lead over Cincinnati by the end of play on August 6, the largest lead that the Pirates had held since the season began.[69]

However, the third victory over Boston was a costly one for the Buccos. During the seventh inning, Glenn Wright injured his ankle while sliding into second base, and Lou Wollen later reported, "An X-ray picture [of the injury] was taken and disclosed a sliver of bone broken from its moorings, besides a severe strain on the ligaments adjoining it."[70] The prognosis for Wright's ankle was not known then, but the star shortstop would not return to the Pirate lineup until August 28 and would not start another game again until September 3, which proved to be a serious blow to Pittsburgh's pennant-winning chances. At the time that Wright got hurt, he was batting .324, with a .350 on-base percentage and a .497 slugging average. He had driven in 72 runs in 94 games and was on course to drive in over 100, so his bat would certainly be missed. Perhaps Chet Smith summed up Wright's offensive worth best when he wrote, "Without Glenn's bat[,] there is a loss of fully 25 per cent [sic] in the strength of the attack."[71] As for Wright's defensive play, though he made more than his share of errors, he also had quite a few assists, and if he had remained healthy and continued to field at the rate that he was fielding going into his injury, he may have recorded over 500 assists for the season.[72] His place would be taken by Hal Rhyne.

But for McKechnie, the worst was yet to come. The day after Wright went down, August 7, Pittsburgh had to face Boston in a doubleheader. Don Songer and Joe Bush pitched for the Bucs, while Johnny Wertz and former infielder Bob Smith took the mound for the Braves. All four hurlers went the distance. All four performed well. But though the Pirate moundsmen were very good, their Brave counterparts were outstanding. Or to be more specific, Songer tossed a seven-hitter, walked two, and gave up only two earned runs. Bush was just as effective: five hits, three walks, and again only two earned runs. Also, both men were aided by the Pirate defense, which did not give up any unearned runs. So, under usual circumstances, holding their opponents to two runs per game combined with a hitting attack that was averaging a little more than five runs per game should have provided the Bucs with two clear-cut victories. But such was not the case because Wertz and Smith threw back-to-back shutouts. Wertz pitched out of various jams to toss the only shutout of his career, whereas Smith, who had whitewashed the Pirates just three days earlier, repeated the feat, despite giving up a one-out triple in the fourth and a one-out double in the seventh. Together they helped to cause Pittsburgh to leave 14 base runners stranded—six on third base—and each man contributed to his own success by driving in a run.[73] Then, if that was not frustrating enough for the Bucs, Earl Smith got tossed out of the first game for shouting an insult from the dugout at Brave manager Dave Bancroft, though the Pirates claimed that Smith was just retorting to something Bancroft had shouted at him, and the second game was called at the end of the eighth inning because of a torrential downpour.[74]

It was after the first game that Clarke turned to McKechnie and suggested that he replace Carey. The suggestion in and of itself was not shocking. At the time that Clarke made it, Carey was 36 years old and a poor imitation of his previous self. He was batting .214, with an on-base percentage of .283 and a slugging average of .288, and Clarke was not the only one saying that the Pirate captain needed to be benched. In his August 9 "Sporting Gossip and Comment" column, James Long, the sports editor of the *Pittsburgh Sun*, wrote:

> Why not give that grand player, Carey, a much-needed rest—play Bigbee in left and Cuyler in center? A rest now might bring Carey around to his form of last year for the drive down the home stretch.... Carey badly needs a rest and ... [McKechnie] has Bigbee on the bench for just such emergencies.[75]

Long went further to say that Cuyler had complained to New York Giant outfielder Emil "Irish" Meusel that having to play "the sun field retarded his batting to a certain extent" and that the correct position for Cuyler was center, so why not move him there?[76]

As for exactly what Clarke said, it all depends on the source. Regis Welsh's informants reported that after Clarke made his suggestion, McKechnie asked him, "Who will we put in?" To which Clarke replied, "Anyone is better than Carey is right now."[77] Ralph Davis' contacts stated that the Clarke-McKechnie conversation went like this:

> CLARKE: "Better get some one [sic] out there to player centerfeild [sic]. Max is having a hard time of it."
> McKECHNIE: "I haven't got anybody" [which sounds fabricated by either Davis or his contacts because Cuyler could have been and was easily moved to center once Carey was removed].
> CLARKE: "Put somebody out there, even if it is a pitcher."[78]

Both accounts—in particular Davis' because of the exposure that it had received by being published in *The Sporting News*—have been used by post–1926 authors writing about the incident. But Clarke himself would later freely admit that he had told McKechnie, "I did say to McKechnie that if I were in his place[,] I would take Carey out, and put anyone, even a batboy in, [sic] as Max was in the worst slump of his career and the balls he was hitting were going straight at a fielder."[79]

Some readers may find Clarke's comment nasty and/or demeaning to the struggling Carey, but this was just Clarke's matter-of-fact way of speaking. Clarke did not mince his words, especially when it came to winning and losing ballgames. Furthermore, his comment was said as a suggestion, a piece of advice, not an order. Clarke was simply carrying out his duties as assistant to the manager. It was up to McKechnie to accept Clarke's advice or ignore it.

In any case, Carey did not hear the remark, but supposedly, Carson Bigbee did and repeated it to the Pirate captain.[80] At this point, Carey could have wisely shrugged it off as something said in the heat of battle or taken the matter up directly with Clarke in the near future. After all, Carey had played for six seasons under Clarke and was groomed by Clarke to be the fiery player-manager's successor in left field, a position at which Carey was the Pirate starter for four years. He was used to Clarke's nature and his way of handling players. But for reasons that will be examined later, Carey chose not to let go of the remark and, instead, allowed it to turn into a series of overreactive measures that would make a mountain out of a mole hill.

The first of these measures, based on what Regis Welsh was able to unearth, was when Bigbee came up with the idea of holding a players' meeting, about which he allegedly told some players that he wanted it called "to talk things over for the benefit of the club," while purportedly telling others that it was "to take a vote on whether the players wanted Clarke to sit on the bench."[81] In Bigbee's mind, the two explanations probably meant the same thing, but according to Welsh's findings, when several players discovered Bigbee's desire to decide Clarke's future in the dugout, they refused to attend the meeting.[82] This refusal may have been the result of Stuffy McInnis' influence, for Welsh would later report that the veteran first baseman had "talked with younger players about the folly of [going against] Clarke" and "counseled [them] not to become embroiled in the insubordination move."[83]

It is not known precisely when Babe Adams was approached, but in all likelihood, it was shortly before Bigbee announced his intention to have a meeting. As the second and third most senior members on the team, it would make sense for Carey and Bigbee to discuss the matter with Adams, the member with the great-

It was Carson Bigbee who repeated Clarke's comment to Carey, and according to Regis Welsh's findings, it was Bigbee who came up with the idea of having a players' meeting to discuss preventing Clarke from continuing to sit on the Pirate bench (National Baseball Hall of Fame Library, Cooperstown, New York).

est number of seasons in a Pirate uniform. And as with Carey, Adams could have ended the issue then by talking Carey and Bigbee out of attempting to remove Clarke from the bench. Having played under Clarke for two more seasons than Carey, Adams, like the Pirate captain, should have understood Clarke's disposition and manner of speaking and not let the incident get out of control. If for no other reasons than Clarke gave Adams his big break by starting him three times in the 1909 World Series and continued to have confidence in him throughout the remainder of Clarke's managerial career, one would think that Adams would have at least tried to talk the matter over with Clarke before any vote was taken. However, he, too, for reasons that will also be examined later, chose to support Bigbee's idea.

The trio's next move was to divulge their plans to McKechnie and ask his permission to hold their meeting, but here is where the details become a he-said, he-said set of differences. In the tell-all article that would appear in the September 30, 1926, issue of the *Pittsburgh Press* and that carried the byline of Ralph Davis, who may have provided information for it, Adams, Bigbee, and Carey said that they had consulted with Jack Onslow before visiting McKechnie and that Onslow had accompanied them to McKechnie's room at the Brunswick Hotel at about 9:00 o'clock on the evening of the 7th.[84] There, they told the Pirate skipper "that a majority of the players felt that Clarke's presence on the bench was a detriment to the club" and asked him his opinion on calling a players' meeting to see what could be done about the matter.[85] They then alleged that McKechnie had not only replied, "Positively; it's the only way to do it," but also that he had decided the meeting would be held at 11:00 o'clock the next morning at Kingston, New York—the town where the Bucs would be playing an exhibition game before traveling to Brooklyn for a three-game series.[86] The trio further alleged, however, that after arriving in Kingston, "McKechnie and Secretary [Sam] Watters called the meeting off, saying they thought they had a 'diplomatic way' of asking Clarke to leave the bench."[87] And, of course, the trio added the self-serving statement that what they did they did for the good of the club: to rid it of dissension, which they believed was caused by Clarke dispensing advice from the bench.[88] To support this belief, the trio also added a statement saying that Watters told them that "he knew of sentiment against Clarke on the bench, and that the club was not playing as it should."[89] But notice how carefully worded the statement was. Whoever wrote it did not say that Watters thought that the sentiment against Clarke sitting on the bench was causing the club not to play as it should. He said that there was "sentiment against Clarke on the bench" AND "the club was not playing as it should," which, without further information, may have been two unrelated observations.

Contrasted with this account, McKechnie reported that the trio without

Onslow approached him when he "was sitting on the porch of the Boston hotel waiting for [the] train to New York," not at 9:00 P.M. in the privacy of his room. After listening to what the threesome suggested, McKechnie claimed:

> I was so stunned by the announcement that, [sic] for a minute I did not realize what they were talking about. Then, after a little more conversation about it, I told them that I would put a stop to any attempt to start a thing of that kind on my ball club [sic], and positively forbid any meeting of any kind.[90]

There was no mention of initially being accommodating to the trio. No mention of any meeting with Sam Watters in Kingston. And no mention of using another way to get Clarke off the bench.

But no matter whose words are to be believed, one thing is for sure: everything that was said was said while Clarke was out of town. Following his suggestion of removing Carey, Clarke left Boston to take a boat trip to New York City with his wife and the wives of George Grantham and Hal Rhyne.[91] He did not travel to Kingston to watch the Bucs lose their exhibition game with the Colonials, Kingston's independent club, but rather reunited with the team for the start of its three-game series with Brooklyn on August 9.[92] So, little did he know what was going on behind his back. As Clarke would state in a lengthy interview that he gave to the Pittsburgh sports media on the evening of September 30, "Neither McKechnie or [sic] Watters ever mentioned to me that there was a meeting brewing."[93]

When Clarke did find out—in McKechnie's room at the Alamac Hotel in New York City—he was shocked, hurt, and puzzled.[94] Shocked because he had been completely blindsided by Adams, Bigbee, and Carey's complaints. Until that time, only one player—George Grantham—had openly resented the advice that Clarke had been dispensing, and to Grantham's credit, he had the guts to tell Clarke to his face to stop trying to help him. Grantham, a left-handed batter, had been hitting the ball very well but then fell into a temporary slump. Clarke, another left-handed batter who knew a thing or two about hitting, attempted to get Grantham hitting again by giving him one or more pointers, but Grantham did not appreciate the suggestion or suggestions and told Clarke, depending on the source, "I wish that you wouldn't say anything to me" or "I wish you wouldn't bother me when I am up there."[95] In either case, Clarke backed off and "from that day o[n,] never did [he] speak a word to Grantham regarding his batting, hitting, style or anything else[,] unless it was a question which came up in the course of the game."[96] But Clarke could not read minds, so if other players felt the same way as Grantham, they were not letting him know.

The hurt came from Clarke's mistaken belief that Adams, Bigbee, and Carey were his friends. As Clarke mentioned in his interview on September 30,

"If someone else had started [the movement to remove me from the bench], I would have counted on [the trio], owing to our friendship, to be with me."[97] This was particularly true of Carey, who Clarke had taken a special interest in early on in the Pirate captain's career. As Carey freely admitted in 1924:

> I owe my success in baseball to Fred Clarke.... I was a raw kid when I joined Pittsburg [sic], with a lot of ambition but little talent. Clarke was the boy who told me about moving around the outfield and playing different positions for certain batters.
>
> Clarke impressed upon me the value of playing a short center field. There are many short flies that fall for cheap base hits because the outfielders are too close to the fences.[98]

Finally, Clarke was puzzled because after discussing the matter with McKechnie on the 9th, he twice asked the Pirate skipper, "What do you want me to do?" And twice McKechnie had no answer for him. The two men discussed the matter further, but McKechnie could not offer a solution to the problem.[99] Though, interestingly enough, McKechnie's version of the meeting does not mention anything about Clarke's questions but does mention that Sam Watters was also present, someone who Clarke does not include in his version.[100]

Clarke then called Adams, Bigbee, and Carey into McKechnie's hotel room—something else that McKechnie left out of his account—and asked them for a solution, but according to Clarke, "None of them said a word to me."[101] To this, Clarke added:

> I was no monster threatening them, but asked them in a way which left no doubt that my chief interest, too, was the winning of the pennant. There they stood and said nothing. Had they said then [that the majority of the players thought that my dispensing of advice from the bench was causing dissension on the team], I would have been off that bench from that minute on, regardless of McKechnie's stand.[102]

After receiving no assistance from McKechnie or the trio on how he should proceed, Clarke went to the Pirates' clubhouse at Ebbets Field and addressed the entire team. In his talk, he discussed the alleged dissension, said that he would no longer sit on the bench, and warned the players not to mention anything to anyone who was not a member of the team because the situation might get misconstrued. As an explanation for those noticing that the assistant to the manager was missing from the bench, Clarke suggested telling them that he had left because he had begun to see himself as a jinx.

Turning his attention to the overall play of the team, Clarke went further to say that he felt that "there were a lot of players on the club who were not giving their best" and that they had better start putting out because each player would have to deal with him, in his capacity as vice president, during the offseason.[103] It appears that Clarke did not mean the last statement to be a threat or a challenge to Adams, Bigbee, and Carey or any other Pirate that wanted him off the bench, but rather to be a general warning to those players who he believed were not contributing as well as they should have to the success of the team. Specifically, Clarke may have been implying the Bucs' recent performances against Philadelphia and Boston: going 5–5 against the eighth-place and seventh-place teams, respectively, and being shut out three times by the Braves. However, that comment would later be held against Clarke by Adams, Bigbee, and Carey, and/or their ghostwriter, Ralph Davis.[104]

After Clarke was finished talking, McKechnie gave a speech of his own in which he allegedly told his men three things: that they had better begin playing winning baseball again or he would lose his job and they would lose theirs; that the Clarke matter was a dead issue; and that if someone leaked what was said at the meeting to the media, that man's stay with the Pirates would be over.[105]

It should be taken into consideration that McKechnie's comments were presented in the trio's tell-all article and that McKechnie neither confirmed nor denied them. McKechnie did say that "[l]ater [presumably on the 9th] a meeting of the players was held [at the Alamac Hotel]" and at that gathering, he told the team, "Clarke and I were the best of friends, that his interest with the club was for the best interests of the team in general and that I would not permit any prejudice toward Clarke or anyone else on the club."[106]

But if McKechnie did indeed make the comments that the trio claimed—and it is conceivable that he did—his line about playing winning baseball again, as well as what Clarke said about players not giving their best, may have had a positive effect on the team because it defeated Brooklyn, 9–3, that afternoon. Still, McKechnie was not totally pleased with what he saw on the field of play,[107] so that evening he suggested to Clarke that he would like to call another team meeting the following morning.[108] Clarke, apparently under the impression that the meeting was going to be used to clear the air about his situation and wanting to know where he stood with the players, not only agreed with McKechnie's idea but also encouraged the Pittsburgh manager to take a vote to see if the majority of the team wanted him to return or stay away from the bench.[109]

And thus the next morning, a meeting was held in McKechnie's hotel room, at the end of which a secret ballot was taken to gauge the feelings of the team towards Clarke's bench presence. Each man was given a slip of paper and asked to write "yes" or "no" on it, and "coaches and others connected with the club" were also permitted to vote if they wanted to.[110] Clarke did not attend the meeting,[111] but Adams, Bigbee, and Carey would later claim that, though McKechnie allowed a baseball discussion, he did not allow the players to discuss the

Clarke matter before they voted.[112] However, in retrospect, the trios' comment, which was meant as criticism of McKechnie, really speaks well of the Pirate leader and sounds like sour grapes on the part of his accusers. If Adams, Bigbee, and Carey were correct in believing that Clarke's presence on the bench was causing dissension on the team, then the players must have already established some view on the subject—even if it was one of indifference. Moreover, Clarke had given his side to the team the previous day. Therefore, to ensure that each man voted his head or heart and was not swayed by either the pro–Clarke or anti–Clarke factions, McKechnie was right to have a secret ballot without any discussion. Besides, from comparing various newspaper accounts, it seems that McKechnie, having declared less than 24 hours earlier that the Clarke matter was finished, had no intention of rehashing what had happened—despite what Clarke thought—he was just carrying out Clarke's request and may have viewed the vote as only an added point to his agenda. After the meeting was over, McKechnie told sportswriters that "some of the players had been making plays that were not correct and it was to remedy this that he decided on the meeting in his room."[113] This may have been just a line to deceive the media and their readers, but it also may have been McKechnie's primary purpose for calling the meeting. And interestingly enough, Adams, Bigbee, and Carey's purported remembrances of what went on at the meeting support this theory: a discussion on baseball, but no discussion of the Clarke matter, only a vote. On the other hand, Clarke's account implies that the meeting was being held to have the team talk about whether his dispensing of advice from the bench was causing dissension.[114] As Clarke would later say, "The meeting, I figured, would bring the whole thing to a head."[115] Unfortunately though for McKechnie, the action of even bringing up the Clarke matter again after he had said that it was a closed issue was probably confusing to the players and may have made the Pirate skipper look inconsistent and not willing to follow his own dictate.

In any case, much to the chagrin of Adams, Bigbee, and Carey, the team voted 18–6 in favor of allowing Clarke to remain on the bench, but because of the secret nature of the ballot and because no voter beyond the trio was willing to publicly disclose how he voted, it will probably never be known who supported Clarke and who did not.[116] James Long reported that even Carey himself lamented "that some who had verbally opposed Clarke's presence on the bench evidently changed their minds and voted the other way when the ballot was taken, and he could not tell what [sic] players had altered their views."[117] What is known is that Johnny Morrison, who still had not rejoined the team, and Glenn Wright, who had been sent back to Pittsburgh the evening of the 9th so that his damaged ankle could receive special treatment, did not take part in the vote.[118] Of course, if Wright had participated, the final tally would have been

19–6. Wright viewed Clarke as a second father[119] and had even dated Clarke's younger daughter, Muriel,[120] so it is not likely that he would have voted against Clarke. Nor was Sam Dreyfuss present for the vote. The Pirate treasurer had returned to Pittsburgh the evening of August 1 and thus missed all the excitement.[121] In fact, he was pleased with what he saw and gave no indication to the press of noticing any form of dissension among his troops.[122]

But because of the lack of public disclosure, rumors abounded. Ralph Davis would later claim that "the names of at least two of [the three other anti–Clarke voters were] generally known,"[123] and Lou Wollen reported on August 16 that "Sam Dreyfuss stated that ... the other three ... were younger players, new to the team."[124] If Wollen was correct in repeating what Dreyfuss said, then Barney's son had been tipped off by someone as to who the voters were, but based on what Wollen's editor, Ralph Davis, wrote in the same issue of the *Press*, Wollen had carelessly or intentionally left out a key phrase in paraphrasing Dreyfuss' statement. According to Davis, Dreyfuss said "that he [did] not know who the other three were ... and that no attempt had been made to find out, inasmuch as they were 'doubtless younger men who were influenced by the older heads.'"[125]

One common belief was that two of the players were George Grantham and Kiki Cuyler, the source of which was the October 1, 1926, *Pittsburgh Gazette Times* column of Chet Smith. In that column, Smith wrote:

> From the very first, it is said, there were members of the Pirates who did not fancy Clarke or his methods. Eddie Moore was one. George Grantham and Ki Cuyler others....
>
> It was George Grantham, it is whispered, who went to Carson Bigbee and declared that he had taken as active a part in the insurrection as any of the trio deposed.[126]

Both Dreyfuss' and Smith's words received wider exposure when Ralph Davis used the former in one of his columns in *The Sporting News* and the same publication reprinted the latter in its "Scribbled by Scribes" column.[127] But if no attempt had been made to find out who the three were, how could Dreyfuss say that "they were 'doubtless younger men who were influenced by the older heads'"? And what did he mean by "younger men"? Younger than Adams, Bigbee, and Carey? Well, everyone on the team was younger than Adams and Carey. Or younger than the team as a whole? As for Smith, he never identified his source or sources, writing only "it is said" and "it is whispered." But said by whom? Whispered by whom? Well, whatever the truth may be, this author has yet to discover any evidence that conclusively proves or disproves that either Grantham or Cuyler were among the anti–Clarke voters.

The initial stage of what would eventually be called the ABC Affair because of the first letters in each of the last names of Adams, Bigbee, and Carey ended when the Bucs left Brooklyn after taking two out of three games from the sixth-place Robins. And interestingly enough, McKechnie started Carey in center field for the entire series, having followed Clarke's advice only for the second half of the doubleheader loss against Boston on the 7th, when he benched the Pirate captain, moved Cuyler to center, and inserted Bigbee in left and had him bat leadoff.

August 12 began as a lull between two storms. Some of the players under the leadership of Sam Watters, Jewel Ens, and Jack Onslow traveled to New Haven, Connecticut, to play an exhibition game against the Profs, while McKechnie, Clarke, Clarke's wife, Hal Rhyne's wife, and nine players, including Max Carey, returned to Pittsburgh, and Joe Bush visited his old stomping grounds in Philadelphia.[128] Also on the 12th, Sam Dreyfuss announced that the Pirates had purchased outfielder Eddie Murphy from the Rochester Tribe of the International League and pitcher Roy Mahaffey, catcher Thomas Farr, and outfielder Lloyd Waner, Paul's brother, from the Columbia Comers of the South Atlantic League. In addition, Dreyfuss stated that he had made arrangements with the Wichita Izzies of the Western League to have Fred Brickell, who had been bought on July 24, report on August 18. Murphy, a 10-year veteran from the American League who had played on four pennant winners and two World Series champions, was 35 years old at the time but was hitting minor league pitching at a .364 clip. Mahaffey, Farr, and Waner were scheduled to report for spring training the following season, though Mahaffey, a six-foot right-hander with a fast-breaking curveball, would be called up by Pittsburgh later that month.[129]

But that afternoon, the *Pittsburgh Chronicle Telegraph*, with a headline on its front page that read "Clarke's Absence from Bench Causes Rumors of Split with Bill M'Kechnie" and a lengthy article by Havey Boyle, broke the story that something was amiss on the Pirate ship. Boyle had perceptively picked up on the fact that Clarke had not been seen on the Bucs' bench for the three-game series with Brooklyn and began to ask questions. As Boyle wrote:

> Yesterday [August 11], in Brooklyn, Clarke sat in a box with Chick Fraser....
> What brought about Clarke's sudden decision to leave the bench and watch the games from the grandstand? Why was no explanatory statement issued, detailing why Clarke, who loves to mingle with the players and get in the thick of every battle, suddenly decided not to don his uniform daily, but instead moved to a grandstand seat?
> If Clarke had done this just one day[,] there would be no cause for suspecting that all was not well in the Pirate camp, but it was noted that on Monday in Brooklyn he was not listed as a bench occupant, that on Tuesday he left the team to visit Newark, and yesterday ... he contented himself with a place in the grandstand with his old friend [and brother-in-law], Chick Fraser.[130]

Boyle went further to say that it was not known yet if Clarke had voluntarily removed himself from the bench, if McKechnie had ordered him off of it, or if certain unnamed players were responsible for his departure, but "[i]n the mind of close observers of Pirate affairs[,] there is no doubt that a rift has appeared in the relations between Clarke and McKechnie, or at least in the relations between Clarke and some of the Pirates."[131] He then interestingly added that "[t]he story that some definite action either by McKechnie or by some of the players was taken to remove Clarke from the bench was bolstered partially at least by an underground rumor which the *Chronicle Telegraph* had access to that a kind of meeting was held by the players at which a very momentous question was taken up."[132] That question, of course, was the one about Clarke leaving the bench, with the resultant 18–6 vote in Clarke's favor, something which Boyle remarkably details, as well as noting that it was three players who had instigated the movement against Clarke, though he still had not discovered their names. The rest of Boyle's article:

- Astutely states that it is "fairly well authenticated [that there exists on the team] a Clarke faction and an anti-Clarke faction led by three rebels, whose identity has not been revealed."

- Raises the questions of if McKechnie was comfortable with Clarke sitting on the bench, why did he not immediately stop Clarke's opponents from attempting to remove him and what will his reluctance not to do so have on his relationship with Clarke.

- Speculates on what effect this matter will have on the success of the team during the rest of the season and on the future of Clarke and the players who voted against him. For example, when and how will Clarke retaliate, and if the situation is not resolved by the time that Barney Dreyfuss returns from Europe, how will he handle it?

- Accurately predicts that "the present story is bound to cause comment in every sphere where baseball is played, and in its wake, doubtless will come stories of widespread dissension, and a possible blow-up of the possible pennant winners."[133]

To write what he did, Boyle had to have had an inside source—an agent who supplied him with the "underground rumor" and more—but who? Later, some Pittsburgh sportswriters would believe that a certain Pirate first baseman was the informant, but at the time, Boyle said that "the players would not dare discuss the trouble with newspaper men."[134] Was that just a line to throw suspicion off his operative, or was Boyle getting his information from someone who was not a player?

Also on the afternoon of the 12th, Clarke claimed that McKechnie approached him (perhaps after reading Boyle's article) and "insisted that [he] come back to the bench and perform [his] usual duties."[135] Clarke, however, refused to do so unless Adams, Bigbee, and Carey were penalized for being disruptive forces. As Clarke explained:

> What I will do all depends on what will be done in order to stifle any attempt of any player to dictate to the manager as to what shall be done with any player on the club, and that includes me in my present capacity....
> I want the Pittsburgh club to win another pennant and another [W]orld [S]eries.... But ... no ball club [sic] that I am on will be ruined by cliques and spats.... Life is too short for such things and it is only fair to the boys who are hustling and trying to give what Pittsburgh wants that these things be stamped out in an emphatic and effective way, so that they will be squelched before the insidious harm of it can become apparent on the playing ability of the club.[136]

This was vintage Clarke: fiery, direct, and not willing to tolerate any player who he viewed as causing disharmony on the team.

Of course, Adams, Bigbee, Carey, and the three other players who voted against Clarke did not see themselves as mutineers. Instead, they saw Clarke's comments from the bench as the source of the disharmony and viewed themselves as the ones trying to rid the team of it by ridding the dugout of Clarke. As Carey said in defense of the ABC trio sometime during the day of the 13th:

> Anything that we did was done because we wanted to see the club win. After we lost that doubleheader in Boston[,] Manager McKechnie suggested that a meeting be held to discuss the welfare of the club. A time was set for the session, but about a half-hour before it was to be held[,] McKechnie called it off.
> Later[,] Clarke came to the clubhouse, [sic] and said he would not appear again on the bench if he was not wanted. The next day[,] a vote was taken by the players as to whether he should be asked to retire. That is all there is to it.
> ...We simply wanted to get results.
> No team can thrive under two managers. That is not said with any special reference to Fred Clarke, for he and I are good friends, but it is a general proposition that holds true on any club. [Apparently Carey forgot about the success that the McKechnie-Clarke duo had had the previous season.] There were conditions existing on our club which were losing games for us, and it was primarily with a view to getting better results that we jumped at McKechnie's suggestion to hold a meeting....[137]

But in opposition to this line of thinking, Clarke countered that he was only doing his job—a job that Barney Dreyfuss had hired him to do and one which McKechnie had gladly agreed to let him do. Clarke would later explain to the Pittsburgh sportswriters and their readers that "Barney Dreyfuss asked me to sit on the bench with the team. I told him I would not unless Bill McKechnie asked me to do so"[138]—something that the Pirate skipper did. In fact, according to Clarke, McKechnie not only asked him to sit on the bench but also said, "I am tickled to death to have you."[139] As for being a source of disharmony, Clarke retorted:

> McKechnie and I have worked in perfect harmony ever since I joined the club last year. We had an understanding before I ever went near the bench[,] and because Bill wanted me there, sort of to bolster the morale of the club, I went there every day, until recently I learned that I was not wanted....
>
> Never have I usurped McKechnie's authority, never have I countermanded one of his orders, always have I tried to work hand-in-hand with him and the players in trying to bring about that which is best for the club.[140]

McKechnie supported Clarke on this matter, stating, "Fred and I have always been friends, and close friends, ever since he came back to the club. Never has there been a word or an argument between us."[141]

After returning to Pittsburgh, Clarke and McKechnie met with Sam Dreyfuss, who was "taken completely by surprise" by what had happened.[142] During the meeting, Clarke insisted that Adams, Bigbee, and Carey be punished, but contrary to popular belief, he did not specify how they should be punished. Clarke believed that since he was the aggrieved party, he should not be the one determining the form of the penalty, so he left that matter in the hands of Dreyfuss and McKechnie, who chose to unconditionally and immediately release Adams and Bigbee and to suspend Carey and place him on waivers.[143] Clarke agreed with their decision,[144] and thus on the evening of August 13, Sam Dreyfuss made the official public announcement regarding the fate of the three perceived troublemakers at a team meeting in the clubhouse at Forbes Field. There, he declared that both he and McKechnie "felt that the attack made upon ... Clarke was totally unnecessary and unwarranted"; that Adams, Bigbee, and Carey would receive the decided-upon punishments; that Pie Traynor would be the new team captain, replacing Carey; that the matter was closed; and that no appeal would be permitted.[145]

In the eyes of Dreyfuss, Clarke, and McKechnie, the club's announcement and the eventual dismissal of Adams, Bigbee, and Carey marked the end of the second and final stage of the ABC Affair and, as Dreyfuss had said, the matter was closed. As of August 14, the club powers did not know who the other three anti–Clarke voters were, nor did they wish them any harm, so there would be no witch hunt. They just wanted to put the affair behind them and move on.[146]

But to their dismay, just the opposite happened. The matter refused to go away, and it refused to go away largely because of five factors:

- The sportswriters and the fans
- The weather

- The prominence of the dismissed players
- The tenacity of Max Carey
- And the crusade by the *Pittsburgh Press* in general and Ralph Davis in particular to vindicate Adams, Bigbee, and Carey and to vilify Clarke and McKechnie

The mainstream Pittsburgh newspapers began giving extensive coverage of the affair shortly after Clarke, McKechnie, Carey, and the other members of the team who had not gone to New Haven returned to Pittsburgh on the 12th. Some sportswriters sided with Clarke, some sided with the ABC trio, but details abounded for anyone interested in reading them. The fans, in turn, divided on the matter, with strong feelings being expressed on both sides, and interest in what had happened was not just confined to Pittsburgh. Regis Welsh, in an article in the August 14 issue of the *Pittsburgh Post*, termed the events "the affair which has not only shocked Pittsburgh fandom, but made food for gossip and opinions throughout the baseball world."[147] He was right and the affair was far from over.

The Pirates had been scheduled to play games on the 13th, 14th, 16th, and 17th, and perhaps if they would have, both the media and fans would have been somewhat distracted by what was occurring on the field, especially if the Bucs went on a four-game winning streak. But such was not the case, as all four contests were rained out, thus giving the sportswriters as well as their readers a lot of time to dwell on what had been said and done and what had not.

More important than the weather, though, was who the players were. As already mentioned twice in this book, Adams, Bigbee, and Carey

Because of his stellar performance in the 1909 World Series and his highly successful career in a Pirate uniform, Babe Adams had become a hero to many Pittsburghers (National Baseball Hall of Fame Library, Cooperstown, New York).

were the members of the team with the most years in a Pirate uniform. Bigbee had been with the club since 1916, Carey since 1910, and Adams briefly in 1907 and then from 1909 through 1916 and continually since 1918. But of greater significance than seasons played was that Adams and Carey had become local heroes and had quite a few fans. Adams' performances during the 1909 World Series helped propel the Bucs to the championship, and over the years, the right-hander with pinpoint control had finished a number of times among the National League's yearly top 10 pitchers in WHIP (10 seasons, five as the league leader), ERA (six, none), adjusted ERA (six, one), shutouts (six, one), and various other positive categories. Based on Wins Above Replacement, he was the most valuable player in the senior circuit in 1913. Carey was arguably the best center fielder in the history of the Pirate franchise and an outstanding base stealer. He was among the NL's yearly top 10 leaders in positive offensive and defensive categories many times—most notably in stolen bases (13 seasons through 1925, 10 as the league leader), walks (11, twice), assists as a center fielder (eight, six), and range factor per game as a center fielder (nine, six)—and, of course, he had played extremely well in the 1925 World Series.[148] These men were memorable players who would not be easily forgotten by the Pirate faithful. Bigbee did not have the stature of Adams and Carey, and if he had been the only one cut, there probably would not have been nearly as much fuss. Still, he had been one of the Pittsburgh starting outfielders for seven years, had all-star seasons in 1921 and 1922, and, as described in the second chapter of this book, came through with a big clutch hit in the seventh game of the '25 Series.

But despite the effect of the previous three factors, in all likelihood the affair would not have dragged out as long as it did if not for the last two: the tenacity of Carey and the zeal of Ralph Davis. Stunned by what he viewed as arbitrary and harsh treatment at the hands of the Pirate power triumvirate, Carey told the Pittsburgh sportswriters on the evening of the 13th that he would discuss the matter with Adams and Bigbee and then the trio would come forth the following day with a statement telling their side of the story, a statement which they hoped would vindicate them in the court of public opinion.[149] But when the next day came, the trio changed their minds and instead sent a telegram to the commissioner of Organized Baseball, Kenesaw Mountain Landis, and asked him: "Will you come to Pittsburgh and give us a hearing immediately? We have been treated unjustly and penalized without a hearing."[150] Landis, who was in New York, wired Carey that he could not travel to Pittsburgh at that time, but if the former Pirate captain would like to come to New York at his own expense, he would meet with him there.[151] This Carey did, leaving the Steel City on the evening of the 15th and arriving in the Big Apple the next morning, where he briefly discussed his concerns with the commissioner. However, unfortunately for Carey, Landis refused to act, declaring that "unless something detrimental to the fundamental interests of baseball [was] involved," he was powerless to assist Carey and his friends, though he suggested that Carey contact John Heydler, the president of the National League.[152]

Heydler was also in New York at that time, so Carey was able to talk to him at 11:00 that same morning and persuade him to hold a hearing at the William Penn Hotel in Pittsburgh the following day.[153] Upon learning about Heydler's decision, Clarke issued a statement on behalf of the Pirate organization, saying that "so far as it was concerned[,] the newspapers could sit in on the meeting, as the club had nothing to hide. It is Mr. Heydler's meeting, however, and should he care to bar newspapers and give out a statement afterward, that is his affair."[154]

At the hearing, which took place where Heydler was staying at the William Penn, beginning sometime between 11:00 A.M. and shortly before noon, depending on the source, and ending sometime between a little after 1:00 P.M. and 1:30 P.M., again depending on the source,[155] the league was represented by Heydler and his secretary, Cullen Cain, while the club was represented by Clarke, McKechnie, Sam Dreyfuss, and Sam Watters. Adams, Bigbee, and Carey represented themselves, with Carey being the leading spokesperson for the trio. Upon his arrival, Heydler was asked by the media if Clarke had a legal right to sit on the bench, to which he explained that Clarke "was signed to a coach's contract, and, therefore, under the rules of the game, was entitled to a seat on the players' bench."[156] Also before any discussion began, Clarke requested that the meeting be open to the 14 sportswriters who had shown up in the outer room of Heydler's quarters, but instead, the league president had a private session with only the above-mentioned individuals present because he felt "that [the] matter purely concern[ed] the internal affairs of the club."[157] Thus, the information that exists about what was said behind closed doors comes from whatever details the participants wished to give the newspapers after the hearing was over, the bits and pieces the sportswriters could pick up by putting their ears against the door where the meeting was being held, and the statement that Heydler issued the evening of the 17th.

Once the hearing was over and the door to the conference room was opened, the club officials emerged: McKechnie looking like a man who had been through a rough time; Clarke smiling and appearing to be in good spirits; and Dreyfuss and Watters also appearing to be in good spirits, though Dreyfuss was said to have had "a set expression." Heydler came out later, told the assembled scribes that he would release a statement that evening, and then returned to the conference room to talk some more with Adams, Bigbee, and Carey. Shortly thereafter, the ABC trio and Heydler left separately, with Heydler going to the Pirate clubhouse to talk with a number of the trio's teammates to see if there were any details to the affair that were not mentioned by either side at the hearing. But with the exception of McKechnie uttering "It's all over," no one said anything to the media, leaving the sportswriters to speculate what occurred during the meeting based on what they could pick up by eavesdropping at the door of the conference room before the hotel authorities prevented them from doing so. And most of what was heard was Carey's loud voice asking McKechnie several questions and putting forth one demand: "Why did you have a feeling in your heart toward me?" "Didn't I ask you in your room a second time?" "Now I want you to answer this." "Why did you call the meeting?" But if McKechnie bothered to respond, he did so in a low enough voice that the media could not make out what he said.[158]

Calling a press conference for 7:00 P.M. that evening, but not appearing until 7:30, Heydler came forth with his official statement, in which he declared that his findings showed:

- "That Clarke [had] an unquestioned right to sit on the bench as advisor to McKechnie under baseball laws."

- "That Clarke was on the bench not alone by orders from ... Barney Dreyfuss, but also at the earnest request of Manager McKechnie."

- That there were disagreements concerning strategy, but these disagreements did not affect the play of the team, which had performed well, especially considering all the illnesses and injuries that it had suffered and the strength of its opponents.

- That a series of misunderstandings led to the ABC Affair.

- That Adams, Bigbee, and Carey were not "guilty of willful insubordination or malicious intent to disrupt or injure [the Pirate] club" but, instead, they sincerely believed that they did what they did to help the team. Thus, "there [was] neither stain nor blemish on their long and honorable baseball career[s]."

- That the ABC trio was, however, guilty of "mistaken zeal" with their actions against Clarke, and that the affair would not have occurred if the trio had taken their complaints directly to Clarke or to Sam Dreyfuss, rather than to McKechnie.

- That the Pirate organization had been "kind in its treatment of both Bigbee and Adams, keeping both of them at a liberal salary when 15 other major league clubs repeatedly declined their services." [In addition to showing the generosity of the Pirate club towards Adams and Bigbee, this state-

- That during the time that Carey was suspended, he was still being paid by the Pirate organization.

- And that he could not "go back [on] the right of the officials of a league club to release, suspend or ask waivers on any of its players, nor would [he] wish to do so if [he] had the right."[159]

Both sides were satisfied with Heydler's pronouncements and each issued its own statement of acceptance. The club's was a two-sentence message which said in part, "We accept [Heydler's] findings in good faith and consider the matter a closed incident."[160] Carey spoke for the trio when he said, "It clears our names. That is all we wanted."[161] Adams and Bigbee agreed with him, and so it appeared that the third stage of the ABC Affair—Carey asking Landis and then Heydler to intervene and Heydler's hearing—was the final one and the matter had ended. But as will be seen, that was not all that the ABC trio had wanted, and the matter would raise its ugly head more than once before the year was over.

And this leads to the role of the *Pittsburgh Press* and Ralph Davis. For some reason, the *Press* and, in particular, Davis decided to become the leading advocates for Adams, Bigbee, and Carey. Perhaps the ill feelings of the *Press* towards the Pirate leadership can be traced back to the falling out that the newspaper had had with Barney Dreyfuss in 1913. According to Fred Lieb:

At one time ... the *Press* was considered the Pirates' official mouthpiece. And when Harry Pulliam[, the Pirate secretary,] was elected

John Heydler, the president of the National League. He ruled that Adams, Bigbee, and Carey were guilty of "mistaken zeal," not "willful insubordination" (National Baseball Hall of Fame Library, Cooperstown, New York).

president of the [National] [L]eague in 1903, Dreyfuss selected the *Press*' sports editor, William Locke, as secretary. Relations between the club and the *Press* continued very close, until Locke left the Pirates in 1913 to become president and part owner of the Phillies. But a chill developed after Dreyfuss appointed Leslie Constans, Locke's brother-in-law, as Will's successor to the Pirate secretaryship.[162]

The situation worsened in 1917 when the Pirates plummeted to the basement of the National League and the *Press* called for Dreyfuss' head. In the words of Lieb:

> The Pittsburgh *Press* printed a front-page story blaming Barney for existing conditions, and voiced the emphatic demand that "Dreyfuss must go." The story went on to say that minority stockholders were much dissatisfied with the way that the club's affairs were conducted, and quoted one of them as saying that a change in the ownership of the Pirates apparently was the only thing that would bring a turn for the better.
> President Oliver S. Hershman and Business Manager [Harry C.] Milholland of the *Press* were stockholders in the Pirates, and no doubt were the minority interests mentioned.[163]

Well, in August of 1926, Hershman was no longer with the *Press*, having sold his interests in the paper to Scripps-Howard Newspapers in 1923, but Milholland remained, holding the positions of vice president and advertising manager.[164] Was he responsible for the stance that the *Press* took?

Or perhaps those in charge of the paper felt sorry for Adams, Bigbee, and Carey. On the evening of August 13, Carey had complained that the newspapers were not treating him fairly, which might have led the *Press* officials to try to rectify the matter by supporting him and the other two members of the ABC trio.[165]

But whatever the cause, as early as the 13th, before many of the details of the affair were known, the *Press* published an editorial, which contained no byline, praising Adams and Carey and stating, "If ... any effort is made to pillory Babe Adams and Max Carey as 'goats[,]' ... the *Press* feels safe in saying—basing the prediction on the sportsmanship and fair play of Pittsburgh fans—that the owners of the club will rue such action."[166]

This threatening prediction was followed by daily columns by Ralph Davis and/or, to a lesser degree, Lou Wollen, in which the two baseball scribes came forth with a barrage of favorable comments about the ABC trio and/or criticisms of Clarke, McKechnie, Sam Dreyfuss, or some combination of the three. Also, in the early days of the affair, articles with or without bylines supporting the side of Adams, Bigbee, and Carey were published. The comments and criticisms ranged from the exaggerated—"Max Carey is in his prime"[167]—to the disparaging—"[Babe Adams] got his chance in the 1909 [World] [S]eries simply because dissipation was rampant on the squad," so "[m]ost of the [other] pitchers weren't in shape to work," and that Clarke "couldn't manage that gang of athletes."[168] Well, the 36-year-old Carey was certainly not in his prime in 1926, and if the latter remarks are true, that leaderless, drunken "gang of athletes" must have succeeded despite themselves, winning 110 regular-season games and the World Series. For that matter, Wollen, who wrote the latter remarks in an attempt to denigrate Clarke's leadership skills, inadvertently maligned Adams in the process.

Truth be told, Clarke had a deep pitching staff in 1909, with a number of effective hurlers, six of whom saw action in the World Series against Detroit. Of those six, just two—Howie Camnitz and Vic Willis—were said to have drinking problems,[169] but Clarke used both of them as starters (Game Two for Camnitz; Game Six for Willis) and relievers (Game Six for Camnitz; Game Two for Willis), something that he would not have done if he thought they were inebriated. However, even if two of his stars were tipsy, Clarke also had Nick Maddox, Lefty Leifield, Deacon Phillippe, and, to a lesser degree, Sam Leever and Sam Frock to open games for him, two of whom did, whereas a third one successfully relieved in two contests. Thus, it was not as if Adams was his only available moundsman for the fall classic.

Now, as for why Clarke selected Adams to start Game One of the Series, Dennis and Jeanne Burke DeValeria persuasively argue that his decision may have been based on how well Adams had performed in August and September,[170] but Clarke himself said many years later:

> Pitching Adams was a decision that a fellow makes once in a lifetime ... when he follows a hunch, and feels that he is right, but cannot convince anybody else he is not crazy.
> ...But I knew that Adams had the kind of curve ball [sic] which had bothered Detroit all season. If he could throw it, I knew he had a chance.[171]

Then, Adams' successful outing in the first game probably convinced Clarke to give him two more starts.

So, what evidence did Wollen have to base his comments on? Apparently three pieces. First, there had been rumors in 1909 that Camnitz had started drinking heavily in early October.[172] Second, despite having outstanding regular seasons, both Camnitz and Willis struggled against Detroit.[173] And finally, an article allegedly penned by Honus Wagner, though sounding ghostwritten, and published in the October 7, 1925, issue of the *Pittsburgh Press* had the former Pirate superstar saying about the '09 Series:

> Pittsburgh faced the great post-season [sic] clash in a bad way for twirlers. We had plenty of them on the roster, but [...] Well, there was no prohibition amend-

ment to the United States Constitution in those days ... and some ballplayers did like some other folks. They didn't think quite as much about business as they did about pleasure.

At any rate, we came to that [S]eries with our twirling department pretty well shot....

Fred [Clarke] didn't have much choice. He was hardly counting on Adams at that time. Babe was rushed into the [S]eries as a last-minute choice, when everything else and everybody else seemed to have failed.[174]

However, as with much of what Davis and Wollen wrote about the ABC Affair, holes appear in Wollen's evidence when it is closely examined. Yes, there were rumors about Camnitz's drinking, but it was known that he was suffering from quinsy before any postseason action began[175] and his illness or the medicine that he was taking for his illness may have adversely affected his pitching. And yes, Camnitz and Willis did not perform well in the World Series, but this may say more about their opponents than it does about them. The 1909 Tigers were one of the strongest contingents put forth by the Detroit franchise. With an overall winning percentage of .645 and a hitting attack, spearheaded by Ty Cobb and Sam Crawford, that led the American League in runs scored, batting average, and on-base percentage, among other categories, the men from the Motor City were a match for any major league pitcher—drunk or sober.[176] As for the newspaper article, it is debatable if Wagner wrote it, but even if he did, he was known for inventing or exaggerating details for the sake of telling a good story. Looking at this particular case, the last two paragraphs of the excerpt quoted above fit the fabricated category. As has been shown, Pittsburgh's pitching corps was not "pretty well shot," and Clarke did have a choice. Nor was Adams "rushed into the [S]eries as a last-minute choice, when everything else and everybody else seemed to have failed." He was Clarke's starter for the first game of the Series, so no one else had been tried yet, let alone failed.

There are far too many other examples of the one-sidedness of Davis' and Wollen's writing to deal with all of them in this chapter, but the following ones are a taste of their handiwork:

- Davis attempting to canonize the ABC trio with such lines as:
  - "[Carey] is ... a man whose private life is and always has been above reproach."[177]
  - "Charles B. 'Babe' Adams is ... a man who is always being held up to younger men as an example of what clean living brings in reward."[178]
  - "There has been absolutely nothing about the course which Max, Babe and Carson have pursued which was not dignified, above board and beyond approach.... There has been nothing vindictive about their course, which is in sharp contrast to that of the man who refused to give an inch when he felt that his vanity had been hurt."[179]

- And "[t]he attitude of the three veterans throughout the controversy has been such as to commend itself to all unbiased and fair-minded fans."[180]

Adams, Bigbee, and Carey taking the high road was a theme that Davis used multiple times in his writings, but he apparently did not see conspiring against a man behind his back and setting into motion a series of events that led to a lot of anguish for a number of people, including themselves, as moral failings.

- Davis sounding like a self-righteous preacher damning the souls of Clarke and McKechnie when he wrote:

> A cold analysis of recent events puts two men in a particularly unfavorable light. One of them is Fred Clarke, who has been branded with the possession of a petty, revengeful spirit, which led him to jeopardize the welfare of the club that he might satisfy it.
> But the most pitiful figure in the whole mess is William B. McKechnie....
> He had the chance to come out of the affair a big man, one who would stand up for and by his friends, regardless of the cost or the consequences. But he passed up that opportunity to "play safe" for himself.
> And yet there is an old biblical saying about the man who would save his life losing it, and perhaps the truth of that will be exemplified in McKechnie's case.
> In fact, it is almost certain to be.[181]

- Davis giving special attention in his column or, in one case, as a separate article in the sports section, letters and other writings that supported Adams, Bigbee, and Carey, and/or demeaned Clarke and/or McKechnie.[182]

- Wollen sarcastically labeling McKechnie as "Lieut. Manager" or "Lieutenant Manager" in several of his columns and referring to the club officials as "under-officials" in one of them.[183]

- Wollen attempting to keep the pot boiling by criticizing both the club officials for wanting to put the incident behind them and their supporters, who said "the fans shouldn't knock, because knocking will kill the Buccos' pennant chances."[184]

Thus, rather than serving the public as responsible journalists presenting both sides of the story and letting their readers decide for themselves, Davis and Wollen became unofficial defense attorneys for Adams, Bigbee, and Carey.

In addition, to add insult to injury, the *Press* printed in its August 15 issue a cartoon of a heroic-looking Carey swinging a bat on the auction block, with Clarke, as the auctioneer, shouting out, "World's greatest base runner. Main spring of the 1925 [w]orld's champions. Going! Going! Going! $4,000."[185]

But leaving aside the *Press*' blatant bias, Carey was certainly going, for the day after Heydler's hearing, he was picked up by the Brooklyn Robins. The Robins and their New York rivals, the Giants, were the only National League teams to lay claim to the former Pirate captain, and since the Robins were lower in the standings, they got him. Other NL clubs may have wanted Carey, but three—Philadelphia, Boston, and St. Louis—were believed to have not been willing to pay his large salary of $16,000 plus a $500 bonus for being the team captain. Of the remaining teams, Chicago, which was higher in the standings than Brooklyn and New York, may have passed on him when it found out that there was no chance that it could acquire him, and Cincinnati felt that it had no need for another outfielder.[186] Nor did any American League team claim him,[187] perhaps for the same reasons.

But Pittsburgh fans had not seen the last of Carey. The aging outfielder would return to Forbes Field in a Robin uniform and amid much fanfare during a four-game series between Brooklyn and Pittsburgh on August 23 (a doubleheader), 24, and 25. Batting second and playing center field in three of the four contests, Carey put on quite a show in the first one and helped to win both it and the final game. In the series opener, he performed like the Carey of younger years, pounding out a single, coaxing two walks, laying down a perfectly placed bunt for another base hit, and scoring two runs. The only thing that he did not do was steal a base. And the fans loved every minute of it, cheering for him as if he were still a Pirate. As James Long described:

> The greeting which he received from the fans must have warmed Carey's heart. No player anywhere ever was given a greater ovation than Max received. He was cheered when he first appeared on the field and every time he emerged from the dugout thereafter, and even when his work in the game meant damage to the Pirate cause, the fans did not fail to applaud.[188]

One of Carey's supporters even proposed having a "Carey Day" to Chet Smith and suggested giving the former star a farewell present.[189] This did not happen, though the 23rd served as an unofficial "Carey Day" and showed that Carey remained a fan favorite despite his dismissal or perhaps more so because of it.

However, not everyone in the Steel City was overcome with sentimentality. The writer of "The Post" column chided the overzealous fans when he wrote, "Loyalty to Carey is a laudable thing, but [certain Pirate players] are working even harder than Max and getting nothing in return for it but a quiet, matter-of-fact recognition for some of the best ball they have flashed this season."[190]

Carey sat out the second game of the series and went hitless with a sacrifice bunt in three plate appearances in the third one, but in the closing contest, he drove in the winning run for the Robins with a smash to Traynor, who knocked the ball down but was unable to throw out the man who he replaced as captain.

Four. *The ABC Affair*   159

For the entire series, Carey had three hits, two walks, and a sacrifice bunt in 12 plate appearances, with two runs scored and one RBI, and his presence alone—not to mention the way that he played—helped to stoke the controversy surrounding the ABC Affair.[191]

No doubt, Carey's warm reception was aided by a call that the ABC trio had strategically made to Ralph Davis on the 21st, in which they gave their "PR man" a formal statement that was printed by Davis in the next day's issue of the *Press*—approximately 24 hours before Carey's debut as a Robin at Forbes Field. Whether Davis was coaching the trio or not is open to debate, but in what was printed, Adams, Bigbee, and Carey said that they had decided not to come forth with "a full and complete statement of the facts" at that time because they did not want to do anything to hurt the chances of the Pirates to win the pennant.[192] Or as the trio or Davis put it, "We ... will not at this time attempt to do that which we tried to prevent."[193] In addition, the trio emphasized that they had been "completely exonerated [by their] worthy president, Mr. Heydler" and that they wished "the Pirates all the success to be had, and that they may finish on top."[194] What the trio did not emphasize was that their "full and complete statement of the facts" would actually be their perception or interpretation of what had happened, and that though Heydler had exonerated them of "malicious intent," he had found them guilty of "mistaken zeal."

However, without attempting to apply any evenhandedness to what he had printed, Davis prefaced the statement with an overly supportive introduction, in which he said, among other things:

> Their statement ... breathes a spirit of loyalty to the club which has discharged the men, which cannot but impress all who read it. It is a show of the finest kind of sportsmanship—a spirit which sinks the private interests of the men and any desire for vengeance which might have actuated them, underneath the bigger, broader desire to see success crown the efforts of their erstwhile mates.[195]

To his schmaltzy prose, Davis should have added that the vengeance would come later, but more on that in the next chapter. For the time being, the *Press* contented itself with two short articles—one on the 24th and the other on the 26th—that highlighted Carey's accomplishments against the Pirates as if he were a Pirate and the Pirates were the opposing team. Neither article contained a byline, though both were no doubt written by Davis or Wollen, and each ended with a jab at Clarke:

- "Carey did this for Brooklyn. He would have been doing it for Pittsburgh but for the fact that he let it be known that, in the interest of the welfare of the Pirates, he thought Fred Clarke should remain off the bench."[196]

- "Carey was wearing a Brooklyn uniform, instead of Pirate toggery, because he had expressed the opinion that Fred Clarke should not sit on the Pirate bench."[197]

Also the day after Heydler's hearing, the Pirates resumed playing major league games, having been idle because of rainy weather since August 11, except for the aforementioned exhibition game against the New Haven Profs on the 12th and another one against the Youngstown General Tires on the 15th.[198] With the ABC trio gone, Dreyfuss, Clarke, and McKechnie began adding some old and new faces to the Pittsburgh roster to strengthen the team for the last five and half weeks of the season. As shown earlier in this chapter, Johnny Morrison was reinstated on August 17. Roy Mahaffey, the young pitcher who Dreyfuss had bought on the 12th, joined the team on the 24th.[199] The next day, Walter Mueller, a fleet-footed outfielder who had been a member of the Pirates from 1922 through 1924, reported to the Corsair management. Mueller had fractured the fifth cervical vertebra in his neck while making a spectacular catch in spring training in 1922, and after his injury had healed, he tore loose the same vertebra in a regular-season game that year, causing him to wear a steel brace for most of the rest of the season. He recovered well enough to play in 102 games over three years for the Bucs but then retired and went into the hauling and moving business in the suburbs of St. Louis. However, after leaving the Pirates, he kept his hand in baseball by performing for a team in one of the semipro leagues in the St. Louis area, and now the Pirate officials turned to him for assistance and asked him to apply for reinstatement. This he did, eventually getting Commissioner Landis' approval and participating in his first game as a resurrected Buc on August 31. It took Mueller longer than expected to rejoin the club because he had inadvertently failed to get permission from the Pirates, who he still belonged to after he had retired, to play independently. This was one of Landis' rules, but once Fred Clarke explained to the commissioner that the Pirate authorities had no problem with what Mueller had done and would have granted him permission if he had asked, the way was cleared for him to come back.[200] On the 26th, Sam Dreyfuss was able to get pitcher Lou Koupal back from the Buffalo Bisons, who, in June, had refused to return him until their season was over.[201] So, on that same day, to keep the roster limit to 25 after Koupal's acquisition and Mueller's anticipated arrival, pitcher Chet Nichols was sent back to New Haven under option.[202]

Besides obtaining the immediate reinforcements, Sam Dreyfuss announced on August 24 that Phil Voyles, who had been playing for the Columbia Comers of the South Atlantic League, had been sent to the Williamsport Grays of the New York-Pennsylvania League as partial payment for two players who were put on the back burner for future use: pitcher Walter Tauscher and outfielder Adam Comorosky, both of whom Pittsburgh had recently acquired from the Grays.[203] Tauscher would not have his major league debut until 1928, but Comorosky would see action with the '26 Bucs in September.

To compensate for the loss of Carey and the absence of Wright, McKechnie altered his batting order to read: Waner, RF; Rhyne, SS; Cuyler, CF; Traynor, 3B; Grantham, 1B; Barnhart, LF; Rawlings, 2B; and Smith/Gooch, C. This order would remain intact for the rest of the month of August with the exception of Grantham and Barnhart exchanging slots on the 19th and maintaining their new slots through the 31st; Murphy playing left field and batting fifth in both games of a doubleheader on the 21st; and McInnis subbing for Grantham at first and batting sixth on the 25th.[204]

The pitching was not adversely affected with Adams' departure—the Babe had been used sparingly as a reliever and had an ERA of 6.14—so for the most part, the major starters stayed the same, with Meadows getting four starts; Kremer, Aldridge, Yde, and Bush getting three apiece; and Songer and Morrison each getting one.[205] Songer would have seen more action, but on August 21 he became the latest Pirate casualty when he wrenched his throwing arm in a game against the Phillies. James Long believed that the injury probably occurred when the left-hander threw wildly to second base, but whatever the cause, Songer went to see Bonesetter Reese the morning of the 24th.[206]

Table 30: National League Standings at the End of the Day on August 31, 1926[207]

Team	Wins	Losses	Ties	Winning Percentage	Games Back	Runs Scored	Runs Allowed
St. Louis	75	54	2	.581	—	669	589
Cincinnati	74	54	2	.578	0.5	647	546
Pittsburgh	71	52	4	.577	1.0	650	560
Chicago	69	58	1	.543	5.0	585	512
New York	60	64	0	.484	12.5	547	559
Brooklyn	60	70	2	.462	15.5	538	603
Philadelphia	47	75	0	.385	24.5	562	730
Boston	48	77	1	.384	25.0	520	619

As for results, once the ABC trio had left, the Bucs finished out the month 10–7–1. Though not a bad record, and in fact, a better winning percentage (.588—ties are not included in baseball winning percentages) than the one they had going into their doubleheader on the 18th (.575), it was not enough to keep pace with the surging Cardinals and Reds. Thus by the time play was finished on August 31, the team from the Steel City found itself in third place, a game out of first (see Table 30).

The race for the NL pennant had turned into a three- or four-team affair, with the month of September serving as the final lap of the event. And to give them added support for the stretch drive, McKechnie's men had a new "weapon": the Pirate Boosters' Club. Formed by Chet Smith the morning of August 13— the day that Adams, Bigbee, and Carey received their walking papers—and having the slogan "Boost—Don't Knock the Pirates," the club's purpose was "to root and boost the Pirates into another world's championship."[208] The *Gazette Times* produced thousands of "Boost the Pirates" buttons, which fans could order for free by simply filling out a coupon printed in various issues of the newspaper and mailing it to Smith.[209] As Smith wrote:

> Now's the time the Pirates need every man-jack [sic] of you behind them. Let's show Skipper Bill and Vice President Clarke and Pie and Glenn and Lee and Ray and Johnny and all the boys that we're with them to the end; that we know they're out there day in and day out plugging their heads off to bring the [New York] Yankees here for the World's Series [at the time of this article, the Yanks were leading the American League by eight and a half games]. Let's show them we have confidence in them; that we appreciate the fact that it's a rocky road to Pennantville, but we're sure they have the stuff to pull them through.[210]

Smith's creation spread like wild fire—in spite of the fans' divisiveness over the ABC Affair. By the 15th, Smith reported:

> From far-away [sic] Florida, from throughout Pennsylvania, from Ohio, from West Virginia and from every nook and cranny of Allegheny County loyal fans are rallying to the "Pirate Boosters [sic] Club," which has for its purpose the welding together of sentiment to cheer the Corsairs to another pennant....
> Literally hundreds of fans have already joined in the procession.... That the club will number thousands within a short time is indicated by the hearty response.[211]

By the 16th, the membership had swelled to more than 10,000.[212] By the 29th, it had grown to over 20,000.[213] So, if fans could win ballgames, the Buccos were in good shape. But would the backing of the boosters equate to victories on the field?

Five

What Becomes of the Brokenhearted

> I am 18 years in baseball without ever opening my mouth, and then when I answer a question, I find myself chucked off the club.
>
> —Babe Adams, 1926

On August 30, Barney Dreyfuss returned to the United States. While in Paris on the 21st getting ready to board the *Columbus*, the ship that would carry him back across the Atlantic two days later, Dreyfuss had publically discussed the ABC Affair for the first time, stating that though he had not been consulted by Clarke, McKechnie, or his son until after the group's decision to release Adams, Bigbee, and Carey, he "thoroughly approve[d]" of what the Pirate management had done.[1] Dreyfuss went further to say:

> I am a sentimental fellow ... and therefore I feel deeply the departure of these players, but sentiment has no place in baseball....
> [From a business standpoint,] Carey's departure by the waiver route means writing a loss of $96,000 in the club's books. I could have sold him for that price last year.... [And] I was considering making [Adams] a pitching coach to keep him on the payroll.
> [As for any previous knowledge of problems on the team,] [w]hen I left Pittsburgh, in June, there was no inkling of dissension. I don't yet know the ground-floor reasons for the trouble, but when trouble breaks out in mid-season, especially when a club is leading the league, it is necessary for a manager to act quickly and efficiently.[2]

Thus, the Pirate owner had spoken and his stance was clear-cut: he supported the dismissal of the ABC trio, and to his way of thinking, neither sentiment nor financial concerns were to be put ahead of obedience to the men running his team.

However, Dreyfuss' explicitness did not stop Adams, Bigbee, and Carey from approaching their former employer shortly after he arrived in Pittsburgh on the 31st and requesting a conference with him. This Dreyfuss consented to, but after listening to the trio's side of the affair and their desire that he make a public statement "clearing them on any wrong in the matter," Dreyfuss told the Pittsburgh sportswriters during an interview following the conference[3]:

- "Before I left for my trip abroad[,] I called a meeting of the players in Brooklyn, and in a talk[,] I pointed out that in my absence Fred Clarke and Sam Dreyfuss were to take my place, and [I] urged the men to follow them as they would follow me if I were here."

- "To have a winner[,] you must have harmony. When you don't have harmony[,] you must take steps to achieve it and this is what Clarke and Sam tried to do."

- "Carey, Bigbee and Adams were personal friends of mine and I regret that they had to be let go, but I can't see what else could have been done under the circumstances."

- "It was too bad that it had to happen at all, but if the players who objected to Clarke had anything on their chests[,] why couldn't they have waited until I got back and given every one [sic] a chance to have the whole thing straightened out when I was here."

Concerning the players' desire for a statement exonerating them, Dreyfuss said that he would do nothing until he talked with his son, McKechnie, and Clarke,[4] all three of whom were out of town at the time—Sam Dreyfuss and McKechnie with the Pirate team in St. Louis and Clarke representing the Pittsburgh club at Walter Mueller's hearing with Commissioner Landis.

Nor did Dreyfuss' explicitness prevent the Pittsburgh scribes from asking him some of the same questions that he was asked when he was in Paris, though in answering two of them, he contradicted his earlier statements. Regarding Carey's value, Dreyfuss said that the former Pirate captain was worth $100,000 in 1923, not 1925, while he did not repeat his idea about possibly offering Adams a coaching position and instead stated that he had no plans for the 44-year-old hurler after the '26 season.[5] Otherwise, he pretty much reiterated what he had said 10 days earlier.

Among the new questions that were raised, the most interesting one involved a story that Ralph Davis reported in his column in the *Press* on August 26. According to Davis, one of the Pirate players was known by the rest of the team to have leaked the details of the vote on Clarke to—in Davis' words—"a newspaper friend here," and that man, who was said to be "a very brainy" infielder, would probably be released within a few days.[6] But when Dreyfuss was asked about the matter, he replied that he knew nothing about it.[7] Of course, Dreyfuss' response does not preclude that the owner's son may have singled out someone to be let go and had not yet discussed the matter with his father, but no infielder—brainy or otherwise—would be released until the season was over, not during late August or early September.

So, the appeal of Adams, Bigbee, and Carey, who had come all the way from his new job in Brooklyn to meet with Dreyfuss, and the subsequent press conference did nothing except to keep the ABC Affair alive.

On the field, matters were no better. A three-game losing streak to end the month of August was the beginning of an 11-game free fall in which the Pirates went 2–9. And if that was not bad enough, six of those nine defeats were to the Cardinals, who by the end of play on September 7 had increased their lead to two games over Cincinnati and four and a half over Pittsburgh.[8]

During this period of decline, the Bucs lost in every way imaginable—close scores, blowouts, and a few games that were in between those two extremes—while their two victories were by one run in 10 innings and two runs in nine innings. They scored a total of only 25 runs, but gave up 59, 14 of them unearned, as they committed 19 errors. Nor did McKechnie's attempts to rectify matters by rearranging his lineup and batting order have much effect on the results. All of which begs the question of what happened.[9]

The traditional view is that the forced departure of Adams, Bigbee, and Carey was key. Although no one would argue that Adams and Bigbee contributed greatly to the on-the-field success of the team or that the Carey of 1926 resembled the Carey of earlier years, the dismissal of the trio is believed to have deprived the Pirates of veteran leadership. According to this line of thinking, it was the intangibles that the ABC trio brought to the ballpark every day that was important, and at first glance, that theory appears to be a good one. After all, the day before the announcement that the trio had been forced to walk the plank, the Pirate ship was playing .575 ball and leading the National League by two games; by the end of play on September 7, it was playing .557 ball and in third place, four and half games behind St. Louis. Once the alleged intangibles were thrown overboard, the ship began to sink.

However, as the science adage says, "correlation does not imply causation," and so it was with the 1926 Pirates. A close examination of the team's misfortunes between August 13 and September 7 shows that other factors were far more likely the cause of the Pirates' troubles than getting rid of Adams, Bigbee, and Carey.

First among these factors was the aforementioned loss of Glenn Wright. Hal Rhyne had a more accurate arm than Wright, but he did not cover as much territory as the veteran shortstop, and no substitute could replace Wright in the batter's box. Nor did Wright's contributions go unnoticed by some of the players and sportswriters. When asked during the latter part of August to predict the result of the National League pennant race, Stuffy McInnis replied:

> In my opinion[,] Pittsburgh will win another pennant. But there's an "if"—a great big "if"—attached to that prediction. If Glenn Wright gets back into the lineup and stays in the lineup for the balance of the season[,] we'll be in. If not[,] it will be bad.
>
> Wright, to my mind, is the key to the whole situation.... He is the big punch of our batting attack, the man we all like to see dig his spikes into the dirt at the plate when the big pinch arrives....
>
> With Wright in there steadily[,] we'd be far in front by now.[10]

Earlier that month, Charlie Grimm had provided a similar analysis when he told Eddie Murphy that "[i]t is not a sure thing that [the Pirates] will hold the lead for the rest of the season. They miss Glenn Wright, and as long as he is out of the game[,] they won't be so formidable."[11] Also in August, James Long devoted part of a lengthy article to arguing that the Pirates' chances of winning a pennant were more dependent on a healthy Wright than on keeping Carey. The thrust of Long's argument was that Pittsburgh was able to secure first place even with Carey "having the poorest season of his entire career, ... hitting only around .200 all season and performing in general far below his standards," but the Bucs had "dropped the majority of their games since [Wright had been] added to the hospital list."[12] Long went further to say, "Not only is the shortfield [i.e., shortstop] position the most important on the field, particularly as Wright plays it, but in addition[,] the Pirates lose through his absence the siege gun of their attack."[13] Chilly Doyle concurred with this view, writing in an article that was published

Glenn Wright, the Bucs' run-producing shortstop. His absence from the Pirate lineup was one of the key reasons why Pittsburgh did not win the pennant in 1926 (National Baseball Hall of Fame Library, Cooperstown, New York).

the next day, "Unless Glnn [sic] Wright is able to take his place in the Pirate lineup in a large majority of the remaining games on the schedule, chances for another pennant in Pittsburgh are seriously imperilled."[14] On September 1, Doyle reiterated his feelings, stating, "If Wright remains out for another week[,] the Pirate flag chances may be at a very low ebb,"[15] and even Lou Wollen, one of Carey's staunchest defenders, admitted on the same day, "Glenn Wright is needed in the Pittsburgh lineup and he is needed badly. He will provide the punch that must be in the makeup of a serious pennant contender."[16]

The Pirate officials also were aware of Wright's value. As McKechnie told one of the *Gazette Times* reporters the evening of August 16, "[Wright's] absence from the lineup leaves a big hole. He drives in a lot of runs and that is what wins games."[17] So, after sending their star shortstop to more than one physician and having his injured ankle receive daily treatments at West Penn Hospital without achieving the recovery that they were hoping for, the Corsair brain trust decided to act upon Fred Clarke's idea of having Wright visit Bonesetter Reese in Youngstown the morning of September 2, with Clarke accompanying him.[18] According to Wright, once at Reese's place, Clarke grabbed his good ankle while Reese worked on his hurt one, and the process was so painful that he thought that the renowned Bonesetter had broken off his hurt one.[19] But the next day, Wright was back in the Pirate starting lineup, playing shortstop and batting cleanup. He cleanly handled five chances—including a one-out grounder over second base with a man on first, which he turned into a brilliant double play—and drove in the Bucs' first run as Pittsburgh squeaked out a 3–2 victory over Chicago in 10 innings.[20]

However, unfortunately for Wright and the rest of the Pirates, not to mention their fans, the euphoria was short-lived, as the good-hitting shortstop's ankle began bothering him again once the game was over. On September 5, Ed Balinger reported, "Glenn Wright said his injured ankle pained him considerably after [the game on the 3rd]. He played with heavier tape on his right foot [in the doubleheader played on the 4th] and at times found it hard to run."[21] Perhaps because of the pain or the tape or the long layoff that he had experienced, Wright did not perform well offensively during the final six games of the Bucs' slide, getting just three hits in 21 at bats and producing only two runs.[22] He was back, but his bat was not, and in part because of it, Pittsburgh lost five of those six games.

A second factor was Don Songer's injury. Although not out as long as Wright—he returned to action on September 4 after missing 14 games—Songer was a valued member of the pitching staff and his absence was felt, too. Also like Wright, once rejoining the team, he was not as effective as he was before his injury, surrendering five earned runs in two and a third innings of relief pitching in games played on September 4, 5, and 6.[23]

To a lesser degree, the loss of Vic Aldridge for several games in early September was another factor. Aldridge was notified that his father was seriously ill and received permission to go to his home in Terre Haute, Indiana, on September 2.[24] He would miss the entire series with Chicago and not be on the mound again until September 7, which proved to be a setback for both him and the Pirates. The former schoolteacher was having an off year, but in his three previous starts before his departure, he had pitched very well, recording a 1.80 ERA and a 0.92 WHIP. There was one catch, though: as Lou Wollen pointed out, "Aldridge need[ed] plenty of work to keep in shape,"[25] and this was something that his trip home deprived him of. He had last pitched on August 29— a three-hitter against St. Louis and Grover Cleveland Alexander, which resulted in a 2–2 tie—and was scheduled to face the Cubs on September 3, but, of course, he was unable to do so. Thus, when he toed the rubber on September 7 in another game against St. Louis, he got pounded, giving up 12 hits, four walks, and six earned runs in an 8–0 pasting.[26]

The fourth factor went beyond individual injuries and family issues and combined two different yet related matters: the schedule and the weather. Because of scheduling and inclement weather, the Pirates were not involved in any major league games from August 12 until they resumed play against Boston on August 18. But beginning on the 18th and continuing through September 7—the period of decline under discussion—Pittsburgh played eight doubleheaders and 10 single games in 21 days, and it appears that the two extremes of not enough playing followed by too much playing had an adverse effect on the team.[27]

But more important than either the schedule or the weather was that St. Louis, Cincinnati, and Chicago were overachieving while the Bucs were slumping. As Table 31 shows, the Cardinals, Reds, and Cubs entered the period under discussion playing winning but not outstanding ball. Then, the first two clubs caught fire and the third elevated its level of play to almost sweep the Pirates when the two teams met for a four-game series between September 3 and September 5. However, what was worse for Pittsburgh than having to face Chicago four times during this stretch of games was having to confront St. Louis nine times, the result of which was a 2–6–1 record for the boys representing the Steel City. Momentum and matchups are important factors in sports for determining wins and losses, but when they combine, the results can be devastating.

There was even a story circulating among Pirate fans that the Buccos were "victims of a concerted, though unorganized, movement by the players of the National League, aimed at the management of the Pittsburgh club in retaliation for the summary dismissal of Carey, Adams, and Bigbee."[29] According to this theory, "a camaraderie [existed] among the players that [was] greater than

Table 31: Records for August 12–September 7, 1926[28]

Team	Wins	Losses	Ties	Winning Percentage	Overall Winning Percentage at the End of Play on August 11, 1926	Overall Winning Percentage at the End of Play on September 7, 1926
St. Louis	20	8	1	.714	.555	.587
Cincinnati	16	6	1	.727	.545	.575
Pittsburgh	12	13	1	.480	.575	.557
Chicago	17	10	0	.630	.523	.544

[O]rganized [B]aseball"—a camaraderie that included "the continued resentment of the players of the power of the owners over the players, without any redress in most instances, of the reserve clause, [and] of the apparent gentlemen's agreement among owners of both leagues to railroad recalcitrant players out of the leagues by the waiver route."[30] So, in reaction to what happened to the ABC trio, the players on other teams in the league were trying to help St. Louis and, to a lesser degree, Cincinnati to win the pennant by not giving their best when competing against those clubs.[31] In all likelihood, this rumor was nothing more than the work of a disgruntled fan with an overactive imagination who could not accept the fact that the Cardinals and the Reds were playing better ball than his beloved Bucs. But if nothing else, it underscores how well St. Louis and Cincinnati were performing.

A related factor working against the lack of leadership theory is the sequence of the results of the games. Once the Pirates resumed playing after the dismissal of the trio, they went 10–4–1 during their first 15 games, for a .714 percentage—much better than their overall percentage of .575 immediately prior to the dismissal. Or if that comparison seems unfair due to the difference in the number of games played for the two percentages, the Bucs' 10 wins and four losses were two games better than their 8–6 record for the last 14 games before the dismissal. There was no sudden collapse as might be expected when three team leaders have been abruptly pushed out the door, but just the opposite. It was not until the second game of the August 30 doubleheader that the tailspin began.

This factor may appear to contradict the importance of Wright not being in the lineup, but remember that Wright's absence overlapped the last five games that the trio were with the Pirates and the first four games of the tailspin. Though Wright saw single at bats as a substitute or a pinch hitter in each of four games during that period, he did not return as a starter until September 3. This means that while he was gone from the cleanup spot and from playing shortstop on a regular basis, Pittsburgh was not much better than a .500 team. For that matter, during the entire season, when Wright started at shortstop, Pittsburgh won 58.9 percent of the time, not counting ties. But in the games that Wright missed and the four where he had just one at bat, Pittsburgh won only 43.9 percent of the time, again not counting ties.[32]

Then there is the question of how much Adams, Bigbee, and Carey were really team leaders. True, they were the senior members on the team in terms of service to the Pittsburgh franchise and, in the case of Adams and Carey, in age as well. And, of course, Carey was the team captain. But did their presence prevent the collapse of the 1921 Pirates or the poor June performance of the 1922 club that led to the resignation of George Gibson? Or how about the late season struggles that contributed to the '22, '23, and '24 teams not winning the pennant?

In fact, one player even said that the ABC trio were just the opposite of team leaders. Upon learning of their dismissal, ex–Pirate Wilbur Cooper sent letters to at least three Pittsburgh papers—the *Sun*, the *Gazette Times* and the *Chronicle Telegraph*—the first two of which in part read:

> I notice in the papers tonight about the big shake-up of the Pirates, and am real glad that the people of Pittsburgh have finally found out the real ones [apparently meaning the ones responsible for dissension on the team], though I have always been the one blamed.
>
> I really feel that this is one of the biggest triumphs I ever had in baseball. They have finally brought to light what I foretold them in a meeting a few years back—the real cause.[33]

While the third, specifically addressed to Havey Boyle, sounds quite similar to the others when Cooper writes:

> Notice in the paper this evening the big shakeup [*sic*] on the Pirates and am sure glad to see the real thing finally come out.
>
> It looks like I was not such a bad fellow after all, though I always got the blame. I feel this is a great triumph for me and hope you can see it the same way.[34]

Were Cooper's words just the grumbling of a bitter former star who was now pitching for Toledo in the American Association, or were they valuable insights into the personalities of the ABC trio? And remember that Cooper had played with Adams, Bigbee, and Carey for a number of years, including on the 1921–1924 teams.

But not everything was gloom and doom during the Pirates' slide from first to third. Between August 18 and September 6, Ray Kremer pitched magnificently, giving up only nine earned runs in 47 and a third innings, having a WHIP of 1.08, and winning five out of the six games in which he appeared, four out of five as a starter.[35] On August 26, Paul Waner went six for six in a game against New York.³⁶ Then, on September 1, Carmen Hill, a bespectacled right-handed pitcher who had seen limited action with the Bucs in four previous seasons—1915, 1916, 1918, and 1919—was purchased from the Indianapolis Indians of the American Association and performed well in helping to defeat the Cubs two days later.³⁷ As Chilly Doyle reported, "Showing the Cubs a smashing fast ball [sic], Carmen also displayed a good curve, and, better still, his control was almost perfect. He walked one batter over the long grind."³⁸

Perhaps these glimmers of hope inspired the Pirates to make one last surge to try to recapture first place. Beginning on September 8 and continuing through the 14th, the team played .636 ball, taking three out of five games from Cincinnati, three out of four from New York, and one out of two from Chicago. Compared to the previous 11 games, the turnaround was dramatic and proved that the Pirate ship was far from dead in the water. During the stretch from the second game of the doubleheader on August 30 through the shutout loss to St. Louis on September 7, Pittsburgh gave up 5.36 runs per game—4.09 of them earned—while scoring only 2.27. But during the September 8–14 period, the numbers changed to 3.64 given up—2.91 of them earned—and 5.00 scored.³⁹ So, what happened this time?

Well, as the statistics suggest, the answer appears to be a combination of strong pitching, better defense, and the awakening of the Pirates' dormant bats. More specifically, regarding the first category, it was either feast or famine for the Corsair staff. In the seven wins amassed from the 8th through the 14th, Meadows (twice), Hill, Bush, Kremer (twice), and Aldridge, with a little assistance from Bush, averaged a 1.00 WHIP and an outstanding 0.86 ERA. These men were scattering hits and walks, but not

The 1926 season left much to be desired for Vic Aldridge. He hurt his elbow; was fined; finished with a 10–13 record, a 4.07 ERA, and a 1.46 WHIP; and suffered the loss of his father, who died while Aldridge was en route to visit him (Library of Congress, George Grantham Bain Collection, LC-DIG-ggbain-38578).

allowing many base runners to cross the plate. In the four losses, Yde (four appearances), Koupal (three), Morrison (two), Songer (two), Hill (two), Mahaffey, and Aldridge averaged a 1.63 WHIP and a 6.69 ERA.[40]

The defense mirrored the pitching. In the seven wins, a total of three errors were made and none of them led to any runs being scored. In the four losses, nine errors were committed and eight unearned runs were given up.[41]

As for the hitting revival, Fred Clarke had predicted on September 2 that "when [the Pirates] start to hit, everything will be all right,"[42] and McKechnie attempted to make Clarke's prediction come true on September 8 by again shuffling his batting order. This time, young Fred Brickell got his first start by being placed in left field and in the leadoff slot. He was followed by Waner in right, Cuyler in center, Wright at shortstop, Grantham at first, Traynor at third, Cronin at second, and Smith behind the plate. That combination would remain the starting batting order for the 11-game period, with the following exceptions: McInnis would play first and bat fifth in the first game on the 9th; Mueller would be the left fielder and bat leadoff for the first game on the 10th; Rhyne would take over at second and bat seventh for the last five games; and Gooch would catch and bat eighth in the second game on the 12th. The results were a collective .298 batting average for the starting nonpitchers—as compared to .214 for the previous 11-game period—with Waner (.409), Brickell (.390), Grantham (.371), and Smith (.345) leading the way.

In addition to the victories, several personnel moves occurred during the upswing:

- The evening of his triumphal performance against the Giants on September 12, Vic Aldridge received word that his father's condition had worsened, causing him to leave New York for Terre Haute on a 3:00 A.M. train the next morning. Sadly, the epilogue to this story was not a pleasant one for either Aldridge or the Pirates. The elder Aldridge died later on the 13th before his son could reach him, and when the younger Aldridge rejoined the team the morning of 20th, he said that his arm was slightly stiff,[43] which was probably the reason that McKechnie did not pitch him anymore.

- Also on the 13th, Adam Comorosky debuted in a Pirate uniform as a pinch hitter.[44]

- Don Songer, whose arm was still bothering him, and who, because of it, had been mostly ineffective since his return to the team (a 6.57 ERA and a 1.54 WHIP in 12 and a third innings pitched), left the evening of the same day to see Dr. Harry Knight, the physician who had treated Aldridge in July,[45] and would not be used for the rest of the season.[46]

- And Eddie Murphy, who had been a bust as a pinch hitter and occasional left fielder (a .118 batting average with a .250 on-base percentage and a .118 slugging average),[47] was sent home on the 14th, with the provision that he would be returned to Rochester once the paperwork was completed.[48]

Despite the pessimism of some of the Pittsburgh press core who thought that the surge was too little too late, the results propelled the Buccos to two and a half games behind the league-leading Reds and two games behind the second-place Cardinals by the end of play on September 14.[49] Moreover, it restored the players' confidence in themselves and, with 12 games remaining for them as well as for Cincinnati and St. Louis, gave them hope that they might still win the race for the National League flag.[50]

But unfortunately for the Pirates and their supporters, what could have been the springboard for a thrilling comeback turned out to be the last hurrah of a bronze medalist. After dropping the final game to the Giants, 6–5, the Bucs lost three out of four to Brooklyn, took two out of three from Philadelphia, and managed to get only one win out of three against Boston. This gave them a disappointing total of four wins and seven losses during the home stretch and left them in third place, four and half games out of first. And what made this late fade even more galling were three other factors: all seven losses came at the hands of second-division teams with losing records; five of the losses were by one or two runs; and neither Cincinnati nor St. Louis had an exceptional finish either. Regarding the last point, the Reds were as bad as the Buccos, going 4–7–1, while the Cardinals had a creditable, though not insurmountable, 7–5 record.[51]

As with their surge, the Pirates' reversal of fortune can be attributed to various reasons, but for the most part, the pitching staff was not to blame. In the three losses to Brooklyn and the first loss to Boston, Meadows, Hill, Yde, and Kremer pitched well enough to win, but the Pittsburgh bats could produce only one run per game in their behalf. In the remaining three defeats, ineffective pitching played a significant role, but in each of two of those contests, the Pirate offense pushed just two runs across the plate. Taken together, in those six losses, the team's ERA was 3.00, while its average runs scored per game equaled 1.33—and this from an offense that averaged a tad more than five runs per game for the entire season.

In the other defeat—the 6–5 setback to the Giants that got the reversal started—Bush was not able to handle the New York hitters, but the Bucs still might have won the game if not for two fielding miscues. Down 4–2 going into the bottom of the fourth, the Giants got three straight singles off Bush to load the bases, but Waner made a great catch of a liner to right center and an equally great throw to hold the New York runner on third from scoring. Bush was then replaced by Johnny Morrison, who did exactly what he was supposed to do: get the batter to hit the ball on the ground to set up a double play. But Rhyne muffed the easy grounder and the runner on third scored with the bases becoming reloaded. The next batter hit a sacrifice fly to Cuyler, who, in the words of Lou Wollen, "whizzed the ball to third somewhat wildly, and the heave permitted a runner who eventually crossed with the winning run, to anchor on second base, instead of being held on the initial cushion had the peg been made to second."[52] One runner scored and the other two advanced to second and third, where they scored when the following hitter whacked a single to right.[53] Pittsburgh managed to get one run back in the top of the sixth but was unsuccessful in pulling out the victory.

Besides the Giant game, fielding woes contributed to six runs in four of the losses, while yet another off-the-field problem has to be factored into the mix. The evening of September 17, Glenn Wright received a telegram from his mother that said that his father, "who [had] been in ill health for many months, had taken a turn for the worse."[54] Wright immediately went to McKechnie, received permission to leave the team, boarded a 3:00 a.m. train on the 18th, headed to his parents' home, and missed the final eight games of the season.[55]

Added to these reasons, it can be argued that timing was partially responsible for the last two losses. Pittsburgh met Boston in Beantown at a time when the Braves had won 14 of their last 19 games, including taking three out of four from St. Louis, four out of five from Chicago, and sweeping Cincinnati. This late-season success prompted Ed Balinger, who enjoyed starting his columns with self-composed rhymes, to introduce what he had written on September 23 for the next day's issue of the *Pittsburgh Post*:

> The Braves might have grabbed off a pennant this fall,
> But they didn't and here is the reason:
> When they started to play the right brand of baseball
> They chose the wrong end of the season.[56]

The Bucs had had problems with the seventh-place Bostonians all year and the fact that the Braves were hot only made trying to beat them more difficult. On the 23rd, in the first match of a four-game series, Kremer lost a 2–1 heartbreaker to 22-year-old Foster Edwards, a former Dartmouth high jumper,[57] when the Pirate bats produced eight hits but just one run and Hal Rhyne's error set up the winning tally for Boston.[58] The second contest, originally planned for the 24th, was cancelled because of wet grounds and not rescheduled. This left the final two games of the series, which were also the last two of Pittsburgh's regular season, as a doubleheader on the 25th. In it, the Pirates won the first game in a slugfest, 11–8, and were aided by five Boston errors, but they lost the second, 5–2, as Emil Yde gave up 12 hits and four walks in eight innings pitched.[59]

That same day, Stuffy McInnis was given his unconditional release.[60] Having not seen action since September 9,[61] the slick-fielding first baseman, who had been nursing a facial injury after having been hit just below one of his eyes by a batted ball during infield practice on September 17,[62] was, according to Barney Dreyfuss, let go as soon as the regular season ended for two reasons:

> In order to give him more time to find something good for himself for next year.... [And because] we are trying to build up with young men and cannot improve the club by retaining the old timber.[63]

Ralph Davis would later argue that the real reason for McInnis' departure had nothing to do with what Dreyfuss had said, but rather with something that McInnis himself had said the previous month. However, more on that matter shortly.

A meaningless exhibition game with an independent team was played in Bridgeport, Connecticut, on the 26th—a game that Pittsburgh won, 3–2[64]—and then the 1926 Pirates were no more. What could have been did not materialize as St. Louis captured the National League flag on September 24 and Cincinnati secured second place on the same day. Mathematically eliminated from the pennant race on the 22nd, the best the Bucs could do was maintain third place, something they did by winning the first half of the doubleheader with Boston on the 25th.

Thus, the Pirates' attempt to repeat as senior circuit champions ended not with a bang but with a whimper. As can be seen from Table 32, there were no outstanding NL teams in 1926. Even St. Louis was not a powerhouse. In fact, in Harry Hollingsworth's 1994 study of the best and worst major league teams between 1901 and 1993, the 1926 Cardinals rank 156th out of 186 pennant winners.[65] Hollingsworth would revise his rating system in 2001, which would result in the '26 Redbirds being moved up to 147th out of 200 pennant winners, but that is still not an impressive ranking for a title holder.[66] Nor did any of the other franchises field a world-beater. So, the competition was not overwhelming and only six more wins would have propelled the Bucs to the top. Believers in fate, like Clarke, may have said that it was not meant to be, but certain other people had a different view as to where the responsibility lay, and these people would provide the off-the-field bang that the Pirates had failed to deliver on the field.

Table 32: Final National League Standings for the 1926 Season[67]

Team	Wins	Losses	Ties	Winning Percentage	Games Back	Runs Scored	Runs Allowed
St. Louis	89	65	2	.578	—	817	678
Cincinnati	87	67	3	.565	2.0	747	651
Pittsburgh	84	69	4	.549	4.5	769	689
Chicago	82	72	1	.532	7.0	682	602
New York	74	77	0	.490	13.5	663	668
Brooklyn	71	82	2	.464	17.5	623	705
Boston	66	86	1	.434	22.0	624	719
Philadelphia	58	93	1	.384	29.5	687	900

On Tuesday, September 28, the editors of the *Pittsburgh Press*, sounding more like the editors of the *National Enquirer* than those of a mainstream metropolitan newspaper, advertised at the bottom of the front page of their issue:

What Caused The Pirate Flare-Up?

Inside Story of the Trouble on the Pittsburgh Baseball Club, Which Culminated in the Release of Carey, Bigbee and Adams, and the Later Release of Stuffy McInnis.

Sensational details of the internal trouble which wrecked a world's championship aggregation and prevented it from repeating its pennant[-]winning feat.

AN EXCLUSIVE PRESENTATION OF FACTS, OVER THE SIGNATURES OF MAX CAREY, CARSON BIGBEE AND BABE ADAMS

IN THE PRESS ONLY, THURSDAY—ORDER YOUR COPY EARLY[68]

This was followed by a similar ad on the first page of the sports section, which read:

The Truth At Last About the Pirates

WHAT WRECKED THE 1926 BUCCANEERS?

That question has been asked a million times since the release of Max Carey, Carson Bigbee and Babe Adams, following the earlier release of Eddie

Moore. It has been asked again, following the recent let-out of Stuffy McInnis.

The question will be answered by the "ABC" combination—Adams[,] Bigbee and Carey—in a sensational disclosure of facts, over their own signatures, which will appear

IN THE PRESS THURSDAY.

If you want the details and undeniable facts, get THE PRESS Thursday. A dispassionate recital of events which led up to the breakup of a great ball club [sic].

The real "inside" story of the strife which set the baseball world talking.[69]

The next day, only one ad appeared and was located at the bottom of the front page of the issue. Worded not much differently from those on the previous day, it was just as melodramatic and laughably full of itself as it purported to have the answers to all the questions:

THE WRECKING OF A WORLD'S CHAMPIONSHIP BALL CLUB [sic]—WHAT CAUSED IT?

THE "INSIDE STORY" of the Dissension which Deprived the Pirates of a chance to win the 1926 pennant, and figure in the World's Series this fall. Adams, Bigbee and Carey tell a straightforward story.

SENSATIONAL DISCLOSURES by "Babe" Adams, Carson Bigbee and Max Carey, who were cast adrift by alarmed and excited under-officials of the Pirates in a desperate effort to "save the sinking Corsair ship."

Read the Real Story of the Reasons for the Blowup Exclusively in Tomorrow's PRESS.[70]

Before continuing, it may be helpful to point out several obvious flaws in the wording of these ads, which, of course, were designed to sell papers, not herald the coming of the true story as to why the '26 Pirates failed to win the pennant. First, though it is important to hear Adams, Bigbee, and Carey's side of the ABC Affair, a side which the trio had been reluctant to go public with in August, to call their perceptions the "truth" or the "real story" simply because they said it is as fallacious as calling Fred Clarke's or Bill McKechnie's side the "truth" or the "real story" simply because they said it. There is an adage that states, "The truth has many faces." Or as Oscar Wilde put it, "The truth is rarely pure and never simple."[71] Second, the men who got rid of the trio were not "under-officials"—they were THE OFFICIALS running the Pittsburgh ballclub during Barney Dreyfuss' absence. As shown earlier in this book, Dreyfuss had temporarily put them in charge of the team until he returned from Europe, and at least publically, he supported their decisions. Thus, they were not overstepping their authority in their dealings with any Pirate player. Third, Adams, Bigbee, and Carey were not "cast adrift in a desperate effort to 'save the sinking Corsair ship.'" At the time the trio was let go, the Bucs were leading the National League by two games. And finally, the ads do not take into account the other factors—such as injuries—that helped to prevent the Pirate franchise from adding another NL flag to its collection.

But the ads were only the tip of the iceberg. On September 30, the article titled "Secret of Pirate Shakeup Revealed" appeared as the lead story on the front page of the *Press*, beating out pieces on the Teapot Dome scandal and Jack Dempsey, among others. Awkwardly organized and at times repetitive, the tell-all account, compiled and written by Ralph Davis and allegedly based on the inside information given to him by Adams, Bigbee, and Carey, whose signatures appear at the end of it, began with a statement of intent:

> Feeling that we [Adams, Bigbee, and Carey] owe the general baseball public of Pittsburgh and the entire nation a statement covering our side of the late controversy between the Pittsburgh baseball club and Adams, Bigbee and Carey, we wish to present at this time the facts pertaining to it as the truth, and nothing but the truth.
> It has been the contention of the officials left in charge of the Pittstburgh [sic] baseball club during Mr. Dreyfuss' absence that the three undersigned players had attempted to put strife and dissension into the Pittsburgh baseball club, and therefore had to be punished.
> In the following statement, it is our purpose to show that strife and dissension already were present on the Pittsburgh baseball club, not only between the players and [Fred] Clarke, but also between [Bill] McKechnie and Clarke, to its detriment, and that any action we took, at the instance of other players, was merely to erase it, so that the ball club [sic] could again play winning ball.[72]

The article then proceeded to blast Clarke for being the source of all morale problems on the Pirate team going back to almost the time that the former player-manager rejoined the Pittsburgh franchise in June of 1925. Specific charges against Clarke included two matters that were dealt with previously in this book and shown to be erroneous—Clarke becoming angry over receiving only $1,000 of the 1925 World Series pot (see Chapter Three) and the reason that Eddie Moore was let go (see Chapter Four)—and will not be repeated here except to say that this was the first time in print that either matter saw the light of day. This lack of attention by the press corps is particularly surprising and supports the argument that the charges were invented or exaggerated to discredit Clarke.

Other matters that were dealt with previously in this book but were given to the court of public opinion for the first time were the details of the ABC trio's version of the events of August 7–9. These details, along with Clarke's and McKechnie's contrasting versions of the same events, can be found in Chapter Four and will also not be repeated here.

But there were some issues found in the article that were not addressed earlier and need to be examined:

- Adams, Bigbee, and Carey claimed that "[Paul] Waner was held back for a long time, because Clarke insisted on him changing his style of hitting"; that "[Kiki] Cuyler told other players repeatedly that he could not hit the way Clarke wanted him to"; and that "[p]ractically every regular player, including Traynor, Wright, Grantham, Cuyler, Waner, Rhyne, Gooch, Rawlings, Yde, Meadows and others, felt that the club was being held back by Clarke's presence on the bench, by his interference, unintentional though it might be."[73]

At face value, these statements appear damning, but a close review of their contents raises various doubts. In responding to the article in a lengthy interview with various Pittsburgh sportswriters the evening of the 30th, Clarke emphatically denied tampering with Waner's style of hitting, declaring:

> Never did I or anyone else, except Carey, try to change Waner's batting style. He is a natural hitter and needs no changing, yet Carey, who never shone as a hitter, ... was the only player on the club who attempted to change Waner's style. Day after day, Carey was at the plate with Waner, making him try to hit a new way. The best proof that Carey was wrong is that after Carey left the club, Waner became the hitting sensation of the league and finished in the first five hitters.[74]

This denial in and of itself would make it only Clarke's word versus that of the trio, except that the facts support what Clarke said. On the evening of the last game that Carey played as a Pirate, Waner was batting .318. But after Carey left, Waner batted .369, which raised his final average to .336 and led to him finishing fifth in the National League in batting average.[75]

Clarke then turned to the comment about Cuyler and said, "The best way to settle that would be to ask Cuyler about it as to who were the ones who insistently demanded that he do something to cut down his numerous strikeouts [Cuyler would finish second in the senior circuit and fifth in the majors in strikeouts]."[76] This does not sound like a man who was trying to cover up anything.

But Clarke did not limit his challenge to asking Cuyler about his version of events. He went further to say:

> As to players sitting on the bench hearing me give orders to a batter going up to the plate conflicting with those flashed by McKechnie from the coaching lines, the best way to shoot this apart would be for you, or any other newspaperman in the country[,] to get hold of these players and ask them. They are free to talk now that some of the others have tried to discolor and misquote things.
>
> The mentioning of Traynor, Wright, Grantham, Cuyler, Waner, Rhyne, Gooch, Rawlings, Yde, Meadows and others looks like a stroke to add body and personality to the stand of the three players. Traynor and Yde were here today to say goodby [to me], Meadows visited me before he left, Wright has wired me that everything is all right. The others, I feel, have no issue to argue with me, but if they have, it is not only their privilege, but their duty now that the others have attempted to place them in a peculiar light, to speak for their own protection or admit, in fact, that the statement of the three players, in substance, is correct. And you can take my word of honor that this is no attempt to discover any players against whom future action might be taken. We may as well have the whole truth.[77]

Clarke was outspoken and not one to sugarcoat his comments, and as has been seen, he had no patience for players who he perceived as being troublemakers, but he was not a liar. A reading of the Pittsburgh papers in the 1920s shows that he was viewed, in the parlance of the day, as a "square shooter"—i.e., an honest person. So, his challenge to the baseball scribes of the country exhibits the confidence of a man not afraid of the answers that they would find.

- The trio went further to say that "[t]he vote [to get Clarke off the bench] was unfair, because the question at hand affected mostly the eight or [10] regular players who were being bothered and made nervous by Clarke's suggestions and orders, some contrary to McKechnie's signals from the coaching line."[78]

But this complaint—if the trio did indeed say it and it was not just Davis grabbing at straws—makes no sense because it is self-critical. Neither Adams nor Bigbee were part of the eight or 10 regular players, so according to what the trio said, neither man should have had a vote in the Clarke matter.

Also, by "regular players," it appears that the trio did not want the pitchers to have a vote either. The regular players would have been Grantham, Rhyne, Wright (who was a Clarke supporter and not present for the vote), Traynor, Cuyler, Carey, Waner, Smith, and Gooch. Does this mean that the pitchers had no problems with Clarke, and if so, what about the trio's earlier statement that Yde and Meadows were part of the group of players who "felt that the club was being held back by Clarke's presence on the bench" (see the first bullet in this section)?

- Then the trio alleged that one of the other Pirate players "spilled the beans" about the ABC Affair to one of the sportswriters, "who broke the story

Five. *What Becomes of the Brokenhearted* 181

in a misrepresenting way."[79] Ralph Davis believed that the leading suspect was Stuffy McInnis and wrote in his "Ralph Davis Says" column on September 27:

> It is known that, before the vote was taken on the question of whether Fred Clarke should be requested to leave the bench or not, the players were warned that any man who talked to the newspaper men about the situation would be summarily fired.
>
> It has been claimed ever since that it was McInnis who was responsible for the story getting out, and those who learned this angle have ever since been waiting for the next move.[80]

But there are two problems with Davis' rhetoric. First, "summarily" means "in a prompt or direct manner," "immediately," or "without notice." Well, whoever leaked the details about the affair did so by August 12, but McInnis did not receive his release until September 25, which is hardly being summarily dismissed. And second, Davis does not cite the source or sources of his information—even in a general way. Was the source a player? Another sportswriter? A gambler who was upset because he lost big-time by betting on the Bucs to go all the way? All Davis says is "It has been claimed." But by whom? Without knowing where Davis got his information, it is impossible to judge the credibility of his claim.

What Davis does not say, however, is that, according to James Long, as early as sometime in July of 1926—remember that the ABC Affair did not begin until August 7—McInnis himself had said that he would probably be gone once the season was over because, in the words of Long who was reporting what the veteran first baseman told him, "George Grantham had developed into a high-grade firstsacker [sic] and the management was naturally endeavoring to build up with young men."[81] McInnis' prediction was supported by something else that Long reported:

Veteran first baseman John "Stuffy" McInnis. What was the real reason Barney Dreyfuss released him (Library of Congress, George Grantham Bain Collection, LC-DIG-ggbain-38573)?

McInnis was one of the players referred to in [t]he *Sun* [on September 14] when it was stated that two veterans would be let go immediately after the final game of the season to make room for the drafting of some minor league youngsters under the 40-player limit.

It is understood that action in the case of the other veteran referred to [probably Johnny Rawlings] has been deferred for a few days until the player in question has succeeded in closing for a new job for himself for next year. He has been promised his release as soon as he desires it.[82]

Nor for some undisclosed reason did McInnis want to return to the Pirates, though his decision had nothing to do with his feelings towards Clarke, who he "was lined up solidly with" in the ABC Affair,[83] or with Barney Dreyfuss. While in Philadelphia on September 20, 21, or 22, McInnis had told Havey Boyle, "[Barney Dreyfuss] gave me the best contract I ever got and that in my fading years, ... and while I do not care to go back[,] I want to make a special point of thanking Mr. Dreyfuss for the kind treatment I received."[84]

Apparently, such information was not what Davis had wanted to hear, so he rejected it, just as he rejected Barney Dreyfuss' statement that "[the ABC Affair] was closed long ago, and the release of McInnis has nothing to do with it."[85] But as Dreyfuss explained, even if McInnis had been the guilty party, the Pirate authorities would not have been able to conclusively prove that it was him because "[25] players knew the result of the balloting at the so-called Clarke meeting [actually only 23 players at most were present for the balloting, but they may have shared the results with the two who were not], so it would be impossible for us to trace any leak on that result to McInnis."[86]

- Moving from the vote to the Heydler hearing, the trio shifted gears temporarily and criticized McKechnie for misleading Clarke by saying that Adams, Bigbee, and Carey were a committee of three—implying that they were representatives of the team as a whole—and not mentioning until the hearing was held that Jack Onslow had accompanied them.[87] But in doing so, they contradicted themselves, stating that "We were not a 'committee'—simply four of the oldest players talking things over with our manager for the sake of harmony."[88] Yet in their statement of intent, Adams, Bigbee, and Carey said that they did what they did "at the instance of other players,"[89] which made them a de facto committee. Thus, the question here is: Did other players request that the trio take their grievances to McKechnie, or did the trio, with or without Onslow, visit McKechnie because they themselves wanted Clarke removed from the bench?

Unfortunately, a clear-cut answer may never be discovered because most of the Pirate players were unwilling to go public with their sides of the story. However, as described in Chapter Four, if Regis Welsh's findings are correct,

Bigbee had initiated the matter by approaching other players, several of whom backed off once they learned that Bigbee had wanted a meeting to vote on Clarke's future.

As for Onslow's part in the affair, it is possible that the scrappy Pirate coach did side with the trio and may have accompanied them when they visited McKechnie. For that matter, he may have been one of the six team members to vote against Clarke. Barney Dreyfuss apparently thought so, because on the day that he released Onslow, almost eight weeks after the Pirates' season had ended, he remarked, "Nothing like doing the job right."[90] But if Onslow's past experiences as a player and later behavior as a major league manager are any indication of his personality, then it is more likely that he sided with Clarke. Onslow had been a substitute catcher for John McGraw in 1917 and was, according to whoever wrote Onslow's obituary for *The Sporting News*, "impressed by the hard-boiled manager's methods of handling his players."[91] This point was elaborated on by Arthur Daley in his May 30, 1950, "Sports of the *Times*" column when he wrote:

> Onslow played briefly for John McGraw as a catcher and it is obvious that the Little Napoleon [one of McGraw's nicknames] made the biggest impression on him.... But Onslow borrowed only McGraw's toughness and few of his other saving graces.
> ...He barred automobiles and wives from camp.... His discipline was unbending. He ran his men bowlegged. Turmoil was his constant companion from the day he arrived.[92]

In addition, Onslow hated what he termed to be "stool pigeons"—players who ran to a higher authority and/or the press with complaints about the manager. Does this sound like a man who would support three players conspiring behind the back of one of their superiors?

Furthermore, it is interesting to note that John C. Hoffman reported in an article in the February 1950 issue of *Baseball Digest* that

> there [were] two schools of thought about Onslow. One is that, as a grizzled prototype of the old school, he is not gifted with the suave demeanor of the modern day manager. Another is that he is a good manager because he plays no favorites, is brutally candid with his players[,] and is well enough versed in the game to win with a good club.[93]

However, no matter which school of thought was correct, either description fits a man who would more likely be found in the pro–Clarke camp than the anti–Clarke one. Of course, this is not to say that a person's personality cannot change over time, so perhaps the Onslow of 1950 was different than the Onslow of 1926, but perhaps not.

- Returning to the topic of the hearing, the trio claimed that "McKechnie admitted [to John Heydler and the others present] that [they and Onslow] had come to him as friends to try [to] help him (not as mutineers), but that his head was in a whirl and that he 'wasn't big enough to handle it.'"[94]

While it is probably true that Adams, Bigbee, and Carey did not view themselves as rebels and that they saw McKechnie as a friend whom they could turn to, it is debatable how much their actions were predicated on their desire to help McKechnie and how much they were based on their desire to help themselves and any other players who did not care for Clarke's presence on the bench.

As for McKechnie's confession that "his head was in whirl and that he 'wasn't big enough to handle [the trio's request to hold a players' meeting to discuss what to do about Clarke],'" the words make perfect sense if McKechnie's version of events is to be believed. Remember, as was first brought forth in Chapter Four, McKechnie had stated for public consumption on August 12—five days before the Heydler hearing—that after being approached by the trio:

> I was so stunned by the announcement that, [sic] for a minute I did not realize what they were talking about. Then, after a little more conversation about it, I told them that I would put a stop to any attempt to start a thing of that kind on my ball club [sic], and positively forbid any meeting of any kind.[95]

According to McKechnie, he had been taken by surprise and, thus, would have been dumbfounded by what he had heard. But it makes no sense whatsoever if the trio's version of events is true and, instead, is another example of the trio contradicting themselves. Again, as can be found in Chapter Four, Adams, Bigbee, and Carey alleged that once McKechnie had heard what they wanted, he said, "Positively; it's the only way to do it" and "that this sentiment [feelings against Clarke sitting on the bench] had been allowed to exist too long as it was," and then he decided when and where to have the meeting.[96] Does this sound like a man whose "head was in a whirl" and who was not strong enough to handle the situation? At least McKechnie's version, whether truthful or not, was consistent.

Of course, McKechnie may have said one thing to the ABC trio and another thing to the press. For that matter, he may have said one thing to the ABC trio and another thing to Clarke, with the hope of appeasing both sides and keeping the peace. Carey's questions directed at the Pirate manager at the Heydler hearing and McKechnie coming out of the conference room looking like he had just undergone some form of mental torture (see Chapter Four)

Five. *What Becomes of the Brokenhearted*

may have been signs that Wilkinsburg Will—McKechnie had multiple nicknames—was caught talking out of both sides of his mouth.

- Finally, the trio ended their article with several more questionable statements:

    - A parting shot at Clarke, saying that he had "[made] a mountain out of a mole-hill [*sic*], to the detriment of Mr. Dreyfuss' best interests."[97] This was the strongest argument that the trio had: that Clarke had overreacted to the situation and that the punishment that they received did not fit their overzealous actions. But Adams and Carey should have known whom they were dealing with. They had played for Clarke for seven and six years, respectively, so they should have been aware that it was not in Clarke's nature to put up with what he perceived to be disruptive forces. Once the vote had been taken and Clarke had learned that 75 percent of the voting members had supported him, he was not going to give the trio another opportunity to undermine him.

    - The martyr-like proclamation that they did what they did "for the best interests of Mr. Dreyfuss and the team."[98] The rhetoric sounds noble, but what has to be kept in mind is that Dreyfuss had appointed Clarke vice president and assistant to the manager, had asked him to sit on the bench, and had designated him as one of the three men in charge of the team while Dreyfuss was in Europe. So, conspiring against and attempting to remove Dreyfuss' handpicked official from a job that Dreyfuss had wanted him to perform without first consulting with Dreyfuss himself was hardly doing something "for the best interests of Mr. Dreyfuss."

    As for the best interests of the team, Adams, Bigbee, and Carey may have convinced themselves that they were helping the ballclub with their plan, but the Bucs were in first place with a two-game lead over second-place Cincinnati when the trio shared their plan with McKechnie. If the team had been mired in sixth place at the time or in the midst of a 10-game losing streak, the trio's explanation for turning on Clarke would have been understandable, but this was not the case. Between July 1 and the end of the day on August 7, Pittsburgh had been playing .641 ball and had weathered various problems to capture the lead in the senior circuit on July 24 and to maintain it despite being swept by Boston on August 7.[99]

    - A blatantly sycophantic tribute to John Heydler: "That President John A. Heydler, in exonerating us, proved to the world that he is a true nobleman, a man unafraid to stand up for right and justice, and by so doing has preserved and kept the national game clean."[100] "Preserved and kept the national game clean"? Clean from what? This was not the Black Sox Scandal, and though Heydler did acquit the trio of being mutineers, he criticized them for "mistaken zeal" and for not first discussing the matter with Clarke or at least with Sam Dreyfuss, rather than running to McKechnie.

- And an expression of thanks to the baseball public in general and, in particular, to "[their] legion of friends, who stood by [them] so staunchly throughout this controversy."[101]

The last two points raise the question of why did Adams, Bigbee, and Carey really come forth with their article or allow Davis to write such a piece with their signatures attached to it. True, they said in their statement of intent that they wanted to tell their side of the story and "to show that strife and dissension already were present on the Pittsburgh baseball club ... and that any action [they] took, at the instance of other players, was merely to erase it, so that the ball club [*sic*] could again play winning ball."[102] But there are several holes in what they or Davis wrote. First, whether or not strife existed on the team prior to their plotting does not exonerate them from the strife that they caused through their recklessness. Second, as mentioned above, though it is not clear who the trio was representing because they contradict themselves, it appears from what Regis Welsh was able to find that Bigbee began the process by going to other players, not that the process was initiated "at the instance of other players." And third, also as mentioned above, the team had been playing well since July 1 and was sitting in first place when the trio approached McKechnie. Thus, to say "that any action we took [was done] ... so that the ball club [*sic*] could again play winning ball" makes no sense.

Moreover, there was no longer any need for Adams, Bigbee, and Carey to defend their actions. Heydler had said at the hearing that they were not "guilty of willful insubordination or malicious intent to disrupt or injure [the Pirate] club" and that "there [was] neither stain nor blemish on their long and honorable baseball career[s]."[103] And both sides of the controversy — the Pirate authorities and the ABC trio — had accepted the ruling. Also, the trio had discussed the situation with Barney Dreyfuss after he had returned to the United States and had learned from him that he was not going to reverse the decision to let them go. So, why write or have written for them the type of article that appeared in the *Press* on September 30? What good would have come from it?

The answer to these questions — beyond just venting for its own sake — may have been twofold: to enact revenge on Clarke and McKechnie, with the hope of driving them from their positions, and to rally public support of the trio's actions of early August so that Dreyfuss would reinstate them. Of course, the trio would never admit to being vengeance seekers or manipulators, but if their motives were indeed revenge and getting reinstated, they were at least partially successful.

Clarke, as shown in the previous two chapters and earlier in this chapter, responded immediately to Adams, Bigbee, and Carey's charges and defended

Five. *What Becomes of the Brokenhearted*   187

himself well in his interview with some of the Pittsburgh scribes on September 30, but in doing so, he let it be known that he had already resigned as assistant to the manager and thus removed himself from sitting on the bench for future seasons. He went further to say that holding that position was "the most disagreeable job that he ever had in his life ... and so far as was within his power[,] he would see to it that no one else would be unfortunate to be in the same position he was this year."[104] To this, Clarke added, depending on the source, "I shall be back here next year"[105]—implying that he would return as vice president and the head of scouting—"What part I shall play in the affairs of the Pirates is not settled yet,"[106] "In what capacity he would serve or whether he would return to the club in any capacity was not determined,"[107] or "It is possible I shall not be connected with the team at all next year."[108] Only time would tell which source had accurately quoted or, in one case, paraphrased Clarke's words.

McKechnie, who was on a hunting trip in Elk County, Pennsylvania, with the future "Voice of the Pirates," A. K. "Rosey" Rowswell, did not respond to the trio's accusations and criticisms, but at about noon on October 18, he was told by Barney Dreyfuss that his contract would not be renewed. For McKechnie, the move came as a surprise,[109] and in certain ways, his reaction was understandable. After all, when Dreyfuss had been asked during a conference with Steel City sportswriters on the evening of September 26 why he thought that the Pirates had not repeated as pennant winners, he told them that the ABC Affair had nothing to do with it.[110] Instead, he said that there were multiple causes, namely Glenn Wright's injury, the troubles suffered by the pitching staff, and Clyde Barnhart's drop-off in offensive production (a .192 batting average, with a .278 on-base percentage, a .207 slugging average, and 10 runs batted in compared to his 1925 stats of .325, .391, .447, and 114, respectively).[111] And though the Pirate magnate refused to disclose if McKechnie would be kept, stating instead that "when we have any announcement to make on that score ... it will be made to the public through the newspapers," he did not say anything negative about the Pirate skipper either.[112]

Asked again about McKechnie's fate on October 1, the day after Adams, Bigbee, and Carey's article was published, Dreyfuss replied:

> I do not know any more than a fly as to what I will do about a manager....
> I have not talked with McKechnie about it, because McKechnie is away, and as far as the baseball season is concerned, the present season is not closed. I have until next February to make a decision on a manager [contracts were sent out in February].[113]

As for any effect that the ABC trio's comments might have on his decision, Dreyfuss said that "from the time this squabble started in the newspapers, I

Was Bill McKechnie a victim of circumstances or was his lack of strong leadership one of the reasons the Pirates failed to repeat as pennant winners in 1926 (National Baseball Hall of Fame Library, Cooperstown, New York)?

have refrained from getting mixed up in it and do not intend to start now"[114] —implying that the trio's criticisms would not be a factor.

It is true that while giving a talk to the Pittsburgh Umpires' Association the evening of September 22, Dreyfuss admitted that there was a lack of harmony on his club during the '26 season.[115] But even here, he did not publically blame McKechnie for anything. For that matter, he disappointed his listeners by not providing them with explicit reasons for the Pirates not recapturing the pennant and instead said that accidents had been a factor and that if he had not gone to Europe, "he would have quieted the uprising [i.e., the ABC Affair] 60 days sooner than [it] was settled."[116]

So, why then did Dreyfuss get rid of Deacon Bill? According to what the Pirate owner told the Pittsburgh media, it was because the Pittsburgh fans no longer had faith in the Wilkinsburg native's ability to captain the Pirate ship. Or as Dreyfuss explained:

> I have high regard for McKechnie as a man and I still have warm friendship for him.
> The public, however, wants a winner, and it is my duty to take whatever steps I can to see that a winner is established here. Judging from the attitude of the fans, they had lost confidence in McKechnie, and there was only one thing to do.[117]

But Dreyfuss' words beg the question of what gave him the impression that fans "had lost confidence in McKechnie." In all likelihood, it was the fans' reactions to the ABC Affair and its ramifications—in particular, the articles and columns that Ralph Davis and, to a lesser extent, Lou Wollen had written about the affair, especially the tell-all account that had been published by the *Press* on September 30. Dreyfuss may have been sincere when he told the press corps on September 26 that the affair had nothing to do with the Pirates' failure to repeat as NL champions and when he said to them on October 1 that he had

Five. *What Becomes of the Brokenhearted*

not made up his mind as to what to do about McKechnie. But he probably was not immune to what he saw as a division among fans concerning McKechnie's leadership qualities. Dreyfuss wanted a strong leader, and even though he may have truly believed that his team would have lost the pennant whether or not the ABC trio had attempted to remove Clarke from the Pirate bench, he was not satisfied with McKechnie's leadership skills in general. Thus, it appears that it was not the ABC Affair per se that hurt McKechnie in Dreyfuss' eyes, but rather the perception that McKechnie gave the public of his inability to handle the affair. No matter whose retelling of events is to be believed—the ABC trio's or Clarke's—McKechnie comes across as indecisive and not in control of the situation. It is likely that the most damning statements in this regard were:

- The trio's accusation that McKechnie had agreed with them to hold a players' meeting to decide if Clarke should be kept on the bench, then cancelling the meeting the next day after saying that he and Sam Watters had a "diplomatic way" to remove Clarke, only to change his mind and eventually invite Clarke back to the bench just five days later. And remember that it was this invitation that led Clarke to tell McKechnie that he would not return until the trio was disciplined.

- After finding out about the movement against him, Clarke's asking McKechnie twice what he should do and McKechnie not having an answer for him. Clarke then discussed the matter further with McKechnie, but the Pirate skipper still did not know what to advise him to do.

- McKechnie's telling the players on August 9 that the Clarke matter was a closed issue but then having the players vote on the 10th on whether they wanted Clarke to return to the bench.

Such accounts of waffling or indecision caused both the supporters of the trio and the supporters of Clarke to criticize McKechnie. Or as an unidentified scribe for the *Pittsburgh Gazette Times*—probably Chet Smith, though possibly Chilly Doyle—put it, "[The trio's partisans and Clarke's partisans] all somehow believ[ed] that McKechnie, had he used a firm hand either on behalf of the players or on behalf of Clarke, might have held back the crisis, or even conquered it."[118] Of course, as was shown in the previous chapter, McKechnie's version of the first bullet differed with that of the trio's, and he never admitted or denied that Clarke had asked him for advice. On top of that, he, too, had supporters. But despite these things and despite the praise that he had received during the previous season, he was still let go.

As for the timing of McKechnie's dismissal, Dreyfuss said:

I selected this time to tell McKechnie of his release so that he would have plenty of time to seek a new field. I don't know if he wants to stay in baseball. If he does want to, I wanted to be sure to give him sufficient time to make his plans for 1927. That is the reason I notified him of his release before I have considered in any definite way his successor.[119]

To McKechnie's credit, he accepted his marching orders philosophically, refusing to issue a statement and instead saying, "There is really nothing to be said. My real friends feel bad, I suppose, but all this is a part of baseball."[120] When asked what his plans for the future were, he replied, "All I can say ... is that it is up to me to look around and endeavor to find a new job."[121] Then he added, "But it's no crime for a fellow to get fired."[122]

As it turned out, McKechnie's ouster may have been a blessing in disguise for the Wilkinsburg native. Not only did he "look around and endeavor to find a new job," but he also embarked on a baseball odyssey during which time he received a number of coaching and managerial positions that led him to greater glory than he had experienced during his Pirate years. Among his accomplishments after leaving the Bucs were managing three pennant winners (1928 St. Louis, 1939 Cincinnati, and 1940 Cincinnati) and a World Series champion (1940 Cincinnati); serving as a coach on another World Series champion (1948 Cleveland); and leading the National League All-Stars to a 4–0 victory over an American League All-Star team that had Joe DiMaggio, Ted Williams, Jimmie Foxx, and Bill Dickey in its starting lineup (the 1940 Major League All-Star Game).

But perhaps McKechnie's most impressive achievements were turning two losing franchises into winners, one more so than the other. In 1930, the former Pirate skipper took over the managerial reins of the Boston Braves, a perennial second-division club that had had one winning season after 1916, and by 1932 had his team playing .500 ball and ending up one game out of fourth place. These marks were topped the next season when the Braves came in fourth with a .539 winning percentage, tying the franchise's highest finish since 1921 and providing its best record since 1916. McKechnie followed this with two more winning seasons (1934 and 1937) and another first-division finish (fourth in 1934), and if his overall record of 560–666 after eight seasons in Beantown does not sound like anything to brag about, the quality of players that McKechnie managed has to be taken into consideration. Blessed with few stars and more than his share of mediocre or worse performers, it is amazing how he transformed most of his teams into groups of overachievers and squeezed every victory that he could out of them. As can be seen in Table 33, the year before McKechnie arrived on the scene, not only were the Braves a bad team, but based on expected won-lost percentage and projected won-lost percentage, they also underachieved. Then, look at the difference under McKechnie's leadership. With the exception of the 1935 season—a year when everything went wrong for the Braves except for the play of Wally Berger—all of McKechnie's teams won more than their statistics would indicate that they should have.

Table 33: Won-Lost Percentages for the Boston Braves, 1929–1937[123]

Season	Won-Lost Percentage	Expected Won-Lost Percentage	Projected Won-Lost Percentage
1929*	.364	.371	.380
1930	.455	.416	.408
1931	.416	.390	.413
1932	.500	.496	.489
1933	.539	.518	.506
1934	.517	.480	.469
1935	.248	.327	.353
1936**	.461	.443	.460
1937**	.520	.519	.511

*The season before McKechnie became manager of the Braves. **Known as the Bees.

In 1938, McKechnie succeeded Charlie Dressen and Bobby Wallace as manager of the Cincinnati Reds, a franchise which had suffered through nine consecutive losing seasons, and within three years led his team to the World Series championship. This rise to fame consisted of a three-step process:

1. In McKechnie's initial year at the helm of the Reds, Cincinnati ended up fourth with a .547 winning percentage.

2. The next season, the Reds captured the National League pennant while increasing their winning percentage to .630.

3. Finally, in 1940, McKechnie's men did it all: amassing 100 wins for the first time in franchise history, having a winning percentage of .654—the best for either major league—defending their NL title, and defeating the Detroit Tigers, four games to three, in the World Series.

No pennant winners would follow that of 1940, but McKechnie was able to have four more first-division finishers in six seasons, each with a .500 or better record. Additionally, as shown in Table 34, he continued, for the most part, to get his teams to play better than their statistics.

Table 34: Won-Lost Percentages for the Cincinnati Reds, 1937–1946[124]

Season	Won-Lost Percentage	Expected Won-Lost Percentage	Projected Won-Lost Percentage
1937*	.364	.435	.436
1938	.547	.560	.543
1939	.630	.614	.593
1940	.654	.630	.597
1941	.571	.540	.502
1942	.500	.485	.489
1943	.565	.552	.514
1944	.578	.530	.534
1945	.396	.384	.415
1946	.435	.461	.475

*The season before McKechnie became manager of the Reds.

Ironically, during the same periods that McKechnie's post–Pirate coaching and managerial career was taking place—1927–1949 and 1952–1953—the Pirates won only one pennant and no World Series championships, though they fielded 15 first-division teams, all of which had winning records. So, would McKechnie's presence have made a difference? Perhaps, though obviously the answer to that question will never be known. What is known is that McKechnie's successes did not go unnoticed. In 1937 and again in 1940, he received *The Sporting News'* Manager of the Year Award, and in 1962, he was elected to the National Baseball Hall of Fame. Other honors included being chosen as one of the 20 best managers of all time by a group of newspaper sportswriters and radio and television sportscasters for Edwin Pope's *Baseball's Greatest Managers* that was published in 1960[125]; being selected as one of the 21 top managers of all time by Harvey Frommer for his book by the same title that was published in 1985[126]; and coming in sixth in Michael D. Koehler's ranking of the greatest professional baseball managers, which can be found in his book, *America's Greatest Coaches*, published in 1990.[127]

Before retiring from Organized Baseball, McKechnie invested in "a large-scale, produce growing and shipping business" in Florida, something that he spent more time with after his retirement until he was bought out in 1956.[128] But despite the career moves that he made, the former Pirate skipper remained a western Pennsylvania boy at heart, not selling his house in Wilkinsburg until the spring of 1947 and later that year moving to Bradenton, Florida.[129] And yet, even then, he would return to Wilkinsburg and other parts of the Pittsburgh area for special occasions, including the 1960 World Series.[130]

Five. *What Becomes of the Brokenhearted*

Of course, McKechnie's affection for the Pittsburgh area was not always reciprocated by everyone living there. One person in particular who was shedding no tears over McKechnie's dismissal was Ralph Davis, who could not resist kicking Wilkinsburg Will while he was down. Not satisfied enough that his preaching had helped stir up the fans' animosity towards McKechnie, which contributed to Dreyfuss' decision to not rehire his manager, Davis now chose to rub salt into the wound. In his October 19 column in the *Press*, the self-righteous scribe pontificated:

> Bill failed to deal with the [ABC Affair] as he should have....
> It was his inability to grasp the seriousness of the situation which cost him his job....
> There is no question that McKechnie was for a time heart and soul with the players who opposed the presence of Fred Clarke on the Pirate bench. He encouraged them when they suggested a conference on the matter.
> But Bill "changes his mind" overnight, and in so doing[,] lost his golden opportunity. Later, too, when the vote on Clarke was taken, McKechnie had an opportunity to stand with his friends, and refuse to sanction the penalties which were inflicted on the trio of veterans.
> He could have told Clarke and Samuel Dreyfuss[,] "If Carey, Adams and Bigbee go, I go, too."
> He would probably have lost out then, but he would have passed out, with the reputation of standing by his friends, by the players who had tried to help him when they saw real trouble staring him in the face.[131]

But Davis was not through yet. Though McKechnie was gone, Clarke was still connected to the club, something which Davis could not stomach. So, he continued in his column:

> Clarke has already stated that he does not plan to return to the Pirate bench next season, but there are thousands of fans [as if Davis counted them] who say that is not going far enough, and that the announcement must come officially from the club that he is in nowise connected with its direction before they will support it again....
> ... so far as public opinion is concerned, the riddance of Clarke is more desired even than that of McKechnie.[132]

As might be expected, Lou Wollen supported this view in an article that he wrote in the same October 19 issue of the *Press*, which stated in part:

> But one thing is certain, according to President Dreyfuss, and that is that Fred Clarke will not be manager of the 1927 Buccaneers. That announcement is mighty pleasing to a majority of Pittsburgh fans, who believe that the meddling fingers of the Kansan were responsible for the eruption in the Pirate ranks and also the firing of McKechnie.

But Clarke in the opinion of those who follow the game closely and know how fatal a double-manager system can be [to] a ball club [*sic*], are also hopeful that Clarke will be kept out of the way next season.[133]

Neither man had to wait long to get what he had crusaded for. On October 27 it was announced that Clarke had submitted his resignation via a letter sent to Barney Dreyfuss the previous week and received by the Pirate owner the evening of the 26th.[134] That same evening, Clarke sent a telegram to the *Pittsburgh Post* that stated:

> Mailed my resignation as vice president and director of the Pittsburgh Athletic Company to Mr. Dreyfuss last week. There is no position on the club that would warrant my staying. Kindest regards.[135]

Although the general impression throughout Pittsburgh was that Clarke would not return to the Pirate club, Dreyfuss publically stated that his friend's decision had taken him by surprise.[136] And despite Chet Smith's belief that Dreyfuss had pushed Clarke out the door by demanding his resignation,[137] it appears that the Corsair magnate was telling the truth. At the time that he had announced McKechnie's dismissal, Dreyfuss had been asked about Clarke's future, and he responded by saying:

> I don't know yet what Clarke plans for next year. I know that he does not care to go on the bench. I can't say at this time what Clarke will be doing next season.[138]

Though, Dreyfuss was certain of one thing about Clarke's future: that the former Pirate manager would not be the new Pirate manager. This was not because Dreyfuss necessarily desired it, but because "Clarke [did] not want the job and never [meaning since he returned to the Pittsburgh club in 1925] has had any ambition for it."[139]

But beyond Dreyfuss' words, Clarke was a man of many interests who had more money than he knew what to do with, and even though baseball was one of his two major passions, he did not need any further aggravation of the type that he had endured during the '26 season. Also, he may have felt that he had been placed in a no-win situation. Brought back by Dreyfuss to supply mental toughness and discipline to a franchise in need of a firm hand, he had been pilloried by certain sportswriters and a number of fans when he had attempted to rid that franchise of what he perceived as disruptive elements. That two of those disruptive elements—Adams and Carey—had been players whose careers he had helped launch and who he had viewed as his friends must of have particularly hurt him. Furthermore, his critics did not seem to remember the successes that he had had a hand in producing during the '25 season and postseason. He was now viewed as a meddler and an ogre. Why return to that environment?

Another possible reason for Clarke's resignation was who Dreyfuss was

Five. What Becomes of the Brokenhearted

considering to be McKechnie's successor. Since Clarke mailed his letter of resignation to the Pittsburgh magnate during the week of October 17, he would not have known that Dreyfuss had chosen Owen "Donie" Bush, the longtime Detroit shortstop who had been a successful minor league manager for three seasons, to be the new Pirate skipper. Dreyfuss announced Bush's hiring the evening of the 25th, so unless he had wired his vice president ahead of time, Clarke would not have found out until after he had severed his ties with the Pittsburgh club. But he probably read the newspapers and saw who the candidates for the managerial position were rumored, in no particular order, to be: Bush, Earl "Greasy" Neale, Art Fletcher, Bill Killefer, Wade Killefer, Dave Bancroft, Casey Stengel, Bill Hinchman, Carlton Molesworth, and Lee Fohl. Seven of these men had no connection with Clarke, and of the three who did—Hinchman, Molesworth, and Fohl—it made sense to use them in different capacities than that of a big league manager. Hinchman, who had one of his two best seasons as a player under Clarke in 1915 and then, of course, served under him as a scout for a season and a half, and Molesworth, a personal friend of Dreyfuss who was part of the Pirates' extended scouting organization,[140] would better benefit the club being left in their current positions. Fohl, who grew up in Pittsburgh, made his major league debut under Clarke in 1902 and later helped Clarke with the development of pitcher Al Mamaux in the 1910s. However, even though he had won three pennants as a minor league manager and had two near misses in the majors, he was considered a better hire as a pitching coach or an advisor.[141] So, that meant that if Clarke had returned, in all likelihood he would have had to deal with someone whom he may not have been comfortable dealing with. Keep in mind that it was George Gibson who had first invited Clarke to attend the Pirates' spring training as an advisor in 1921, and it was Bill McKechnie who Clarke had assisted. Both men had broken into the majors under Clarke and both men had played several (McKechnie) or a number of (Gibson) years for Clarke. These were men who Clarke had felt close to, in the way that a teacher feels close to his former students. But this would not be the case with the majority of men who Dreyfuss was considering for McKechnie's job.

Whatever Clarke's reason or reasons for not returning to the Pirates, his resignation was accepted by the club's board of directors[142] and Clarke turned his attention to ranching, being involved in Winfield community activities, pursuing his varied interests, holding leadership positions with the National Baseball Congress,[143] and enjoying time with his family. During those years, and in one case posthumously, he was honored by being elected to the Kansas Baseball Hall of Fame (1939), the National Baseball Hall of Fame (1945), the Iowa Sports Hall of Fame (1951), and the Kansas Sports Hall of Fame (1963).

But neither Clarke's separation from the Pirate club nor his involvement

An excellent trapshooter, Fred Clarke had a number of interests and did not need the headaches of being a baseball executive (Library of Congress, National Photo Company Collection, LC-DIG-npcc-01609).

in non–Organized Baseball activities could prevent a rumor from starting in October of 1927 that his friend, oil millionaire Lewis Wentz, was attempting to buy the Bucs from Barney Dreyfuss, and if he succeeded, he would appoint Clarke "to direct the destinies of the Pirates from a playing point of view."[144] Nothing came of this tale as Wentz openly and emphatically denied it in a statement that he issued to the Pittsburgh sportswriters on October 11,[145] though a part of the rumor is worth considering. According to United Press sports editor, Frank Getty, if Clarke did return to the Pirates in a leadership capacity, Kiki Cuyler, who had incurred the enmity of Donie Bush and was on the trading block at that time, would be kept by the Corsairs and used as the starting center fielder. The reason: in Getty's words, "It is no secret ... that Clarke considers Cuyler just about the most valuable player on the pay roll [sic]."[146] This statement implies that if Cuyler did indeed harbor any animosity toward Clarke, it does not seem that the feeling was mutual.

Leaving the rumor aside, Adams, Bigbee, and Carey and their defense attorneys in the court of public opinion, Davis and Wollen, had achieved their first goal of removing Clarke as well as McKechnie. But their second goal, that of rejoining the Pirates, was not as easy to attain.

Hoping that Dreyfuss would reinstate them, Adams and Bigbee initially turned down minor league offers for their services.[147] But no invitation came. So, Adams, who owned land in Missouri and Kansas, spent the '27 season playing semiprofessional ball in the Show-Me State and performing for two minor league teams—Johnstown, Pennsylvania, for which he pitched and managed until June 4, and Springfield, Missouri, for which he pitched but did not manage—and then returned to farming.[148] Luther Spoehr and later Pete Cava and Paul Sandin have written that, in addition to tilling the soil, Adams became a sports reporter, and during both World War II and the Korean War, he used his reporting skills as a war correspondent.[149] But Adams' granddaughter, Libby Henderson, disagrees. Instead, she claims that Adams continued to farm uninterrupted until 1958 when he and his wife, Blanche, moved to Silver Spring, Maryland, to live with their elder daughter, Mary Elizabeth Denham.[150]

Bigbee considered returning to the University of Oregon and resuming his course work in medicine to complete the degree that he had not finished by the time he had entered Organized Baseball in 1916,[151] but after reconsidering his options, he signed with the Seattle Indians of the Pacific Coast League.[152] According to an article in the April 7, 1927, issue of the *Milwaukee Journal*, "He had dickered with several Coast clubs, but his terms were regarded as too high."[153] The former Pirate outfielder played for both Seattle and Portland, Oregon, during the '27 season and for Portland and Los Angeles in 1928 before calling it quits as a professional baseballer.[154] By 1940, he had become a used-car salesman,[155] but in 1948, he managed the Springfield, Illinois, Sallies of the All-American Girls Professional Baseball League (AAGPBL) and then served as the skipper of the Muskegon, Michigan, Lassies of the same league in 1949.[156]

Neither Adams nor Bigbee was inducted into the National Baseball Hall of Fame, though Adams was on the Baseball Writers' Association of America's (BBWAA's) ballots 15 times, with his most successful year being 1947, when he received 13.7 percent of the votes.[157] After his death, he also received consideration from the Hall's Historic Overview Committee,[158] and a black marble monument was erected to him in Mount Moriah, Missouri, the village to which he had moved at the age of 16 and near where he had his farm.[159] He was further honored when, in 2002, the Missouri General Assembly named a section of U.S. Route 136 the Babe Adams Highway.[160]

Max Carey's situation was somewhat different from those of his ABC Affair mates. After finishing his playing days with the Robins in 1929 and losing over $100,000 in the stock market crash that same year,[161] Carey attempted to get a job managing in the majors but was unable to do so.[162] It was at that time that Barney Dreyfuss decided to let bygones be bygones and hired Carey to be a Pirate coach, announcing the news on January 31, 1930.¹⁶³ As Dreyfuss told Carey in a letter dated March 5 of that year:

> I have forgotten 1926 long ago, only hope that 1930 will turn out to be a successful year for us all. You can make yourself quite useful to the club—this is entirely up to you.
>
> I have left everything up to Jewel [Ens] and Sam [Dreyfuss], work hand in hand with them, and you will get along with me allright [*sic*][.] [I]f they want any advice from me[,] it is there for the asking[;] however[,] I will not interfere unless I am asked.¹⁶⁴

So, for the 1930 season—a season in which the Bucs finished in the second division for the first time since 1917—Carey was once again a member of the Pirate ship. But his tour of duty did not last long. On October 31, he was unconditionally released by the Corsair management. No reason was given, though it was reported that he had no problems with the players, Manager Ens, or the Dreyfuss family.¹⁶⁵

In October of the following year, Carey resurfaced in Organized Baseball as the new manager of the Brooklyn Dodgers, a position that he held until he was fired in February of 1934. And interestingly enough, though the specific details are different, Carey's experiences as a manager had certain karmic elements to them. Like Clarke, Carey had inherited a team not known for its mental toughness.¹⁶⁶ Like Clarke, he had instilled discipline in his charges and remained optimistic when the team did not perform well.¹⁶⁷ Like Clarke, he was praised during his first season when the team was successful and criticized during his second season when the team could not duplicate or better its previous year's finish because "some of the key players were injured and others tailed off badly."¹⁶⁸ Like Clarke, who was accused of alienating various Pirate players, Carey was reported to have been dismissed "due to his inability to get along with the Brooklyn players."¹⁶⁹ Finally, like Clarke, whose image was tarnished by the writings of Ralph Davis and Lou Wollen, Carey must have been plagued by his own "Davis" and "Wollen," for as one of his biographers, John Bennett, writes, "Carey later remarked that 'he was the first manager fired by the newspapers.'"¹⁷⁰

But also like Clarke, Carey was a man of many interests who did not let his setbacks keep him down for long. Following his ouster by the Dodgers (once Wilbert Robinson was gone, the team's nickname changed back to one of its pre–Robinson sobriquets), Carey applied his talents to a variety of money-making endeavors. For example, he shared a patent on liniment that he and his partner sold to Bristol-Myers, served as the field director of the Amateur Baseball Congress, raised lime and avocado plants, managed three different minor league teams and rose to be the general manager of one of them, became a special

Five. *What Becomes of the Brokenhearted*

instructor for three major league franchises and a scout for one of them, wrote a baseball instructional book, authored and co-authored articles, and worked as an official for the Florida State Dog Racing Commission, among other things.[171]

However, Carey's fondest moments were spent as the manager of the 1944 Milwaukee Chicks and the 1950 and 1951 Fort Wayne Daisies of the AAGPBL and as the president of the league from 1945 through 1949.[172] In his former capacity, he led the Chicks to the second-half, league, and playoff championships.[173] In his latter capacity, he had a variety of duties. As he told Pittsburgh sportswriter Roy McHugh:

> My job was to pick the managers, chaperones, umpires and players. I developed an ability-rating chart and set up a scouting organization and we brought 80 girls to Florida for spring training. We taught them baseball and these girls were terrific. They could really play. We drew a million people one year in a 126-game schedule and later we took the girls to Central and South America.[174]

Beyond his duties, Carey did his best to make the women's game appear to be as exciting as the men's. In 1949, he revealed that by diminishing the distance between the bases to 72 feet, reducing the pitching distance to 50 feet, and using a less lively ball than the one currently being used in the majors, the league had deceived the spectators into believing that the women's brand of ball was just as fast as what was being played by their male counterparts.[175]

During his playing days, Carey had finished in the top 10 in his league in positive offensive categories 134 times, including leading the senior circuit in stolen bases 10 of those times and in four other categories six more times.[176] Defensively, he was the top National League outfielder in putouts nine times, assists four times, double plays five times, and range factor six times.[177] As just a left fielder, his numbers in these categories were once in assists and twice in double plays as well as once in fielding percentage, while as a center fielder, he was the leader seven times in putouts, six in assists, five in double plays, and six in range factor.[178] But despite these accomplishments, the National Baseball Hall of Fame selectors delayed in choosing Carey for induction into the national pastime's pantheon.[179] On the BBWAA's ballot 14 years between 1937 and 1958, he never received more than 51.1 percent of the votes and had to wait until 1961 when he was elected by the Veterans Committee.[180]

Though, after he was elected, Carey made the most of the situation, using his induction speech to promote two of his ideas to improve the game that he loved. First, he wanted the return of the spitball. No lover of the home run and a man who hit only 70 homers in 20 seasons in the majors, Carey argued:

> I think the spit ball [sic] should come back but not under that name.... Maybe we should call it the emory [sic] ball or the saliva ball. It would help the pitchers stop some of those home runs. I think a lot of people like to see the kind of game we

used to play when there was suspense about your ability to score a run. I believe in running bases.[181]

And second, he proposed a new baseball statistic: Total Advanced Bases or TAB. An accomplished bunter who enjoyed batting second and who is 13th on the all-time list of sacrifice hits,[182] Carey desired a stat that would give credit to players who advanced a runner and TAB was it.[183]

Another matter that Carey was outspoken about was the failure to include the players of his day in the pension plan that former major leaguers received. In particular, he believed that the National Baseball Hall of Fame and the club owners should help financially needy Hall of Famers.[184] As Carey explained:

> The oldtimers [sic] in the Hall of Fame don't share pension benefits and some are needy....
>
> The All-Star receipts go to the player pension fund which was instituted long after some of the Hall of Famers ended their careers....
>
> In 1933, I was a member of the committee for the first All-Star [G]ame. I was unsuccessful at persuading my colleagues to divert some of the receipts for needy oldtimers [sic]....
>
> I think the [Hall of Fame should pay benefits to members and the] club owners should contribute to hardship cases.[185]

A little more than 18 months following his induction into the Hall of Fame, Carey received the Retroactive Award from the New York chapter of the BBWAA.[186] Established to honor players who had excelled, for the most part, before the BBWAA started its Most Valuable Player Award in 1931, the Retroactive Award was given to Ty Cobb in 1960 and Rogers Hornsby in 1962, with no

Despite playing 20 seasons in the National League, being one of the stars of a World Series championship team, and managing and serving in other capacities in both the majors and the minors, Max Carey said that his most enjoyable time in baseball was when he was involved with the All-American Girls Professional Baseball League (Library of Congress, George Grantham Bain Collection, LC-DIG-ggbain-38581).

one getting it in 1961.[187] For Carey, the presentation ceremony occurred only five days after he had celebrated his 50th wedding anniversary on January 22, 1963, thus providing him with a personal "Triple Crown" achievement in approximately a year and a half.[188]

As for the rest of the team, 23 players who performed in at least one game for the '26 Pirates returned the following season to be part of the '27 team that edged out the Cardinals and the Giants for the National League pennant and was later swept by the Yankees in the World Series.[189] But for most of these men, 1927 was the last time that they would experience the exhilaration of being on a big league pennant winner, and of the exceptions, only Roy Mahaffey would play on a future World Series champion. This peculiar twist of fate or piece of bad luck was particularly painful to Pie Traynor, Jewel Ens, Johnny Gooch, Bill Hinchman, and Paul Waner. These men, as the manager, two of the coaches, one of the scouts, and the starting right fielder of the 1938 Pirates, respectively, were part of a team that failed to maintain the seven-game lead that it had on September 1 and ended up in second place, two games behind the Chicago Cubs.[190] Though what made the outcome even harder to accept for the Buccos and their fans was that the '38 team still held a two-game lead at the end of play on September 25 but then proceeded to lose six of its last seven games to bring back unpleasant memories of other Pirate collapses.[191]

Nor did the players on the '26 team who did not come back in '27 fare any better. Of the nine men who were part of the Pirate crew in 1926 but either were let go during that season or did not win a spot on the 1927 roster—not including Adams, Bigbee, and Carey, whose post–1926 lives have already been dealt with—none of them would wear the uniform of a major league championship team during any succeeding years.[192]

Of course, this is not to say that what lay in store for the remaining members of the '26 Pirates or former '26 Pirates was dismal or unfulfilling. Besides Carey, Joe Cronin, Kiki Cuyler, Pie Traynor, and Paul Waner all had Hall of Fame playing careers, with Cronin being elected to the Cooperstown shrine in 1956, Cuyler posthumously in 1968, Traynor in 1948, and Waner in 1952. Cronin would also become the player-manager of the Washington Senators, leading his 1933 team to the American League pennant; the player-manager, then bench manager, and finally general manager of the Boston Red Sox, capturing the AL pennant in 1946; and eventually the president of the American League.[193] Cuyler followed his playing days in the majors by becoming a minor league manager for Chattanooga and Atlanta of the Southern Association and a coach for the Chicago Cubs and the Boston Red Sox.[194] Traynor and Waner spent all (Traynor) or over two-thirds (Waner) of their remaining seasons with the Pirates, with Traynor serving as the Corsairs' player-manager in 1934, 1935, and 1937 and as their bench manager in 1936, 1938, and 1939. Subsequently, he was one of their scouts from 1939 through 1942[195] and again between 1947 and his death in 1972 (though he did less and less scouting as the years went on) and a guest instructor at their spring training camps from 1957 until his death.[196]

Waner did no managing in the majors or scouting, but he was the player-manager and part-owner of the Miami Sun Sox of the Florida International League in 1946.[197] More importantly, he became a hitting instructor for various major league clubs and their minor league affiliates, especially for the Milwaukee Brave organization, and helped to revolutionize the teaching of batting skills.[198] As Clifton Blue Parker wrote:

> So Paul began a second career—as a hitting coach. He would be one of the first such specialists in major league baseball....
> Paul had a missionary zeal about the role of batting instruction in the majors. As late as the 1950s, teams usually did not employ full-time hitting coaches. That began to change with the spreading of the gospel by Paul Waner and others. During the 1950s[,] he published a 34-page pamphlet on hitting, *Paul Waner's Batting Secrets*....
> In his booklet, Waner summarized the gospel of hitting according to Big Poison[.][199]

At the opposite end of the spectrum were seven team members who ended or virtually ended their major league playing careers during the '26 season. In addition to Bigbee, whose final big league game was August 7, and Adams, whose last one was August 11, Tom Sheehan, Bud Culloton, Red Oldham, Eddie Murphy, Johnny Rawlings, and Walter Mueller would not return to the majors in a playing capacity after 1926, and Stuffy McInnis would appear in only one major league game once he left the Pirates. However, even with most of these men, their time in professional baseball was not yet over. With the exception of Culloton, who got his law degree from the Fordham University School of Law in 1928 and eventually became a judge,[200] all of these former Buccaneers played one or more seasons in the minors. Also, Sheehan had a lengthy career as a major league coach and scout, a minor league manager, and, for several months in 1960, the skipper of the San Francisco Giants.[201] And McInnis served as the player-manager of the Philadelphia Phillies in 1927 and of the Salem Witches of the New England League in 1928 and then was the head baseball coach at Norwich University, Brooks School, Amherst College, and Harvard University.[202]

Between these two extremes—Hall of Fame playing careers and no more major league playing careers—was everyone else. Performing in all or part of one to 10 seasons in the majors and two to 12 seasons in the minors after the '26 season, these men attained varying degrees of post–1926 success. None would ever be called superstars, though some—Bush, Grantham, Kremer, Meadows, Smith, and Wright—did receive token support in one or more National Baseball Hall of Fame elections. Wright in particular was honored in such a fashion, being nominated on at least one ballot for 12 years between 1948 and 1962. But the most votes he ever got, which were the most votes that any member of this subgroup received, were 18 in 1960, the year that the Pirates won their next World Series championship.[203] Of course, if Wright had not suffered the injuries that he did, he might have put up the numbers to be enshrined in Cooperstown. Besides the mishaps he sustained during the '26 season, Wright was plagued with weak ankles, experienced a severe beaning in 1927, and separated his shoulder playing handball during the offseason between the '28 and '29 seasons, and all these misfortunes took their toll on both his body and his playing time.[204]

Wright was also part of a subgroup of this group who managed in the minors.[205] The others were Joe Bush, Johnny Gooch, Lee Meadows, Hal Rhyne, Earl Smith, Emil Yde, and, surprisingly, Eddie Moore.[206] In addition, Wright was a scout for the Boston Red Sox,[207] while Gooch served as a coach for the Buccos for three seasons under his good friend Pie Traynor before being a Pirate scout for over a year.[208]

As for the coaches and scouts, Jewel Ens spent the rest of his life in Organized Baseball, coaching for Pittsburgh, Detroit, Cincinnati, and the Boston Braves, scouting for Cincinnati, managing minor league teams in the Cincinnati organization and winning three league championships with them, and even managing the Pirates for more than two seasons.[209] For his efforts, he was inducted into the International League Hall of Fame in 1950, and that same year, he received one vote for election into the National Baseball Hall of Fame.[210]

Jack Onslow was released by the Pirates in November of 1926 and accepted a job as a coach with the Washington Senators for the 1927 season.[211] Then, for 21 of the next 33 years, he coached for the St. Louis Cardinals, the Philadelphia Phillies, and the Boston Red Sox, managed Hartford, Waterloo—winning the league championship there in 1947—Memphis, Chattanooga, and the Chicago White Sox, and scouted for the Bosox.[212]

Like Ens and Onslow, Chick Fraser and Bill Hinchman were baseball lifers. Fraser continued to scout for the Pirates until he was released at the end of the 1930 season, managed Peoria in 1931, and then was a scout for the Dodgers and later the Yankees.[213] Hinchman remained a scout for the Pittsburgh club until 1958 or 1959, depending on the source.[214]

On the other hand, like McKechnie, Clarke, and the ABC trio, there was life after Organized Baseball for some of the rest of the '26 Bucs.[215] For example:

- Vic Aldridge and, as mentioned earlier in this chapter, Bud Culloton earned law degrees, with Aldridge becoming a state senator in Indiana[216] and Culloton a judge in Kingston, New York, and the deputy commissioner of Motor Vehicles and chief administrative officer of the New York State Department of Taxation and Finance.[217]

- Clyde Barnhart found employment as a press operator for a rubber manufacturer[218] and then got a job with the Maryland Correctional Institution.[219]

- Fred Brickell became a meter repairman for the Wichita water plant[220] before being a sales manager for a wholesale tobacco company.[221]

- Joe Bush held various jobs, including working for what is believed to be a bituminous coal company, being a timekeeper in a Philadelphia shipyard, having a position with the Bureau of Recreation in Philadelphia, and clerking at racetracks in New Jersey and Florida.[222]

- Adam Comorosky ran a store in Swoyersville, Pennsylvania.[223]

- Johnny Gooch operated the Gooch Manufacturing Company in Nashville, Tennessee, which produced baseball bats, and then became the owner and president of the Gooch Lamp Company, which was located in Brentwood, a suburb of Nashville.[224]

- George Grantham managed the menswear department of the Commercial Clothing Store in Kingman, Arizona, a store that he was part owner of.[225]

- Carmen Hill got a job as merchant policeman[226]—something that the author of his obituary in *The Sporting News* called a safety inspector[227]—for the General Motors plant in Indianapolis, Indiana.

- Lou Koupal began a career as a carpenter.[228]

- Ray Kremer delivered mail for the United States Post Office Department in Berkeley and the Bay area in California.[229]

- Roy Mahaffey managed a petroleum station[230] and then worked as a brick mason.[231]

- Lee Meadows became a deputy clerk for the Internal Revenue Service.[232]

- Walter Mueller went back to being a hauling contractor.[233]

- Eddie Murphy supervised the recreation division of the Works Progress Administration (renamed the Work Projects Administration in 1939) in

Lackawanna County, Pennsylvania, held a job with the Grumman Aircraft Engineering Corporation, and, during World War II, served with the United Services Organizations Inc.[234]

- Chet Nichols found employment as a laborer with Slater Dyer Works, Inc., in Pawtucket, Rhode Island.[235]
- Red Oldham became a retail salesman for menswear[236] and then got a job as a security officer for the Lockheed Corporation in California,[237] whereas Hal Rhyne got a job as a guard at Folsom Prison, also in California.[238]
- Johnny Rawlings sold insurance,[239] clerked for a wholesale produce company,[240] managed the Grand Rapids Chicks and the Rockford Peaches of the AAGPBL,[241] and worked in the ticket department at the Los Angeles Sports Center.[242]
- Don Songer owned and operated Billy-Don's restaurant in Kansas City, Missouri.[243]
- Pie Traynor started a new career as a radio and television personality in Pittsburgh[244] following employment as a car salesman—which overlapped with the last third of his first stint as a scout—and as a lathe operator who made parts for airplanes.[245] In addition, he spent about 18 months as the recreation supervisor for the Parks Department of Allegheny County.[246] Of course, since Traynor was serving as a scout for the Pirates during much of his time as a local media star, this was not exactly life after Organized Baseball. But as James Forr has noted, "Traynor's responsibilities were light; he ran tryout camps and baseball schools, and represented the team at public events."[247]

Many Pittsburghers who were alive in the 1960s may not recognize the young Pie Traynor, but they probably do remember the older Pie as the spokesperson for the American Heating Company ads that were shown during *Studio Wrestling* on WIIC-TV (National Baseball Hall of Fame Library, Cooperstown, New York).

- Emil Yde became the manager of a fruit packing house[248] and then a real estate investor.[249]

By January 2, 1990, the 1926 Pirates no longer existed, with Carmen Hill, the "last man standing," dying on New Year's Day. The first to go was Chick Fraser, who passed away in 1940, the victim of a blood disease which claimed the lower part of his right leg before taking his life.[250] Other early departures were Jewel Ens and Kiki Cuyler in 1950, Adam Comorosky in 1951, and George Grantham in 1954.

However, it was the 1960s that were particularly cruel to the team, with 19 members dying during that decade, including four of the five individuals involved in the ABC Affair: Fred Clarke (1960), Carson Bigbee (1964), Bill McKechnie (1965), and Babe Adams (1968).[251] Max Carey would join them in 1976, as a total of 11 members would exit this world by the end of the '70s,[252] leaving only Clyde Barnhart, Joe Cronin, Carmen Hill, Chet Nichols, Tom Sheehan, and Glenn Wright. Of those six, all but Hill died during the first half of the '80s, with Cronin following Wright as he had done as a rookie.[253] Wright told Eugene Murdock that when Cronin joined the Bucs in 1926, he "followed me around like a little dog."[254] Wherever Wright went, Cronin went. Of course, Wright did not know it at the time, but Cronin was purposely shadowing him because he was trying to keep the star shortstop from drinking alcohol.[255] Later the roles would be reversed,[256] but in 1984 they ended the way they had begun, with Wright giving up the ghost in April and Cronin following him in September.

Six

Making Sense of It All

> Much of what we do in life requires a willingness to reconsider our narratives, our understandings based on new evidence, and new ways of thinking.
> —James Grossman, 2014

The 1926 Pirates were gone, but a number of questions about them remain. *First, when all the rhetoric is stripped away, can the Bucs' inability to defend their National League title be explained statistically?* This question is best answered by looking at the same statistical criteria that was used to examine the 1921–1925 seasons:

- Comparing Pittsburgh's various won-lost records (e.g., home, away, and in one-run games) with its leading competitors—in this case, St. Louis and Cincinnati

- Comparing Pittsburgh's, St. Louis,' and Cincinnati's won-lost records against each other and against the other teams in the NL

- And comparing other select statistics (e.g., runs scored, adjusted ERA, and fielding wins) for the three teams

To begin, as can be seen from Table 35, the Pirates had higher home and one-run won-lost percentages than the NL champion Cardinals and played over .620 ball against the losing teams in their league but did not fare well on the road or against the league's stronger teams. Nor did they lead the league in any of the chosen categories, as did the Cardinals and the Reds.

However, the most telling stats were expected won-lost record and projected won-lost record, which, when compared to the actual won-lost record, show the Pirates to have performed as well as they were expected to and five and a half games better than they were projected to. This means that whether

Table 35: The Won-Lost Records of the 1926 St. Louis Cardinals, Cincinnati Reds, and Pittsburgh Pirates[1]

Team	Won-Lost Record	Home Won-Lost Record	Away Won-Lost Record	Won-Lost Record in One-Run Games	Won-Lost Record Against Teams That Were .500 or Better	Won-Lost Record Against Teams That Were Under .500	Expected Won-Lost Record	Projected Won-Lost Record
St. Louis	**89-65**	47-30	42-35	19-23	32-34	**57-31**	**90-64**	85.5-68.5
Cincinnati	87-67	**53-23**	34-44	**26-18**	**36-30**	51-37	87-67	**89.6-64.4**
Pittsburgh	84-69	49-28	35-41	22-18	30-36	54-33	84-69	78.5-74.5

Or if these numbers were converted to percentages, the results would be as follows:

Team	Won-Lost Percentage	Home Won-Lost Percentage	Away Won-Lost Percentage	Won-Lost Percentage in One-Run Games	Won-Lost Percentage Against Teams That Were .500 or Better	Won-Lost Percentage Against Teams That Were Under .500	Expected Won-Lost Percentage	Projected Won-Lost Percentage
St. Louis	**.578**	.610	**.545**	.452	.485	**.648**	**.584**	.555
Cincinnati	.565	**.697**	.436	**.591**	**.545**	.580	.565	**.582**
Pittsburgh	.549	.636	.461	.550	.455	.621	.549	.513

League leaders are in boldface.

their anticipated won-lost record is based on the number of runs they scored and allowed or on their batting, pitching, and fielding, the Bucs performed at an equal or greater level than they should have—indicating that they played at a level reflective of their statistics or that they OVERACHIEVED. Pirate fans and Pittsburgh sportswriters may have viewed the Corsairs as a group of frustrating underachievers because of the high expectations that they had placed upon the team, but the statistics tell a different story. Plagued by illnesses and injuries, the best numbers the Buccaneer crew could put forth were not disappointing at all but, because of intangible factors and/or luck, rather commendable, considering the circumstances. In fact, depending on what system is preferred, it was St. Louis or Cincinnati that had underachieved.

Without knowing the final won-lost records and just looking at the other statistics found in Table 35, a reader would think that the Reds edged out the Cardinals for the NL championship. But the Reds' Achilles' heel was their away won-lost record, whereas the Redbirds did not do well in one-run games or games against the tougher teams in the league.

Turning to Table 36, it is evident that the Pirates had no problem handling their old nemesis New York, taking 16 out of 22 contests from McGraw's men. They also did well against their cross-state rivals, Philadelphia, and Wilbert Robinson's Brooklyn Robins. But they struggled against fourth-place Chicago and, surprisingly, sixth-place Boston, winning their seasonal series with both of those clubs by close margins. More significantly, they went 18–26 against St. Louis and Cincinnati.

Comparatively, the Cardinals lost their seasonal series to the Reds and split with the Cubs, but made up ground against the second-division clubs and held the crucial 13–9 edge over Pittsburgh. And keep in mind that the Pirates finished four and a half games out of first, so turning that 13–9 margin into an 11–11 standoff would have gone a long way in helping the Bucs to capture the National League flag.

The Reds were the oddest of the three teams under consideration. Coming within two games of catching the Cardinals, they lost three seasonal series, more than either St. Louis or Pittsburgh, and all three were to teams that ended up lower than them in the standings. But they won their series against the Cardinals and the Pirates. So, if they had taken some combination of three games more from the Cubs, the Giants, or the Braves, they would have been the senior circuit champs.

Table 37 reinforces the view that the Bucs were either fortunate or moved by some intangible factor or factors to have finished as high as they did, especially considering how bad their hitting and fielding stats were. In adjusted on-base plus slugging average, batting wins, and fielding wins, they were below average, and when their runs allowed is subtracted from their runs scored, they were only a +80, not much more than half a run per game to the good. Conversely, just the year before, the team had led the National League in the first two categories (108 and 5.8, respectively), as well as in runs scored (912) and run differential (197), with the latter equaling a robust 1.29 runs per game.

If taken a step further and examined at the individual level, much of this contrast can be attributed to the decline in the quality of offensive production by Clyde Barnhart, Max Carey, Eddie Moore, Stuffy McInnis, and, to a lesser extent, Johnny Gooch. But even one of the better performers, Kiki Cuyler, saw his batting average, on-base percentage, and slugging average drop from .357, .423, and .598 in 1925 to .321, .380, and .459, despite being the National League leader in stolen bases and runs scored.[2]

Of course, not all the Pittsburgh hitters were slumping that season. Paul Waner had a sensational rookie year. Putting his eye-hand coordination to great use, Waner led his league in triples, came in second in walks and runs scored, third in on-base percentage and slugging average, fourth in doubles, and fifth in batting average. Applying current means to evaluate his performance, Waner finished first in Wins Above Replacement for nonpitchers and third in WAR for all players who were National Leaguers, second in adjusted batting runs and adjusted batting wins in the NL, and fourth in adjusted on-base plus slugging average in his league.[3]

Table 37 also shows that even though Pittsburgh's pitching stats did not measure up to those of the previous season, it was pitching that was the strength of the team. What the table does not show, however, is that, in particular, Ray Kremer was superb. Leading the league in ERA, wins (tied with Lee Meadows and two others), and winning percent-

The ace of the Pirate pitching staff in 1926, Ray Kremer was the top hurler in the voting for the National League Award, coming in third behind St. Louis catcher Bob O'Farrell and Cincinnati second baseman Hughie Critz (National Baseball Hall of Fame Library, Cooperstown, New York).

age, coming in second in WHIP and saves (tied with one other), and fourth in shutouts, Kremer finished third in the NL most valuable player voting (i.e., the National League Award). In recent times, he was rated second to former Pirate pitcher Hal Carlson in WAR for the senior circuit. Other current statistical measurements have him first in adjusted ERA, adjusted pitching runs, and adjusted pitching wins for his league. In addition, the native Californian hit well for a hurler, batting .253, with 14 runs scored, 14 RBI, and even one homer.[4]

Of course, the pitching could have been even more effective if Alvin Crowder had been retained and/or Grover Cleveland Alexander had been acquired. But such was not the case.

As for fielding wins, the Pirates as a team left something to be desired, but interestingly enough, their score here was no worse than their score in 1925, indicating that slightly below average fielding in and of itself was not a factor in preventing the Bucs from capturing another pennant. In fact, several Pirates were among the top three in fielding in the NL for their respective positions. Smith was tied for third in putouts and third outright in double plays for catchers. Traynor was first in putouts, second in assists, first in double plays, and third in range factor for third basemen. Cuyler was tied for third in assists and second in double plays for left fielders.[5] And Waner was first in range factor and second in putouts and fielding percentage for right fielders. Furthermore, if outfield statistics are combined, Cuyler was second in putouts and third in range factor and Waner was tied for third in assists.[6]

Overall, four Pirates—Cuyler, Kremer, Smith, and Traynor—were good enough to make both *Baseball Magazine's* National League All-Star Team and its Major League All-America Team.[7] Also, Traynor was chosen as the top third baseman on *The Sporting News'* Major League All-Star Team.[8]

Returning to Table 37, it can be seen that of the three leading clubs battling it out for the National League pennant, it was Cincinnati, not St. Louis, that was the strongest. The Reds had better hitting, pitching, and fielding than the Cardinals and led the league in more positive categories than St. Louis did, though the Cards scored more runs and had a better run differential.

In conclusion, based strictly on statistics, it is a wonder that the Pirates finished third at all, again pointing the finger to intangibles and/or good fortune as their benefactors. This, of course, indicates quite the opposite of what Davis, Wollen, and other proponents of the theory that the major reason the Pirates did not win the pennant was because of intangibles—i.e., dissension caused by Fred Clarke's presence on the bench—and leads into the next question: *Did Dreyfuss' appointment of Clarke as assistant to the manager adversely affect the*

Table 36: The Won-Lost Records of the 1926 St. Louis Cardinals, Cincinnati Reds, and Pittsburgh Pirates Versus the Other Teams in the National League[9]

Team	Boston	Brooklyn	Chicago	Cincinnati	New York	Philadelphia	Pittsburgh	St. Louis
St. Louis	15–7	15–7	11–11	8–14	12–10	15–7	13–9	
Cincinnati	10–12	18–4	9–13		7–15	16–6	13–9	14–8
Pittsburgh	11–10	13–9	12–10	9–13	16–6	14–8		9–13

Table 37: Team Statistics for the 1926 St. Louis Cardinals, Cincinnati Reds, and Pittsburgh Pirates[10]

Team	Runs Scored	Runs Allowed	AOPS	AERA	Batting Wins	Pitching Wins	Fielding Wins	Number of Positive Categories That the Team Led the League In
St. Louis	817	678	107	106	4.7	3.5	0.3	9
Cincinnati	747	651	110	108	**6.9**	4.3	1.3	**15**
Pittsburgh	769	689	99	107	-1.2	4.1	-0.9	2

League leaders are in boldface.

performance of the Bucs, which, in turn, is reflected in the statistics that were just examined?

The major point to keep in mind in attempting to answer this question is that Clarke reboarded the Pirate ship not on Opening Day of the 1926 season, but rather on June 12 of the previous season. Also, because of his duties as assistant to the president—a position from which he was later elevated to vice president—and head of scouting, Clarke was not in uniform for every game that the Bucs played during his second coming, and he certainly was not on the bench during Pittsburgh's second game of its doubleheader with Boston on August 7 or its three-game series with Brooklyn on August 9, 10, and 11. But for the sake of argument, if all the games from his arrival until his departure are considered, including the seven-game World Series against Washington, the Pirates won slightly more than 59 percent of their matches—a percentage that would have captured National League pennants in both 1925 and 1926—with them having a combined .649 record for regular-season and postseason play in '25.[11] In comparison, the Corsair teams of 1921–1924 had an average winning percentage of .573.[12]

Now, neither the job description for the assistant to the manager nor Clarke changed between 1925 and 1926, so if the Skipper McKechnie-First Mate Clarke arrangement not only worked but was also praised for being one of the key factors for the Pirates' great success in '25, why was it now being denigrated for being such a terrible idea? The answer here is simple: because the Pirates equaled or exceeded what was expected of them in 1925, but they did not live up to expectations in 1926, and something or someone or both had to be blamed for this disappointment. In this case, it was both, with the something being the manager-assistant-to-the-manager system that Dreyfuss had instituted and the someone being Fred Clarke.

In reality, Dreyfuss was ahead of his time. By establishing Clarke as assistant to the manager, he was one of the first to use what is today called a "bench coach"—something that has gone unnoticed by most baseball historians. In an article published in the August 19, 2012, issue of the *New York Times*, Stuart Miller wrote:

> Through much of baseball history, the manager was seen as a solitary figure, making decisions without help. These days, though, many are pictured as attached at the hip to their bench coaches, who ponder every possible situation, evaluate statistics, time a pitcher's speed to the plate, shift infielders, keep role players informed and offer tactical ideas.
>
> "They're not just making suggestions; that's not really the right word," said Houston Astros Manager Brad Mills, who was a bench coach in Montreal in 2003 and in Boston from 2004 to 2009. "It's a constant conversation, a flow."[13]

Miller reveals in the article that, like what Clarke was accused of doing, bench coaches will disagree with their managers and suggest different options that the manager may not have thought of. He cites several examples of this:

- "[Joe] Torre had been a conservative manager, and he credited [his bench coach Don] Zimmer with pushing him to be more aggressive."
- Terry Francona saying that one of the prerequisites for anyone who's going to be his bench coach is, "You need to have a big enough voice and a strong enough personality to stand up to me and tell me when I'm wrong."
- And Dave Martinez discussing his role as bench coach for Joe Maddon. "Joe liked that I could see things before they happened, but he also wanted someone who was opinionated.... And I always ask Joe why whenever he makes or doesn't make a move."[14]

Dreyfuss was also a trailblazer in pairing an older, more experienced assistant to the manager/bench coach with a younger, less experienced manager. Another owner to do the same thing was Cleveland's Bill Veeck, who in the late 1940s ironically appointed Bill McKechnie as the right-hand man in the dugout to the 29-year-old Lou Boudreau. Although referred to by some later writers as Boudreau's pitching coach, McKechnie was actually Boudreau's chief lieutenant, with Mel Harder being the official pitching coach for most of the time that Wilkinsburg Will was with the Tribe. The former Pirate leader was now placed into a similar situation that Clarke had been placed into during the mid-1920s, but he did not turn down the job or tell Veeck that such a plan could not work. Instead, he made it clear that he was not after Boudreau's position and then proceeded to do his part to help the Indians win the American League pennant and the World Series championship in 1948. Of course, despite what McKechnie said about his role, baseball journalist Bob Bloss writes that Boudreau's "assistant manager" "was widely, but unofficially, credited with 'managing' yet [another] pennant winner,"[15] much in the same way that Clarke was praised after the 1925 season.

Over 30 years later, Veeck would repeat himself by choosing veteran minor league manager Loren Babe to be Tony La Russa's bench coach, when the latter was the rookie pilot of the Chicago White Sox.[16] Other times, managers themselves would bring in someone who they valued to be their bench coaches, with Walt Alston choosing Pete Reiser, Billy Martin choosing Yogi Berra, and Joe Torre choosing Don Zimmer as prime examples of this practice.[17]

However, Dreyfuss was not the only one ahead of his time. John McGraw had hired Christy Mathewson as assistant manager of the Giants in 1919,[18] and when Mathewson was diagnosed with tuberculosis in 1920, McGraw brought in his old friend Hugh Jennings to be his assistant manager for the next five seasons before Jennings also became afflicted with TB.[19] For all intents and purposes, Bill Killefer was Rogers Hornsby's assistant manager as well as his pitching coach on the 1926 Cardinals and was referred to as such,[20] and Earle Mack held the position for his father's Philadelphia Athletics for a number of years.[21]

All told, the examples given in the previous paragraph helped to produce eight pennant winners. Thus, despite what the naysayers said, the system worked, and based on the results that the Pirates had in 1925, Clarke did not adversely affect the Pirates' performance as exhibited in the team's batting and pitching statistics. *But what then caused the drop-off in those statistics?*

The answer here appears to be the pairing of two factors—illnesses and injuries and the inability of most of the replacement players to perform at a pennant-winning level—with high expectations likely being another culprit. When it comes to illnesses and injuries, there can be no question that they took their toll on what could have been an unstoppable Pirate team. At one time or another during the '26 preseason and season, a countless number of Bucs suffered maladies and mishaps, as shown in the previous three chapters. The most significant of these casualties, based on importance of the player and/or extent of the illness or injury, were, in alphabetical order, Vic Aldridge, Max Carey, Ray Kremer, Eddie Moore, Johnny Morrison, Hal Rhyne, Don Songer, and Glenn Wright. Kremer recovered nicely to have the second best season of his career, but the others were not so fortunate. And of those others, five of them, in addition to Kremer, were mainstays for the '25 club. The two that were not—Rhyne and Songer—were a highly touted rookie and a pitcher who was having a productive season before he got hurt.

Another mainstay from 1925 whose '26 performance seems to have been severely affected by an injury was Clyde Barnhart. As

Clyde Barnhart: How serious was the injury to his elbow (Library of Congress, George Grantham Bain Collection, LC-DIG-ggbain-38569)?

described in the third chapter of this book, Barnhart had been hit so hard on the right elbow by a Phil Morrison pitch during spring training that it was feared that his arm had been fractured. The official report after the elbow was x-rayed said that the damage was a bad bruise, but over 53 years later, Barnhart's wife told Eugene Murdock that she thought that 1926 was the year that her husband had broken his elbow,[22] and though this might have been an exaggeration or the muddled recollections of an old woman, two pieces of evidence suggest otherwise. First, Chilly Doyle's account of the injury states that "a minute after the impact of the ball[,] there arose on Barney's arm a lump as big as a doorknob and he suffered intensely."[23] Doyle went further to say, "Barnhart had trouble moving his arm shortly after it was struck."[24] These words imply that what had happened was more than a bad bruise. And second, Barnhart's subsequent batting stats support this assessment. A lifetime .295 hitter who had batted .325 in 1925, with a .391 on-base percentage and 114 runs driven in, the quiet Pennsylvanian could not raise his batting average above .205 at any time during the '26 season and finished at .192, with a .278 on-base percentage and only 10 runs driven in. It is known today that the injury that Eddie Moore had sustained in '26 had been misdiagnosed, and the same thing could have happened to Barnhart's injury. Further support of this theory is that Barnhart regained his batting stroke in 1927, hitting .319, with a .384 on-base percentage, and 54 RBI in 108 games, mostly from the second and sixth slots in the batting order.[25]

Besides Barnhart, the mishap that befell Tom Sheehan in April of '26—also described in the third chapter of this book—possibly led to his later poor performances and eventual release, while other Bucs suffered less debilitating, though frustrating, medical problems. Thus, McKechnie was hard-pressed to field a consistent starting nine.

Of course, if the bench support had been more effective and/or if a greater number of acquisitions procured during the season had performed better, the team's final won-lost record may have improved. Perhaps the best way of assessing this matter is to use the Wins Above Replacement statistical category found at Baseball-Reference.com. Here, simply put, a score of 0.0 is average, with anything above it being above average and anything below it being below average. Well, the 20 men who would be considered reserves for the Pirates—pitchers with less than 100 innings pitched and nonpitchers who did not play the most games at their particular positions—totaled a score of -2.9, with 13 of them having below average marks.[26]

Unfortunately, it is impossible to quantify the stress created by the high expectations placed upon the team, and obviously this stress would vary from player to player, but it would be naive to think that there was not some level of pressure present which may have caused the team to try too hard. Such pressure may have been exacerbated by the illness-injury situation and could have contributed to the team as a whole not performing as well as it did in 1925.

But if this is true, what then brought about the ABC Affair and what effect did the affair have on the Pirates' performance? The ABC Affair was brought about by a number of factors, which, when combined, produced the baseball equivalent of a perfect storm. None of these factors in and of itself was particularly deadly, but when each of them intersected with the others in August of 1926, they created a series of incidents which swallowed up all the major participants. To fully understand this personal catastrophe, it is necessary to look at the factors individually, of which there were six:

- *The changing generational and educational environment on the 1925 and 1926 Pirate teams that Fred Clarke encountered after his return to the Pittsburgh club.* As described in detail in the second chapter of this book, there were two problematic issues regarding Clarke and many of the other Buccaneers: differences in attitude between members of an idealist generation and those of a reactionary one and educational differences.

To reiterate, Clarke came from an idealist generation, a type of generation which has among its common traits being principled, resolute, and ruthless. Just as importantly, in general, idealists have a vision based upon their set of values of how things should be and, if in a position of power, will attempt to enforce that ideal. Of course, as emphasized in the second chapter, not every person who belongs to an idealist generation is a clone. Genes, birth order, environmental factors, and personal experiences will shape an individual's personality and there are nonconformists in all generations. However, in the case of Clarke, he was no exception to the traits just mentioned.

On the other hand, as can be seen in Table 38, 80 percent of all players on the active roster of the 1926 Pirates and 83 percent of the men on the team when the ABC Affair occurred came from a reactive generation,[27] a type of generation known for being savvy, practical, and unfeeling, among other things, and for placing emphasis on liberty, survival, and honor. Reactives in general are not fond of idealists and would be reluctant to accept the vision and advice that an idealist would thrust upon them, especially if they felt that it opposed or limited what they wanted to do. Thus, with such a difference between a superior and his subordinates, it is a wonder that there were not more clashes and/or that there were not more men who voted against Clarke. That there were not implies that Clarke may have gotten along better with more members of the team than his opponents would like to admit.

But turning to the clash that did occur, it is evident that Clarke had his vision of how the team should operate and could be resolute and ruthless in trying to enforce that vision. Conversely, Carey and Bigbee—both reactives—viewed themselves as being savvy and practical in their attempt to remove Clarke from the Pittsburgh bench and were being unfeeling at the same time. Their reaction to the Pirate authorities getting rid of them was a fight to defend their liberty and honor as well as to survive as paid employees in the major leagues.

Furthermore, it is interesting to note that the Bucs who had been disciplinary problems before the ABC Affair had occurred—Yde, Moore, Aldridge, and Morrison—were all reactives, as were the two players who were suspected of joining Adams, Bigbee, and Carey in voting against Clarke: Grantham and Cuyler.

Table 38: Generational Types of the Players on the 1926 Pittsburgh Pirate Active Roster*[28]

Type	Entire Season**	On August 7**
Idealist	3%	4%
Reactive	80%	83%
Civic	17%	13%
Adaptive	0%	0%

* Percentages have been rounded and may not equal 100 percent.
** Players had to have performed in at least one game.

As for education, Clarke went no further than the eighth grade, but as Table 39 shows, 43 percent of all players on the active roster of the '26 Pirates and 50 percent of the men on the team when the ABC Affair happened had been exposed to some form of higher education,[29] while 43 percent and 38 percent, respectively, had at least attended high school.[30] Again as described in the second chapter of this book, Clarke had managed some college men when he had been the skipper of the Pirate ship, but the majority of the men under his command had elementary school or high school educations. Now he was faced with a new type of player who would not be as accepting of Clarke's old school methods and direct approach to dispensing advice. For example, when Glenn Wright, someone extremely loyal to Clarke and one who called him "a great man," was asked about problems on the '26 team, he replied, "Some of the fellows resented [Clarke's] advice because when Fred told you something, he just ... told it like [Rogers] Hornsby would: right straight out."[31] Hornsby, a tremendous right-handed hitter and the man who led the '26 Cardinals to the World Series championship, was not noted for his tact, and neither was Clarke. For that matter, when Clarke was defending himself against the attack launched in the September 30 issue of the *Press*, he argued that at the Heydler hearing, "Carey said nothing then about anything [involving me] other than I had been hollering at players and they did not like it."[32]

The epitome of this new ballplayer was Carson Bigbee. A reactive who was the son of schoolteachers, he had attended the University of Oregon where he was pursuing a degree in medicine. And as described earlier in this book, it was Bigbee who was bothered enough by Clarke's comment about replacing Carey that he shared Clarke's words with the Pirate captain, and from all available evidence, it was Bigbee who came up with the idea of how to remove Clarke from the Bucs' bench.

Table 39: Highest Level of Education of the Players on the 1926 Pittsburgh Pirate Active Roster*[33]

Level	Entire Season**	On August 7**
Seminary	3%	4%
College or University	29%	29%
Normal School	11%	17%
High School	43%	38%
Eighth Grade	9%	8%
Sixth Grade	3%	0%
Elementary School	3%	4%

*Percentages have been rounded and may not equal 100 percent.
**Players had to have performed in at least one game.

Regional origins and social backgrounds probably played less of a divisive role. As Table 40 highlights, the plurality of the players came from the Midwest, as did Clarke. Similarly, as shown by Table 41, the plurality of players came from multiple social levels, though not shown is that all of them had been part of the working and/or farming class at one time, just like Clarke, the son of a blacksmith-farmer. Another 26 percent and 21 percent were raised only on farms, whereas 20 percent and 25 percent grew up solely in working class families. So, Clarke should have been able to relate to these men and vice versa. But it is possible that some of the players were envious of Clarke's wealth and may have resented him because of it. When Clarke was managing the Pirates from 1900 through 1915, he was acquiring land at 160 acres per year, a process which eventually led to a total of 1,320 acres, making him a very rich man. But it was not until 1917, the year after oil was discovered on his land and two years after he retired from managing, that he became a millionaire and was elevated to an even higher social and economic status.

Table 40: Regional Origins of the Players on the 1926 Pittsburgh Pirate Active Roster*[34]

Region	Entire Season**	On August 7**
Northeast	20%	17%
Southeast	20%	21%
Midwest	34%	33%
Southwest	3%	4%
West Coast	11%	17%
Multiple	11%	8%

*Percentages have been rounded and may not equal 100 percent.
**Players had to have performed in at least one game.

Table 41: Social Backgrounds of the Players on the 1926 Pittsburgh Pirate Active Roster*[35]

Background	Entire Season**	On August 7**
Upper Class	0%	0%
Middle Class	20%	17%
Working Class	20%	25%
Farming Class	26%	21%
Multiple	34%	38%

*Percentages have been rounded and may not equal 100 percent.
**Players had to have performed in at least one game.

The odd man out in these matters was Babe Adams. Born in the last year of Clarke's generation and having no postsecondary education, Adams was a calm fellow who, according to Art McKennan, had a pulse rate of 58.[36] Also, like Clarke, he was from the Midwest and a farming family. So, why was he involved with the movement against Clarke? The answer to this question leads into the second factor:

- *The state of mind of Adams, Bigbee, and Carey on August 7.* Since to this author's knowledge, none of these men left a written record of his feelings at the time of the incident, it is impossible to determine exactly what went through the minds of the ABC trio on that fateful day in August. But what is known is that Adams and Carey had played under Clarke and that Clarke had been more than supportive of them. As described earlier in this book, it was Clarke who launched their major league careers and whose confidence in their ability helped to turn the duo into beloved sports stars for the Pittsburgh fans. True, they had to perform well to achieve the level of success that they did, but without being given the opportunity to perform, they would never have been able to show their stuff. They, in turn, gave Clarke the perception that they were his friends as well as his loyal subordinates. Adams was known to have been an admirer of Clarke.[37] Carey, along with Bigbee, Traynor, and Yde, went duck hunting on the Little Pirate Ranch in November of 1924, and while there, he and his teammates were "royally entertained at Clarke's residence" and given a tour of Winfield.[38] And even as late as August 13 of 1926, Carey said that "[Fred Clarke] and I are good friends."[39] So, if there were problems with Clarke, why did Adams and Carey not approach their former benefactor and someone who they supposedly thought well of rather than attempting to organize a meeting of players to rid him of a position that he was assigned to and complaining about him behind his back to McKechnie? What made them take such drastic steps? Were they afraid of Clarke? Or was there something else going on?

Perhaps the answer lies in where Adams, Bigbee, and Carey were in their lives in 1926. All three men were former stars—Bigbee for just a few seasons, but still briefly a star—who were now in the last stages of their major league careers. Adams and Bigbee, Pirate starters for multiple seasons, had been relegated to only occasional appearances and to watching others get the attention and the accolades, and this may have caused them some frustration. Carey's situation was different but no less frustrating. The team captain of the Buccos and a World Series hero, Carey had one of his finest seasons in 1925. But 1926 was not 1925, and Carey had been troubled with respiratory and sinus problems and

Why did Babe Adams side with Bigbee and Carey (Library of Congress, George Grantham Bain Collection, LC-DIG-ggbain–36172)?

then could not extricate himself from a hitting rut that left him with a .222 batting average, a .288 on-base percentage, and a .296 slugging average.

All three men were also the senior members of the team. Combined they had 43 years of service with the Pittsburgh club, and they presumably viewed themselves as the voices of experience. McKechnie himself as a player, coach, and manager had the same number of seasons in a Pirate uniform as did Bigbee and seven and six seasons less than Adams and Carey, respectively. Moreover, leaving aside the three games that he had played for the Bucs in 1907, McKechnie's true rookie season was the year after Adams' and the year before Carey's.[40] Because of this, the trio may have viewed McKechnie more as a peer or a first among equals rather than a superior whom they had to defer to.

And all three men were proud individuals when it came to baseball, and rightly so. They each had performed well for their club over the years and expected to be treated in a manner that reflected their contributions.

But Clarke's arrival changed the environment for the ABC trio. The fiery ex-player-manager now had McKechnie's ear and his direct approach to doing things did not include massaging the egos of former stars or team elders. Clarke was an optimist, but he did not mince words, no matter whom he was dealing with. Nor was he a sentimentalist, which means that he probably was not adverse to the Pirates' attempts to waive Adams and Bigbee (twice) before the ABC Affair had occurred.[41] Exactly when the waivers had been obtained and how much Clarke may have had a hand in obtaining them has not been found by this author, but if the decision for either or both men was made after Clarke had come on board the Pirate ship, he may have been perceived as suggesting that course of action or at least supporting it. Also, his dispensing of advice may have been seen as annoying or interfering to three such veteran players as the ABC trio. That they tolerated Clarke until August 7 was in all likelihood because the team was winning ballgames. After great success in 1925 following Clarke's joining the team, the Bucs had weathered a storm of injuries, illnesses, and personnel issues to regain the top spot in the National League and to have a three-game lead going into their doubleheader on the 7th. But the straw that broke the camel's back was Clarke's comment to McKechnie that the Pirate skipper remove Carey and "put anyone, even a batboy[,] in." Once Carey had learned about the comment from Bigbee, the wounded old warhorse had had enough, and even though it seems that it was Bigbee's idea to call a players' meeting, Carey did nothing to dissuade him. Benefactor or no benefactor, friend or no friend, he refused to be treated in the manner that Clarke had suggested. He found Clarke's remark demeaning and he was going to put an end to what he viewed as an unwelcome guest in the dugout. Obviously, Bigbee and Adams were also disturbed by the remark and willing to assist Carey.

That the trio went to McKechnie rather confronting Clarke may have been because they viewed Deacon Bill as being one of them. Yes, he was their manager, but he had been their teammate and coach prior to taking the helm of the Pirate ship, and he, too, had served under Clarke as a player. They figured that he would sympathize with their plight, and that since he was known to be a players' manager—as opposed to Clarke, who believed, "To the men must come the realization that the manager knows more [about baseball] than they do, otherwise the cogs will never work well"[42]—he would agree with their plan. This trust in McKechnie would bring into play the third factor, which would only exacerbate the problem:

- *Bill McKechnie's personality.* McKechnie was a brilliant tactician who genuinely cared about his players, but his personality was ill-suited to handle the type of issue that the ABC trio dumped in his lap. No disciplinarian, he did not want to alienate the three most senior members of his team or any other members who may have sided with them, but he did not want to alienate Clarke either. Like Adams and Carey, McKechnie had received a chance to perform in the majors because of Clarke, and like Adams and Carey, he had played under Clarke. But unlike Adams and Carey, he was the one who had invited his former manager to sit on the bench. Thus, McKechnie was caught between a rock and a hard place, and if the evidence from all parties involved is pieced together, it appears that he tried to extricate himself by appeasing both the trio and Clarke.

It is conceivable to believe that when McKechnie was approached by Adams, Bigbee, Carey, and possibly Onslow, he initially acquiesced to their request to have a players' meeting. But then, after giving the subject more thought, he waffled, called off the meeting, and told the ABC trio that he had come up with a diplomatic way of getting Clarke to leave the bench. That his diplomatic way consisted of telling Clarke that the trio wanted him gone apparently was not enough to get Clarke to step down on his own—something that McKechnie may have secretly desired. However, when Clarke gave the Pirate skipper a golden opportunity to express his true feelings by asking him twice what he wanted Clarke to do, McKechnie's fear of alienating Clarke overcame him and he said nothing. Even discussing the predicament further did not help Deacon Bill to arrive at a solution that would keep everyone happy.

Nor did McKechnie's inconsistency between his words on August 9—that the Clarke problem was a dead issue—and his actions on August 10—giving in to Clarke's request that a secret ballot be held to determine where his assistant stood with the team—do anything but make the situation worse. For that matter, when Clarke misunderstood the nature of the meeting, McKechnie should have set him straight, but again it appears that the Pirate manager was attempting to be a pleaser rather than a leader.

Finally, according to Clarke, it was McKechnie who precipitated the next stage of the ABC Affair by "insist[ing] that [Clarke] come back to the bench and perform [his] usual duties."[43] In doing so, was McKechnie trying to put an end to the suspicion raised by Havey Boyle's article in the *Pittsburgh Chronicle Telegraph* on August 12 that something was amiss on the Pirate ship, or was he trying to undo the hurt that Clarke must have felt because of the trio's actions? Perhaps it was both, or perhaps he sincerely wanted Clarke's assistance in running the team, but whatever his reason or reasons, his urging opened the door for the fourth factor to come to the forefront:

- *Fred Clarke's personality.* The two biggest weapons wielded by Clarke's critics are both in the form of questions: Why did Clarke not step down on August 9 after McKechnie told him what the ABC trio had planned? And why did Clarke insist upon punishing the trio after learning that three-fourths of the team that voted on August 10 wanted him to remain on the bench? Or in other words, once Clarke knew that he had the upper hand, why did he not leave well enough alone?

The answer to these questions is the same: the nature of Clarke's personality. When Clarke was appointed assistant to the manager by Barney Dreyfuss, who requested that he sit next to McKechnie, he refused to do so until he received McKechnie's permission, something that the Pirate manager readily gave. This is why Clarke twice asked McKechnie, "What do you want me to do?" He was deferring to the man who had allowed him to sit on the bench to begin with. Based on what is known about Clarke, if McKechnie would have responded by recommending that his assistant stay out of the dugout, Clarke would have done so. For that matter, even though McKechnie offered no guidance whatsoever, Clarke still removed himself from the bench for the three-game series held against Brooklyn on August 9–11 and may have stayed away if McKechnie had not insisted that he return. In his role as assistant to the manager, Clarke saw himself as answerable to only Barney Dreyfuss and McKechnie, but he later admitted that if Adams, Bigbee, and Carey had told him when he confronted them in McKechnie's room on the 9th that the majority of the players no longer wanted him on the bench and dispensing advice, "[he] would have been off that bench from that minute on, regardless of McKechnie's stand."[44] But the trio said nothing, and not knowing exactly where he stood with the majority of the players, Clarke chose to take a quiet leave of absence from the Pirate dugout. Furthermore, it was the not knowing part that motivated him to ask McKechnie to conduct the secret-ballot vote on the 10th after he had misunderstood McKechnie's intention for calling the meeting. However, even armed with the news that 18 out of 24 team members had no objection to him being a bench coach, Clarke still stayed away until McKechnie urged him to come back.

It was at this time that Clarke let it be known that he would not return until the ABC trio was punished. Again, this was vintage Fred the Fearless. In his eyes, Adams, Bigbee, and Carey were disruptive forces who, instead of carrying out the orders of their superiors, were trying to dictate policy to their manager. He now knew that they did not have the backing of the majority of their teammates—at least based on the results of the vote taken on the 10th—and he was going to show them that the crew did not captain the ship.

As was discussed earlier in this book, Clarke did not choose the specific punishment for the trio, but he

If the problems between Fred Clarke and some of the Pirate players went back to 1925, as Babe Adams, Carson Bigbee, and Max Carey said they did, why did Bigbee wait until early August of 1926, when Barney Dreyfuss was in Europe, to attempt to call a players' meeting to remove Clarke from the Bucs' bench (Library of Congress, George Grantham Bain Collection, LC-DIG-ggbain–38566)?

did agree with it, and left to his own devices, he probably would have arrived at the same penalty. He was shrewd enough not to give the trio another opportunity to knife him in the back or to stir up trouble of some other sort. Thus for Clarke, it was never a matter of leaving well enough alone, it was a matter of removing the sources of dissension before they caused more divisiveness among their fellow players.

Turning up the heat to the previous four factors was something that was partially beyond the control of the people involved in the ABC Affair:

- *Pressure caused by a combination of high expectations and the inability to live up to them because of illnesses and injuries.* Not enough can be said about the effect that illnesses and injuries had on the 1926 Pirates. As the defending World Series champion and a team chosen by the majority of prognosticators and many Pittsburgh fans, not to mention Fred Clarke himself, to repeat as at least pennant winners, McKechnie's men had a lot of pressure placed upon them, and this pressure was increased exponentially by the maladies and mishaps that they had suffered. Though it is true that they were in first place on August 7, getting there had been a struggle—and the Reds and the Cardinals were not going away. This pressure had to have put the team on edge. And the force that pushed a few members (i.e., Bigbee and Carey) over the edge was the doubleheader shutout loss to Boston, at that time a seventh-place team with a 43–62 record.

The final factor was one that was not something that was present within the team, but rather just the opposite:

- *The absence of Barney Dreyfuss.* Could the presence of the Pirate owner have prevented the ABC Affair from occurring?

Obviously, the answer will never be known, but Dreyfuss himself apparently thought so when he told the Pittsburgh Umpires' Association on September 22 of 1926 that "he would have quieted the uprising 60 days sooner than [it] was settled."[45] It seems that Dreyfuss viewed the "uprising" settled with the announcement on August 13 that Adams and Bigbee had been released and Carey had been placed on waivers, which means that he believed that he would have taken care of the matter about the time that he left for Europe on June 10. This expression of self-confidence may very well have been more than just hubris. All the parties involved in the affair had a friendly relationship with the Pirate owner, who had known each man for a number of years. Dreyfuss was the one who had given Clarke the advice that set the young Louisville player on the course that led to his eventual induction into the National Baseball Hall of Fame. Dreyfuss was the one who had taken a chance on McKechnie by appointing him George Gibson's successor in 1922. Dreyfuss was the one who would later hire Carey to coach for the Pirates, despite supporting the decision to let him go in 1926.

And the fact that Dreyfuss had kept Adams and Bigbee on his payroll when no other major league team wanted them speaks for itself. So, Dreyfuss was the voice that all the parties would have listened to. However, the Pirate magnate's statement assumes that the ABC trio would have come to him with their concerns on June 10 or earlier—something that they, or at least Carey as the team captain, should have done if they felt that Clarke was interfering with the success of the team. But they did not. As Dreyfuss told the Pittsburgh sportswriters on August 31, "It was too bad that it had to happen at all, but if the players who objected to Clarke had anything on their chests[,] why couldn't they have waited until I got back and given every one [sic] a chance to have the whole thing straightened out when I was here."[46] Thus, see Dreyfuss before he left the country or wait until he returned. But Adams, Bigbee, and Carey did neither, and the question is why. It was not the position of the team at either time because, ironically, the Pirates had exactly the same winning percentage and led Cincinnati by almost the same number of percentage points on the day before Dreyfuss embarked on his vacation as on the day he walked down the gangplank to set foot again on American soil. At the close of play on June 9, the Bucs were in first place with a .587 winning percentage, while the Reds, in the words of the late, great sportscaster Bob Prince, were a gnat's eyelash behind them at .580. At the close of play on August 30, Pittsburgh was again in first place with a .587 winning percentage, while Cincinnati was then at .583. This means that in spite of all the personnel and personal upheavals that had happened during Dreyfuss' absence, very little had changed with respect to records. But it does not explain why the ABC trio did not approach Dreyfuss in April, May, or June or wait until the end of August. If Clarke's behavior was seriously affecting the harmony that existed among the Pirate players and/or undermining McKechnie's authority, surely one or more of the three senior members on the team should have approached Dreyfuss about the matter before June 10. Or if Clarke's behavior was annoying certain members of the team but not hurting the team's pennant chances, then why not wait until August 30 and discuss the matter with Dreyfuss at that time? Apparently it was neither, which suggests that if Dreyfuss had remained in Pittsburgh, Adams, Bigbee, and Carey would have kept their feelings to themselves, or if they had complained to McKechnie, they would not have planned to have a players' meeting to remove Clarke from the Pirate bench.

This scenario also suggests that Clarke was not an obstacle to the team's success and that Carey's overreaction to what Bigbee told him on August 7 was no more than an attempt to defend his status and his livelihood. In this quest, he was able to get his good friend Bigbee, fellow longtime veteran Adams, and three other team members to side with him, but these men did not speak for the team as whole.

Now, what about the second part of the question: what effect did the affair have on the Pirates' performance? In an article written by John Kieran that was published in the May 15, 1937, issue of the *New York Times*—an article that contains its share of errors—Pie Traynor is reported to have said to Kieran that because of the ABC Affair:

We'd lost our spirit, we had no zip. We slopped around and finished third when we had the best team in the league.

The players began to slump off individually—you never saw a great club melt away so fast.... [I]t only goes to show how a ball club [sic] that looks good for years can be wrecked in a season.[47]

Unfortunately for Traynor, if he did indeed make those comments, he appears to have been suffering from long-term memory loss. As shown earlier in this book, there was no sudden or complete collapse of the team immediately after Adams, Bigbee, and Carey had stopped wearing Pirate uniforms, something that might be expected of a club that had lost its spirit. Instead, the Buccos experienced a four-phase roller-coaster ride, going 10–4–1, 2–9, 7–4, and 4–7 between the time that the ABC trio walked the plank and the end of the season. And if they tired along the way, it was probably because they had to play 11 doubleheaders and 35 games in 26 days from August 18 through September 12. Furthermore, the absence of Wright, Songer, and Aldridge added to their frustrations and wore them down, as did the pressure applied by St. Louis and Cincinnati, teams that refused to go away. However, the brutal schedule, the injuries, and the opponents who would not let up would have been the same whether or not the ABC threesome had stayed. True, there were individual slumps, but like the team's play as a whole, these slumps did not begin immediately after the dismissal of Adams, Bigbee, and Carey. For example, George Grantham's batting, on-base, and slugging averages on August 18 were .332, .421, and .518, whereas as late as September 14, they were .337, .416, and .520, before dropping to .318, .401, and .490 for the season.[48] Or Emil Yde lowered his ERA from 3.64 on August 19 to 3.52 on September 6 before raising it to 3.67 on September 25.[49] Nor did everyone slump. Kremer and Waner, for example, did not. Finally, Traynor's or Kieran's ludicrous statements that "you never saw a great club melt away so fast" and that "it only goes to show how a ball club [sic] that looks good for years can be wrecked in a season," do nothing but demonstrate how quickly the 1927 Pirates had been forgotten. Returning over 65 percent of the players from the '26 team, including all its stars, the '27 Bucs went on to capture the National League pennant before losing the World Series to a legendary New York Yankee contingent. That the franchise did not win another pennant until 1960 had nothing to do with McKechnie, Clarke, Adams, Bigbee, or Carey, but rather with various problems beyond the scope of this book. So, the bottom line is that, contrary to the rhetoric provided by Ralph Davis, Lou Wollen, and certain other sportswriters, the ABC Affair, though hurtful and unsettling to the people directly involved in it, did not prevent the '26 Pirates from repeating as pennant winners.

But if this conclusion is correct, then why have various baseball historians bought into Davis et al.'s rhetoric and perpetuated the traditional tale of how Clarke's meddling brought about the affair, which in turn prevented a powerful Pirate team from claiming another National League flag and maybe even another World Series title? As with the previous question, there is no single answer here. But instead of a series of disparate factors coming together to form a perfect storm, the answer lies in the compounding effect of various connected factors.

The first of these factors was *the persistence of Ralph Davis,* who repeated in writing his version of why the '26 Pirates were not in the World Series every time that he could work it into one of his columns. Then, in spreading the gospel according Ralph, Davis was benefitted by three other factors:

- *The popularity of the Pittsburgh Press.* As was shown in note 61 of Chapter Four, based on circulation statistics of the five mainstream Pittsburgh newspapers in 1926, the *Press* was the most read, leading its top rival, the *Post,* 183,495 to 143,739 in weekday copies and 243,688 to 188,342 in Sunday ones. In comparison, the *Chronicle Telegraph* was third during weekdays (108,194 copies), but it had no Sunday edition; the *Gazette Times* was a close fourth during weekdays (101,574) but third overall because of its Sunday edition (150,443); and the *Sun* was dead last during weekdays (79,860) and, like the *Chronicle Telegraph,* it had no Sunday edition.[50] These numbers increase if the "pass-along rate" is considered. According to McInnis & Associates, a training firm specializing in newspaper advertising sales, the average number of readers of any copy of a newspaper will be two and a half times the circulation number.[51] So, weekday issues of the *Press* would have been read by approximately 458,737 people, while Sunday ones would have had a readership of 609,220.

- *Two pulpits to preach from.* If being the sports editor of the *Press* did not provide Davis with a large enough readership, he was also the Pittsburgh correspondent to *The Sporting News,* which gave him national exposure, something that the journalists who supported Clarke did not have.

- *The* Press *and* The Sporting News *have been digitized.* Even after death, Davis and his fellow *Press* scribe Lou Wollen have had the good fortune of having their writings digitized, making them easily accessible to researchers, who do not have to leave the comfort of their homes to view them. On the other hand, the *Post* and the *Sun,* papers favorable to Clarke, are not online, forcing researchers to ignore them if they do not choose to travel to Pittsburgh or order them through interlibrary loan. Of the remaining two mainstream Steel City papers, the *Gazette Times* has been digitized, but at the time this book was written, the *Chronicle Telegraph* had not.

The final factor is the nature of previous research on the issue or issues. A complete picture of the 1926 Pirates in general and the ABC Affair in particular cannot be painted without examining all five mainstream Pittsburgh papers. However, the ease of using the *Press* and *The Sporting News* coupled with the fact that the previous works that have dealt with the '26 Bucs and the ABC Affair have done so as part of a bigger story—e.g., a history of the Pirates or the biography of a particular player—has limited the range of sources examined. This is no slight to the authors of such works but simply an explanation of why a certain line of thinking persists. Obviously, if someone is writing the life of a player on the '26 Pittsburgh ballclub, he or she is not going to have the time to explore five newspapers and various other primary writings to compose what may occupy a small section of one chapter of a 300-page book. It would be far less tedious and complicated to read the online versions of the *Press* and *The Sporting News*, summarize Davis' and Wollen's accounts, and move on to the next topic. Or, at the very least, take most of his or her information from those two sources. And for some 21st-century writers, this is what has happened.

To show the continuing effect of what Davis and, to a lesser degree, Wollen wrote, the author of this book has examined seven relatively recent works that include the 1926 Pirates and the ABC Affair. All were published between 2010 and 2012. All of them were written by reputable authors, the majority of whom belong to the Society for American Baseball Research. All of them are documented to varying degrees. All of them are either biographies of members of the '26 Bucs or books on broader topics that take in the '26 Bucs. And when the sources cited in the endnotes that apply to their sections pertaining to the 1926 Pirate team are totaled, over 85 percent of them are found to have come from the *Pittsburgh Press* or *The Sporting News*. In comparison, slightly less than two percent of the same notes came from the *Pittsburgh Post* and none from any other Pittsburgh paper.

Other writers of the 20th or 21st centuries who deal with the '26 Pirates do not document their books and/or articles, but most of these publications also espouse some version of the traditional storyline, suggesting the influence of possibly the *Press*, though more likely that of *The Sporting News*, on their work.

It was the purpose of this book to show that the saga of the 1926 Pirates was much more complex than the traditional storyline and that Fred Clarke was not the villain who brought about the ruination of a great team. As James

Grossman, the executive director of the American Historical Association, has written, "Much of what we do in life requires a willingness to reconsider our narratives, our understandings based on new evidence, and new ways of thinking.... To think historically is to understand the nature and necessity of revisionism."[52] And though, ultimately, the overwhelming majority of readers will believe what they want to believe and ignore any efforts to convince them otherwise, it is the hope of this author that whoever reads this book will view the 1926 Pirates and the ABC Affair in a different light.

Key to the Abbreviations Used in the Appendices

A	Assists	PB	Passed Balls
AB	At Bats	PO	Putouts
BA	Batting Average	POS	Position
BB	Base on Balls or Walks	R	Runs
BFP	Batters Faced by the Pitcher	RBI	Runs Batted In
BK	Balks	RF	Right Field or Right Fielder
C	Catcher	RF-G	Games Played in Right Field
CF	Center Field or Center Fielder	RF/G	Range Factor per Game
CF-G	Games Played in Center Field	RS	Run Support
CG	Complete Games	SB	Stolen Bases
DP	Double Plays	SH	Sacrifice Hits
E	Errors	SHO	Shutouts
ER	Earned Runs	SLG	Slugging Average
ERA	Earned Run Average	SO	Strikeouts
FA	Fielding Average	SO/BB	Strikeouts Divided by Walks
G	Games	SS	Shortstop
GF	Games Finished	SV	Saves
GS	Games Started	T	Tied
H	Hits	TB	Total Bases
HBP	Number of Times Hit by a Pitch (for hitters); Hit Batsmen (for pitchers)	W	Wins
		WHIP	Walks Plus Hits Divided by Innings Pitched
HR	Home Runs	WP	Wild Pitches
IP	Innings Pitched	W%	Winning Percentage
L	Losses	1B	First Base or First Baseman
LF	Left Field or Left Fielder	2B	Second Base or Second Baseman (for positions); Doubles (for hitters)
LF-G	Games Played in Left Field		
NA	Not Applicable		
OBP	On-Base Percentage	3B	Third Base or Third Baseman (for positions); Triples (for hitters)
OF	Outfield or Outfielder		
P	Pitcher		
PA	Plate Appearances		

Appendix A

Biographical Information for the 1926 Pirates

The information for this appendix came from a variety of sources, including, among others, Eugene Murdock's interviews with Clyde Barnhart, Carmen Hill, Eddie Moore, Eddie Onslow, and Glenn Wright; e-mail exchanges and/or telephone conversations with personnel at academic institutions, relatives of some of the players and nonplayers, and residents of the localities where some of the players and nonplayers had lived; player files from the National Baseball Hall of Fame Library; the United States Federal Census records; draft registration cards; death certificates; book-length biographies of and/or biographical articles about some of the players and nonplayers; issues of *Baseball Magazine*, *The Sporting News*, and the major Pittsburgh newspapers; the player pages at www.baseball-reference.com; Strauss and Howe's *Generations: The History of America's Future, 1584 to 2069*; and Strauss and Howe's *The Fourth Turning: An American Prophecy*.

Nicknames are listed in alphabetical order. Some of them are less well-known sobriquets that were used by one or more teammates or sportswriters. For example, "Peanuts," "Big Semipro," and "Little Semipro" were what Earl Smith called Eddie Moore, Tom Sheehan, and Paul Waner, respectively.

The generation descriptors, which are based on year of birth, were created by the late historian, sociologist, and author William Strauss and the historian, economist, and demographer Neil Howe and are used in their books on generations. Strauss and Howe argue that there are four basic kinds of generations—idealist, reactive, civic, and adaptive—that have, with one exception, repeated themselves in cyclical fashion throughout American history. For more details, including the general traits of each type of generation, see the second and sixth chapters of this book.

Attendance does not necessarily mean graduation. For example, Pie Traynor went to Somerville High School for less than two months.

Players

Name	Charles Benjamin "Babe" or "Charley" ("Charlie") Adams
Year of Birth	1882
Type of Generation	Idealist
Place of Birth	According to his granddaughter, Libby Henderson, Adams was born in Moorefield, Indiana, but moved with his family first to Tipton, Indiana, when he was one year old, and then to Mount Moriah, Missouri, in March of 1898.
Social Background	His father was a farmer.
Academic Institution Attended Before 1926 that Provided the Highest Level of Education	Mount Moriah High School, Mount Moriah, Missouri

Name	Victor "The Hoosier Schoolmaster" or "Vic" Aldridge. According to his grandson, Victor Aldridge III, Aldridge "had no middle name. His mother's maiden name, Eddington, is sometimes mistakingly [sic] listed as his middle name, or 'E.' as a middle initial. It has been suggested that he, at times, used this middle initial because he felt it filled his name out."
Year of Birth	1893
Type of Generation	Reactive
Place of Birth	Indian Springs, Indiana, but he grew up in Cale, Indiana
Social Background	His father was a farmer who later worked in a handle factory and then became a self-employed handle maker.
Academic Institution Attended Before 1926 that Provided the Highest Level of Education	Central Normal College, Danville, Indiana

Name	Clyde Lee "Barney" ("Barnie") or "Pooch" Barnhart
Year of Birth	1895
Type of Generation	Reactive
Place of Birth	Buck Valley, Pennsylvania
Social Background	His father was a farmer.
Academic Institution Attended Before 1926 that Provided the Highest Level of Education	Cumberland Valley State Normal School, Shippensburg, Pennsylvania

Name	Carson Lee "Skeeter" Bigbee
Year of Birth	1895

Type of Generation	Reactive
Place of Birth	Depending on the source, Lebanon, Waterloo, or Sweet Home, Oregon. For example, Lebanon is written on Bigbee's 1917 draft registration card, but his 1919 passport application and his 1942 draft registration card say Waterloo, and his death certificate states Sweet Home.
Social Background	His parents were schoolteachers.
Academic Institution Attended Before 1926 that Provided the Highest Level of Education	University of Oregon, Eugene, Oregon

Name	George Frederick "Fred" Brickell
Year of Birth	Several sources say or imply 1907, but most sources say or imply 1906.
Type of Generation	Civic
Place of Birth	Saffordville, Kansas, but moved with his family to Emporia, Kansas, by January 19, 1920, and to Wichita, Kansas, by an unknown date in 1923
Social Background	His father was a farmer who became a county treasurer and then a hardware merchant.
Academic Institution Attended Before 1926 that Provided the Highest Level of Education	Wichita High School, Wichita, Kansas

Name	Leslie Ambrose "Bullet Joe" or "Joe" Bush
Year of Birth	1891, 1892, or 1893, depending on the source, though most sources say or imply 1892
Type of Generation	Reactive
Place of Birth	Gull River, Minnesota, but he grew up mostly in Brainerd, Minnesota
Social Background	His father was a railroad conductor.
Academic Institution Attended Before 1926 that Provided the Highest Level of Education	Brainerd High School, Brainerd, Minnesota

Name	Maximilian George "Max" or "Scoops" Carnarius (Carey). Sources vary as to the spelling of Carey's given first name. The most common spelling is "Maximilian," but the 1910 United States Federal Census records have "Maxmilian," while other sources have Maximillian or Maxmillian.
Year of Birth	1890
Type of Generation	Reactive
Place of Birth	Terre Haute, Indiana
Social Background	Two of Carey's biographers, John Bennett and

	Luther Spoehr, say that Carey's father was a contractor, an occupation that, according to Bennett, he had after he emigrated from Prussia to the United States in 1886. However, the Hamburg Passenger Lists, 1850–1934, the New York Passenger Lists, 1820–1957, and the 1900 United States Federal Census records list him as a plumber, a tinman, and a tinner, respectively.
Academic Institution Attended Before 1926 that Provided the Highest Level of Education	Concordia Seminary, St. Louis, Missouri

Name	Adam Anthony "Commy" or "The Polish Flier (Flyer)" Comorosky
Year of Birth	The standard baseball reference works and sites say 1904 or 1905 and Comorosky's death certificate says that he was born in 1904 and died at the age of 47. However, the month of Comorosky's birth was December and he died in March of 1951, which would indicate that his year of birth was 1903. Also, the 1920 United States Federal Census records state that he was 16 years old in January of 1920, thus supporting a 1903 birth year. As for Comorosky himself, he told his wife that the correct year was 1905.
Type of Generation	Civic
Place of Birth	Swoyersville, Pennsylvania
Social Background	His father was a coal miner. In an article published in the July 31, 1932, issue of the *Brooklyn Daily Eagle*, Harold Burr wrote that Comorosky's father was the chief of police of Swoyersville at that time, but the Swoyersville authorities have no record of him ever holding such a position. Nor did the author find any evidence to support Burr's statement.
Academic Institution Attended Before 1926 that Provided the Highest Level of Education	He had no formal schooling after the sixth grade, but the author did not find the name of the last school that he had attended. Two sources in Comorosky's player file in the National Baseball Hall of Fame Library say that Comorosky had been enrolled at Wyoming Seminary Prep School in Kingston, Pennsylvania. However, John Shafer, vice president of advancement at Wyoming Seminary, reviewed all his school's academic records and yearbooks from the mid-1910s through the mid-1920s and could not find any evidence that Comorosky had been a student at that institution.

Name	Joseph Edward "Joe" Cronin
Year of Birth	1906
Type of Generation	Civic
Place of Birth	San Francisco, California
Social Background	His father was a teamster.
Academic Institution Attended Before 1926 that Provided the Highest Level of Education	Mission High School, San Francisco, California; then transferred to Sacred Heart High School, San Francisco, California

Name	Bernard Aloysius "Bud" Culloton
Year of Birth	1896, 1897, or 1898, depending on the source, though almost all the primary sources that the author looked at say or imply 1897
Type of Generation	Reactive
Place of Birth	Kingston, New York
Social Background	His father was a grocer, but by June 1, 1905, Culloton, his mother, and some of his siblings were living with his maternal grandfather, who was the proprietor of a hotel. By June 1, 1915, Culloton and certain members of his family were still living with his grandfather, but his uncle had taken control of the hotel. However, the 1920 United States Federal Census records contain no mention of the hotel, and based on the information provided by that census, the Culloton household, with a few changes, was probably being supported by Culloton's sister, who was a secretary, and Culloton's brother, who was an engineer.
Academic Institution Attended Before 1926 that Provided the Highest Level of Education	Columbia University, New York City, New York, and Fordham University, New York City, New York

Name	Hazen Shirley "Cuy," "Ki," or "Kiki" Cuyler
Year of Birth	Of all the sources that the author found, one implied 1897, but the others divide almost evenly between 1898 and 1899.
Type of Generation	Reactive
Place of Birth	Sturgeon Point, Michigan, but moved with his family to Harrisville, Michigan, in 1906
Social Background	Cuyler's father had various occupations before Cuyler was born and after Cuyler got married and left Harrisville, including being a semiprofessional baseball player prior to emigrating from Canada to the United States in 1885. However, while Cuyler lived with his family, his father was a member of a ship rescue service and a register of deeds.

Academic Institution Attended Before 1926 that Provided the Highest Level of Education	United States Military Academy, West Point, New York

Name	John Beverley "Johnny" Gooch
Year of Birth	1897
Type of Generation	Reactive
Place of Birth	Smyrna, Tennessee
Social Background	His father was a farmer.
Academic Institution Attended Before 1926 that Provided the Highest Level of Education	Wallace University School, Nashville, Tennessee

Name	George Farley "Boots" Grantham
Year of Birth	1900
Type of Generation	Reactive
Place of Birth	Galena, Kansas, but moved to Goldroad, Arizona, with his family when he was three years old and then later to Kingman, Arizona
Social Background	His father was a laborer in Kansas who, after relocating to Arizona, became an electrician in a gold mine and then an engineer in an electric plant, before dying in 1917. At the time of the 1920 United States Federal Census, Grantham was living with his mother, a landlady in Kingman.
Academic Institution Attended Before 1926 that Provided the Highest Level of Education	Northern Arizona Normal School, Flagstaff, Arizona

Name	Carmen Proctor "Bunker" or "Specs" Hill
Year of Birth	1895
Type of Generation	Reactive
Place of Birth	Royalton, Minnesota, but moved with his family to Corry, Pennsylvania, when he was three years old
Social Background	The 1900 and 1910 United States Federal Census records state that his father was a carpenter, but Hill himself said that his father was "a contractor and builder."
Academic Institution Attended Before 1926 that Provided the Highest Level of Education	Corry High School, Corry, Pennsylvania

Name	Louis Ladislaus (Ladidaus? Ladilaus?) (Laddie) "Kool" or "Lou" Koupal
Year of Birth	1898

Type of Generation	Reactive
Place of Birth	Tabor, South Dakota
Social Background	His father was a farmer.
Academic Institution Attended Before 1926 that Provided the Highest Level of Education	Columbus College, Chamberlain, South Dakota

Name	Remy Peter "Bush Wiz," "Ray," "The Frenchman," or "Wiz" Kremer
Year of Birth	The standard baseball reference works and sites say 1893, but almost all the primary sources that the author viewed, including the 1900, 1910, 1920, and 1940 United States Federal Census records and Kremer's draft registration cards for both World Wars, say or imply 1895.
Type of Generation	Reactive
Place of Birth	Oakland, California
Social Background	His father was the co-owner of a zinc and brass foundry.
Academic Institution Attended Before 1926 that Provided the Highest Level of Education	St. Ignatius College, San Francisco, California. For whatever reason or reasons, Kremer did not mention attending college to the 1940 United States Federal Census taker who recorded his demographic information. But the University of San Francisco archivist, Fr. Michael Kotlanger, SJ, found evidence that Kremer had attended St. Ignatius College (the University of San Francisco today) during the 1913–1914 academic year.

Name	Lee Roy "Popeye," "Roy," "Speed," or "Workhorse" Mahaffey
Year of Birth	1904
Type of Generation	Civic
Place of Birth	Belton, South Carolina
Social Background	His father was a farmer who became a brick mason.
Academic Institution Attended Before 1926 that Provided the Highest Level of Education	He completed four years of high school, but the author did not find the name of the school.

Name	John Phalen "Jack" or "Stuffy" McInnis
Year of Birth	1890
Type of Generation	Reactive
Place of Birth	Gloucester, Massachusetts
Social Background	His father was a caretaker of a stable of driving horses, a chauffeur, and a fireman.
Academic Institution Attended	Gloucester High School, Gloucester,

Before 1926 that Provided the Highest Level of Education	Massachusetts
Name	Henry Lee "Specs," "The Eye-Glassed Twirler," or "The Four-Eyed Pitcher" Meadows
Year of Birth	1894
Type of Generation	Reactive
Place of Birth	Oxford, North Carolina
Social Background	His father was a leaf tobacco dealer who later became a bottling works manufacturer and then a tobacco buyer.
Academic Institution Attended Before 1926 that Provided the Highest Level of Education	Horner Military School, Oxford, North Carolina. According to the 1940 United States Federal Census records, Meadows had attended a postsecondary institution for two years, but the author found no evidence that he did so before 1926.
Name	Graham Edward "Eddie" or "Peanuts" Moore
Year of Birth	1899
Type of Generation	Reactive
Place of Birth	Barlow, Kentucky, but moved with his family to Mississippi sometime between 1910 and 1912
Social Background	His father was a farmer.
Academic Institution Attended Before 1926 that Provided the Highest Level of Education	A prep school in Mississippi, but the author did not find its name
Name	John Dewey "Johnny," "Jughandle," or "Jughandle Johnny" Morrison
Year of Birth	1895
Type of Generation	Reactive
Place of Birth	Pellville, Kentucky, but he was living with his family in Patesville, Kentucky, by June 28, 1900, in Deanefield, Kentucky, by April 18, 1910, and in Owensboro, Kentucky, by January 27, 1920
Social Background	His father was a farmer who became an engineer, also referred to as a mechanic, in a distillery.
Academic Institution Attended Before 1926 that Provided the Highest Level of Education	He had no formal education after the eighth grade, but the author did not find the name of the last school that Morrison had attended.
Name	Walter John Edward "Heinie" Mueller
Year of Birth	1894
Type of Generation	Reactive
Place of Birth	Central Township, Saint Louis County, Missouri
Social Background	His father was a farmer who became a grocer.
Academic Institution Attended	He had no formal schooling after the eighth

Before 1926 that Provided the Highest Level of Education	grade, but the author did not find the name of the last school that Mueller had attended.
Name	John Edward "Eddie" or "Honest Eddie" Murphy
Year of Birth	1891
Type of Generation	Reactive
Place of Birth	Hancock, New York, but was living in Sidney, New York, by June 28, 1900, and then moved with his family to White Mills, Pennsylvania, sometime between June 28, 1900, and an unknown date in 1907
Social Background	His father ran a hotel.
Academic Institution Attended Before 1926 that Provided the Highest Level of Education	Villanova University, Villanova, Pennsylvania
Name	Chester Raymond "Chet" or "Nick" Nichols, Sr.
Year of Birth	1897
Type of Generation	Reactive
Place of Birth	Woonsocket, Rhode Island
Social Background	His father was a piano tuner.
Academic Institution Attended Before 1926 that Provided the Highest Level of Education	New York State School of Agriculture on Long Island, East Farmingdale, New York
Name	John Cyrus "Red" Oldham
Year of Birth	1893
Type of Generation	Reactive
Place of Birth	Zion, Maryland, but moved with his family to Rising Sun, Maryland, by June 11, 1900, and to Upper Providence Township, Pennsylvania, sometime between June 11, 1900, and April 25, 1910
Social Background	His father was a farmer.
Academic Institution Attended Before 1926 that Provided the Highest Level of Education	He completed four years of high school, but the author did not find the name of the school.
Name	John William "Johnny" or "Red" Rawlings
Year of Birth	1892
Type of Generation	Reactive
Place of Birth	Bloomfield, Iowa, but moved with his family to Los Angeles, California, sometime before his junior year in high school
Social Background	His father was a farmer who became a grocer and then a fruit salesman.
Academic Institution Attended	University of Southern California School of Law,

Biographical Information for the 1926 Pirates

Before 1926 that Provided the Highest Level of Education	Los Angeles, California
Name	Harold J. "Hal" Rhyne. Most of the standard baseball reference works and sites have Rhyne's middle initial as "J," though none of them spells out what the "J" is an abbreviation for. However, the name may be "Jacob." The 1900 United States Federal Census records list Rhyne as "Jacob H.," indicating that his first name was Jacob. But subsequent census records that include Rhyne and four of the six other primary sources that the author found that mention Rhyne have his first name as "Harold" and do not have a middle name or an initial.
Year of Birth	1899
Type of Generation	Reactive
Place of Birth	Paso Robles, California, but moved with his family to San Jose, California, sometime before September 12, 1918, and then to Lindsay Township, California, by January 8, 1920
Social Background	His father was a farmer.
Academic Institution Attended Before 1926 that Provided the Highest Level of Education	San Jose High School, San Jose, California

Name	Thomas Clancy "Big Semipro" or "Tom" Sheehan
Year of Birth	1894
Type of Generation	Reactive
Place of Birth	Grand Ridge, Illinois
Social Background	His father was a farmer.
Academic Institution Attended Before 1926 that Provided the Highest Level of Education	A 10th-grade education from Grand Ridge High School, Grand Ridge, Illinois. In addition, he may have gone to 11th and 12th grades at another high school, but the author found no evidence to confirm this possibility.

Name	Earl Sutton "Oil" or "Smitty" Smith
Year of Birth	1897
Type of Generation	Reactive
Place of Birth	Sheridan, Arkansas, but his father died in 1898, and by June 12, 1900, he, his mother, and his brother Luther were living with his maternal grandparents in Center Township, Arkansas. Then, his mother remarried on November 27, 1905, and by April 19, 1910, he, his mother, and his brother Rufus were living with his stepfather in Hot Springs, Arkansas.

Social Background	His maternal grandfather was a farm laborer, whereas his stepfather was a farm laborer who became a driver for a transportation company, a carpenter, and a self-employed teamster.
Academic Institution Attended Before 1926 that Provided the Highest Level of Education	Jones School, Hot Springs, Arkansas, an elementary school that is no longer open. According to an article in the June 1927 issue of *Baseball Magazine*, Smith attended high school for two years, and Edward Balinger in his "Champtown Chatter" column in the February 13, 1926, issue of the *Pittsburgh Post* extended Smith's schooling when he wrote that the "belligerent backstop ... complet[ed] his high school course...." However, the author could not find any corroborating evidence to support either assertion.

Name	Donald C. "Don" Songer. Almost all the standard baseball reference works and sites have Songer's middle initial as "C," though none of them spells out what the "C" is an abbreviation for. However, the author did not find any primary sources that include a middle initial, let alone a middle name.
Year of Birth	1899
Type of Generation	Reactive
Place of Birth	Walnut, Kansas, but moved with his family to Kansas City, Missouri, sometime between June 22, 1900, and an unknown month and day in 1910
Social Background	On June 22, 1900, he and his parents were living with his uncle, who was an insurance agent, but sometime between that date and an unknown month and day in 1910, his father became a teamster for an ice company and then rose to be a foreman for that company by January 3, 1920.
Academic Institution Attended Before 1926 that Provided the Highest Level of Education	He completed three years of high school, but the author did not find the name of the school.

Name	Roy Hampton Spencer
Year of Birth	1900
Type of Generation	Reactive
Place of Birth	Scranton, North Carolina, but grew up in Norfolk, Virginia
Social Background	His father was a farmer who became a house carpenter by May 6, 1910, and then became a ship carpenter sometime between May 6, 1910, and April 4, 1930.
Academic Institution Attended	He had no formal schooling after the eighth

Biographical Information for the 1926 Pirates 245

Before 1926 that Provided the Highest Level of Education	grade, but the author did not find the name of the last school that he had attended.

Name	Harold Joseph "Pie" or "Pie Man" Traynor
Year of Birth	1898
Type of Generation	Reactive
Place of Birth	Framingham, Massachusetts
Social Background	His father was a compositor for a manufacturing company, a newspaper, a printing company, and/or a publishing house, depending on the source.
Academic Institution Attended Before 1926 that Provided the Highest Level of Education	Somerville High School, Somerville, Massachusetts

Name	Paul Glee "Big Poison" or "Little Semipro" Waner
Year of Birth	1903
Type of Generation	Civic
Place of Birth	About two miles from Harrah, Oklahoma
Social Background	His father was a farmer.
Academic Institution Attended Before 1926 that Provided the Highest Level of Education	East Central State Normal School, Ada, Oklahoma

Name	Forest or Forrest (depending on the source) Glenn "Buckshot" Wright
Year of Birth	1901
Type of Generation	Civic
Place of Birth	Archie, Missouri
Social Background	His father operated a lumber yard and a hardware store.
Academic Institution Attended Before 1926 that Provided the Highest Level of Education	University of Missouri, Columbia, Missouri

Name	Emil Ogden Yde. The 1910 United States Federal Census records say that Yde's first name was "Ulf," but he apparently never used it.
Year of Birth	1900
Type of Generation	Reactive
Place of Birth	Great Lakes, Illinois
Social Background	His father was a caretaker at the Great Lakes Naval Station and then became a coal yard superintendent.
Academic Institution Attended Before 1926 that Provided the Highest Level of Education	University of Wisconsin, Madison, Wisconsin, and University of Illinois, Urbana-Champaign, Illinois

Nonplaying Personnel

Name	William Boyd "Bill," "Deacon," "Deacon Bill," "Wilkinsburg Bill," or "Wilkinsburg Will" McKechnie
Year of Birth	1886 or 1887, depending on the source, though the majority of sources say or imply 1886
Type of Generation	Reactive
Place of Birth	Wilkinsburg, Pennsylvania
Social Background	His father was a laborer.
Academic Institution Attended Before 1926 that Provided the Highest Level of Education	He had an eighth-grade education, but he attended Wilkinsburg High School in Wilkinsburg, Pennsylvania, to play for the school's baseball team.

Name	Fred Clifford "Cap" Clarke
Year of Birth	1872
Type of Generation	Idealist
Place of Birth	Near Winterset, Iowa, but raised mostly near Winfield, Kansas, and in Des Moines, Iowa
Social Background	His father was a blacksmith and a farmer.
Academic Institution Attended Before 1926 that Provided the Highest Level of Education	He had no formal schooling after the eighth grade. Clarke's younger daughter, Muriel, told historian David Porter that her father had attended Dickenson public schools after moving to Des Moines, but the author did not find any evidence of the Dickenson public schools in the Des Moines area.

Name	Jewel Ens. The standard baseball reference works and sites say that his middle name was Willoughby or Winklemeyer, but no primary evidence seen by the author shows any middle name, though in the 1940 United States Federal Census records, he is listed as "Jewel W. Ens."
Year of Birth	1889
Type of Generation	Reactive
Place of Birth	St. Louis, Missouri
Social Background	His father was a millwright who became a machinery salesman.
Academic Institution Attended Before 1926 that Provided the Highest Level of Education	Based on the information pieced together from the sources that the author viewed, Ens completed four years of high school in St. Louis, but the author did not find the name of the school. However, according to Bill Lamb, Ens' son would later claim that "Ens had no secondary-school education."

Biographical Information for the 1926 Pirates

Name	John James "Happy Jack," "Honest John," or "Jack" Onslow
Year of Birth	Most of the sources that the author looked at, including two draft registration cards signed by Onslow himself, say or imply 1888, but in a letter that Onslow sent to Earl Hillegan on October 17, 1948, he wrote that he was born in 1889.
Type of Generation	Reactive
Place of Birth	Scottdale, Pennsylvania, but grew up in several towns in western Pennsylvania and eastern Ohio
Social Background	His father was the superintendent of an oil company.
Academic Institution Attended Before 1926 that Provided the Highest Level of Education	In an article published in the May 31, 1925, issue of the *Pittsburgh Post*, John Gruber stated that Onslow had been a member of the baseball team at Scio College in Scio, Ohio, which merged with Mount Union College (the University of Mount Union today) in 1911. Al Abrams went further than that to report in his column in the December 24, 1960, issue of the *Pittsburgh Post-Gazette* that Onslow played football as well as baseball for Scio. However, the Office of the Registrar at the University of Mount Union has no record of Onslow ever being enrolled at Scio, and Onslow's niece, Nancy Purviance, says that her uncle was never a student at Scio. According to Purviance, Onslow attended but probably did not graduate from Scio School, and the Harrison Hills City School District has records of his attendance at Scio School for only 1900–1901, when he was in the fourth grade, and 1901–1902, when no grade level was given. The confusion about Onslow's schooling may have come from the fact that Onslow's brother, Eddie, served as the mascot for the Scio College baseball team and sometimes the players would allow him to participate in their games.

Name	Charles Carrolton "Chic" ("Chick") Fraser
Year of Birth	Of the sources that the author looked at, a few imply 1870 and a few others imply 1872, but the majority divide evenly between 1871 and 1873.
Type of Generation	Idealist
Place of Birth	Chicago, Illinois
Social Background	His father was a laborer who became a stationary engineer.
Academic Institution Attended	Bryant & Stratton's Chicago Business College,

Before 1926 that Provided the Highest Level of Education	Chicago, Illinois
Name	William White "Big Bill" or "Bill" Hinchman
Year of Birth	1883
Type of Generation	Reactive
Place of Birth	Philadelphia, Pennsylvania
Social Background	The author did not find any information on the occupations of Hinchman's parents.
Academic Institution Attended Before 1926 that Provided the Highest Level of Education	The author did not find any information on Hinchman's schooling either. As of January 15, 2015, Baseball-Reference.com said that Hinchman attended Midwest City High School in Oklahoma City, Oklahoma, but Midwest City High School was not established until 1943.

Appendix B

Offensive Statistics

The table on the following four pages runs across the two-page spreads left to right.

POS	Primary Starting Nonpitchers	G	PA	AB	H	2B	3B	HR
C	Earl Smith*	105	331	292	101	17	2	2
1B	George Grantham*	141	523	449	143	27	13	8
2B-SS-3B	Hal Rhyne	109	425	366	92	14	3	2
SS	Glenn Wright	119	493	458	141	15	15	8
3B-SS	Pie Traynor	152	639	574	182	25	17	3
CF-LF-RF	Kiki Cuyler	**157**	694	614	197	31	15	8
CF	Max Carey#	86	370	324	72	14	5	0
RF-LF	Paul Waner*	144	618	536	180	35	**22**	8

POS	Reserves	G	PA	AB	H	2B	3B	HR
C	Johnny Gooch#	86	247	218	59	15	1	1
LF-RF	Clyde Barnhart	76	234	203	39	3	0	0
2B	Johnny Rawlings	61	209	181	42	6	0	0
1B	Stuffy McInnis	47	138	127	38	6	1	0
2B-3B-SS	Eddie Moore	43	149	132	30	8	1	0
LF-CF	Carson Bigbee*	42	72	68	15	3	1	2
2B-SS	Joe Cronin	38	92	83	22	2	2	0
C	Roy Spencer	28	47	43	17	3	0	0
LF	Fred Brickell*	24	60	55	19	3	1	0
LF-RF	Walter Mueller	19	62	62	15	0	1	0
LF	Eddie Murphy*	16	22	17	2	0	0	0
LF	Adam Comorosky	8	16	15	4	1	1	0

POS	Pitching Staff	G	PA	AB	H	2B	3B	HR
P	Emil Yde#	43	82	74	17	5	2	0
P	Ray Kremer	37	90	83	21	4	1	1
P	Lee Meadows*	36	93	88	20	0	0	0
P	Don Songer*	35	41	38	4	0	1	0
P	Vic Aldridge	30	75	71	16	1	1	0
P	Bullet Joe Bush	28	50	49	13	4	0	1
P	Johnny Morrison	26	41	39	3	0	0	0
P	Babe Adams*	19	9	9	2	0	0	0
P	Red Oldham#	17	11	9	2	1	0	0
P	Tom Sheehan	9	11	9	1	0	0	0
P	Carmen Hill	6	17	17	3	0	0	0

TB	BB	HBP	SB	SH	SO	R	RBI	BA	OBP	SLG
128	28	2	1	9	7	29	46	.346	.407	.438
220	60	1	6	12	42	66	70	.318	.400	.490
118	35	6	1	18	21	46	39	.251	.327	.322
210	19	0	6	16	26	73	77	.308	.335	.459
250	38	1	8	26	14	83	92	.317	.361	.436
282	50	9	35	21	66	113	92	.321	.380	.459
96	30	0	10	16	14	46	28	.222	.288	.296
283	66	4	11	12	19	101	79	.336	.413	.528

TB	BB	HBP	SB	SH	SO	R	RBI	BA	OBP	SLG
79	20	3	1	6	14	19	42	.271	.340	.362
42	23	1	1	7	13	26	10	.192	.278	.207
48	14	0	3	15	10	27	20	.232	.287	.265
46	7	0	1	4	3	12	13	.299	.336	.362
40	12	0	3	5	6	19	19	.227	.292	.303
26	3	1	2	0	0	15	4	.221	.264	.382
28	6	0	0	3	15	9	11	.265	.315	.337
20	1	0	0	2	0	5	4	.395	.409	.465
24	3	2	0	0	6	11	4	.345	.400	.436
17	0	0	0	0	2	8	3	.242	.242	.274
2	3	0	0	2	0	3	6	.118	.250	.118
7	1	0	1	0	2	2	0	.267	.313	.467

TB	BB	HBP	SB	SH	SO	R	RBI	BA	OBP	SLG
26	5	0	0	2	7	11	4	.230	.278	.351
30	1	0	0	6	20	14	14	.253	.262	.361
20	2	2	0	1	5	11	9	.227	.261	.227
6	3	0	0	0	4	3	2	.105	.171	.158
19	0	0	1	4	6	8	7	.225	.225	.268
20	1	0	0	0	10	5	7	.265	.280	.408
3	2	0	0	0	13	1	0	.077	.122	.077
2	0	0	0	0	0	1	0	.222	.222	.222
3	1	0	0	1	1	0	1	.222	.300	.333
1	0	0	0	2	0	1	1	.111	.111	.111
3	0	0	0	0	4	0	3	.176	.176	.176

POS	Pitching Staff	G	PA	AB	H	2B	3B	HR
P	Lou Koupal	6	5	4	1	0	0	0
P	Roy Mahaffey	4	1	2	0	0	0	0
P	Bud Culloton	4	0	NA	NA	NA	NA	NA
P	Chet Nichols	3	3	3	1	0	0	0
	Team Totals	**157**	**5970**	**5312**	**1514**	**243**	**106**	**44**
	Rank in the National League	1st T	3rd	3rd	3rd	5th	2nd	5th

*Batted left-handed. #Batted both left-handed and right-handed. League leaders are in boldface. Statistics were taken from "1926 Pittsburgh Pirates," www.baseball-reference.com (accessed on December 3, 2014) and "The 1926 Pittsburgh Pirates Regular Season Roster," www.retrosheet.org (accessed on December 3, 2014), but see "Discrepancy File for 1926 Pittsburgh Pirates" at www.retrosheet.org. Statistical categories were selected and organized by the author.

TB	BB	HBP	SB	SH	SO	R	RBI	BA	OBP	SLG
1	0	1	0	0	0	1	0	.250	.400	.250
0	0	0	0	0	0	0	0	.000	.000	.000
NA	NA	NA	NA	NA	NA	NA	NA	NA	NA	NA
1	0	0	0	0	0	0	0	.333	.333	.333
2101	434	33	91	190	350	769	707	.285	.343	.396
3rd	5th	2nd	2nd	5th	6th	2nd	2nd	3rd	3rd	3rd

Appendix C

Pitching Statistics

Pitching Statistics

Name	G	GS	CG	GF	IP	BFP	WP	BK	SO	BB	SO/BB	HBP
Ray Kremer	37	26	18	8	231.1	955	0	0	74	51	1.45	4
Emil Yde*	37	22	12	8	187.1	812	2	0	34	81	0.42	2
Lee Meadows	36	31	15	2	226.2	967	3	0	54	52	1.04	4
Don Songer*	35	15	5	12	126.1	547	1	0	27	52	0.52	11
Vic Aldridge	30	26	12	2	190.0	837	0	0	61	73	0.84	4
Johnny Morrison	26	13	6	6	122.1	513	1	0	39	44	0.89	2
Bullet Joe Bush	19	12	9	4	110.2	459	0	0	38	35	1.09	2
Babe Adams	19	0	0	14	36.2	164	0	0	7	8	0.88	0
Red Oldham*	17	2	0	7	41.2	185	0	0	16	18	0.89	1
Tom Sheehan	9	2	1	2	31.0	139	0	0	16	12	1.33	2
Carmen Hill	6	6	4	0	39.2	164	1	1	8	9	0.89	2
Lou Koupal	6	2	1	2	19.2	87	0	0	7	8	0.88	1
Roy Mahaffey	4	0	0	3	4.2	20	0	0	3	1	3.00	1
Bud Culloton	4	0	0	3	3.2	21	0	1	1	6	0.17	0
Chet Nichols	3	0	0	1	7.2	43	1	0	2	5	0.40	0
Team Totals	157	157	83	74	1379.1	5913	9	2	387	455	0.85	36
Rank in the National League	1st T	1st T	3rd T	5th	3rd	4th	8th	2nd T	6th	3rd T	7th	1st T

Appendix C

Name	H	HR	WHIP	R	ER	ERA	W	L	W%	SHO	SV	RS
Ray Kremer	221	9	1.176	79	67	**2.61**	**20**	6	**.769**	3	5	5.00
Emil Yde*	181	3	1.399	97	76	3.65	8	7	.533	1	0	5.18
Lee Meadows	254	10	1.350	125	100	3.97	**20**	9	.690	1	0	6.16
Don Songer*	118	4	1.346	60	44	3.13	7	8	.467	1	2	4.53
Vic Aldridge	204	7	1.458	100	86	4.07	10	13	.435	1	1	4.62
Johnny Morrison	119	3	1.332	52	46	3.38	6	8	.429	2	2	3.15
Bullet Joe Bush	97	7	1.193	45	37	3.01	6	6	.500	2	3	4.00
Babe Adams	51	5	1.609	32	25	6.14	2	3	.400	0	3	NA
Red Oldham*	56	1	1.776	27	26	5.62	2	2	.500	0	2	4.00
Tom Sheehan	36	0	1.548	24	23	6.68	0	2	.000	0	0	5.50
Carmen Hill	42	1	1.286	17	15	3.40	3	3	.500	1	0	5.83
Lou Koupal	22	0	1.525	9	7	3.20	0	2	.000	0	0	1.50
Roy Mahaffey	5	0	1.286	4	0	0.00	0	0	NA	0	0	NA
Bud Culloton	3	0	2.455	4	3	7.36	0	0	NA	0	0	NA
Chet Nichols	13	0	2.348	11	7	8.22	0	0	NA	0	0	NA
Team Totals	1422	50	1.361	686	562	3.67	84	69	.549	12	18	4.90
Rank in the National League	6th	4th T	4th	4th	5th T	3rd T	3rd	6th	3rd	3rd	1st	2nd

*Threw left-handed. League leaders are in boldface. All rankings are based on most to fewest or highest to lowest except for ERA and WHIP, which are based on lowest to highest. Statistics were taken from "1926 Pittsburgh Pirates," www.baseball-reference.com (accessed on December 3, 2014) and "The 1926 Pittsburgh Pirates Regular Season Roster," www.retrosheet.org (accessed on December 3, 2014), but see "Discrepancy File for 1926 Pittsburgh Pirates" at www.retrosheet.org. Statistical categories were selected and organized by the author.

Appendix D

Fielding Statistics

Appendix D

Name	POS	G	GS	CG	PO	A	E	DP	PB	FA	RF/G	LF-G	CF-G	RF-G
Babe Adams	P	19	0	0	0	7	1	0		0.875	0.37			
Vic Aldridge	P	30	26	12	0	42	3	3		0.933	1.40			
Bullet Joe Bush	P	19	12	9	5	21	0	1		1.000	1.37			
Bud Culloton	P	4	0	0	0	1	0	0		1.000	0.25			
Carmen Hill	P	6	6	4	2	16	0	1		1.000	3.00			
Lou Koupal	P	6	2	1	1	4	0	0		1.000	0.83			
Ray Kremer	P	37	26	18	4	46	1	0		0.980	1.35			
Roy Mahaffey	P	4	0	0	0	0	1	0		0.000	0.00			
Lee Meadows	P	36	31	15	9	69	3	6		0.963	2.17			
Johnny Morrison	P	26	13	6	2	20	0	3		1.000	0.85			
Chet Nichols	P	3	0	0	0	3	0	0		1.000	1.00			
Red Oldham*	P	17	2	0	3	9	1	1		0.923	0.71			
Tom Sheehan	P	9	2	1	0	7	1	0		0.875	0.78			
Don Songer*	P	35	15	5	1	36	2	2		0.949	1.06			
Emil Yde*	P	37	22	12	10	47	4	3		0.934	1.54			
Johnny Gooch	C	81	59	53	202	38	5	6	2	0.980	3.00			
Earl Smith	C	97	93	64	307	63	14	10	7	0.964	3.78			
Roy Spencer	C	16	5	4	29	3	1	0	0	0.970	2.67			
George Grantham	1B	132	130	117	1203	66	13	106		0.990	9.61			
Stuffy McInnis	1B	40	27	25	300	17	4	32		0.988	7.93			
Joe Cronin	2B	27	22	19	54	74	3	18		0.977	4.74			
Eddie Moore	2B	24	22	21	49	63	11	15		0.911	4.67			
Johnny Rawlings	2B	59	54	48	126	164	9	25		0.970	4.92			
Hal Rhyne	2B	66	59	52	167	220	13	46		0.968	5.86			

Fielding Statistics

Name	POS	G	GS	CG	PO	A	E	DP	PB	FA	RF/G	LF-G	CF-G	RF-G
Joe Cronin	SS	7	0	0	1	8	0	1		1.000	1.29			
Eddie Moore	SS	1	1	1	2	3	2	1		0.714	5.00			
Hal Rhyne	SS	44	38	35	102	123	13	28		0.945	5.11			
Pie Traynor	SS	3	3	3	9	15	1	1		0.960	8.00			
Glenn Wright	SS	116	115	104	242	382	49	82		0.927	5.38			
Eddie Moore	3B	9	9	9	5	20	1	0		0.962	2.78			
Hal Rhyne	3B	1	0	0	2	3	0	0		1.000	5.00			
Pie Traynor	3B	148	148	147	182	279	23	32		0.952	3.11			
Clyde Barnhart	LF	54	47	38	94	4	1	1		0.990	1.81			
Carson Bigbee	LF	18	13	10	24	2	1	0		0.963	1.44			
Fred Brickell	LF	14	13	11	20	3	2	1		0.920	1.64			
Adam Comorosky	LF	6	2	2	7	0	0	0		1.000	1.17			
Kiki Cuyler	LF	64	63	59	156	9	6	2		0.965	2.58			
Walter Mueller	LF	14	12	8	27	2	1	0		0.967	2.07			
Eddie Murphy	LF	3	2	2	5	0	0	0		1.000	1.67			
Paul Waner*	LF	6	5	5	8	2	0	0		1.000	1.67			
Carson Bigbee	CF	4	0	0	2	0	0	0		1.000	0.50			
Max Carey	CF	82	80	75	225	8	14	3		0.943	2.84			
Kiki Cuyler	CF	79	77	75	214	9	7	1		0.970	2.82			
Clyde Barnhart	RF	8	7	5	7	1	0	0		1.000	1.00			
Kiki Cuyler	RF	18	17	17	35	1	1	1		0.973	2.00			
Walter Mueller	RF	1	1	1	2	0	0	0		1.000	2.00			
Paul Waner*	RF	133	132	131	299	19	8	3		0.975	**2.39**	**54**	**0**	**8**
Clyde Barnhart	OF	61	54	43	101	5	1	1		0.991	1.74			

Name	POS	G	GS	CG	PO	A	E	DP	PB	FA	RF/G	LF-G	CF-G	RF-G
Carson Bigbee	OF	22	13	10	26	2	1	0		0.966	1.27	18	4	0
Fred Brickell	OF	14	13	11	20	3	2	1		0.920	1.64	14	0	0
Max Carey	OF	82	80	75	225	8	14	3		0.943	2.84	0	82	0
Adam Comorosky	OF	6	2	2	7	0	0	0		1.000	1.17	6	0	0
Kiki Cuyler	OF	**157**	**157**	**151**	405	19	14	4		0.968	2.70	64	79	18
Walter Mueller	OF	15	13	9	29	2	1	0		0.969	2.07	14	0	1
Eddie Murphy	OF	3	2	2	5	0	0	0		1.000	1.67	3	0	0
Paul Waner*	OF	139	137	136	307	21	8	3		0.976	2.36	6	0	133
Team Totals		157	1413	1224	4144	1929	220	158#	9	0.965	NA			
Rank in the National League		1st T	1st T	3rd	3rd	6th	3rd	3rd#	7th	6th	NA			

*Threw left-handed. #The standard baseball reference works and sites credit the Pirates with 161 double plays, which would put them in second place in the National League in that category. However, a close examination of the box scores and play-by-play accounts show that the Bucs completed only 158 twin killings, which would demote them to third place. League leaders are in boldface. Statistics were taken from "1926 Pittsburgh Pirates," www.baseball-reference.com (accessed on December 3, 2014) and "The 1926 Pittsburgh Pirates Regular Season Roster," www.retrosheet.org (accessed on December 3, 2014), but see "Discrepancy File for 1926 Pittsburgh Pirates" at www.retrosheet.org. Statistical categories were selected and organized by the author.

Chapter Notes

Introduction

1. Adams, Bigbee, and Carey, or Ralph Davis, the sports editor of the *Pittsburgh Press* and the Pittsburgh correspondent to *The Sporting News*, who may have supplied some of the details that appear in the article bearing Davis' byline that was published in the September 30, 1926, issue of the *Pittsburgh Press*, would later claim that coach Jack Onslow was also part of the group that approached McKechnie on the 7th. Ralph S. Davis, "Secret of Pirate Shakeup Revealed," *Pittsburgh Press*, September 30, 1926.

2. Regis M. Welsh, "Discharged Bucs Take Case to Judge Landis," *Pittsburgh Post*, August 15, 1926. For the purposes of this book, it will be assumed that Bigbee was the messenger and "allegedly" will not be repeated when the author addresses this topic.

3. The usual line credited to Adams is "Well, I think the manager should manage, and no one else should interfere"—a quotation apparently first published by Fred Lieb in his history of the Pirates and then repeated by other authors, sometimes with the "Well" and/or the second comma missing. However, Lieb does not cite the source of the quotation and may have invented the words himself. David Finoli and Bill Ranier in their encyclopedia on the Pirates have Adams saying, "No one should tell the manager what to do," but they, too, do not cite the source of the quotation. And Dick Bartell, who was on the roster of the Pirates for the last few weeks of the 1927 season, told Norman Macht that he believed Adams had said, "The manager is the manager. Nobody else should interfere." But Bartell was not a member of the '26 Pirates and had to have gotten his information from someone else. So, it is difficult, if not impossible, to know exactly what Adams said, though since he supported Carey and Bigbee, it can be assumed that he must have said something to the effect that there should be only one manager on the team. Cf. Frederick G. Lieb, *The Pittsburgh Pirates* (New York: G. P. Putnam's Sons, 1948; reprint, Carbondale: Southern Illinois University Press, 2003), 223 (this reference and all future references are to the reprint edition); Clifton Blue Parker, *Big and Little Poison: Paul and Lloyd Waner, Baseball Brothers* (Jefferson, NC: McFarland, 2003), 59; James Forr and David Proctor, *Pie Traynor: A Baseball Biography* (Jefferson, NC: McFarland, 2010), 93; David Finoli and Bill Ranier, *The Pittsburgh Pirates Encyclopedia* (Champaign, IL: Sports Publishing, 2003), 52; and Dick Bartell, with Norman L. Macht, *Rowdy Richard: A Firsthand Account of the National League Baseball Wars of the 1930s and the Men Who Fought Them* (Berkeley: North Atlantic Books, 1987), 43.

4. Davis, "Secret of Pirate Shakeup Revealed."

5. Regis M. Welsh, "Clarke Denies Statements of Discharged Pirates," *Pittsburgh Post*, October 1, 1926.

6. Forr and Proctor, 74–75.

7. "All-Around Class of Pirates Makes Them Favorites to Repeat; Macks, Slowly Developed, Choice in American," *Pittsburgh Post*, March 30, 1926.

8. Ibid.

9. Daniel M. Daniel, "How Fred Clarke Taught the Pirates Confidence," *Baseball Magazine* 36, no. 4 (March 1926): 444.

Chapter 1

1. There has been quite a bit of controversy among sabrmetricians over whether the peak

age of a major leaguer is 27 or 29. Cf. Steve Walters, "It Ain't Necessarily So," *The Wages of Wins Journal*, www.wagesofwins.com/2007/04/21/it-aint-necessarily-so/ (accessed on November 10, 2014); Mitchel Lichtman, "How Do Baseball Players Age? (Part I)," *The Hardball Times*, December 21, 2009, www.hardballtimes.com/main/article/how-do-baseball-players-age-part–1/ (accessed on November 10, 2014); Mitchel Lichtman, "How Do Baseball Players Age? (Part II)," *The Hardball Times*, December 29, 2009, www.hardballtimes.com/main/article/how-do-baseball-players-age-part–2 (accessed on November 10, 2014); J. C. Bradbury, "How Do Players Age?" *Baseball Prospectus*, January 11, 2010, www.baseballprospectus.com/article.php?articleid=9933 (accessed on November 10, 2014); Russell A. Carleton, "Baseball Therapy: That Peak Age Thing, Part I," *Baseball Prospectus*, February 15, 2010, www.baseballprospectus.com/article.php?articleid=10058 (accessed on November 10, 2014); and Tangotiger, "When Do Pitchers Peak?" *The Book: Playing the Percentages in Baseball*, April 8, 2010, www.insidethebook.com/ee/index.php/site/comments/when_do_pitchers_peak/ (accessed on November 10, 2014). However, no matter whether the age of the entire team or just the age of its starters is emphasized, an argument can be made that the 1920 Pirates were on the verge of peaking. Nor did the Maranville trade or any other personnel changes drastically alter the age of either group for the next season. The average age of the 1921 Pirates as a team was 26.82, while that of its main performers—five infielders, three outfielders, a catcher, and seven pitchers—averaged 28.94. Ages are based on the July 1-June 30 year. For specific ages, see "1921 Pittsburgh Pirates," www.baseball-reference.com (accessed on November 10, 2014), though the author's averages disagree with the averages found there.

2. "All-Time Pirate Line Ups [sic]," http://home.mindspring.com/~gearhard/pilineup.html (accessed on November 10, 2014).

3. John J. Ward, "The Best Curve Ball Since Mordecai Brown," *Baseball Magazine* 31, no. 4 (September 1923): 450; Irving E. Sanborn, "The Decline of Curve Ball [sic] Pitching," *Baseball Magazine* 32, no. 5 (April 1924): 484.

4. Ralph S. Davis, "Pirates Are Made If They Get a Catcher," *The Sporting News*, February 3, 1921, 5. The date of the column should have been January 31, not January 21, as was printed, and what Davis was referring to in the title of his column was the Pirates getting another experienced backstop to help Walter Schmidt.

5. The best American League franchise was Philadelphia, with 1123 wins, 785 losses, a .589 winning percentage, and a 2.5 average placement.

6. The statistics used in this table were taken from "Complete Baseball Team and Baseball Team Encyclopedias," www.baseball-reference.com (accessed on November 24, 2014).

7. Bezdek had already begun coaching football at Penn State in 1918.

8. Gibson would have been Clarke's starting catcher for all 10 seasons, but he broke his ankle in 1913 and was replaced by Mike Simon.

9. Forr and Proctor, 50, and Finoli and Ranier, *The Pittsburgh Pirates Encyclopedia*, 442.

10. "The 1921 Pittsburgh Pirates Regular Season Game Log," www.retrosheet.org (accessed on December 21, 2014). In addition to the statistics listed on the "Game Log" page for this note and future notes, any "Game Log" citation may include statistics accessed through the "Date" and "Box" and/or "PBP" links.

11. Ralph S. Davis, "Pirates Can Jog to Flag in Last Month," *The Sporting News*, August 25, 1921, 3.

12. James C. Isaminger, "Pirates Show Fast Pace Against Phils," *The Sporting News*, August 25, 1921, 3.

13. "The 1921 Pittsburgh Pirates Regular Season Game Log" and "Standings At Close of Play of October 2, 1921," www.retrosheet.org (accessed on January 6, 2015).

14. The statistics used in this paragraph were taken from "The 1922 Pittsburgh Pirates Regular Season Game Log," "Standings At Close of Play of September 21, 1922," and "Standings At Close of Play of October 1, 1922," www.retrosheet.org (accessed on January 6, 2015).

15. The statistics used in this paragraph were taken from "Standings At Close of Play of September 15, 1923," "The 1923 Pittsburgh Pirates Regular Season Game Log," and "Standings At Close of Play of October 7, 1923," www.retrosheet.org (accessed on January 6, 2015).

16. The statistics used in this paragraph were taken from "The 1924 Pittsburgh Pirates Regular Season Game Log," "Standings At

Close of Play of September 20, 1924," and "Standings At Close of Play of September 30, 1924," www.retrosheet.org (accessed on January 6, 2015).

17. Charlie Grimm, with Ed Prell, *Jolly Cholly's Story: Grimm's Baseball Tales* (Notre Dame, IN: Diamond Communications, 1983; originally published under the title of *Jolly Cholly's Story: Baseball, I love You!* [Chicago: Henry Regnery, 1968], 15–16 [this reference and all future references are to the 1983 edition].

18. Pitchers Hal Carlson, Whitey Glazner, Earl Hamilton, Remy Kremer, Lee Meadows, Emil Yde, and Jimmy Zinn; catcher Johnny Gooch; infielders George Cutshaw, Johnny Rawlings, Cotton Tierney, Pie Traynor, and Glenn Wright; third baseman-outfielder Clyde Barnhart; infielder-outfielder Possum Whitted; and outfielders Carson Bigbee and Kiki Cuyler.

19. In descending order, Adams, Traynor, Carey, Cooper, Kremer, Cuyler, Wright, Bigbee, Meadows, Maranville, Barnhart, Grimm, and Schmidt. Finoli and Ranier, *The Pittsburgh Pirates Encyclopedia*, 260–262, 269–270, 272–275, 277–278, 282–283, 306, 332–333, 338–339, 342–344, 358, 360–361, and 362–363.

20. "1921 National League Team Statistics and Standings," "1922 National League Team Statistics and Standings," "1923 National League Team Statistics and Standings," and "1924 National League Team Statistics and Standings," www.baseball-reference.com (accessed on November 23, 2014).

21. The statistics used in this table, with the exception of Projected Won-Lost Record, which came from Gary Gillette and Pete Palmer, eds., *The ESPN Baseball Encyclopedia*, 5th ed. (New York: Sterling, 2008), 174, 176, 178, 180, were taken from "1921 National League Team Statistics and Standings," "1922 National League Team Statistics and Standings," "1923 National League Team Statistics and Standings," and "1924 National League Team Statistics and Standings," www.baseball-reference.com (accessed on November 23, 2014). The conversions were done by the author, and the definitions were taken from "1921 National League Team Statistics and Standings," www.baseball-reference.com (accessed on November 23, 2014) and Gillette and Palmer, 7.

22. The statistics used in this table were taken from "The 1921 Pittsburgh Pirates," "The 1922 Pittsburgh Pirates," "The 1923 Pittsburgh Pirates," and "The 1924 Pittsburgh Pirates," www.retrosheet.org (accessed on November 23, 2014).

23. Grimm, 16.

24. The statistics used in this table were taken from Gillette and Palmer, 174, 176, 178, 180. The definitions were taken from Gillette and Palmer, 6–7.

25. The statistics used in this table, with the exception of Projected Won-Lost Record, which came from ibid., 180, were taken from "1921 National League Team Statistics and Standings," www.baseball-reference.com (accessed on November 23, 2014). The conversions were done by the author.

26. The statistics used in this table were taken from "The 1921 New York Giants" and "The 1921 Pittsburgh Pirates," www.retrosheet.org (accessed on November 23, 2014).

27. The statistics used in this table were taken from Gillette and Palmer, 180.

28. The information used in this paragraph was taken from "1922 Pittsburgh Pirates," "Cotton Tierney," "Carson Bigbee," and "Max Carey," www.baseball-reference.com (accessed on January 6, 2015).

29. The statistics used in this table, with the exception of Projected Won-Lost Record, which came from Gillette and Palmer, 178, were taken from "1922 National League Team Statistics and Standings," www.baseball-reference.com (accessed on November 23, 2014). The conversions were done by the author.

30. The statistics used in this table were taken from "The 1922 New York Giants," "The 1922 Cincinnati Reds," and "The 1922 Pittsburgh Pirates," www.retrosheet.org (accessed on November 23, 2014).

31. The statistics used in this table were taken from Gillette and Palmer, 178.

32. The statistics used in this table, with the exception of Projected Won-Lost Record, which came from ibid., 176, were taken from "1923 National League Team Statistics and Standings," www.baseball-reference.com (accessed on November 23, 2014). The conversions were done by the author.

33. The statistics used in this table were taken from "The 1923 New York Giants," "The 1923 Cincinnati Reds," and "The 1923 Pittsburgh Pirates," www.retrosheet.org (accessed on November 23, 2014).

34. The statistics used in this table were taken from Gillette and Palmer, 176.

35. The statistics used in this table, with

the exception of Projected Won-Lost Record, which came from ibid., 174, were taken from "1924 National League Team Statistics and Standings," www.baseball-reference.com (accessed November 23, 2014). The conversions were done by the author.

36. The statistics used in this table were taken from "The 1924 New York Giants," "The 1924 Brooklyn Robins," and "The 1924 Pittsburgh Pirates," www.retrosheet.org (accessed on November 23, 2014).

37. The statistics used in this table were taken from Gillette and Palmer, 174.

38. John Thorn and John Holway, *The Pitcher* (New York: Prentice Hall, 1987), 247.

39. Forr and Proctor, 47.

40. Glenn Wright, interviewed by Eugene Converse Murdock, Fresno, California, June 23, 1978, Cleveland Public Library, Cleveland, Ohio.

41. Bill Veeck, with Ed Linn, *Veeck—As in Wreck: The Autobiography of Bill Veeck* (Chicago: University of Chicago Press, 2001; originally published under the same title, New York: G. P. Putnam's Sons, 1962), 31 (this reference and all future references are to the 2001 edition).

42. Depending on the source, YellowHorse's first name is given as "Mose" or "Moses" and his last name is spelled "YellowHorse," "Yellow Horse," or "Yellowhorse," but for the purposes of this book, he will be referred to as "Mose YellowHorse," the way two of his biographers, Todd Fuller and Ralph Berger, refer to him.

43. Todd Fuller, *60 Feet, 6 Inches and Other Distances from Home: The (Baseball) Life of Mose YellowHorse* (Duluth: How Cow! Press, 2002), 99–100.

44. Walter "Rabbit" Maranville, *Run, Rabbit, Run: The Hilarious and Mostly True Tales of Rabbit Maranville*, ed. John Holway (Cleveland: Society for American Baseball Research, 1991), 46, and Don Connery, "Hey, Mr. Banjo!" *Sports Illustrated*, September 19, 1955, www.si.com/vault/1955/09/19/604983/hey-mr-banjo (accessed on November 23, 2014). However, Connery is incorrect in writing that Grimm sang baritone. Both Maranville and Grimm himself said that Grimm sang bass. See Maranville, 46, and Grimm, 15.

45. Finoli and Ranier, *The Pittsburgh Pirates Encyclopedia*, 343.

46. Ralph S. Davis, "Pittsburgh Satisfied with Eastern Test," *The Sporting News*, July 28, 1921, 3, and ibid., 343.

47. Bill James, *The New Bill James Historical Baseball Abstract*, updated ed. (New York: Free Press, 2003), 130.

48. During spring training in 1922, Johnny Morrison's brother, Phil, who played guitar, was also part of the group. See the caption under the photograph titled "Glee Club Supplants Quartet," *Pittsburgh Post*, April 7, 1922. The caption did not mention Tierney and Maranville, but in all likelihood, both of them were members.

49. Edward F. Balinger, "Champtown Chatter," *Pittsburgh Post*, February 16, 1926.

50. Lewis Burton, "Too Many Jugs Fanned 'Jughandle' Morrison," *New York Journal-American*, January 14, 1944; Art McKennan, interviewed by Rob Roberts, Pittsburgh, Pennsylvania, July 14, 1994, Oral History Research Committee of the Society for American Baseball Research; and Jack Kavanaugh, "Johnny Morrison," www.baseballlibrary.com (accessed on July 10, 2012).

51. Burton.

52. Ralph S. Davis, "M'Kechnie Hears Shouting of Mob," *The Sporting News*, October 9, 1924, 1.

53. Wright, interview.

54. Ibid.

55. Lieb, *The Pittsburgh Pirates*, 191–192.

56. Grimm, 17–18.

57. Jimmy Zinn, interviewed by Mark Bernstein, Memphis, Tennessee, October 7, 1989, Oral History Research Committee of the Society for American Baseball Research.

58. Ibid.

59. Grimm, 15.

60. Wright, interview.

61. Chilly Doyle, "Chilly Sauce," *Pittsburgh Gazette Times*, January 15, 1922. Depending on the date, the column could be titled "Chilly Sauce," "Chillysauce," or "Training Camp Chillysauce."

62. Lawrence S. Ritter, *The Glory of Their Times: The Story of the Early Days of Baseball Told by the Men Who Played It*, new enlarged ed. (New York: Vintage, 1984), 77.

63. Ibid., 76.

64. Lyle Spatz and Steve Steinberg, *1921: The Yankees, the Giants, and the Battle for Baseball Supremacy in New York* (Lincoln: University of Nebraska Press, 2010), 80.

65. Ralph S. Davis, "Second If Not First Place for Pirates," *The Sporting News*, April 21, 1921, 3.

66. Cf. Henry L. Farrell, "Pennant No Cinch for Any Starter in Senior League," *Pitts-*

burgh Sun, April 11, 1922; "Outlook Is Bright for St. Louis Clubs," *New York Times*, April 11, 1922; Ralph S. Davis, "Gibson Decided on His Pitching Only," *The Sporting News*, April 13, 1922, 3; and W. A. Phelon, "Who Will Win the Big League Pennants?" *Baseball Magazine* 28, no. 6 (May 1922): 819–822, 851–852.

67. "Major League Moguls Air Views on Eve of Opening," *Los Angeles Times*, April 16, 1923.

68. Cf. "League Teams Set for Season's Start," *New York Times*, April 15, 1923, and W. A. Phelon, "Who Will Win the Big League Pennants of 1923?" *Baseball Magazine* 30, no. 6 (May 1923): 531–533, 563–564.

69. W. A. Phelon, "Who Will Win the Big League Pennants?" *Baseball Magazine* 32, no. 6 (May 1924): 531–533, 571.

70. Cf. Frank Smith, "Indians 'Doped' to Nose Out Yanks," *Chicago Daily Tribune*, April 13, 1924; Ralph S. Davis, "Bucs Get Acid Test First Three Weeks," *The Sporting News*, April 17, 1924, 3; and Reed Browning, *Baseball's Greatest Season, 1924* (Amherst: University of Massachusetts Press, 2003), 2–9.

71. F. C. Lane, "The All-America Baseball Club of 1921," *Baseball Magazine* 28, no. 1 (December 1921): 585–587.

72. Based on the income index of the GDP per capita. "Purchasing Power of Money in the United States from 1774 to Present," www.measuringworth.com/ppowerus (accessed on November 24, 2014). GDP per capita=gross domestic product per person.

73. Regis M. Welsh, "Buc Owner Silent on Status of Schmidt," *Pittsburgh Post*, April 18, 1922.

74. For support of this theory, see Ralph S. Davis, "Players of Schmidt Type Are Drawbacks," *The Sporting News*, January 26, 1922, 3; Ralph S. Davis, "Pirates Start on Their Second Stage," *The Sporting News*, March 16, 1922, 3; and Ralph S. Davis, "Gibby Hasn't Lost Faith in His Team," *The Sporting News*, April 27, 1922, 3.

75. "Pirates Get Walt Schmidt," *Los Angeles Times*, September 12, 1915; "Walter Schmidt to Join Pittsburgh Nine," *Los Angeles Times*, April 14, 1920; and Doyle, "Chilly Sauce," January 15, 1922.

76. "Davy Robertson Is Unconditionally Released by Bucs," *Pittsburgh Post*, April 19, 1922.

77. Doyle, "Chilly Sauce," January 15, 1922.

78. William A. White, "'Will Not Join Pirates in Chicago or Anywhere Else'—Walter Schmidt," *Pittsburgh Post*, April 24, 1922.

79. William A. White, "Walter Schmidt, Corsair Holdout, Reported Ready to Accept Club's Terms," *Pittsburgh Post*, April 22, 1922.

80. "Pirates Seek Both Wagner and Schmidt," *The Sporting News*, July 13, 1922, 1; "Stubborness [*sic*] Never Pays," *The Sporting News*, July 20, 1922, 1; and Ralph S. Davis, "Pittsburg[h]'s Change Brings No Success," *The Sporting News*, July 27, 1922, 3. Schmidt resumed catching for the Bucs on August 7.

81. Even before he resumed his position behind home plate, Schmidt was working with the Pirate pitchers and catcher Johnny Gooch. For an appraisal of Schmidt and his value to the Pirate team, see "Catcher Walter Schmidt May Rejoin Pittsburgh Pirates," *Washington Post*, July 9, 1922, and "Walter Schmidt Plays with Pittsburgh Club," *Washington Post*, August 8, 1922.

82. "Carson Bigbee," www.baseball-reference.com (accessed on November 24, 2014). This number does not include at bats and plate appearances.

83. Ibid. (accessed on November 24, 2014). This number does not include defensive games as a left fielder.

84. Lane, "The All-America Baseball Club of 1921," 585–586, and F. C. Lane, "The All-America Baseball Club of 1922," *Baseball Magazine* 30, no. 1 (December 1922): 308.

85. Lane, "The All-America Baseball Club of 1922," 310. This book's author has not been able to locate any all-star teams that McGraw and Bancroft selected for 1921.

86. Ralph S. Davis, "It's Not Peeve That Makes Pirates Lose," *The Sporting News*, June 22, 1922, 3.

87. Ralph S. Davis, "Shakeup in Pirates Demanded by Fans," *The Sporting News*, October 6, 1921, 2.

88. "Giants and Robins Named in Scandal," *New York Times*, January 4, 1927.

89. "Still Fighting," *Pittsburgh Post*, May 5, 1922.

90. W. A. Phelon, "How the Pennant Tide Ebbed and Flowed Through 1922," *Baseball Magazine* 29, no. 6 (November 1922): 558.

91. Finoli and Ranier, *The Pittsburgh Pirates Encyclopedia*, 45.

92. Wright, interview.

93. William Peet, "Treat 'Em Rough," *Pittsburgh Post*, March 3, 1925.

94. Smith, "Indians 'Doped' to Nose Out Yanks."

95. "Big Leagues Ready for Pennant Races," *New York Times*, April 13, 1924.

96. Phelon, "Who Will Win the Big League Pennants?" *Baseball Magazine* 32, no. 6 (May 1924): 533.
97. W. A. Phelon, "The New York Clubs Against the Field," *Baseball Magazine* 33, no. 4 (September 1924): 480.
98. William Peet, "What the Post Clock Saw," *Pittsburgh Post*, August 19, 1924.
99. F. C. Lane, "Wrecking Baseball's Greatest Infield," *Baseball Magazine* 34, no. 4 (March 1925): 469.
100. Grimm may have been better known for his banjo playing, but he also performed on the ukulele, and according to one Pittsburgh scribe, the fancy-fielding first baseman could play "any musical instrument under the sun." See the caption under the photograph titled "Glee Club Supplants Quartet."
101. Noel Hynd, *The Giants of the Polo Grounds: The Glorious Times of Baseball's New York Giants* (New York: Doubleday, 1988), 222.
102. Maranville, 48.
103. Fuller, 98.
104. "Pirate Notes," *Pittsburgh Post*, August 26, 1921.
105. Irving Vaughan, "Pirates Hard Band to Dope; Morale of Men Great Big?" *Chicago Daily Tribune*, March 28, 1922.
106. "Pirates Recover and Beat Robins," *New York Times*, August 29, 1921.
107. Zinn, interview.
108. Ibid.
109. Eddie Moore, interviewed by Eugene Converse Murdock, Ironton, Ohio, June 13, 1975, Cleveland Public Library, Cleveland, Ohio.
110. Ralph S. Davis, "One Thing Pirates Won't Argue About," *The Sporting News*, October 18, 1923, 3.
111. Lou Wollen, "M'Kechnie Lays Down Law to Team," *Pittsburgh Press*, March 2, 1925.
112. "Pirates Seek Both Wagner and Schmidt," 1.
113. Francis C. Richter, "Casual Comment," *The Sporting News*, July 27, 1922, 4.
114. Ralph S. Davis, "Pirates Refuse to Be Counted Out Yet," *The Sporting News*, August 9, 1923, 3.
115. Ralph S. Davis, "It's Plain M'Kechnie Has Big Job on Hand," *The Sporting News*, July 13, 1922, 3.
116. Ibid.
117. "Pittsburg [sic] Pirates' Wives Must Stay Home When Team Travels," *Boston Daily Globe*, May 13, 1923.
118. Ibid.
119. Edward F. Balinger, "Will Pirates Be Stronger or Weaker Than They Were Last Year?" *Pittsburgh Post*, February 17, 1922.
120. Lieb, *The Pittsburgh Pirates*, 117.
121. After playing in the American Association for one season and in the National League for nine more—one as a player-manager—McGraw jumped to the American League in 1901 to become the player-manager of the Baltimore Orioles. There he remained until he jumped back to the National League in July of 1902 to assume the duties of player-manager of the New York franchise. His playing days ended in 1906, but he remained as the manager of the Giants until June 3, 1932.

Chapter 2

1. For the reaction to the trade, see L. H. Wollen, "Pirate-Cub Deal Leaves Fans Divided," *Pittsburgh Press*, October 28, 1924; Ralph Davis, "Sport Chat," *Pittsburgh Press*, October 28, 1924; "Fear Pirate Club Gave Away More Than It Received," *Pittsburgh Sun*, October 28, 1924; James J. Long, "Sporting Gossip and Comment," *Pittsburgh Sun*, October 28, 1924; Regis M. Welsh, "Recent Pirate Trade Sets Baseball Fans Arguing Over Merits," *Pittsburgh Post*, October 29, 1924; Edward F. Balinger, "Flag Talk Waxes Loud in Cubland Since Recent Wholesale Swap," *Pittsburgh Post*, October 30, 1924; Ralph S. Davis, "Anyway, Big Swap Satisfies Barney," *The Sporting News*, November 6, 1924, 1; Irving Vaughan, "Three-Three Swap Pleases Cub Fans," *The Sporting News*, November 6, 1924, 3; and Lane, "Wrecking Baseball's Greatest Infield," 453.
2. For the defensive rankings of the Pirate infielders in the categories covered in this paragraph, see "1924 Major League Baseball Fielding Leaders" and "1924 National League Fielding Leaders," www.baseball-reference.com (accessed on November 24, 2014) and *The Baseball Encyclopedia: The Complete and Official Record of Major League Baseball* (Toronto: Macmillan, 1969), 264–267.
3. Cf. Gillette and Palmer, 174, and "1924 Major League Baseball Batting Leaders," www.baseball-reference.com (accessed November 24, 2014).
4. Lane, "Wrecking Baseball's Greatest Infield," 453.
5. Ibid.

Notes—Chapter 2

6. Ibid.
7. Ibid.
8. Ibid., 453, 469.
9. Chester L. Smith, "First-Basing That Fairly Glitters," *Baseball Magazine* 33, no. 4 (September 1924): 448.
10. Al Abrams, "Sidelights on Sports," *Pittsburgh Post-Gazette*, January 27, 1959.
11. "Wilbur Cooper," www.baseball-reference.com (accessed on November 24, 2914).
12. Ibid., www.baseball-reference.com (accessed on December 2, 2014). These numbers do not include games played, innings pitched, games started, complete games, and games finished, in which Cooper came in the top 10 five, eight, eight, eight, and four times, respectively, and led the league once in innings pitched and twice each in games started and complete games.
13. Ibid., www.baseball-reference.com (accessed on November 24, 2014).
14. Finoli and Ranier, *The Pittsburgh Pirates Encyclopedia*, 274–275.
15. "All-Time Pirate Line Ups [*sic*]," http://home.mindspring.com/~gearhard/pilineup.html (accessed on November 24, 2014).
16. Davis, "Anyway, Big Swap Satisfies Barney," 1.
17. Wright, interview.
18. "George Grantham," www.baseball-reference.com (accessed on November 24, 2014).
19. Glenn Wright called Grantham "one of the best fastball hitters that [he had] ever [seen]." Wright, interview.
20. "George Grantham," www.baseball-reference.com (accessed November 24, 2014).
21. Ibid. (accessed on November 24, 2014). Striking out 92 and 63 times may not seem like a lot compared to 21st-century batters who lead the majors with anywhere from 168 to over 200 K's, but during the first half of the 1920s, the range for major league leaders was 81 to 98.
22. Davis, "Anyway, Big Swap Satisfies Barney," 1.
23. Lieb, *The Pittsburgh Pirates*, 202.
24. Davis, "Gibby Hasn't Lost Faith in His Team," 3.
25. Finoli and Ranier, *The Pittsburgh Pirates Encyclopedia*, 41, 42.
26. In addition to YellowHorse, Pittsburgh gave Sacramento three minor leaguers—Bill Hughes, Claude Rohwer, and Harry Brown—and $7,500 for pitcher Earl Kunz. Ralph S. Davis, "Pirates Do Well in the Slave Market," *The Sporting News*, December 21, 1922, 5.
27. Lieb, *The Pittsburgh Pirates*, 191.

28. Davis, "Anyway, Big Swap Satisfies Barney," 1.
29. Edward F. Balinger, "Champtown Chatter," *Pittsburgh Post*, February 22, 1926.
30. Ralph S. Davis, "Barney and Pirates Beam on Each Other," *The Sporting News*, March 22, 1923, 3; Ralph S. Davis, "Win Them at Home and Fans Come Out," *The Sporting News*, June 7, 1923, 3; and Ralph S. Davis, "Pirate Squad Cut Before Going West," *The Sporting News*, January 31, 1924, 3.
31. Ralph S. Davis, "Schmidt's Salary Works Against Him," *The Sporting News*, December 25, 1924, 1.
32. Finoli and Ranier, *The Pittsburgh Pirates Encyclopedia*, 338.
33. Eugene Murdock, *Baseball Between the Wars: Memories of the Game by the Men Who Played It* (Westport, CT: Meckler, 1992), 179. For the audio version of Hill's interview with Murdock, see Carmen Hill, interviewed by Eugene Converse Murdock, Indianapolis, Indiana, February 21, 1975, Cleveland Public Library, Cleveland, Ohio.
34. In June, both Koupal and Songer would be optioned to minor league clubs, but with the provision that they could be recalled on 48 hours notice. Koupal went to Kansas City of the American Association on June 21, while Songer was sent to Oklahoma City of the Western League on June 10. "Koupal, Young Bucco Hurler, Is Released," *Pittsburgh Press*, June 21, 1925, and "Baseball Gossip of the Major Leagues," *Pittsburgh Press*, June 11, 1925.
35. Clifford Blau, "Brief History of Roster Limits," www.dmbforum.yuku.com/topic/7848 (accessed on November 3, 2014).
36. Edward F. Balinger, "Jack Onslow, Veteran Catcher, Signed as Coach for Pirates," *Pittsburgh Post*, December 2, 1924, and Edward F. Balinger, "Tame Yearly Conference Concluded by National League Magnates," *Pittsburgh Post*, December 11, 1924. The seventh edition of *Total Baseball*, the fifth edition of Gillette and Palmer, and www.retrosheet.org say that Land was a coach with the Pirates in 1914 instead of 1924, but this is an error. As multiple sources show, Land was the starting catcher for the Brooklyn Tip-Tops of the Federal League for the entire 1914 season. Cf. Balinger, "Tame Yearly Conference Concluded by National League Magnates"; John Thorn, Pete Palmer, and Michael Gershman, eds., *Total Baseball*, 7th ed. (Kingston, NY: Total Sports, 2001), 933, 2359, 2444; Gillette and Palmer, 662, 1639, 1712; "Grover Land,"

www.retrosheet.org (accessed on November 3, 2014); box score records for the 1914 Brooklyn Tip-Tops as found in various issues of *The Sporting News*; *The Baseball Encyclopedia: The Complete and Official Record of Major League Baseball*, 224, 1101; and "Grover Land," www.baseball-reference.com (accessed on November 3, 2014).

37. William Peet, "Treat 'Em Rough," *Pittsburgh Post*, December 2, 1924; William Peet, "Treat 'Em Rough," *Pittsburgh Post*, December 4, 1924; Balinger, "Jack Onslow, Veteran Catcher, Signed as Coach for Pirates"; and Ralph S. Davis, "Pirates All Set, Is View of Owner," *The Sporting News*, December 11, 1924, 2.

38. Chester L. Smith, "Barney Dreyfuss Unearths a Player Gold Mine," *Baseball Magazine* 34, no. 5 (April 1925): 489.

39. The statistics used in this paragraph were taken from "Kiki Cuyler," www.baseball-reference.com (accessed on November 3, 2014).

40. "Eddie Moore," www.baseball-reference.com (accessed on November 3, 2014).

41. "Emil Yde" and "Ray Kremer," www.baseball-reference.com (accessed on November 3, 2014).

42. The standard baseball reference works and sites say 1893, but almost all the primary sources that the author viewed, including the 1900, 1910, 1920, and 1940 United States Federal Census records and Kremer's draft registration cards for both World Wars, say or imply 1895.

43. Lieb, *The Pittsburgh Pirates*, 199.

44. Ward Mason, "Ray Kremer, Pittsburgh's Veteran Ace," *Baseball Magazine* 43, no. 4 (September 1929): 449, 474, and John J. Ward, "The Pitcher With the Deceiving Delivery," *Baseball Magazine* 34, no. 6 (May 1925): 558.

45. Lane, "Wrecking Baseball's Greatest Infield," 469.

46. "Major Leagues Open Title Races Tuesday," *New York Times*, April 12, 1925.

47. W. A. Phelon, "Who Will Win the Big League Pennants in 1925," *Baseball Magazine* 34, no. 6 (May 1925): 571.

48. "Major Leagues Open Title Races Tuesday."

49. Phelon, "Who Will Win the Big League Pennants in 1925," 531–534, 571–573.

50. Ralph Davis, "Sport Chat," *Pittsburgh Press*, October 20, 1925.

51. "Major Leagues Open Title Races Tuesday"; John McGraw, "Close Races Predicted," *Los Angeles Times*, April 12, 1925; "American and National League Pennant Races Will Get Under Way Next Tuesday," *Los Angeles Times*, April 12, 1925; "Big League Ball Teams Open Fire," *Los Angeles Times*, April 14, 1925; and "In the Press Box with Baxter," *Washington Post*, April 15, 1925.

52. "Major Leagues Open Title Races Tuesday."

53. Ralph S. Davis, "Big League Moguls Will Confer," *Pittsburgh Press*, December 7, 1924.

54. Ralph S. Davis, "Long Arid Stretch Ahead for Pirates," *The Sporting News*, March 12, 1925, 1.

55. Wollen, "M'Kechnie Lays Down Law to Team."

56. Ibid.

57. The statistics used in this sentence were taken from "The 1925 PIT N Pitching Splits for Vic Aldridge," www.retrosheet.org (accessed on November 28, 2014), but the calculations were made by the author.

58. Lou Wollen, "Niehaus' Injury May Cause Big Shift," *Pittsburgh Press*, April 11, 1925.

59. Lou Wollen, "Injuries Increase Woes of Corsairs," *Pittsburgh Press*, May 9, 1925.

60. "The 1925 PIT N Regular Season Batting Log for Al Niehaus" and "The 1925 PIT N Regular Season Fielding Log for Al Niehaus," www.retrosheet.org (accessed on November 24, 2014).

61. Charles Rigler, Umpires' Daily Official Report, May 14, 1925, Earl Smith, Player File, National Baseball Hall of Fame Library, Cooperstown, New York; John A. Heydler to Barney Dreyfuss, Western Union Telegram, May 15, 1925, Earl Smith, Player File, National Baseball Hall of Fame Library, Cooperstown, New York; and S. E. Watters to John A. Heydler, Letter, July 21, 1925, Earl Smith, Player File, National Baseball Hall of Fame Library, Cooperstown, New York.

62. Charles Rigler, Umpires' Daily Official Report, May 14, 1925, Earl Smith, Player File, National Baseball Hall of Fame Library, Cooperstown, New York.

63. Charles Rigler, Umpires' Daily Official Report, May 14, 1925, Earl Smith, Player File, National Baseball Hall of Fame Library, Cooperstown, New York; John A. Heydler to Earl Smith, Western Union Telegram, May 18, 1925, Earl Smith, Player File, National Baseball Hall of Fame Library, Cooperstown, New York; John A. Heydler to William McKechnie,

Western Union Telegram, May 18, 1925, Earl Smith, Player File, National Baseball Hall of Fame Library, Cooperstown, New York; and John A. Heydler to Charles Rigler, Letter, May 18, 1925, Earl Smith, Player File, National Baseball Hall of Fame Library, Cooperstown, New York.

64. "Earl Smith's Case Again Continued," *Boston Globe*, August 26, 1925; "Smith's Accuser Again Absent," *Boston Globe*, August 27, 1925; and "National League," *The Sporting News*, September 10, 1925, 7. According to an unsigned note found in Smith's player file in the National Baseball Hall of Fame Library, the case had been dismissed when Lewis failed to appear on August 26, but this information is obviously incorrect. An unsigned note dated August 26, 1925, found in Earl Smith, Player File, National Baseball Hall of Fame Library, Cooperstown, New York.

65. Charles Rigler, Umpires' Daily Official Report, May 14, 1925, Earl Smith, Player File, National Baseball Hall of Fame Library, Cooperstown, New York.

66. Jack Ryder, "Reds Seen as Keen Factor in National League Race," *Washington Post*, April 2, 1925.

67. For examples of this relationship, see Barney Dreyfuss to August Herrmann, Letter, October 18, 1907, Barney Dreyfuss, Player File, National Baseball Hall of Fame Library, Cooperstown, New York; Barney Dreyfuss to August Herrmann, Letter, October 28, 1907, Barney Dreyfuss, Player File, National Baseball Hall of Fame Library, Cooperstown, New York; Barney Dreyfuss to August Herrmann, Letter, November 25, 1907, Barney Dreyfuss, Player File, National Baseball Hall of Fame Library, Cooperstown, New York; Barney Dreyfuss to August Herrmann, Letter, December 26, 1907, Barney Dreyfuss, Player File, National Baseball Hall of Fame Library, Cooperstown, New York; Barney Dreyfuss to August Herrmann, Letter, January 10, 1908, Barney Dreyfuss, Player File, National Baseball Hall of Fame Library, Cooperstown, New York; Barney Dreyfuss to August Herrmann, Letter, January 13, 1908, Barney Dreyfuss, Player File, National Baseball Hall of Fame Library, Cooperstown, New York; August Herrmann to Fred C. Clarke, Western Union Telegram, January 14, 1908, Barney Dreyfuss, Player File, National Baseball Hall of Fame, Cooperstown, New York; Barney Dreyfuss to August Herrmann, Letter, May 6, 1910, Barney Dreyfuss, Player File, National Baseball Hall of Fame, Cooperstown, New York; Barney Dreyfuss to August Herrmann, Letter, June 6, 1910, Barney Dreyfuss, Player File, National Baseball Hall of Fame, Cooperstown, New York; and Barney Dreyfuss to August Herrmann, Letter, June 8, 1910, Barney Dreyfuss, Player File, National Baseball Hall of Fame, Cooperstown, New York.

68. Ronald T. Waldo, *The Battling Bucs of 1925: How the Pittsburgh Pirates Pulled Off the Greatest Comeback in World Series History* (Jefferson, NC: McFarland, 2012), 73.

69. Edward F. Balinger, "Pirates Trade Maranville, Cooper and Grimm to Cubs," *Pittsburgh Post*, October 28, 1924.

70. Waldo, *The Battling Bucs of 1925: How the Pittsburgh Pirates Pulled Off the Greatest Comeback in World Series History*, 73.

71. Davis, "Anyway, Big Swap Satisfies Barney," 1.

72. James J. Long, "Sporting Gossip and Comment," *Pittsburgh Sun*, October 31, 1924.

73. "Fred Clarke: The Baseball Capitalist," *New York Herald*, March 5, 1911, Magazine Section, 7.

74. Depending on the source, the Clarke name can be found with or without an "e" at the end of it. However, since Fred included the "e" when signing his name, "Clarke" will be used throughout this book for purposes of consistency.

75. Edward C. Papenfuse, Alan F. Day, David W. Jordan, and Gregory A. Stiverson, *A Biographical Dictionary of the Maryland Legislature, 1635–1789*, Volume 1 (Baltimore: The Johns Hopkins University Press, 1979), 223–224. See also "The Clarke Family," biographical information compiled from data that belonged to William Howard Scarff, one of Clarke's brothers-in-law, and given to the author by Margaret Donahoe Burroughs, and "The Clarke Family Tree," constructed and given to the author by Margaret Donahoe Burroughs.

76. "The Clarke Family."

77. For information on Sarah Ann Elizabeth Dickinson, see ibid.

78. Most secondary works that mention William say that he was a farmer, but in the United States Federal Census records for 1860–1880, William's profession is listed as a blacksmith. Cf. Frederick G. Lieb, "Fred Clarke," *Baseball Magazine* 4, no. 4 (February 1910): 47; David. L. Porter, "Fred Clifford 'Cap' Clarke," in *Biographical Dictionary of American Sports: Baseball*, edited by David L.

Porter (Westport, CT: Greenwood Press, 1987), 94; John Pletchette, "Fred Clifford Clarke, Major League Baseball Hall of Famer," a timeline compiled for the 150th anniversary of the founding of Winterset, Iowa, Madison County Historical Society, Winterset, Iowa, 1; Bob Hartley, *Winfield's Golden Era of Sports: How Five Decades of Champions, Heroes and Dynasties Shaped One of the Richest Athletic Traditions in Kansas* (Westminster, CO: Sniktau Publications, 2009), 11; and 1860–1880 United States Federal Census. For more information on William, see "The Clarke Family."

79. "The Clarke Family."

80. Madison County Recorder, Madison County Court House, Winterset, Iowa.

81. Northeast Quarter, Section 12, Township 32, Range 3. Register of Deeds Office, Cowley County Court House, Winfield, Kansas, Book E, 356.

82. No one knows the exact time when the Clarke family went back to Iowa. Clarence Miller, writing in 1909, said 1880, but baseball historian Frank Phelps, Winterset native John Pletchette, and journalist and book publisher Robert Hartley later wrote that it was 1879. Historian David Porter said that the Clarkes travelled to southern Kansas when Fred was two — which would have been sometime between October 3, 1874, and October 2, 1875 — and returned five years later, meaning 1879 or 1880. However, the 1880 United States Federal Census records have the Clarkes living in Kansas as of June 21, 1880, and William and Lucy Clarke sold the last piece of land that they owned in the Sunflower State on July 2, 1881, to a resident of Polk County, Iowa, the county where Des Moines is located. So, the most likely time was between mid–1880 and mid–1881. Cf. Clarence W. Miller, "Fred Clarke — Ball Player [sic], Ranchman — Kansan," *Kansas Magazine* (November 1909): 46; Frank V. Phelps, "Fred Clifford Clarke," in *Baseball's First Stars*, edited by Frederick Ivor-Campbell, Robert L. Tiemann, and Mark Rucker (Cleveland: Society for American Baseball Research, 1996), 29; Pletchette, 1; Hartley, 11–12; Porter, 94; 1880 Untied States Federal Census; and Register of Deeds, Cowley County Kansas, Winfield, Kansas, Book S, 447.

83. For details on Clarke's rise to baseball prominence, see Angelo Louisa, "Fred Clarke," SABR Baseball Biography Project, http://sabr.org/bioproject, and Angelo Louisa, "Fred Clarke: It All Began in Iowa," The Field of Dreams Chapter of the Society for American Baseball Research, http://chapters.sabr.org/fieldofdreams.

84. Ralph J. Christian, "Edward Grant Barrow: The Des Moines Years," paper presented at the Society for American Baseball Research National Convention, Scottsdale, AZ, 1999, 2–3.

85. For more information on Barrow and his relationship with Clarke, see Edward Grant Barrow, with James M. Kahn, *My Fifty Years in Baseball* (New York: Coward-McCann, 1951); Daniel R. Levitt, *Ed Barrow: The Bulldog Who Built the Yankees' First Dynasty* (Lincoln: University of Nebraska Press, 2008); Dan Levitt, "Ed Barrow," SABR Baseball Biography Project, http://sabr.org/bioproject; and Christian. However, Levitt is wrong in writing on page 14 of his book that "Clarke quickly established himself as the team's first baseman and part-time pitcher." Actually, Clarke was the team's second baseman and part-time catcher. Also, the team that Levitt is referring to is the Des Moines Mascots. Ed Barrow later claimed that Clarke had played for the Des Moines Stars, but Ralph Christian has found no newspaper evidence to corroborate Barrow's claim. The biggest difficulty, according to Christian, is "the lack of published box scores for both [the Mascots and the Stars]." Cf. Barrow, 16; Christian, 4; "Once Grocery Clerk," *Washington Post*, July 30, 1911; Ralph Christian to Angelo Louisa, e-mail message of September 22, 2001; and announcements and game results for the Mascots found in "Among the Amateurs," *Iowa State Register*, April 20, 1890; "Mascots vs. Juniors," *Iowa State Register*, July 2, 1890; "The City League," *Iowa State Register*, July 26, 1890; "The City League," *Iowa State Register*, July 27, 1890; "The World of Sport," *Iowa State Register*, August 2, 1890; "The Amateurs," *Iowa State Register*, August 12, 1890; and "The Amateurs," *Iowa State Register*, August 27, 1890.

86. Clarke played for Hastings of the Nebraska State League in 1892 and St. Joseph of the Western Association and Montgomery of the Southern League in 1893. The first two leagues folded on July 13 and June 19 of their respective years — though Benjamin Barrett Sumner and www.baseball-reference.com state that the Western Association ceased operating on the 20th, while Lloyd Johnson and Miles Wolff (referring to the group of teams as the Western League) maintain it was the 30th — and the third one ended its season on August 12 because of a yellow fever outbreak. How-

ever, after the Western Association became defunct, St. Joseph played a best-of-seven series with Kansas City, which ended on July 4 with Kansas City as the champion, four games to two. For the Nebraska State League, see Gregory Bond, "'Too Much Dirty Work': Race, Manliness, and Baseball in Gilded Age Nebraska," *Nebraska History* 85 (Winter 2004): 183. For the Western Association, cf. Benjamin Barrett Sumner, *Minor League Baseball Standings: All North American Leagues, Through 1999* (Jefferson, NC: McFarland, 2000), 568; "Western Association," www.baseball-reference.com (accessed on November 3, 2014); Lloyd Johnson and Miles Wolff, eds., *Encyclopedia of Minor League Baseball*, 3d ed. (Durham, NC: Baseball America, 2007), 164; "The Western League," *Kansas City Star*, June 20, 1893; and "Another Western Association," *Reach's Official Base Ball Guide for 1894* (Philadelphia: A. J. Reach, 1894), 35–36. And for the Southern League, see "Southern League Meeting," *The Sporting News*, August 19, 1893, 3.

87. The official name of this section is the Cherokee Outlet, an area in northern Oklahoma that was made available for white settlement via a land rush on September 16, 1893.

88. Phelps, 29.

89. Ibid.

90. "Fred Clarke: The Baseball Capitalist," Magazine Section, 7.

91. The statistics used in this paragraph were taken from "Fred Clarke," www.baseball-reference.com (accessed on December 7, 2014).

92. The Louisville directors, of which Dreyfuss was a member, made the official decision, but it appears that Dreyfuss was the driving force behind that decision.

93. Not including games played and plate appearances, in which he was in the top 10 twice for both. "Fred Clarke," www.baseball-reference.com (accessed on December 23, 2014), and Joseph L. Reichler, *The Great All-Time Baseball Record Book* (New York: Macmillan, 1981), 112.

94. "Fred Clarke," www.baseball-reference.com (accessed on November 24, 2014). Clarke's 362 putouts and .987 fielding percentage in 1909 led outfielders in both major leagues. Also that season, he came in second in range factor per game for major league outfielders.

95. Not including defensive games as an outfielder, in which he was in the top five three times. Ibid. (accessed on November 24, 2014).

96. Reichler, *The Great All-Time Baseball Record Book,* 269, and Morris Eckhouse and Carl Mastrocola, *This Date in Pittsburgh Pirates History* (New York: Stein and Day, 1980), 25, 60.

97. "Fred Clarke," www.baseball-reference.com (accessed on November 25, 2014).

98. H. Perry Lewis, "'Smile! Smile! No Matter How Things Break,' Clarke's Motto," [Philadelphia] *Public Ledger*, May 23, 1915.

99. Ibid.

100. Ibid.

101. Ibid.

102. Margaret Donahoe Burroughs, interviewed by Angelo J. Louisa and Pamela A. Louisa, Pittsburgh, Pennsylvania, June 8, 2008.

103. Lewis.

104. For an example of Clarke criticizing himself, see Lieb, *The Pittsburgh Pirates*, 130.

105. Nick Acocella and Donald Dewey, *The "All-Stars" All-Star Baseball Book* (New York: Avon, 1986), 38.

106. Letter from Fred C. Clarke to Ernest Lanigan, January 14, 1947, found in Fred Clarke, Player File, National Baseball Hall of Fame Library, Cooperstown, New York. Also, in 1951, Clarke provided Joe King with an all-time all-star team of "only men [he] had a chance to follow through a season," and again he picked Waddell as his number one left-hander. Joe King, "'The Wonder Man' of Pittsburgh: Life Story of Fred Clarke, Famed Pirate," *The Sporting News*, March 28, 1951, 22.

107. Lewis.

108. "Sun Glasses," *Sporting Life*, February 10, 1912, 14; Ed A. Goeway, "The Old Fan Says," *Leslie's Illustrated Weekly Newspaper*, August 6, 1914, 134; "Playing Sunfield Detrimental to Batting; Hooper, Red Sox, One of Most Adept on Job," *Washington Post*, November 5, 1916; F. C. Clarke, Sliding Pad for Base Ball Players, etc., U.S. Patent 1,044,494, filed May 24, 1911, issued November 19, 1912; "Ball Game [sic] of To-Day [sic] Postponed," *Pittsburgh Sun*, April 21, 1911; F. C. Clarke, Diamond Cover, U.S. Patent 983,857, filed June 7, 1909, issued February 7, 1911; Judy Welch, "Cowley County's Fred Clarke Brought Fame, Glory to Pittsburgh Pirates," *Arkansas City* (KS) *Traveler*, November 8, 1976; Dennis DeValeria and Jeanne Burke DeValeria, *Honus Wagner: A Biography* (New York: Henry Holt, 1995), 200–201. For Harry Hooper's endorsement of Clarke's sunglasses, see "Playing Sunfield Detrimental to Batting; Hooper, Red Sox, One of Most Adept on Job."

109. Based on the income index of the GDP per capita. "Purchasing Power of Money in the United States from 1774 to Present," www.measuringworth.com/ppowerus (accessed November 28, 2014).

110. Sally Wilcox, *Winfield and the Walnut Valley* (Arkansas City, Kansas: Gilliland's Publishing, 1975), 117, 124, 129; Beverly and Scott Reiter, interviewed by Angelo J. Louisa and David Cicotello, Winfield, Kansas, August 15, 2007; "Winfield Country Club History," www.winfieldcountryclub.com (accessed on November 24, 2014); and Burroughs, interview. Clarke had an Airedale that he would sic on Klan members who came to his ranch to harass him.

111. "Crown Wagner Diamond's King," *Chicago Daily Tribune*, February 25, 1917.

112. "Johnny Evers Urges Aggressive Ball," *Boston Daily Globe*, February 25, 1917.

113. Ralph S. Davis, "Dreyfuss Spoils a Fresh Line of Dope," *The Sporting News*, October 26, 1916, 3; Ralph S. Davis, "Injections of Cheer for Pirate Fandom," *The Sporting News*, January 31, 1918, 5; and I. E. Sanborn, "Comiskey Predicts Rough Going for Major Leagues," *Chicago Daily Tribune*, December 13, 1919. However, according to Joe King, the second rumor was more than just hearsay. See Joe King, "Fred, With $3,000,000 Cash in Hand, Couldn't Buy Bucs," *The Sporting News*, March 21, 1951, 16.

114. Ralph S. Davis, "Gibby Enthuses as Rooks Show Paces," *The Sporting News*, March 24, 1921, 3.

115. Ralph S. Davis, "Pirates Absolutely Right for a Start," *The Sporting News*, April 14, 1921, 3, and Ralph Davis, "Sport Chat," *Pittsburgh Press*, August 27, 1925.

116. Davis, "Sport Chat," August 27, 1925.

117. Edward F. Balinger, "Buccaneer Outfit Lands at Hot Springs for Final Training Grin [sic]," *Pittsburgh Post*, March 13, 1922, and Ralph S. Davis, "M'Kechnie Proves a Great Diplomat," *The Sporting News*, March 15, 1923, 3.

118. Thorn, Palmer, and Gershman, 2479–2480. A review of issues of *The Sporting News* for those years supports this information.

119. Ralph S. Davis, "Two Bound to Make M'Graw Miserable," *The Sporting News*, August 30, 1923, 3.

120. For examples of Clarke's sojourns to California prior to choosing a new spring training site, see "Fred Clarke Is Among Us," *Los Angeles Times*, June 14, 1919; "Fred Clarke Now a Scattergunner," *Los Angeles Times*, June 23, 1919; and Joe Bush, "Pittsburg [sic] Boss Talks to Bushers," *Los Angeles Times*, July 30, 1923.

121. Davis, "One Thing Pirates Won't Argue About," 3, and Thorn, Palmer, and Gershman, 2480.

122. Edward F. Balinger, "Fred Clarke to Tell Fans About World Series Games Exclusively in the *Post*," *Pittsburgh Post*, October 1, 1922.

123. "F. Clarke Still Likes to Play," *Atlanta Constitution*, September 8, 1922, and Balinger, "Fred Clarke to Tell Fans About World Series Games Exclusively in the *Post*."

124. "Clarke Signs Up to Write Series at Polo Grounds," *Pittsburgh Post*, September 29, 1922; "Fred Clarke's Pen as Mighty as Bat He Used to Wield," *Pittsburgh Post*, September 30, 1922; and Balinger, "Fred Clarke to Tell Fans About World Series Games Exclusively in the *Post*."

125. Balinger, "Fred Clarke to Tell Fans About World Series Games Exclusively in the *Post*."

126. "Clarke May Come Back," *Los Angeles Times*, December 29, 1922.

127. Ibid.

128. Bill Henry, "Coast League Confab Opens," *Los Angeles Times*, November 12, 1923.

129. "Fred Clarke, Ex-Pirate Boss, May Buy Philly Nationals," *Chicago Daily Tribune*, November 6, 1924.

130. Daniel, 444.

131. "Fred Clarke Seeks Baseball Come-Back [sic]," *Washington Post*, October 30, 1924.

132. "Yanks Get Holiday to Join Mardi Gras," *New York Times*, March 5, 1924, and "Fred Clarke Advocates Shift to the Outfield for Sisler," *New York Times*, March 20, 1924.

133. "McGraw Selects All-National Team," *Atlanta Constitution*, November 8, 1922.

134. W. B. Hanna, "The Twenty-five Greatest Players," *Baseball Magazine* 33, no. 1 (June 1924): 299–300.

135. "Fred Clarke to Coach," *New York Times*, February 26, 1922, and Balinger, "Buccaneer Outfit Lands at Hot Springs for Final Training Grin [sic]."

136. "Clarke Awaits Oldtime [sic] Game to Show Form," *Pittsburgh Post*, June 1, 1925, and Edward F. Balinger, "Pirates Loaf Today; Phils Open Invasion of East Tomorrow," *Pittsburgh Post*, June 3, 1925.

137. "Clarke Returns to Buccaneers," *Pittsburgh Press*, June 13, 1925.

138. Ralph Davis, "Sport Chat," *Pittsburgh Press*, June 15, 1925.
139. "Fred Clarke Returns to Corsairs in Official Capacity," *Pittsburgh Post*, June 13, 1925.
140. Ibid.
141. Ibid.
142. Ibid.
143. Ralph S. Davis, "Clarke Goes Back with His Old Team," *The Sporting News*, June 18, 1925, 3.
144. According to Ralph Davis, "[In 1925,] there [were] few better propositions than the [Pittsburgh] club, from a monetary standpoint." Davis, "Sport Chat," June 15, 1925.
145. Daniel, 444.
146. "Fred Clarke, Ex-Pirate Boss, May Buy Philly Nationals."
147. Daniel, 444.
148. "Will He Quit?" *Chicago Daily Tribune*, September 4, 1925.
149. "Sam Dreyfuss Dies Here of Pneumonia," *Pittsburgh Press*, February 23, 1931.
150. "Sam Dreyfuss Dead; A Baseball Notable," *New York Times*, February 23, 1931.
151. "Caught on the Fly," *The Sporting News*, October 22, 1925, 6.
152. "Sam Dreyfuss Dies Here of Pneumonia."
153. Davis, "M'Kechnie Hears Shouting of Mob."
154. Jenifer Langosch, "Dreyfuss A Baseball Pioneer," http://m.pirates.mlb.com/news/article/2305042/ (accessed on November 24, 2014).
155. 1940 United States Federal Census. Despite what Edwin Pope wrote in his *Baseball's Greatest Managers*, Clarke did not drop out of school after the sixth grade. Cf. 1940 United States Federal Census, with Clarke's last name spelled without the "e," and Edwin Pope, *Baseball's Greatest Managers* (Garden City, NY: Doubleday, 1960), 39.
156. For the purpose of this book, the Midwest has been defined as consisting of the states of Illinois, Indiana, Iowa, Kansas, Michigan, Minnesota, Missouri, Nebraska, North Dakota, Ohio, South Dakota, and Wisconsin.
157. For the purpose of this book, the farming class has been defined as people who work on, manage, and/or own farms.
158. For the purpose of this book, the working class has been defined as craftsmen and skilled and unskilled laborers.
159. William Strauss and Neil Howe, *Generations: The History of America's Future, 1584 to 2069* (New York: William Morrow, 1991) and William Strauss and Neil Howe, *The Fourth Turning: An American Prophecy* (New York: Broadway Books, 1997).
160. Strauss and Howe, *The Fourth Turning: An American Prophecy*, 98.
161. Strauss and Howe, *Generations: The History of America's Future, 1584 to 2069*, 113–343. In *The Fourth Turning: An American Prophecy*, the authors go as far back as the late Middle Ages with generational types. See Strauss and Howe, *The Fourth Turning: An American Prophecy*, 123–138.
162. Strauss and Howe, *Generations: The History of America's Future, 1584 to 2069*, 137–143, 172–180, and Strauss and Howe, *The Fourth Turning: An American Prophecy*, 128–132.
163. This percentage would be higher if it could be conclusively proven that Lee Meadows had attended a postsecondary institution prior to 1926. According to the 1940 United States Federal Census records, Meadows had been a student for two years at an institution of higher education, generically referred to as a college, but the author has found no evidence to show that he was there before the 1926 season.
164. It can be documented that Earl Smith had attended Jones School in Hot Springs, Arkansas, an elementary school that is no longer open. However, according to an article in the June 1927 issue of *Baseball Magazine*, Smith had also gone to high school for two years, and Ed Balinger extended Smith's schooling when he wrote that the "belligerent backstop ... complet[ed] his high school course." But the author could not find any corroborating evidence to support either assertion. Liz Robbins, e-mail message to the author, December 10, 2014; "'Oil' Smith, the Pirates Colorful Catcher," comprising an interview with Earl Smith, *Baseball Magazine* 39, no. 1 (June 1927): 312; and Edward F. Balinger, "Champtown Chatter," *Pittsburgh Post*, February 13, 1926.
165. Anne Elise Morris, telephone conversation with the author, May 14, 2014.
166. Carol McKechnie Montgomery, with Jerry Hanks, *"The Deacon's" Daughter: "Daddy's Girl" Relives Her Life with Hall of Fame Baseball Manager Bill McKechnie* (West Conshohocken, PA: Infinity, 2011), 38.
167. Anne Elise Morris, telephone conversation with the author, May 14, 2014.
168. Anne Elise Morris, e-mail message to the author, May 15, 2014.
169. United States Federal Census.

170. According to Onslow's niece, Nancy Purviance, the Pirate coach attended but probably did not graduate from Scio School in Scio, Ohio, and the Harrison Hills City School District has records of his attendance at Scio School for only 1900–1901, when he was in the fourth grade, and 1901–1902, when no grade level is given. Nancy Purviance, interviewed by Angelo J. Louisa, by telephone, October 13, 2014, and Jenny Gibson, e-mail message to the author, November 20, 2014.

171. Though Onslow grew up in several towns in western Pennsylvania and eastern Ohio.

172. Murdock, *Baseball Between the Wars: Memories of the Game by the Men Who Played It*, 93, and Nancy Purviance, interviewed by Angelo J. Louisa, by telephone, October 13, 2014.

173. See Appendix B for more information on Fraser.

174. The information for this table came from a variety of sources including, among others, Eugene Murdock's interviews with Clyde Barnhart, Eddie Moore, and Glenn Wright; e-mail exchanges and/or telephone conversations with personnel at academic institutions, relatives of some of the players, and residents of the localities where some of the players had lived; player files from the National Baseball Hall of Fame Library; the United States Federal Census records; draft registration cards; death certificates; book-length biographies of and/or biographical articles written about some of the players; issues of *Baseball Magazine*, *The Sporting News*, and the major Pittsburgh newspapers; and the player pages at www.baseball-reference.com.

175. For the purpose of this book, the subdivisions of the regional origin category have been defined as follows:

Northeast = Connecticut, Delaware, Maine, Massachusetts, New Hampshire, New Jersey, New York, Pennsylvania, Rhode Island, and Vermont

Southeast = Alabama, Arkansas, Florida, Georgia, Kentucky, Louisiana, Maryland, Mississippi, North Carolina, South Carolina, Tennessee, Virginia, and West Virginia

Midwest = Illinois, Indiana, Iowa, Kansas, Michigan, Minnesota, Missouri, Nebraska, North Dakota, Ohio, South Dakota, and Wisconsin

Southwest = Arizona, New Mexico, Oklahoma, and Texas

West Coast = California, Oregon, and Washington

No player on either the 1925 or 1926 Pirates came from any other geographic region. However, George Grantham and Johnny Rawlings were born in one region and then moved to another at the age of three and sometime before entering his junior year in high school, respectively, and have been classified as "multiple."

176. For the purpose of this book, the subdivisions of the social background category have been defined as follows:

Upper Class = Industrialists and owners of other big businesses, capitalists, and owners of large tracts of land

Middle Class = Small businessmen, merchants, salesmen, and professionals

Working Class = Craftsmen and skilled and unskilled laborers

Farming Class = People who work on, manage, and/or own farms

Multiple = The head of the household started in one class but moved to one or more others.

177. George "Mule" Haas, John "Red" Oldham, and Lafayette Fresco "Tommy" Thompson.

178. The statistics used in this paragraph were taken from "The 1925 Pittsburgh Pirates Regular Season Game Log," www.retrosheet.org (accessed on December 6, 2014).

179. "Pirates Smear Fading Giants," *Boston Globe*, August 25, 1925.

180. The statistics used in this table, with the exception of Projected Won-Lost Record, which came from Gillette and Palmer, 172, were taken from "1925 National League Team Statistics and Standings," www.baseball-reference.com (accessed November 28, 2014). The conversions were done by the author.

181. The statistics used in this table were taken from "The 1925 Pittsburgh Pirates" and "The 1925 New York Giants," www.retrosheet.org (accessed on November 3, 2014).

182. The statistics used in this table were taken from Gillette and Palmer, 172.

183. The statistics and rankings used in this paragraph were taken from "1925 Pittsburgh Pirates," "1925 National League Team Statistics and Standings," and "1925 National League Batting Leaders," www.baseball-reference.com (accessed on December 5, 2014); where Traynor and Wright hit in the batting order was taken from "The 1925 PIT N Batting Splits for Traynor" and "The 1925 PIT N

Batting Splits for Wright," www.retrosheet.org (accessed on December 5, 2014).

184. The rankings used in this paragraph were taken from "1925 National League Pitching Leaders," www.baseball-reference.com (accessed on December 1, 2014).

185. The rankings used in this paragraph were taken from "1925 National League Fielding Leaders," www.baseball-reference.com (accessed on December 1, 2014).

186. The statistics used in this paragraph were taken from "Clyde Barnhart" and "Max Carey," www.baseball-reference.com (accessed on December 2, 2014).

187. Jim Steinman, "Two Out of Three Ain't Bad," *Bat Out of Hell*, Epic Records/CBS Inc., 1977.

188. The statistics and rankings used in this paragraph were taken from "George Grantham," "Vic Aldridge," "Charlie Grimm," "Rabbit Maranville," and "Wilbur Cooper," www.baseball-reference.com (accessed on December 1, 2014).

189. "Stuffy McInnis," www.baseball-reference.com (accessed on December 2, 2014).

190. "Red Oldham," www.baseball-reference.com (accessed on December 2, 2014).

191. www.baseballchronology.com/Baseball/Awards/TSN-AllStars.asp (accessed on November 24, 2014), and F. C. Lane, "The All America [sic] Baseball Club of 1925," *Baseball Magazine* 36, no. 1 (December 1925): 305–308, 332, 334.

192. "Baseball Awards Voting for 1925," www.baseball-reference.com (accessed on November 25, 2014).

193. "Three Pirates on All-League Team," *Pittsburgh Gazette Times*, October 20, 1925; "Traynor, Wright Voted League's Best," *Pittsburgh Gazette Times*, October 23, 1925; and "National League Says Cuyler Leads All," *Pittsburgh Gazette Times*, October 25, 1925.

194. "Three Pirates on All-League Team," and "Hornsby and Cobb Most Feared Batsmen," *Pittsburgh Gazette Times*, October 27, 1925.

195. F. C. Lane, "Babe Adams' All But Miraculous Control," *Baseball Magazine* 35, no. 6 (November 1925): 545–546; John J. Ward, "The Third Member of the Pirates Great Outfield," *Baseball Magazine* 35, no. 6 (November 1925): 547; "A Word on the Proper Batting Stance," from an interview with Hazen Cuyler, *Baseball Magazine* 35, no. 6 (November 1925): 542; and John J. Ward, "Has Pittsburgh Found a Worthy Successor to Hans Wagner?" *Baseball Magazine* 35, no. 6 (November 1925): 538, 568.

196. "Pitcher Aldridge, Who Was Well Named 'Victor,'" from an interview with Victor Aldridge, *Baseball Magazine* 36, no. 1 (December 1925): 304; John J. Ward, "The Hero of the 1925 World's Series," *Baseball Magazine* 36, no. 1 (December 1925): 297, 335; "How Lee Meadows Rose Above All Handicaps to Become a Star Pitcher," comprising an interview with Lee Meadows, *Baseball Magazine* 36, no. 1 (December 1925): 310, 325; and James M. Gould, "Baseball's Greatest Infield," *Baseball Magazine* 36, no. 4 (March 1926): 447–448.

197. Ralph S. Davis, "There's Something To Those Pirates," *The Sporting News*, June 25, 1925, 1. Although published on June 25, the dateline of Davis' column was June 22.

198. Jack Gallagher, "Scared of the Pirates," *Los Angeles Times*, July 5, 1925.

199. "Pirates Have Upset the Dope: Clarke Will Help in National League Race," *Washington Post*, July 5, 1925.

200. Daniel, 443–444.
201. Ibid., 444.
202. Ibid.
203. Ibid.
204. Ibid.

205. Ralph Davis, "Sport Chat," *Pittsburgh Press*, September 24, 1925.

206. Waldo, *The Battling Bucs of 1925: How the Pittsburgh Pirates Pulled Off the Greatest Comeback in World Series History*, 142.

207. "Pirates Clinch Flag; Beat the Phils, 2–1," *New York Times*, September 24, 1925.

208. "Pirate Victory Popular," *Pittsburgh Press*, September 24, 1925, and "Pirates Clinch Flag; Beat the Phils, 2–1."

209. The statistics and rankings used in this paragraph were taken from "1925 American League Batting Leaders," "Joe Judge," "1925 American League Fielding Leaders," and "1925 American League Pitching Leaders," www.baseball-reference.com (accessed on December 6, 2014).

210. "Baseball Writers Concede Pirates Slight Advantage in World's Series," *The Sporting News*, October 1, 1925, 3, 5.

211. W. B. Hanna, "Strong Points and Weaknesses of Baseball's Four Most Prominent Clubs," *Baseball Magazine* 35, no. 6 (November 1925): 535–536.

212. Ibid., 536.

213. "Carey Improving at Mercy Hospital," *Pittsburgh Press*, October 27, 1925.

214. Les Biederman, "Right Price Can Buy Any Business[,] but Pirates Lack Bona Fide [sic] Offer," an article presumably from the *Pittsburgh Press* found in Barney Dreyfuss, Player File, National Baseball Hall of Fame Library, Cooperstown, New York. The name of the paper and the date have been cut off of the clipping, but "1945" has been printed on it.
215. Chilly Doyle, "Chillysauce," *Pittsburgh Gazette Times*, March 4, 1926.
216. William B. McKechnie, "M'Kechnie Expects Mad Hitting Spree," *Pittsburgh Press*, October 9, 1925.
217. Arthur Daley, "Sports of *The Times*," *New York Times*, February 8, 1962.
218. Daniel, 443.
219. "Nats' Twirler Fans Ten Bucs in Winning First Contest," *The Sporting News*, October 15, 1925, 3.
220. Ralph Davis, "Sport Chat," *Pittsburgh Press*, October 12, 1925.
221. Daniel, 444.
222. "Forbes Field a Lake," *Chicago Daily Tribune*, October 15, 1925.
223. Ralph Davis, "Sport Chat," *Pittsburgh Press*, February 23, 1926.
224. Daniel, 444.

Chapter 3

1. "Pirates' Boss Says Team Won. Not He," *Chicago Daily Tribune*, October 18, 1925.
2. Ralph S. Davis, "Clarke to Return as M'Kechnie's Aid," *The Sporting News*, December 17, 1925, 1.
3. Ibid.
4. Edward F. Balinger, "Champtown Chatter," *Pittsburgh Post*, November 3, 1925.
5. Davis, "Secret of Pirate Shakeup Revealed."
6. The 21 players were Babe Adams, Vic Aldridge, Clyde Barnhart, Carson Bigbee, Max Carey, Bud Culloton, Kiki Cuyler, Johnny Gooch, George Grantham, Ray Kremer, Stuffy McInnis, Lee Meadows, Eddie Moore, Johnny Morrison, Johnny Rawlings, Tom Sheehan, Earl Smith, Roy Spencer, Pie Traynor, Glenn Wright, and Emil Yde. Lou Koupal and Don Songer received nothing because they had been optioned to Kansas City and Oklahoma City, respectively, during the course of the season.
7. Edward F. Balinger, "Champtown Chatter," *Pittsburgh Post*, October 23, 1925. For information on Devine, see Dwayne Kling, "Joe Devine," in *Can He Play? A Look at Baseball Scouts and Their Profession*, edited by Jim Sandoval and Bill Nowlin (Phoenix: Society for American Baseball Research, 2011), 41–42, and Dwayne Kling, "Joe Devine," SABR Baseball Biography Project, http://sabr.org/bioproject.
8. Davis, "Secret of Pirate Shakeup Revealed."
9. Havey J. Boyle, "Through the Sport Lens," *Pittsburgh Chronicle Telegraph*, October 29, 1925.
10. Welsh, "Clarke Denies Statements of Discharged Pirates."
11. Ibid.
12. Edward F. Balinger, "Fred Clarke Officially Severed from Pirates, Resignation Accepted," *Pittsburgh Post*, October 29, 1926.
13. Ralph S. Davis, "Clarke Not Likely to Desert Pirates," *The Sporting News*, November 12, 1925, 1. For a humorous account of Dreyfuss dealing with rumors, see "Corsair Club Office Becomes Bureau for Denial of Rumors," *Pittsburgh Chronicle Telegraph*, November 3, 1925.
14. Walter M. Langford, *Legends of Baseball: An Oral History of the Game's Golden Age* (South Bend, IN: Diamond Communications, 1987), 32–33.
15. Johnson and Wolff, 296.
16. The Observer, "Casual Comment," *The Sporting News*, December 10, 1925, 4.
17. "Dugdale Gives Rhyne Edge over La Zerre [sic] as Shortstop," *The Sporting News*, November 5, 1925, 5.
18. Johnson and Wolff, 296.
19. Ralph S. Davis, "Winter Fiction, Says Dreyfuss of Report on Moore and Bigbee," *The Sporting News*, November 5, 1925, 1.
20. "Pirates Sell Thompson to Buffalo Club," *Pittsburgh Post*, December 11, 1925.
21. "Pirates Release Haas to Atlanta," *Pittsburgh Gazette Times*, February 14, 1926.
22. Ralph S. Davis, "B. Dreyfuss Holds Jubilee of His Own," *The Sporting News*, February 11, 1926, 1.
23. Ibid.
24. Ralph S. Davis, "Dreyfuss and M'Kechnie Can Laugh Matters Off Nowadays," *The Sporting News*, February 25, 1926, 1. Stuffy McInnis would be the next-to-the-last Pirate to sign. "M'Innis Signs Buc Contract," *Pittsburgh Gazette Times*, February 17, 1926.
25. "Rhyne, Last Pirate to Sign Contract, Ready for Training," *Pittsburgh Gazette Times*, February 24, 1926.

26. "Fred Clarke Will Remain with Pirates," *Pittsburgh Post*, December 11, 1925.
27. Edward F. Balinger, "Champtown Chatter," *Pittsburgh Post*, March 17, 1926.
28. Davis, "Dreyfuss and M'Kechnie Can Laugh Matters Off Nowadays," 1.
29. Edward F. Balinger, "Champtown Chatter," *Pittsburgh Post*, February 26, 1926.
30. James J. Long, "Pirates Have Specialized in Brothers as Pitchers," *The Sporting News*, March 9, 1922, 8.
31. Leonard Wise, "Dunn Means a Lot of Work for Barons," *The Sporting News*, February 22, 1923, 5.
32. Lou Wollen, "Pitcher Phil Morrison Sent to Indianapolis," *Pittsburgh Press*, April 6, 1926.
33. Morrison would die in 1955 of mesenteric artery thrombosis, which caused gangrene in 12 feet of his small intestine. At the time of his death, he had also been suffering from syphilis of his central nervous system for 15 years. Certificate of Death, Commonwealth of Kentucky, Frankfort, Kentucky, found in Phil Morrison, Player File, National Baseball Hall of Fame Library, Cooperstown, New York. However, it is not known if either ailment had anything to do with Morrison's lifestyle or physical condition in the 1920s.
34. Forr and Proctor, 91.
35. Ibid., 90.
36. Ibid., 89.
37. Ralph S. Davis, "M'Kechnie Hoping It'll Be a 'Big Five,'" *The Sporting News*, March 25, 1926, 1.
38. Ibid. It is interesting to note that Davis was not with the Pirates during spring training, so he must have been receiving his information from someone who was there.
39. Edward F. Balinger, "Aldridge to Start, Waner and Rhyne in Opener Tuesday," *Pittsburgh Post*, April 11, 1926. And Balinger was with the team during spring training.
40. Lou Wollen, "Pirates' Opening Lineup Is Still Unsettled," *Pittsburgh Press*, April 11, 1926.
41. Edward F. Balinger, "Champtown Chatter," *Pittsburgh Post*, April 7, 1926. For more information on Phil Morrison, see Phil Morrison, Player File, National Baseball Hall of Fame Library, Cooperstown, New York, and "Phil Morrison," www.baseball-reference.com.
42. Balinger, "Aldridge to Start, Waner and Rhyne in Opener Tuesday." For more information on Arthur Traynor, cf. Edward F. Balinger, "Champtown Chatter," *Pittsburgh Post*, August 10, 1926, and Forr and Proctor, 89–91,
43. Davis, "M'Kechnie Hoping It'll Be a 'Big Five,'" 1.
44. Edward F. Balinger, "Champtown Chatter," *Pittsburgh Post*, March 23, 1926.
45. Lou Wollen, "Four Buccaneers Still Unfit for Strenuous Duty," *Pittsburgh Press*, March 23, 1926.
46. Balinger, "Champtown Chatter," March 23, 1926.
47. Edward F. Balinger, "Champtown Chatter," *Pittsburgh Post*, April 12, 1926.
48. Edward F. Balinger, "Eddie Hock Released Outright to Oklahoma City; Game Called Off," *Pittsburgh Post*, April 1, 1926. For more information on Hock, see Ed Hock, Player File, National Baseball Hall of Fame Library, Cooperstown, New York; Clifford Blau, "Leg Men: Career Pinch-Runners in Major League Baseball," *The Baseball Research Journal* 38, no. 1 (Summer 2009): 70–71; and "Ed Hock," www.baseball-reference.com.
49. Edward F. Balinger, "Champtown Chatter," *Pittsburgh Post*, April 3, 1926.
50. Lou Wollen, "Manager M'Kechnie Names His Lineup with Opening Game with Cardinals," *Pittsburgh Press*, April 12, 1926. For more information on Pierson, see William Pierson, Player File, National Baseball Hall of Fame Library, Cooperstown, New York; "Obituary," *The Sporting News*, March 4, 1959, 28; and "1926 Columbia Comers," www.baseball-reference.com.
51. "Pirates Drop Kissinger and Phil Voyles," *Pittsburgh Post*, April 4, 1926; Davis, "M'Kechnie Hoping It'll Be a 'Big Five,'" 1; and Edward F. Balinger, "'Pie' Traynor Injured as Pirate Yanigans Win First Game, 1–0," *Pittsburgh Post*, March 11, 1926. For more information about Kissinger, see Edward F. Balinger, "Champtown Chatter," *Pittsburgh Post*, March 4, 1926, and "George Kissinger," www.baseball-reference.com. For more information about Voyles, see Phil Voyles, Player File, National Baseball Hall of Fame Library, Cooperstown, New York; Davis, "M'Kechnie Hoping It'll Be a 'Big Five,'" 1; and "Phil Voyles," www.baseball-reference.com.
52. Chilly Doyle, "Training Camp Chillysauce," *Pittsburgh Gazette Times*, March 2, 1926; James M. M'Afee, "Oldham-Gooch Are Busy Again Despite Hurts," *Pittsburgh Sun*, March 9, 1926; James M. M'Afee, "Practice Drill Is Substituted for Contest," *Pitts-

burgh Sun, March 16, 1926; Davis, "M'Kechnie Hoping It'll Be a 'Big Five,'" 1; and Ralph S. Davis, "Pirates Get Test from Very Start," *The Sporting News*, April 15, 1926, 1.

53. Lou Wollen, "McKechnie Worried Over His Opening Day Lineup," *Pittsburgh Press*, April 8, 1926. For more information on Brown, see Charles F. Doyle, "Seals to Get Pirate Rookies—Not Stars," *Pittsburgh Gazette Times*, November 1, 1925; Chilly Doyle, "Training Camp Chillysauce," *Pittsburgh Gazette Times*, March 1, 1926; Doyle, "Training Camp Chillysauce," March 2, 1926; and "Joe Brown," www.baseball-reference.com.

54. Lou Wollen, "Buccaneers Travel to Little Rock for Game Today," *Pittsburgh Press*, April 7, 1926.

55. Wollen, "Manager M'Kechnie Names His Lineup with Opening Game with Cardinals." For more information on Cook, see Doyle, "Seals to Get Pirate Rookies—Not Stars."

56. Edward F. Balinger, "Pirates Leave Hot Springs; To Open Series with Louisville Today," *Pittsburgh Post*, April 9, 1926.

57. "All-Around Class of Pirates Makes Them Favorites to Repeat; Macks, Slowly Developed, Choice in American."

58. Ibid.

59. "Max Carey in Hospital," *Pittsburgh Gazette Times*, October 25, 1925, and "Carey Improving at Mercy Hospital."

60. Edward F. Balinger, "Carey, Stricken on Way to Camp, in St. Louis Hospital," *Pittsburgh Post*, March 3, 1926.

61. Edward F. Balinger, "M'Kechnie Facing Task of Re-Making [sic] World Champions," *Pittsburgh Post*, March 23, 1926.

62. Lou Wollen, "Carey Will Not Play in Season's Opening Game," *Pittsburgh Press*, April 4, 1926.

63. Davis, "Pirates Get Test from Very Start."

64. Edward F. Balinger, "Champtown Chatter," *Pittsburgh Post*, June 3, 1926.

65. Chilly Doyle, "Training Camp Chillysauce," *Pittsburgh Gazette Times*, March 7, 1926, and Edward F. Balinger, "Champtown Chatter," *Pittsburgh Post*, March 15, 1926.

66. Charles J. Doyle, "Buc Pitcher Suffers Grippe Attack; Gunmen, Card Sharps Hold Sway," *Pittsburgh Gazette Times*, February 24, 1926, and Charles J. Doyle, "Pirates, in Arizona Desert, Fast Nearing Journey's End," *Pittsburgh Gazette Times*, February 25, 1926.

67. Lou Wollen, "Double Session for Buccaneer Battery Men Today, Then Rest Period Until Monday," *Pittsburgh Press*, February 27, 1926.

68. Ralph S. Davis, "Carey Still Hears from Injured Ribs," *The Sporting News*, March 11, 1926, 1, and Edward F. Balinger, "M'Kechnie Faced with Task of Figuring Out First and Second Teams," *Pittsburgh Post*, March 9, 1926.

69. Charles J. Doyle, "Adams Hurt When Traynor Liner Hits Him on Leg," *Pittsburgh Gazette Times*, March 6, 1926, and Doyle, "Training Camp Chillysauce," March 7, 1926.

70. Balinger, "'Pie' Traynor Injured as Pirate Yanigans Win First Game, 1–0," Lou Wollen, "Traynor's Condition Is Latest Worry for M'Kechnie," *Pittsburgh Press*, March 26, 1926; and Lou Wollen, "Pirates Score Close Victory Over Indianapolis," *Pittsburgh Press*, April 4, 1926.

71. Lou Wollen, "Another Change Made in Pirate Program," *Pittsburgh Press*, April 5, 1926.

72. Chilly Doyle, "Training Camp Chillysauce," *Pittsburgh Gazette Times*, March 9, 1926.

73. Balinger, "'Pie' Traynor Injured as Pirate Yanigans Win First Game, 1–0."

74. Balinger, "Champtown Chatter," March 23, 1926.

75. Davis, "Carey Still Hears from Injured Ribs," 1.

76. Edward F. Balinger, "Eddie Moore Injured as Regulars Trounce Yanigans, 7–1," *Pittsburgh Post*, March 14, 1926.

77. Eugene Murdock, *Baseball Players and Their Times: Oral Histories of the Game, 1920–1940* (Westport, CT: Meckler, 1991), 178. For the audio version of Moore's interview with Murdock, see Moore, interview.

78. Davis, "Carey Still Hears from Injured Ribs," 1.

79. Edward F. Balinger, "Two More Cripples are Added to Pirates' Casualty List," *Pittsburgh Post*, March 16, 1926.

80. Ibid.

81. Balinger, "Champtown Chatter," March 23, 1926.

82. Balinger, "Champtown Chatter," March 23, 1926, and Edward F. Balinger, "Western Storm Grips Pirates," *Pittsburgh Post*, March 31, 1926.

83. Wollen, "Carey Will Not Play in Season's Opening Game."

84. Lou Wollen, "M'Kechnie Calls Off Pirate Game Scheduled Today," *Pittsburgh Press*, March 24, 1926.

85. Ibid.

86. Edward F. Balinger, "Waner, Struck in

Face by Batted Ball, Suffers Serious Injury," *Pittsburgh Post*, April 10, 1926.

87. Edward F. Balinger, "Champtown Chatter," *Pittsburgh Post*, March 29, 1926.

88. Balinger, "M'Kechnie Facing Task of Re-Making [sic] World Champions."

89. Wollen, "Four Buccaneers Still Unfit for Strenuous Duty."

90. Balinger, "Eddie Hock Released Outright to Oklahoma City; Game Called Off," and Ralph S. Davis, "Inferiority Complex Overcome, Pirates Now 'Know They're Good,'" *The Sporting News*, April 8, 1926, 1.

91. Lou Wollen, "Pirates' Exhibition Game at Wichita Today Is Cancelled," *Pittsburgh Press*, March 31, 1926.

92. Wollen, "Buccaneers Travel to Little Rock for Game Today"; Wollen, "McKechnie Worried Over His Opening Day Lineup"; and Balinger, "Champtown Chatter," April 12, 1926.

93. "Pirates Inaugurate 1926 Campaign with Two Spirited Drills," *Pittsburgh Gazette Times*, February 27, 1926.

94. Ibid.

95. Balinger, "M'Kechnie Faced with Task of Figuring Out First and Second Teams."

96. Ralph S. Davis, "Fred Clarke Puts His Seal on Waner," *The Sporting News*, March 18, 1926, 2.

97. "No Eastern Team Will Beat Out Pirates in Pennant Race, New York Critic Avers," *Pittsburgh Gazette Times*, March 9, 1926.

98. Irving Vaughan, "Three Cornered [sic] Fights Loom in Major League Flag Wars," *Chicago Daily Tribune*, April 11, 1926.

99. Ibid.

100. Ibid.

101. Frederick G. Lieb, "Pirates-Yanks Picked to Win by Lieb," *Pittsburgh Gazette Times*, April 14, 1926, and Hugh Fullerton, "Hugh Fullerton Picks Athletic and Pirates," *The Sporting News*, April 29, 1926, 2.

102. Davis J. Walsh, "M'Kechnie's Outfit Picked for 1926 Flag," *Pittsburgh Sun*, March 30, 1926.

103. "Writers Pick Pirates and Athletics," *The Sporting News*, April 15, 1926, 3.

104. Cf. "McGraw Adds Cards to Annual Threat of Pirates; Satisfied with Flag Chances," *Pittsburgh Post*, March 20, 1926; "Pirates to be Tested by Giants, Reds, Cards, Baseball Critics Hold," *Pittsburgh Post*, March 21, 1926; and "Giants, Cards, Reds Menace Bucs; Macks, Yankees Dangerous," *Pittsburgh Post*, April 11, 1926.

105. "Giants, Cards, Reds Menace Bucs; Macks, Yankees Dangerous."

106. "Major Races Open Tuesday," *Los Angeles Times*, April 11, 1926.

107. Richards Vidmer, "Major Leagues Open Season This Week," *New York Times*, April 11, 1926.

108. James M. Gould, "Who Will Win the Big League Pennants in 1926?" *Baseball Magazine* 36, no. 6 (May 1926): 531.

109. Ibid., 533, 564.

110. Ibid., 533.

111. Ibid., 531–532.

112. "Giants and Macks Picked to Win Major League Flags," *Pittsburgh Post*, April 11, 1926.

113. "Wall Street Favors Giants Over Pirates," *Pittsburgh Press*, March 25, 1926; "Giants and Macks Made Favorites by Wall St. Bettors," *Pittsburgh Post*, April 4, 1926; "Giants Are 8 to 5 Favorites in Wall Street to Win Flag; Senators and Athletics, 2 to 1," *New York Times*, April 13, 1926.

114. "Major Leagues Begin Season's Grind Today," *Pittsburgh Post*, April 13, 1926.

115. Ralph Davis, "Sport Chat," *Pittsburgh Press*, April 13, 1926.

116. L. J. O'Conner, "Pirates Will Repeat, Says M'Kechnie: Claims Team Is 25 Per Cent [sic] Better," *Pittsburgh Sun*, March 4, 1926.

117. The statistics used in this paragraph were taken from "The 1926 Pittsburgh Pirates Regular Season Game Log," www.retrosheet.org (accessed on November 6, 2014).

118. The statistics used in this paragraph were taken from "The Regular Season Splits for 1926 Pittsburgh Pirates," "The 1926 PIT N Pitching Splits for Johnny Morrison," "The 1926 PIT N Pitching Splits for Vic Aldridge," "The Regular Season Batting/Fielding Log for 1926 Pittsburgh Pirates," and "The 1926 Pittsburgh Pirates Regular Season Game Log ," www.retrosheet.org (accessed on November 6, 2014).

119. Lou Wollen, "World's Champions Close Series with Reds Today," *Pittsburgh Press*, April 20, 1926.

120. Edward F. Balinger, "Champtown Chatter," *Pittsburgh Post*, April 19, 1926; Lou Wollen, "Pirates Must Take Two More Games from Reds to Reach Even-Break Mark," *Pittsburgh Press*, April 19, 1926; Edward F. Balinger, "Wright Spiked on Hand as Pirates Go Down Before Reds, 2–1," *Pittsburgh Post*,

April 20, 1926; Edward F. Balinger, "Champtown Chatter," *Pittsburgh Post*, April 22, 1926; Edward F. Balinger, "Crash Over Left Field Wall Gives Keen Another Win," *Pittsburgh Post*, April 23, 1926; Edward F. Balinger, "Champtown Chatter," *Pittsburgh Post*, April 23, 1926; Lou Wollen, "Pirates Show Improvement in Hitting in Home Opener," *Pittsburgh Press*, April 23, 1926; and Edward F. Balinger, "Champtown Chatter," *Pittsburgh Post*, April 24, 1926.

121. Lou Wollen, "Johnny Morrison Due to Pitch Against Cardinals Today," *Pittsburgh Press*, April 15, 1926.

122. Balinger, "Champtown Chatter," March 15, 1926; Ralph S. Davis, "Usual Slow Start for Pirate Champs," *The Sporting News*, April 22, 1926, 3; Doyle, "Training Camp Chillysauce," March 9, 1926; and Wollen, "Johnny Morrison Due to Pitch Against Cardinals Today."

123. Balinger, "Champtown Chatter," March 15, 1926.

124. "Al Crowder Released to Birmingham," *Pittsburgh Post*, April 15, 1926.

125. Davis, "Usual Slow Start for Pirate Champs," 3.

126. For more information on Crowder, see Alvin Crowder, Player File, National Baseball Hall of Fame Library, Cooperstown, New York.

127. Regis M. Welsh, "31,000 See Pirates Open Season with 5–3 Loss," *Pittsburgh Post*, April 23, 1926, and "Wounded Vets To Be Guests at Game Today," *Pittsburgh Post*, April 22, 1926.

128. Welsh, "31,000 See Pirates Open Season with 5–3 Loss."

129. The statistics used in this paragraph were taken from "1926 National League Attendance & Miscellaneous" and "Pittsburgh Pirates Attendance, Stadiums, and Park Factors," www.baseball-reference.com (accessed on November 7, 2014), but the National League average attendance was calculated by the author.

130. For an example of this activity, see "Fans Interested in Giant Series," *Pittsburgh Press*, June 18, 1926.

131. "Improved Attack Encourages Buccaneers," *Pittsburgh Press*, April 27, 1926.

132. For information on the Pirate batting orders, see the box scores found at "The 1926 Pittsburgh Pirates Regular Season Game Log," www.retrosheet.org (accessed on November 27, 2014).

133. The statistics used in this table were taken from "Standings At Close of Play of April 30, 1926," www.retrosheet.org (accessed on November 6, 2014).

134. The statistics used in this paragraph were taken from "The Regular Season Splits for 1926 Pittsburgh Pirates," box scores found at "The 1926 Pittsburgh Pirates Regular Season Game Log," "The 1926 PIT N Regular Season Batting Log for Clyde Barnhart," and "The 1926 PIT N Regular Season Batting Log for Stuffy McInnis," www.retrosheet.org (accessed on December 25, 2014).

135. The statistics used in this paragraph were taken from "The Regular Season Splits for 1926 Pittsburgh Pirates" and the regular season splits for the other 1926 National League teams, www.retrosheet.org (accessed on December 24, 2014).

136. The statistics used in this sentence were taken from "The 1926 PIT N Batting Splits for Glenn Wright," "The 1926 PIT N Batting Splits for Pie Traynor," "The 1926 PIT N Batting Splits for Kiki Cuyler," "The 1926 PIT N Batting Splits for Paul Waner," and "The 1926 PIT N Batting Splits for Earl Smith," www.retrosheet.org (accessed on December 24, 2014), but the runs produced numbers were calculated by the author.

137. The statistics used in this sentence were taken from "The 1926 PIT N Regular Season Fielding Log for Hal Rhyne," www.retrosheet.org (accessed on December 24, 2014), but the range factor was calculated by the author.

138. Ralph S. Davis, "Hal Rhyne Chases Moore Off Second," *The Sporting News*, May 13, 1926, 3.

139. "Playing the Game with the Pirates," *Pittsburgh Press*, May 12, 1926.

140. The statistics used this paragraph were taken from "The 1926 PIT N Pitching Splits for Lee Meadows," "The 1926 PIT N Pitching Splits for Ray Kremer," "The 1926 PIT N Pitching Splits for Don Songer," "The 1926 PIT N Pitching Splits for Johnny Morrison," and "The 1926 PIT N Regular Season Pitching Log for Don Songer," www.retrosheet.org (accessed on November 28, 2014), but some of the calculations were done by the author.

141. "Onslow, Tyson to Be Honored by Tarentum," *Pittsburgh Post*, April 28, 1926; "Playing the Game with the Pirates," *Pittsburgh Press*, May 19, 1926; "Onslow and Tyson to Be Honored at Giant Game Today," *Pittsburgh Gazette Times*, May 19, 1926; "The Post," *Pitts-*

burgh Post, May 20, 1926; John H. Gruber, "Jack Onslow, Popular Pirate Coach, Commenced Career in Texas League Where Star Players Were Developed," *Pittsburgh Post*, May 31, 1925; "The History of Tarentum," www.tarentumboro.com/index.php/documents?task=document.viewdoc&id=20 (accessed on November 8, 2014); and Balinger, "Jack Onslow, Veteran Catcher, Signed as Coach for Pirates."

142. "Onslow and Tyson to Be Honored at Giant Game Today."

143. Lou Wollen, "Pirates Celebrate Winning of World's Title," *Pittsburgh Press*, May 27, 1926. What the Pirates received has been described as an emblem, a medallion, a medal, or a fob, depending on the sportswriter. Cf. Edward F. Balinger, "Champtown Chatter," *Pittsburgh Post*, May 25, 1926; Wollen, "Pirates Celebrate Winning of World's Title"; Chester L. Smith, "Baseball's Ritziest Feet Tread Forbes Field As Pirates Hoist World's Championship Flag," *Pittsburgh Gazette Times*, May 28, 1926; caption under "Raising World Championship Emblem," *Pittsburgh Post*, May 28, 1926; Edward F. Balinger, "Cubs Mar World Series Celebration by Upsetting Champions, 5–2," *Pittsburgh Post*, May 28, 1926; and Ralph S. Davis, "Pirate-Giant Trade? Never, So They Say," *The Sporting News*, June 3, 1926, 1.

144. "The 1926 PIT N Batting Splits for Max Carey" and "The 1926 PIT N Regular Season Fielding Log for Max Carey," www.retrosheet.org (accessed on November 27, 2014).

145. "The Regular Season Batting/Fielding Log for 1926 Pittsburgh Pirates," www.retrosheet.org (accessed on November 27, 2014).

146. Lou Wollen, "Harold Carlson to Face Pirates in Philly Farewell," *Pittsburgh Press*, May 13, 1926.

147. Ralph S. Davis, "Fans Wait for Bucs to Begin Real Drive," *The Sporting News*, May 20, 1926, 1.

148. Davis, "Pirate-Giant Trade? Never, So They Say," 1, and Balinger, "Champtown Chatter," May 25, 1926.

149. Lou Wollen, "World's Champions Leave for Cincinnati Tonight," *Pittsburgh Press*, May 29, 1926.

150. David Anderson, "Bonesetter Reese," SABR Baseball Biography Project, http://sabr.org/bioproject (accessed on November 27, 2014). For more information about Reese, see ibid., and David L. Strickler, *Child of Moriah: A Biography of John D. "Bonesetter" Reese, 1855–1931* (n.p.: D. L. Strickler, 1984).

151. The statistics used in this table were taken from "Standings At Close of Play of May 31, 1926," www.retrosheet.org (accessed on November 7, 2014).

152. The statistics used in this paragraph was taken from "The 1926 Pittsburgh Pirates Regular Season Game Log," www.retrosheet.org (accessed on January 26, 2015), and "Standings At Close of Play of June 9, 1926"-"Standings At Close of Play of Play June 22, 1926," www.retrosheet.org (accessed on January 26, 2015).

153. "The 1926 PIT N Regular Season Pitching Log for Don Songer," www.retrosheet.org (accessed on January 26, 2015).

154. The statistics used in this paragraph were taken from "The 1926 Pittsburgh Pirates Regular Season Game Log," www.retrosheet.org (accessed on December 25, 2014). For information on the Pirate batting orders, see the box scores found at "The 1926 Pittsburgh Pirates Regular Season Game Log," www.retrosheet.org (accessed on November 27, 2014).

155. Edward F. Balinger, "Champtown Chatter," *Pittsburgh Post*, June 4, 1926.

156. Lou Wollen, "Ray Kremer to Try Today to Avenge Defeat of Mates," *Pittsburgh Press*, June 7, 1926.

157. "The 1926 PIT N Regular Season Pitching Log for Vic Aldridge," www.retrosheet.org (accessed on January 26, 2015).

158. Ibid. (accessed on January 26, 2015), and "The 1926 Pittsburgh Pirates Regular Season Game Log," www.retrosheet.org (accessed on January 26, 2015).

159. Edward F. Balinger, "Champtown Chatter," *Pittsburgh Post*, June 6, 1926.

160. Lou Wollen, "Traynor's Knee Still Very Sore," *Pittsburgh Press*, June 20, 1926.

161. For information on Dreyfuss' vacation, see "Caught on the Fly," *The Sporting News*, June 10, 1926, 10, and Ralph S. Davis, "Dreyfuss Goes on His Way Rejoicing," *The Sporting News*, June 17, 1926, 1.

162. "The 1926 Pittsburgh Pirates Regular Season Game Log," and "Standings At Close of Play of June 9, 1926," www.retrosheet.org (accessed on January 26, 2015).

163. Davis, "Dreyfuss Goes on His Way Rejoicing," 1.

164. For the complete list of the names on the message, see Edward F. Balinger, "Champtown Chatter," *Pittsburgh Post*, June 10, 1926.

165. Sheehan's 1926 ERA is usually seen as 6.68, but as the Retrosheet discrepancy page for Sheehan points out, Babe Adams' pitching

stats for the April 24 game against St. Louis were mistakenly added to Sheehan's. "Discrepancy File for Tom Sheehan," www.retrosheet.org (accessed on November 27, 2014).

166. "The 1926 PIT N Regular Season Pitching Log for Tom Sheehan," www.retrosheet.org (accessed on January 26, 2014), and "The 1926 PIT N Regular Season Fielding Log for Tom Sheehan," www.retrosheet.org (accessed on January 26, 2014).

167. "The 1926 PIT N Regular Season Pitching Log for Tom Sheehan," www.retrosheet.org (accessed on January 26, 2014).

168. Ralph S. Davis, "Fate of Pirates in Hands of Pitchers," *The Sporting News*, June 24, 1926, 3.

169. Frank Finch, "'Old Pete': Intimate Details of Former Pitcher's Life Related by Alexander's Ex-Wife," *The Sporting News*, May 2, 1951, 13.

170. "The 1926 CHI N Regular Season Pitching Log for Pete Alexander," www.retrosheet.org (accessed on January 26, 2014), but the calculations were done by the author.

171. Mitchell Conrad Stinson, *Deacon Bill McKechnie: A Baseball Biography* (Jefferson, NC: McFarland, 2012), 129.

172. John C. Skipper, *Wicked Curve: The Life and Troubled Times of Grover Cleveland Alexander* (Jefferson, NC: McFarland, 2006), 103.

173. For information on the Pirates not getting Alexander, see "Standings At Close of Play of June 21, 1926," www.retrosheet.org (accessed on January 27, 2015); "Victory Cost Buccaneers Services of Alexander," *Pittsburgh Press*, June 23, 1926; and Ralph S. Davis, "Pirates Feel Sure Worst Is Now Over," *The Sporting News*, July 1, 1926, 3. However, it is interesting to note that the day after Alexander was claimed by the Cardinals, the Cub president, William Veeck, Sr., said, "St. Louis was the only club to claim Alexander by waivers. If the Cardinals hadn't claimed him, he would have been given his unconditional release." "Alexander Released to Cards," *Pittsburgh Post*, June 23, 1926. Also, Ed Balinger reported in his column dated the same day as Veeck's comments, "It is said here that Grover was claimed by the Reds as well as the Cardinals when waivers were asked by the Cubs. None of the other teams filed applications." Edward F. Balinger, "Champtown Chatter," *Pittsburgh Post*, June 24, 1926. For more information about Alexander, see Finch, 13–14; Jerry E. Clark and Martha Ellen Webb, *Alexander the Great: The Story of Grover Cleveland Alexander* (Omaha: Making History, 1993); Jack Kavanagh, *Ol' Pete: The Grover Cleveland Alexander Story* (South Bend, IN: Diamond Communications, 1996); and Skipper.

174. Lou Wollen, "Nichols Deal Is Closed," *Pittsburgh Press*, June 25, 1926.

175. Edward F. Balinger, "Champtown Chatter," *Pittsburgh Post*, July 1, 1926.

176. The statistics used in this paragraph were taken from "The 1926 Pittsburgh Pirates Regular Season Game Log," "The Regular Season Batting/Fielding Log for 1926 Pittsburgh Pirates," and "The Regular Season Pitching Log for 1926 Pittsburgh Pirates," www.retrosheet.org (accessed on November 27, 2014), but the calculations were done by the author.

177. The statistics used in this table were taken from "Standings At Close of Play of June 30, 1926," www.retrosheet.org (accessed on November 7, 1926).

178. Lou Wollen, "League Leaders Give World's Champs Fine Lacing," *Pittsburgh Press*, June 27, 1926.

179. The statistics used in this paragraph were taken from the batting/fielding logs for the National League teams, www.retrosheet.org (accessed on December 25, 2014), but the calculations were done by the author.

180. Edward F. Balinger, "Champtown Chatter," *Pittsburgh Post*, June 13, 1926; Edward F. Balinger, "Pirates Grab First Place, Beating Phils as Reds Lose Another," *Pittsburgh Post*, June 10, 1926; Balinger, "Champtown Chatter," June 24, 1926; Edward F. Balinger, "Champtown Chatter," *Pittsburgh Post*, June 25, 1926; Edward F. Balinger, "Champtown Chatter," *Pittsburgh Post*, June 7, 1926; Edward F. Balinger, "Pirates Offer Another Weird Exhibition as Reds Win, 9–1," *Pittsburgh Post*, June 27, 1926; Edward F. Balinger, "Pirates Subjected to Crushing 16–0 Defeat as Four Pitchers Fail," *Pittsburgh Post*, June 28, 1926; Edward F. Balinger, "Champtown Chatter," *Pittsburgh Post*, June 29, 1926; Edward F. Balinger, "Champtown Chatter," *Pittsburgh Post*, June 30, 1926; and Balinger, "Champtown Chatter," July 1, 1926.

181. "The Post," *Pittsburgh Post*, June 26, 1926. At one time, William Peet had been the author of "The Post" column when it was called "What the Post Clock Saw," but by 1926, Peet was no longer working for the *Post*, and though "What the Post Clock Saw" was used during 1926 as the title of the column on subsequent pages, the title on the page where

the column began was "The Post" followed by "Most News" and "Keep Post-ed." So, for the purposes of this book, the column in 1926 will be referred to as "The Post."

182. For the diagnosis and treatment of Kremer, Morrison, and Rhyne, see Edward F. Balinger, "Champtown Chatter," *Pittsburgh Post*, June 26, 1926.

183. For the continuing misfortunes of Kremer, Morrison, and Rhyne, see Edward F. Balinger, "Pirates Drop Fifth Straight in Series Final at Cincinnati, 6–3," *Pittsburgh Post*, June 30, 1926, and Edward F. Balinger, "Champtown Chatter," *Pittsburgh Post*, June 28, 1926.

184. "Onslow and Snyder Engage in Fist Fight Before Game," *Pittsburgh Post*, June 21, 1926.

185. Edward F. Balinger, "Champtown Chatter," *Pittsburgh Post*, June 22, 1926; Edward F. Balinger, "Champtown Chatter," *Pittsburgh Post*, July 27, 1926; "The 1926 NY N Regular Season Batting Log for Frank Snyder," www.retrosheet.org (accessed on November 25, 2014); and ibid. Apparently, no rematch ever occurred.

186. Balinger, "Champtown Chatter," June 3, 1926. Although Balinger does not specifically say that Clarke was in Columbia in May, it can be assumed that because of the date of Balinger's article and because the head of scouting, in all likelihood, would have waited several weeks for the players to acclimate themselves to their new team, Clarke was there in May and not April.

187. "Playing the Game with the Pirates," *Pittsburgh Press*, June 29, 1926.

188. "Ralph Davis Says," *Pittsburgh Press*, June 30, 1926.

189. Ralph S. Davis, "All Isn't So Well in Pirate Menage," *The Sporting News*, July 8, 1926, 1.

190. "Ralph Davis Says," June 30, 1926.

Chapter 4

1. "Bush Signs Pirate Contract," *Pittsburgh Post*, July 1, 1926.

2. "Bullet Joe Bush," www.baseball-reference.com (accessed on November 25, 2014), and Bill Deane, *Award Voting: A History of the Most Valuable Player, Rookie of the Year, and Cy Young Awards* (Kansas City: Society for American Baseball Research, 1988), 7.

3. "Bush Signs Pirate Contract."

4. The statistics used in this paragraph were taken from "The 1926 Pittsburgh Pirates Regular Season Game Log," www.retrosheet.org (accessed on February 2, 2015).

5. The statistics used in this paragraph were taken from "The Regular Season Splits for 1926 Pittsburgh Pirates," the regular season splits for the other 1926 National League teams, and "Standings At Close of Play of July 31, 1926," www.retrosheet.org (accessed on December 9, 2014), but the calculations were done by the author.

6. The statistics used in this table were taken from "Standings At Close of Play of July 31, 1926," www.retrosheet.org (accessed on November 7, 2014).

7. For the batting orders and statistics used in this paragraph, see the "The 1926 Pittsburgh Pirates Regular Season Game Log," and the box scores found there, www.retrosheet.org (accessed on February 4, 2015).

8. "The Post," *Pittsburgh Post*, July 3, 1926.

9. The statistics used in this table were taken from "The 1926 PIT N Batting Splits for Paul Waner," "The 1926 PIT N Batting Splits for Kiki Cuyler," "The 1926 PIT N Batting Splits for Pie Traynor," "The 1926 PIT Batting Splits for George Grantham," "The 1926 Batting Splits for Earl Smith," and "The 1926 Batting Splits for Johnny Gooch," www.retrosheet.org (accessed on November 26, 2014).

10. Lou Wollen, "Victory Today Will Send Buccaneers into Second Place," *Pittsburgh Press*, July 3, 1926.

11. The statistics used in this paragraph were taken from "The 1926 PIT N Pitching Splits for Ray Kremer," "The 1926 PIT N Pitching Splits for Don Songer," "The 1926 PIT N Pitching Splits for Emil Yde," and "The 1926 PIT N Pitching Splits for Bullet Joe Bush," www.retrosheet.org (accessed on December 8, 2014).

12. Edward F. Balinger, "Champtown Chatter," *Pittsburgh Post*, July 13, 1926; Lou Wollen, "Fighting Qualities Make Braves Worthy Foemen," *Pittsburgh Press*, July 17, 1926; Lou Wollen, "Playing the Game with the Pirates," *Pittsburgh Press*, July 19, 1926; Lou Wollen, "Cubs Wind Up Stay Here with Double-Header [sic]," *Pittsburgh Press*, July 6, 1926; Lou Wollen, "Playing the Game with Pirates," *Pittsburgh Press*, July 22, 1926; Balinger, "Champtown Chatter," July 27, 1926; Edward F. Balinger, "Champtown Chatter,"

Pittsburgh Post, July 28, 1926; Ralph S. Davis, "M'Kechnie Wields an Iron Fist to Restore Champions to Order," *The Sporting News*, July 29, 1926, 1; Edward F. Balinger, "Champtown Chatter," *Pittsburgh Post*, August 1, 1926; Edward F. Balinger, "Champtown Chatter," *Pittsburgh Post*, July 6, 1926; Lou Wollen, "Pirates and Quakers Grapple in Second Battle," *Pittsburgh Press*, July 8, 1926; and "The 1926 PIT N Regular Season Batting Log for Glenn Wright," "The 1926 PIT N Regular Season Fielding Log for Glenn Wright," "The 1926 PIT N Regular Season Batting Log for Hal Rhyne," "The 1926 PIT N Regular Season Fielding Log for Hal Rhyne," "The 1926 PIT N Regular Season Pitching Log for Chet Nichols," "The 1926 PIT N Regular Season Pitching Log for Vic Aldridge," and "The 1926 PIT N Regular Season Pitching Log for Johnny Morrison," www.retrosheet.org (accessed on December 8, 2014).

13. Edward F. Balinger, "Champtown Chatter," *Pittsburgh Post*, July 8, 1926.

14. Lou Wollen, "Playing the Game with the Pirates," *Pittsburgh Press*, July 15, 1926.

15. "The Post," *Pittsburgh Post*, July 15, 1926.

16. Ralph S. Davis, "They'll Be Careful Now, If Not Serious," *The Sporting News*, July 22, 1926, 1.

17. Ralph S. Davis, "Bucs Now Bearing More Serious Mien," *The Sporting News*, August 5, 1926, 1.

18. Havey J. Boyle, "Through the Sport Lens," *Pittsburgh Chronicle Telegraph*, July 23, 1926.

19. The rankings used in the paragraph were taken from "Eddie Moore," www.baseball-reference.com (accessed on November 27, 2014).

20. Murdock, *Baseball Players and Their Times: Oral Histories of the Game, 1920–1940*, 179. Also found in Moore, interview.

21. Jimmy Connors, *The Outsider: A Memoir* (New York: HarperCollins, 2013), 53.

22. Davis, "They'll Be Careful Now, If Not Serious," 1.

23. Murdock, *Baseball Players and Their Times: Oral Histories of the Game, 1920–1940*, 181. Also found in Moore, interview.

24. Ibid. Also found in Moore, interview.

25. Davis, "They'll Be Careful Now, If Not Serious," 1.

26. Lou Wollen, "Pirates and Giants End Series Today," *Pittsburgh Press*, July 15, 1926.

27. Ibid.; "Moore-Yde Fined," *Pittsburgh Post*, July 15, 1926; "Eddie Moore Is Through As Corsair," *Pittsburgh Press*, July 18, 1926; and as the box scores show, after playing in the game on July 14 which led to McKechnie's ire, Moore did not play another game in a Pirate uniform.

28. Davis, "They'll Be Careful Now, If Not Serious," 1.

29. "Eddie Moore Is Through As Corsair."

30. Lou Wollen, "Playing the Game with the Pirates," *Pittsburgh Press*, July 21, 1926.

31. Davis, "Secret of Pirate Shakeup Revealed."

32. Ralph S. Davis, "Only One Part of It in Minds of Pirates," *The Sporting News*, October 25, 1923, 3.

33. Welsh, "Clarke Denies Statements of Discharged Pirates."

34. "Braves Claim Eddie Moore by Waiver; To Play at Third," *Pittsburgh Post*, July 21, 1926.

35. Murdock, *Baseball Players and Their Times: Oral Histories of the Game, 1920–1940*, 179. Also found in Moore, interview.

36. Davis, "M'Kechnie Wields an Iron Fist to Restore Champions to Order," 1.

37. Regis M. Welsh, "Following through," *Pittsburgh Post*, July 19, 1926.

38. "The Post," *Pittsburgh Post*, July 22, 1926.

39. Ibid.

40. Wollen, "Playing the Game with the Pirates," July 22, 1926.

41. "Pitcher Aldridge, Who Was Well Named 'Victor,'" 304.

42. Chilly Doyle, "Chillysauce," *Pittsburgh Gazette Times*, May 16, 1926.

43. Lou Wollen, "Playing the Game with the Pirates," *Pittsburgh Press*, July 23, 1926.

44. Edward F. Balinger, "Champtown Chatter," *Pittsburgh Post*, July 24, 1926.

45. "Morrison Handed Suspension by Bucs," *Pittsburgh Post*, July 25, 1926.

46. Davis, "M'Kechnie Wields an Iron Fist to Restore Champions to Order," 1.

47. "Morrison Is Out for Season, Report," *Pittsburgh Post*, July 28, 1926.

48. Davis, "Bucs Now Bearing More Serious Mien," 1.

49. Lou Wollen, "Pirates Believe They Are in First Place to Stay," *Pittsburgh Press*, July 30, 1926.

50. "National League Standing on Tuesday Morning," *The Sporting News*, August 12, 1926, 7.

51. "Morrison Forgiven as Champs Rest

and Sign Recruit," *Pittsburgh Post*, August 18, 1926.

52. The statistics used in this paragraph were taken from "The 1926 PIT N Regular Season Pitching Log for Emil Yde," www.retrosheet.org (accessed on December 8, 2014), but the calculations were done by the author.

53. "Clubs Play Double Bill Tomorrow," *Pittsburgh Sun*, July 23, 1926.

54. "Speaker Makes His 3,000th Safe Drive," *Cleveland Plain Dealer*, May 18, 1925.

55. Edward F. Balinger, "Champtown Chatter," *Pittsburgh Post*, July 30, 1926.

56. Balinger, "Champtown Chatter," August 1, 1926.

57. "Ralph Davis Says," *Pittsburgh Press*, July 23, 1926.

58. Charles J. Doyle, "Hughey Critz Central Figure in Reds' Fight to Hold Top Position," *Pittsburgh Gazette Times*, July 18, 1926.

59. Lou Wollen, "Playing the Game with the Pirates," *Pittsburgh Press*, July 24, 1926.

60. "The Post," July 15, 1926.

61. Obviously, it is impossible to tell which readers were reading which columnists, but based on circulation statistics for the five mainstream Pittsburgh newspapers in 1926, the *Press* (weekdays: 183,495; Sundays: 243,688); the *Post* (weekdays: 143,739; Sundays: 188,342); and the *Gazette Times* (weekdays: 101,574; Sundays: 150,443) were the top three. In comparison, the *Chronicle Telegraph* was third during weekdays (108,194), but it had no Sunday edition, and the *Sun* was a distant fifth during weekdays (79,860) and it, too, had no Sunday edition. *N. W. Ayer & Son's American Newspaper Annual and Directory* (Philadelphia: N. W. Ayer & Son, 1927), 947, 949.

62. "Ralph Davis Says," *Pittsburgh Press*, July 17, 1926.

63. "Ralph Davis Says," *Pittsburgh Press*, August 2, 1926.

64. Wollen, "Pirates and Giants End Series Today," "Red Oldham Released to Kansas City," *Pittsburgh Post*, July 20, 1926; and "Red Oldham, Heroic Figure in World's Series, Passes Out of Fold of Champions," *Pittsburgh Gazette Times*, July 20, 1926.

65. In addition to his baseball skills, Brickell excelled at track and, according to the *Pittsburgh Post*, was regarded as probably the best high school football player to come out of the state of Kansas as of 1926. "Pirates Buy Outfield Star from Wichita," *Pittsburgh Post*, July 24, 1926, and "Brickell, New Buc, in First Year of League Baseball," *Pittsburgh Post*, July 26, 1926.

66. "Pirates Buy Outfield Star from Wichita."

67. Ibid.

68. "Fred Brickell," www.retrosheet.org (accessed on November 27, 2014).

69. The statistics used in this paragraph were taken from the box scores found at "The 1926 Pittsburgh Pirates Regular Season Game Log," "The 1926 Cincinnati Reds Regular Season Game Log," "Standings At Close of Play of August 6, 1926," and standings for the 1926 season prior to August 6, www.retrosheet.org (accessed on December 8, 2014).

70. Lou Wollen, "Pirates and Braves Are Playing Another Bargain Matinee," *Pittsburgh Press*, August 7, 1926.

71. Chester L. Smith, "Sport Shafts," *Pittsburgh Gazette Times*, August 20, 1926.

72. The statistics used in this paragraph were taken from "The 1926 PIT N Regular Season Batting Log for Glenn Wright" and "The 1926 PIT N Regular Season Fielding Log for Glenn Wright," www.retrosheet.org (accessed on December 9, 2014), but the projections were done by the author.

73. For details, see the box scores for the two games played by Pittsburgh and Boston on August 7, 1926, found at "The 1926 Pittsburgh Pirates Regular Season Game Log," www.retrosheet.org (accessed on December 9, 2014), and Edward J. Balinger, "Champtown Chatter," *Pittsburgh Post*, August 8, 1926.

74. Balinger, "Champtown Chatter," August 10, 1926, and "Pirate Detail," *Pittsburgh Post*, August 8, 1926.

75. James J. Long, "Sporting Gossip and Comment," *Pittsburgh Sun*, August 9, 1926.

76. Ibid.

77. Welsh, "Discharged Bucs Take Case to Judge Landis."

78. "Carey Wages Fight in Rebellion Ouster," *The Sporting News*, August 19, 1926, 1. Davis' byline was not on the article, but since the article was published next to his piece titled "Guillotine Quickly Puts Down Pirate Anti-Clarke Rebellion," and since he was the Pittsburgh correspondent to *The Sporting News*, in all likelihood, the article was written by him.

79. Welsh, "Clarke Denies Statements of Discharged Pirates."

80. Welsh, "Discharged Bucs Take Case to Judge Landis."

81. Ibid.

82. Ibid.

83. Regis M. Welsh, "M'Innis' Release Start of Pirate Shakeup," *Pittsburgh Post*, September 27, 1926.
84. Davis, "Secret of Pirate Shakeup Revealed."
85. Ibid.
86. Ibid.
87. Ibid.
88. Ibid.
89. Ibid.
90. Regis M. Welsh, "Clarke Demands Disciplinary Action Following Expulsion Request," *Pittsburgh Post*, August 13, 1926.
91. Balinger, "Champtown Chatter," August 8, 1926.
92. "Bucs Are Beaten in Kingston Exhibition," *Pittsburgh Sun*, August 9, 1926.
93. Welsh, "Clarke Denies Statements of Discharged Pirates."
94. Welsh, "Clarke Demands Disciplinary Action Following Expulsion Request."
95. There are two somewhat different versions of the interview that Clarke gave the evening of September 30, 1926. Cf. "Clarke May Quit Pirates, He Asserts," *Pittsburgh Gazette Times*, October 1, 1926, and Welsh, "Clarke Denies Statements of Discharged Pirates."
96. Welsh, "Clarke Denies Statements of Discharged Pirates."
97. "Clarke May Quit Pirates, He Asserts."
98. "Max Set Fly Chasers New Pace in National," *The Sporting News*, February 14, 1924, 7.
99. The details for Clarke's attempts to get McKechnie to suggest a solution come from Welsh, "Clarke Demands Disciplinary Action Following Expulsion Request."
100. Welsh, "Clarke Demands Disciplinary Action Following Expulsion Request."
101. Welsh, "Clarke Denies Statements of Discharged Pirates." For McKechnie's account, see Welsh, "Clarke Demands Disciplinary Action Following Expulsion Request."
102. Welsh, "Clarke Denies Statements of Discharged Pirates."
103. The details for Clarke's talk to the Pirate team on August 9 come from ibid.
104. Davis, "Secret of Pirate Shakeup Revealed."
105. Ibid.
106. Welsh, "Clarke Demands Disciplinary Action Following Expulsion Request."
107. "Yde Opposes Brooklyn in Final Clash," *Pittsburgh Sun*, August 11, 1926.
108. Welsh, "Clarke Denies Statements of Discharged Pirates."
109. Ibid.
110. For details about the voting, see James J. Long, "Sporting Gossip and Comment," *Pittsburgh Sun*, August 16, 1926, though Long does not specify who the "others connected with the club" were.
111. Welsh, "Clarke Denies Statements of Discharged Pirates."
112. Davis, "Secret of Pirate Shakeup Revealed."
113. "Yde Opposes Brooklyn in Final Clash."
114. Davis, "Secret of Pirate Shakeup Revealed," and Welsh, "Clarke Denies Statements of Discharged Pirates."
115. Welsh, "Clarke Denies Statements of Discharged Pirates."
116. Long, "Sporting Gossip and Comment," August 16, 1926.
117. Ibid.
118. Ibid., and Balinger, "Champtown Chatter," August 10, 1926.
119. Wright, interview.
120. Langford, 32.
121. Balinger, "Champtown Chatter," August 1, 1926.
122. James J. Long, "Sporting Gossip and Comment," *Pittsburgh Sun*, August 2, 1926.
123. Davis, "Secret of Pirate Shakeup Revealed."
124. Lou Wollen, "Playing the Game with the Pirates," *Pittsburgh Press*, August 16, 1926.
125. "Pirate Fans Express Their Views," *Pittsburgh Press*, August 16, 1926. This section contained an introduction with no byline followed by letters to the sports editor, but since Davis was the sports editor, he probably wrote the introduction, which included Dreyfuss' statement.
126. Chester L. Smith, "Sport Shafts," *Pittsburgh Gazette Times*, October 1, 1926.
127. See Ralph S. Davis, "Guillotine Quickly Puts Down Pirate Anti-Clarke Rebellion," *The Sporting News*, 1, and "Scribbled by Scribes," *The Sporting News*, October 7, 1926, 4.
128. Edward F. Balinger, "Champtown Chatter," *Pittsburgh Post*, August 12, 1926.
129. All the information found in this paragraph on Murphy, Mahaffey, Farr, and Waner was taken from Edward F. Balinger, "Murphy, Sensation of Internationals Bought by Champs," *Pittsburgh Post*, August 13, 1926, and it is interesting to note that Farr was a member of the Burlington Bees of the Mississippi Valley League when he was bought by Pittsburgh, but the Pirates had to purchase

him from Columbia because the Comers owned him, though he did not play for them that season.

130. Havey J. Boyle, "Clarke's Absence from Bench Causes Rumors of Split with Bill M'Kechnie," *Pittsburgh Chronicle Telegraph*, August 12, 1926.

131. Ibid.

132. Ibid.

133. Ibid.

134. Ibid.

135. Welsh, "Clarke Demands Disciplinary Action Following Expulsion Request."

136. Ibid.

137. Charles J. Doyle, "Max Carey Seen as Victim Rather Than Instigator of Rebellion; Penalty Severe," *Pittsburgh Gazette Times*, August 14, 1926.

138. "Clarke May Quit Pirates, He Asserts."

139. Welsh, "Clarke Denies Statements of Discharged Pirates."

140. Welsh, "Clarke Demands Disciplinary Action Following Expulsion Request."

141. Ibid.

142. Edward F. Balinger, "Adams, Bigbee Released, Waivers Asked on Carey," *Pittsburgh Post*, August 14, 1926.

143. "Clarke May Quit Pirates, He Asserts," and Welsh, "Clarke Denies Statements of Discharged Pirates."

144. "Clarke May Quit Pirates, He Asserts."

145. "How the Iron Hand of Discipline Was Clamped on Pirate Mutiny; Treasurer Dreyfuss' Speech," *Pittsburgh Post*, August 14, 1926.

146. For statements by Clarke and McKechnie supporting Dreyfuss' pronouncement that the matter was closed, see "Deposed Pirates Plan to Strike Back," *Pittsburgh Sun*, August 14, 1926.

147. Regis M. Welsh, "Wholesale Explanations Only Method of Clearing Up Dismissals," *Pittsburgh Post*, August 14, 1926.

148. The statistics for Adams were taken from "Babe Adams," www.baseball-reference.com (accessed on December 8, 2014); those for Carey were taken from "Max Carey," www.baseball-reference.com (accessed on December 8, 2014).

149. "Censured Players Will Talk Today," *Pittsburgh Post*, August 14, 1926.

150. Welsh, "Discharged Bucs Take Case to Judge Landis."

151. "Heydler to Attempt to Settle Pirate Row," *Pittsburgh Sun*, August 16, 1926.

152. Regis M. Welsh, "Heydler to Hear Buc Revolt Today," *Pittsburgh Post*, August 17, 1926.

153. Charles J. Doyle, "Carey May Stay; Heydler Here Today," *Pittsburgh Gazette Times*, August 17, 1926.

154. Welsh, "Heydler to Hear Buc Revolt Today."

155. Starting times vary from 11:00 A.M. to about 11:00 A.M., 11:30 A.M., and shortly before noon, while the ending times are reported to have been shortly after 1:00 P.M., after 1:00 P.M., about 1:20 P.M., shortly before 1:30 P.M., and 1:30 P.M. Cf. "Carey and M'Kechnie Clash at Hearing," *Pittsburgh Press*, August 17, 1926; "Heydler Probes Pirate Row; Decision Tonight," *Pittsburgh Sun*, August 17, 1926; "Heydler Statement on Buc Fuss Tonight," *Pittsburgh Chronicle Telegraph*, August 17, 1926; Charles J. Doyle, "Heydler Clears Players, Upholds Club," *Pittsburgh Gazette Times*, August 18, 1926; and Regis M. Welsh, "Heydler Clears Pirate Trio But 'Firing' Stands," *Pittsburgh Post*, August 18, 1926. It amazes this author that five sportswriters could disagree so much on the time of the meeting. Saying it began at 11:00 A.M. or about 11:00 A.M. is close enough, but there is a big difference between 11:00 A.M. and shortly before noon or between a little after 1:00 P.M. and 1:30 P.M.

156. "Carey and M'Kechnie Clash at Hearing."

157. Welsh, "Heydler Clears Pirate Trio But 'Firing' Stands," and "Heydler Probes Pirate Row; Decision Tonight."

158. The information on the hearing was taken from ibid.; "Carey and M'Kechnie Clash at Hearing"; Chester L. Smith, "Sport Shafts," *Pittsburgh Gazette Times*, August 18, 1926; and Edward F. Balinger, "Champtown Chatter," *Pittsburgh Post*, August 18, 1926. For specific quotations used, "a set expression" came from Smith; "It's all over" came from Welsh; and the questions and demand came from Welsh, but the first two questions and the demand were also found in Doyle, "Heydler Clears Players, Upholds Club."

159. "Heydler Statement Clears Pirate Players' Names," *Pittsburgh Gazette Times*, August 18, 1926.

160. Welsh, "Heydler Clears Pirate Trio But 'Firing' Stands."

161. "Deposed Bucs Exonerated by Heydler," *Pittsburgh Sun*, August 18, 1926.

162. Lieb, *The Pittsburgh Pirates*, 178.

163. Ibid.

164. Masthead, *Pittsburgh Press*, August 1, 1926.

165. Welsh, "Wholesale Explanations Only Method of Clearing Up Dismissals."
166. "There Must Be No 'Goats,'" *Pittsburgh Press*, August 13, 1926.
167. Ralph S. Davis, "Baseball Fandom Shocked by Upheaval on Pittsburgh Club," *Pittsburgh Press*, August 15, 1926.
168. Lou Wollen, "Playing the Game with the Pirates," *Pittsburgh Press*, August 14, 1926.
169. "Boozers' Day on Pirate Payroll Ended Forever," *Pittsburgh Press*, October 9, 1910, and DeValeria and DeValeria, 242. Also, during the 1908 season, Lefty Leifield was rumored to have been suffering the effects of alcohol abuse when he compiled a 15–14 record, with a below National League average WHIP of 1.162 (average was 1.141). But in October of that year, Clarke vehemently denied the gossip, saying that "I am as positive as I am of anything that [Leifield] has not touched a drop of intoxicating liquor since last June. He never did use it to excess, but when he saw that his taking a drink of beer was starting ugly stories about his habits, he cut it out altogether." A better explanation for Leifield's statistics is that he was battling arm ailments and poor run support (3.15 runs per game compared to 4.81 for Nick Maddox, 4.00 for Vic Willis, and an average of 3.77 for all Pirate hurlers). Furthermore, not all his numbers were disappointing. For example, he posted a 2.10 ERA (the National League average was 2.35), and based on Wins Above Replacement for pitchers, he was the third best twirler on a Pirate team that almost won the pennant. "1908 Pittsburgh Pirates," www.baseball-reference.com (accessed on February 3, 2015); "1908 National League Team Statistics and Standings," www.baseball-reference.com (accessed on February 3, 2015); Ralph S. Davis, "Fought to Finish," *The Sporting News*, October 8, 1908, 4; David Finoli and Bill Ranier, *When Cobb Met Wagner: The Seven-Game World Series of 1909* (Jefferson, NC: McFarland, 2011), 198; and "The 1908 Pittsburgh Pirates Regular Season Roster," www.retrosheet.org (accessed on February 3, 2015).
170. DeValeria and DeValeria, 219–221.
171. Joe King, "'The Wonder Man' of Pittsburgh: Life Story of Fred Clarke, Famed Pirate," *The Sporting News*, March 21, 1951, 15.
172. DeValeria and DeValeria, 219,
173. During the regular season, Camnitz had a 25–6 won-lost record, with a 1.62 ERA and a 0.972 WHIP, while Willis was 22–11, 2.24, and 1.125. But during the Series, their statistics were 0–1, 13,50, and 3.000, and 0–1, 4.63, and 1.543, respectively. "1909 Pittsburgh Pirates" and "1909 World Series (4–3): Pittsburgh Pirates (110–42) over Detroit Tigers (98–54)," www.baseball-reference.com (accessed January 31, 2015).
174. Hans Wagner, "Pirates Better Off for Slabbists Than in 1909," *Pittsburgh Press*, October 7, 1925.
175. "Late News," *The Sporting News*, October 7, 1909, 1; "Do the Pirates of 1925 Outrank the Pirates of 1909?" from an interview with Fred Clarke, *Baseball Magazine* 36, no. 1 (December 1925): 303; Lieb, *The Pittsburgh Pirates*, 140, 142.
176. "1909 American League Team Statistics and Standings," www.baseball-reference.com (accessed on January 30, 2015).
177. "Carey and Adams Outstanding Figures in Baseball World," *Pittsburgh Press*, August 13, 1926. Though there is no byline for the lengthy caption under the photographs of Carey and Adams, the writing style is undoubtedly that of Davis.
178. "Carey and Adams Outstanding Figures in Baseball World."
179. "Ralph Davis Says," *Pittsburgh Press*, August 19, 1926.
180. "Ralph Davis Says," *Pittsburgh Press*, August 21, 1926.
181. Ralph S. Davis, "Not Much Sentiment in Baseball, but Plenty on Part of Fans," *Pittsburgh Press*, August 22, 1926.
182. For examples, see "Girl Fan Writes She'd Like to Give Fred Clarke Good Shaking," *Pittsburgh Press*, August 15, 1926; "Ralph Davis Says," August 21, 1926; and "Ralph Davis Says," *Pittsburgh Press*, August 24, 1926.
183. Lou Wollen, "Playing the Game with the Pirates," *Pittsburgh Press*, August 18, 1926; Lou Wollen, "Playing the Game with the Pirates," *Pittsburgh Press*, August 19, 1926; [No byline, but it is Wollen's column], "Playing the Game with the Pirates," *Pittsburgh Press*, August 22, 1926; and Lou Wollen, "Playing the Game with the Pirates," *Pittsburgh Press*, September 8, 1926.
184. [No byline, but it is Wollen's column], "Playing the Game with the Pirates," August 22, 1926.
185. "Carey Offered for Sale for $4,000," *Pittsburgh Press*, August 15, 1926.
186. Edward F. Balinger, "Champtown Chatter," *Pittsburgh Post*, August 17, 1926. For Carey's salary, see "The Post," *Pittsburgh Post*, August 24, 1926.

187. "Carey Awarded to Brooklyn," *Pittsburgh Press*, August 18, 1926.
188. James J. Long, "Sporting Gossip and Comment," *Pittsburgh Sun*, August 24, 1926.
189. "Pittsburgh Fan Starts Move for 'Carey Day,'" *Pittsburgh Gazette Times*, August 20, 1926.
190. "The Post," *Pittsburgh Post*, August 25, 1926.
191. The statistics used in this paragraph were taken from "The 1926 BRO N Regular Season Batting Log for Max Carey," www.retrosheet.org (accessed on February 2, 2015).
192. Ralph S. Davis, "Carey, Bigbee and Adams Make Formal Statement," *Pittsburgh Press*, August 22, 1926.
193. Ibid.
194. Ibid.
195. Ibid.
196. "Here's What Carey Did for Brooklyn," *Pittsburgh Press*, August 24, 1926.
197. "What Carey Did," *Pittsburgh Press*, August 26, 1926.
198. "Pirates Down General Tires in Exhibition," *Pittsburgh Post*, August 16, 1926.
199. Chilly Doyle, "Chillysauce," *Pittsburgh Gazette Times*, August 25, 1926.
200. For information on Mueller, see Walter Mueller, Player File, National Baseball Hall of Fame Library, Cooperstown, New York; Edward F. Balinger, "Champtown Chatter," *Pittsburgh Post*, August 22, 1926; "Playing the Game with the Pirates," *Pittsburgh Press*, September 1, 1926; Edward F. Balinger, "Champtown Chatter," *Pittsburgh Post*, September 1, 1926; and "Walter Mueller," www.baseball-reference.com.
201. For information on Koupal rejoining the Pirates, see Chilly Doyle, "Chillysauce," *Pittsburgh Gazette Times*, August 26, 1926, and Edward F. Balinger, "Champtown Chatter," *Pittsburgh Post*, August 26, 1926.
202. For information on Nichols' departure, see Edward F. Balinger, "Champtown Chatter," *Pittsburgh Post*, August 27, 1926; Lou Wollen, "Playing the Game with the Pirates," *Pittsburgh Press*, August 27, 1926; and Chilly Doyle, "Chillysauce," *Pittsburgh Gazette Times*, August 27, 1926.
203. "Voyles Reclaimed and Then Swapped," *Pittsburgh Post*, August 25, 1926.
204. For information on the Pirate batting orders, see the box scores found at "The 1926 Pittsburgh Pirates Regular Season Game Log," www.retrosheet.org (accessed on February 4, 2015).
205. All the information concerning the batting orders and pitching starts was taken from the box scores found at "The 1926 Pittsburgh Pirates Regular Season Game Log," www.retrosheet.org (accessed on December 10, 2014).
206. Long, "Sporting Gossip and Comment," August 24, 1926.
207. The statistics used in this table were taken from "Standings At Close of Play of August 31, 1926," www.retrosheet.org (accessed on November 8, 2014).
208. Chester L. Smith, "Boosters [sic] Club Rallies to Help Bucs Win Flag," *Pittsburgh Gazette Times*, August 14, 1926.
209. "Don't Knock—Join the 'Pirate Boosters,'" *Pittsburgh Gazette Times*, August 13, 1926.
210. Smith, "Boosters [sic] Club Rallies to Help Bucs Win Flag."
211. Chester L. Smith, "Boost Buccos to Another Pennant Proves Popular War Cry with Fans," *Pittsburgh Gazette Times*, August 15, 1926.
212. Chester L. Smith, "Boosters Club Membership Mounts to 10,000 as Fans Rally to Support of Bucs," *Pittsburgh Gazette Times*, August 16, 1926.
213. "Spirit of Boosters with Bucs Today," *Pittsburgh Gazette Times*, August 29, 1926.

Chapter 5

1. "'No Sentiment in Baseball'—President Dreyfuss," *Pittsburgh Press*, August 22, 1926.
2. Ibid.
3. "Pirate 3 Told They're Fired, Stay Fired," *Pittsburgh Gazette Times*, September 1, 1926.
4. "Dreyfuss Has No Statement," *Pittsburgh Press*, September 1, 1926.
5. James F. Murray, "Carey Appeals to Dreyfuss," *Pittsburgh Post*, September 1, 1926.
6. "Ralph Davis Says," *Pittsburgh Press*, August 26, 1926.
7. Murray.
8. The statistics used in this paragraph were taken from "The 1926 Pittsburgh Pirates Regular Season Game Log" and "Standings At Close of Play of September 7, 1926," www.retrosheet.org (accessed on November 4, 2014).
9. The information used in this paragraph was taken from "The 1926 Pittsburgh Pirates Regular Season Game Log," "The Regular Season Pitching Log for 1926 Pittsburgh Pirates," and "The Regular Season Batting/

Fielding Log for 1926 Pittsburgh Pirates," www.retrosheet.org (accessed on November 29, 2014).

10. James J. Long, "Sporting Gossip and Comment," *Pittsburgh Sun*, August 26, 1926.

11. Long, "Sporting Gossip and Comment," August 16, 1926.

12. James J. Long, "Bucs Strong Enough To Win Without Carey But Not Without Wright; No Player on Pirate Roster Has Been Here Longer Than Six Years," *Pittsburgh Sun*, August 21, 1926.

13. Ibid.

14. Charles J. Doyle, "Shortstop's Presence in Lineup Necessary To Bolster Champions," *Pittsburgh Gazette Times*, September 2, 1926.

15. Chilly Doyle, "Chillysauce," *Pittsburgh Gazette Times*, September 2, 1926. Doyle's column was published on the 2nd, but its dateline is September 1.

16. Wollen, "Playing the Game with the Pirates," September 1, 1926.

17. "'Won't Resign, No Matter How Case Ends, They'll Have to Fire Me,' McKechnie Says," *Pittsburgh Gazette Times*, August 17, 1926.

18. "Wright Likely Out of Game for Week," *Pittsburgh Post*, August 8, 1926; Balinger, "Champtown Chatter," August 10, 1926; Balinger, "Adams, Bigbee Released, Waivers Asked on Carey"; Lou Wollen, "Playing the Game with the Pirates," *Pittsburgh Press*, August 15, 1926; Lou Wollen, "Playing the Game with the Pirates," *Pittsburgh Press*, August 17, 1926; Lou Wollen, "Playing the Game with the Pirates," *Pittsburgh Press*, August 21, 1926; [no byline, but this is Lou Wollen's column], "Playing the Game with Pirates," August 22, 1926; "Pirates Buy Carmen Hill from A. A. Club," *Pittsburgh Post*, September 2, 1926; Doyle "Chillysauce," September 2, 1926; and "Wright May Play for Bucs Today," *Pittsburgh Gazette Times*, September 3, 1926.

19. Wright, interview.

20. "It's Not Hits, But Runs That Count," *Pittsburgh Post*, September 4, 1926, and Edward F. Balinger, "Champtown Chatter," *Pittsburgh Post*, September 4, 1926.

21. Edward F. Balinger, "Champtown Chatter," *Pittsburgh Post*, September 5, 1926.

22. "The 1926 PIT N Regular Season Batting Log for Glenn Wright," www.retrosheet.org (accessed on November 4, 2014).

23. The statistics used in this paragraph were taken from "The 1926 PIT N Regular Season Pitching Log for Don Songer," www.retrosheet.org (accessed on November 4, 2014).

24. Edward F. Balinger, "Champtown Chatter," *Pittsburgh Post*, September 3, 1926.

25. Wollen, "Playing the Game with the Pirates," September 8, 1926.

26. The statistics used in this paragraph were taken from "The 1926 PIT N Regular Season Pitching Log for Vic Aldridge," www.retrosheet.org (accessed on November 30, 2014), but the calculations were done by the author.

27. The statistics used in this paragraph were taken from "The 1926 Pittsburgh Pirates Regular Season Game Log," www.retrosheet.org (accessed on November 4, 2014).

28. The statistics used in this table were taken from "The 1926 St. Louis Cardinals Regular Season Game Log," "The 1926 Cincinnati Reds Regular Season Game Log," "The 1926 Pittsburgh Pirates Regular Season Game Log," and "The 1926 Chicago Cubs Regular Season Game Log," www.retrosheet.org (accessed on November 4, 2014).

29. "Pirates' Slump Linked with Firing of Carey, Adams, Bigbee," *Pittsburgh Gazette Times*, September 2, 1926.

30. Ibid.

31. Ibid.

32. The statistics used in this paragraph were taken from "The 1926 PIT N Regular Season Batting Log for Glenn Wright" and "The 1926 Pittsburgh Pirates Regular Season Game Log," www.retrosheet.org (accessed on December 10, 2014), but the calculations were done by the author.

33. "Wilbur Cooper Says Pirate Upheaval 'Shows Real Ones,'" *Pittsburgh Sun*, August 16, 1926, and "Wilbur Cooper Revels in Pirates' Plight; Says Persons Responsible for Conditions for Which He Was Blamed Have Been Exposed," *Pittsburgh Gazette Times*, August 17, 1926.

34. "Views on Pirate Situation Stated by 'Tele' Readers," *Pittsburgh Chronicle Telegraph*, August 17, 1926.

35. The statistics used in this sentence were taken from "The 1926 PIT N Regular Season Pitching Log for Ray Kremer," www.retrosheet.org (accessed on November 27, 2014), but Kremer's WHIP was calculated by the author.

36. "The 1926 PIT N Regular Season Batting Log for Paul Waner," www.retrosheet.org (accessed on November 27, 2014).

37. "Pirates Buy Carmen Hill from A. A. Club," *Pittsburgh Post*, September 2, 1926, and

"The 1926 PIT N Regular Season Pitching Log for Carmen Hill," www.retrosheet.org (accessed on November 30, 2014). Hill was the second 20th-century major leaguer to wear glasses while playing, debuting on August 24, 1915, four months and five days after his equally bespectacled teammate Lee Meadows made his debut.

38. Chilly Doyle, "Chillysauce," *Pittsburgh Gazette Times*, September 4, 1926.

39. The statistics used in this paragraph were taken from the box scores for September 8–14, 1926, found at "The 1926 Pittsburgh Pirates Regular Season Game Log," www.retrosheet.org (accessed on November 29, 2014), but the calculations were done by the author.

40. The statistics used in this paragraph were taken from ibid. (accessed on December 1, 2014), but the calculations were done by the author.

41. The statistics used in this paragraph were taken from ibid. (accessed on December 1, 2014).

42. "Clarke, Wright Pay Flying Visit Here," *Pittsburgh Post*, September 3, 1926.

43. "Aldridge Loses Race with Death; Father Expires in Indiana," *Pittsburgh Chronicle Telegraph*, September 13, 1926, and Lou Wollen, "Pirates Eager to Make Third Place Secure in Race," *Pittsburgh Press*, September 21, 1926.

44. "Pirate Detail," *Pittsburgh Post*, September 14, 1926.

45. Lou Wollen, "Double Victory Rekindles Pennant Hopes of World Champs," *Pittsburgh Press*, September 13, 1926.

46. The statistics used in this sentence were taken from "The 1926 PIT N Regular Season Pitching Log for Don Songer," www.retrosheet.org (accessed on November 27, 2014), but the calculations were done by the author.

47. "The 1926 PIT N Regular Season Batting Log for Eddie Murphy," www.retrosheet.org (accessed on December 31, 2014).

48. "Pirates Send Murphy Home; Fails to Deliver," *Pittsburgh Chronicle Telegraph*, September 14, 1926.

49. "Standings At Close of Play of September 14, 1926," www.retrosheet.org (accessed on November 27, 2014).

50. Lou Wollen, "Pirates Still Believe They Are in Pennant Battle," *Pittsburgh Press*, September 15, 1926.

51. The statistics used in this paragraph were taken from "The 1926 Pittsburgh Pirates Regular Season Game Log," "Standings At Close of Play of September 29, 1926," "The 1926 Cincinnati Reds Regular Season Game Log," and "The 1926 St. Louis Cardinals Regular Season Game Log," www.retrosheet.org (accessed on December 31, 2014).

52. Lou Wollen, "Playing the Game with the Pirates," *Pittsburgh Press*, September 16, 1926.

53. The play-by-play account of the inning was taken from "Burn Up Extra Bleachers; Our Chance Is About Gone," *Pittsburgh Post*, September 16, 1926.

54. Edward F. Balinger, "Champtown Chatter," *Pittsburgh Post*, September 19, 1926.

55. Ibid.

56. Edward F. Balinger, "Champtown Chatter," *Pittsburgh Post*, September 24, 1926.

57. Ibid.

58. "Pirate Detail," *Pittsburgh Post*, September 24, 1926.

59. "Pirate-Brave Dual Bill—Play by Play," *Pittsburgh Press*, September 26, 1926.

60. Welsh, "M'Innis' Release Start of Pirate Shakeup."

61. "The 1926 PIT N Regular Season Batting Log for Stuffy McInnis" and "The 1926 PIT N Regular Season Fielding Log for Stuffy McInnis," www.retrosheet.org (accessed on November 27, 2014).

62. Edward F. Balinger, "Champtown Chatter," *Pittsburgh Post*, September 18, 1926.

63. James J. Long, "Sporting Gossip and Comment," *Pittsburgh Sun*, September 27, 1926.

64. "Pirates Wind Up Deplorable Season Taking Listless Exhibition from Bridgeport," *Pittsburgh Post*, September 27, 1926.

65. Hollingsworth used 11 statistical measures: percentage of games won (which he weighted as 25 percent of the total score), games ahead of second place (15 percent), games won minus games lost in the World Series (5 percent), runs scored (5 percent), net runs scored (i.e., "subtracting the average number of runs scored by all the teams in its given league that year from the number of runs scored by the team in question"; 5 percent), batting average (5 percent), net batting average (5 percent), net slugging average (5 percent), net home runs (5 percent), earned run average (5 percent), and net earned run average (20 percent). Harry Hollingsworth, *The Best and Worst Baseball Teams of All Time* (New York: S.P.I. Books, 1994), 15–24, 167–171.

66. The author received a copy of Hollingsworth's revised rankings from a friend who wishes to remain anonymous.

67. The statistics used in this table were taken from "Standings At Close of Play of September 27, 1926," www.retrosheet.org (accessed on November 4, 2014).
68. "What Caused The Pirate Flare-Up?" *Pittsburgh Press*, September 28, 1926.
69. "The Truth At Last About the Pirates," *Pittsburgh Press*, September 28, 1926.
70. "The Wrecking of a World's Championship Ball Club [sic]—What Caused It?" *Pittsburgh Press*, September 29, 1926.
71. Oscar Wilde, *The Importance of Being Earnest and Related Writings*, ed. Joseph Bristow (London: Routledge, 1992), 33.
72. Davis, "Secret of Pirate Shakeup Revealed."
73. Ibid.
74. Welsh, "Clarke Denies Statements of Discharged Pirates."
75. The statistics used in this paragraph were taken from "The 1926 PIT N Regular Season Batting Log for Paul Waner," www.retrosheet.org (accessed on November 30, 2014) and "Paul Waner," www.baseball-reference.com (accessed on November 30, 2014).
76. Welsh, "Clarke Denies Statements of Discharged Pirates."
77. Ibid.
78. Davis, "Secret of Pirate Shakeup Revealed."
79. Ibid.
80. Ralph Davis, "Ralph Davis Says," *Pittsburgh Press*, September 27, 1926.
81. Long, "Sporting Gossip and Comment," September 27, 1926.
82. Ibid.
83. Havey J. Boyle, "Through the Sport Lens," *Pittsburgh Chronicle Telegraph*, September 28, 1926.
84. Ibid.
85. Long, "Sporting Gossip and Comment," September 27, 1926.
86. "Dreyfuss Denies Revolt Lost Flag," *Pittsburgh Gazette Times*, September 27, 1926.
87. Davis, "Secret of Pirate Shakeup Revealed."
88. Ibid.
89. Ibid.
90. Lou Wollen, "Pirates Release Onslow," *Pittsburgh Press*, November 19, 1926.
91. "John J. (Jack) Onslow," *The Sporting News*, December 28, 1960, 26.
92. Arthur Daley, "Sports of the *Times*," *New York Times*, May 30, 1950.
93. John C. Hoffman, "Onslow's 64th Victory," *Baseball Digest*, February 1950, 17.
94. Davis, "Secret of Pirate Shakeup Revealed."
95. Welsh, "Clarke Demands Disciplinary Action Following Expulsion Request."
96. Davis, "Secret of Pirate Shakeup Revealed."
97. Ibid.
98. Ibid.
99. "The 1926 Pittsburgh Pirates Regular Season Game Log," www.retrosheet.org, and "Standings at Close of Play of July 24, 1926" and "Standings at Close of Play of August 7, 1926," www.retrosheet.org (accessed on January 29, 2015).
100. Davis, "Secret of Pirate Shakeup Revealed."
101. Ibid.
102. Ibid.
103. "Heydler Statement Clears Pirate Players' Names."
104. Welsh, "Clarke Denies Statements of Discharged Pirates."
105. Ibid.
106. "Clarke to Stay Off Bench Next Year," *Pittsburgh Chronicle Telegraph*, September 30, 1926.
107. "Won't Sit On Pirate Bench Next Season, Clarke Avers," *Pittsburgh Sun*, September 30, 1926.
108. "Clarke May Quit Pirates, He Asserts."
109. "None of Those Named in Rumors Is Likely to Be Successor to M'Kechnie," *Pittsburgh Sun*, October 19, 1926.
110. "Dreyfuss Denies Revolt Lost Flag."
111. Ibid. and "Clyde Barnhart," www.baseball-reference.com (accessed on November 4, 2014).
112. "Dreyfuss Denies Revolt Lost Flag."
113. "No 1927 Pirate Pilot Chosen," *Pittsburgh Chronicle Telegraph*, October 1, 1926.
114. Ibid.
115. Paul A. R. Kurtz, "'No Harmony,' Barney Tells Local Umps," *Pittsburgh Press*, September 23, 1926.
116. Ibid.
117. "Bill McKechnie, Pirates' Manager, Fired," *Pittsburgh Gazette Times*, October 19, 1926.
118. Ibid.
119. "M'Kechnie Hopefully Looks Toward Future," *Pittsburgh Chronicle Telegraph*, October 19, 1926.
120. Ibid.
121. "Bill Surprised," *Pittsburgh Post*, October 19, 1926.

122. "No Crime to Lose Job, Asserts Bill; Future Undecided," *Pittsburgh Gazette Times*, October 19, 1926.

123. The statistics for this table were taken from "Atlanta Braves Team History & Encyclopedia," www.baseball-reference.com (accessed on November 26, 2014) and Gillette and Palmer, 148, 150, 152, 154, 156, 158, 160, 162, 164, but the percentages for the latter source were calculated by the author.

124. The statistics for this table were taken from "Cincinnati Reds Team History & Encyclopedia," www.baseball-reference.com (accessed on November 26, 2014) and Gillette and Palmer, 130, 132, 134, 136, 138, 140, 142, 144, 146, 148, but the percentages for the latter source were calculated by the author.

125. Pope, 184–194.

126. Harvey Frommer, *Baseball's Greatest Managers* (New York: Franklin Watts, 1985), 174–181.

127. Michael D. Koehler, *America's Greatest Coaches* (Champaign, IL: Leisure Press, 1990), 23–24.

128. Stinson, 198, 207.

129. Montgomery, 59–60.

130. Ibid., 86–88, and Stinson, 209–210, 215, 217, 218–219.

131. Ralph Davis, "Ralph Davis Says," *Pittsburgh Press*, October 19, 1926.

132. Ibid.

133. Lou Wollen, "Naming M'Kechnie's Successor Pastime of Fans," *Pittsburgh Press*, October 19, 1926.

134. "Fred Clarke Resigns from Pirates," *Pittsburgh Gazette Times*, October 27, 1926.

135. Edward F. Balinger, "Fred Clarke Severs Connections with Pirates," *Pittsburgh Post*, October 27, 1926.

136. "Fred Clarke Resigns from Pirates."

137. Chester L. Smith, "Sports Shafts," *Pittsburgh Gazette Times*, October 28, 1926.

138. "Bill McKechnie, Pirates' Manager, Fired."

139. Ibid.

140. Besides his two main finders of talent, Chick Fraser and Bill Hinchman, Barney Dreyfuss employed various other scouts, including Molesworth, Frank Haller, Tom McNamara, and the aforementioned Joe Devine. For more information about Dreyfuss' scouts, see Chester L. Smith, "The Village Smithy," *Pittsburgh Press*, July 29, 1951; "Dragging for the Victims of River Accident," *Pittsburgh Press*, May 12, 1909; "Judges Relieve Wagner from Jury," *Pittsburgh Press*, March 3, 1911; "How the Baseball Scouts Work," *Reading Eagle*, January 27, 1914; "Pittsburgh Scout Tells Why Baseball Material Is Scarce," *Ludington* [Michigan] *Daily News*, October 8, 1922; "Brilliant Record Is Made by Joe Devine as Pittsburgh Scout," *Pittsburgh Sun*, March 11, 1926; Jack Sell, "Searches Two Years in Vain, Uncovers Star in Home Town," *Pittsburgh Post-Gazette*, July 21, 1943; Tom McNamara, Player File, National Baseball Hall of Fame Library, Cooperstown, New York; Carlton Molesworth, Player File, National Baseball Hall of Fame Library, Cooperstown, New York; Bill Lamb, "Carlton Molesworth," SABR Baseball Biography Project, http://sabr.org/bioproject; Kling, "Joe Devine," in *Can He Play? A Look at Baseball Scouts and Their Profession*; Kling, "Joe Devine," SABR Baseball Biography Project; and "Chick Fraser," "Bill Hinchman," and "Carlton Molesworth," www.baseball-reference.com (accessed on November 4, 2014); as well as Fraser's and Hinchman's player files in the National Baseball Hall of Fame Library.

141. Charles J. Doyle, "Fohl, Here for Parley with Dreyfuss, May Sign as New Manager of the Pirates," *Pittsburgh Gazette Times*, October 21, 1926, and Charles J. Doyle, "Dreyfuss Selects New Pirate Manager," *Pittsburgh Gazette Times*, October 22, 1926.

142. Balinger, "Fred Clarke Officially Severed from Pirates, Resignation Accepted."

143. See "Clarke in Baseball Post," *New York Times*, January 5, 1937; "Clarke Heads Board of Semi-Pro Congress," an undated article from an unknown source, Fred Clarke, Player File, National Baseball Hall of Fame Library, Cooperstown, New York; "Six Countries to Compete in Semi-Pro Meet," *Chicago Daily Tribune*, January 30, 1939; "Fred Clarke to Head New Baseball Veterans' Group," *Chicago Daily Tribune*, December 17, 1944; "Fred Clarke Stays as Sandlot Leagues' Head," *Chicago Daily Tribune*, February 27, 1955; "Fred Clarke to Be Feted at Non-Pro Baseball Meet," an article dated August 3, 1959, from an unknown source, Fred Clarke, Player File, National Baseball Hall of Fame Library, Cooperstown, New York; and "Bucs to Honor Clarke, 86," an undated article from an unknown source, Fred Clarke, Player File, National Baseball Hall of Fame Library, Cooperstown, New York.

144. Frank Getty, "Sale of Pirates Would Put Cuyler Back in Buc Lineup," [St. Petersburg, FL] *Evening Independent*, October 14, 1927.

145. Regis M. Welsh, "Wentz, Going Home, Denies Dickering for Local Club," *Pittsburgh Post-Gazette*, October 12, 1927.
146. Getty.
147. "Veterans Are Hopeful," *Reading Eagle*, August 30, 1926.
148. Pete Cava and Paul Sandin, "The First Babe," *Sports Collectors Digest*, April 7, 1995, 168; "Babe Adams Pitches No-Hit Game but Is Beaten, 3–1, as His Semi-Pros Err Often," an article from an unknown source with a dateline of July 6, on which someone wrote 1927, Babe Adams, Player File, National Baseball Hall of Fame Library, Cooperstown, New York; "A 'Babe Adams Day' at Bethany," an article from an unknown source with a dateline of July 9 that lacks a year but is known from internal evidence to have been published in 1927, Babe Adams, Player File, National Baseball Hall of Fame Library, Cooperstown, New York; "Babe Adams Signed to Manage Johnstown," *Milwaukee Journal*, February 3, 1927; "'Babe' Adams Succeeded as Manager by Bender," *New York World*, June 5, 1927; and "Springfield Signs Adams," *New York World*, July 31, 1927.
149. Luther W. Spoehr, "Charles Benjamin 'Babe' Adams," in Porter, *Biographical Dictionary of American Sports: Baseball*, 3, and Cava and Sandin, 168.
150. Libby Henderson, "Charles Benjamin Adams: A Humble, Honorable Hero," www.babeadams.com (accessed on November 29, 2014). Henderson also claims that her grandfather did not manage in the minors, but there is enough evidence to prove that he did.
151. "Ralph Davis Says," *Pittsburgh Press*, February 17, 1927.
152. "Bigbee with Seattle," *Milwaukee Journal*, April 7, 1927.
153. Ibid.
154. "Carson Bigbee," www.baseball-reference.com (accessed on November 4, 2014).
155. 1940 United States Federal Census.
156. "Sports Briefs," *Owosso (MI) Argus-Press*, December 22, 1948, and "Carson Bigbee," www.aagpbl.org (accessed on November 29, 2014).
157. The 15 times include the BBWAA's nominating ballot in 1946. "Babe Adams," www.baseball-reference.com (accessed on November 4, 2014).
158. In addition, Adams may have received consideration from the Committee on Baseball Veterans, commonly referred to as the Veterans Committee, prior to the establishment of the Historic Oversight Committee, but this author has found no evidence to either confirm or refute this possibility.
159. Brian Stevens, "Babe Adams," SABR Baseball Biography Project, http://sabr.org/bioproject (accessed on November 27, 2014).
160. Ibid. (accessed on November 27, 2014).
161. Lester J. Biederman, "Election to 'Hall' Gives Max Carey His Greatest Thrill," *Pittsburgh Press*, January 31, 1961.
162. Edward F. Balinger, "Carey Returns to Pirates in Capacity of Coach," *Pittsburgh Post-Gazette*, February 1, 1930.
163. Ibid.
164. Barney Dreyfuss to Max Carey, Letter, March 5, 1930, Barney Dreyfuss, Player File, National Baseball Hall of Fame, Cooperstown, New York.
165. "Carey Released as Coach by Pirate Management," *Pittsburgh Press*, October 31, 1930, and "Walks Pirate Plank," *The Sporting News*, November 6, 1930, 8.
166. Frank Graham, "Graham's Corner," *New York Journal-American*, February 1, 1961.
167. Ibid., and Charles E. Parker, "Dodger Pilot Ends Age-Old Controversy," an undated article from an unknown source, Max Carey, Player File, National Baseball Hall of Fame Library, Cooperstown, New York.
168. Graham.
169. "Brooklyn Dismisses Max Carey as Manager," *Pittsburgh Press*, February 21, 1934.
170. John Bennett, "Max Carey," SABR Baseball Biography Project, http://sabr.org/bioproject (accessed on November 27, 2014).
171. Biederman, "Election to 'Hall' Gives Max Carey His Greatest Thrill"; "District Baseball Stars Get Olympic Games Try," *Pittsburgh Press*, July 9, 1935; "Max Carey Grows Limes Big as Baseballs," an article from an unknown source dated July 15, 1937, Max Carey, Player File, National Baseball Hall of Fame Library, Cooperstown, New York; "Max Carey Wants Job in Baseball," *Milwaukee Journal*, February 28, 1940; "Max Carey Lifetime Records," an undated compilation with no byline, Max Carey, Player File, National Baseball Hall of Fame Library, Cooperstown, New York; "Max Carey," www.baseball-reference.com (accessed on November 29, 2014); Jimmy Jordan, "Pie, Carey Swap Tales of Old Bucs," *Pittsburgh Post-Gazette*, February 5, 1968; "Carey Writing Fiction," an article from an unknown source dated November 30, 1944, Max Carey, Player File, National Baseball Hall of Fame Library, Cooperstown, New York; Ed

Pollock, "Playing the Game" an article from an unknown source dated October 23, 1955, Max Carey, Player File, National Baseball Hall of Fame Library, Cooperstown, New York; and "Max Carey," www.baseballindex.org.

172. Bennett (accessed November 27, 2014), and "Max Carey," www.aagpbl.org (accessed on November 29, 2014).

173. "1944 Season," www.aagpbl.org (accessed on November 29, 2014).

174. Roy McHugh, "Miami Beach from Carey to Nixon," *Pittsburgh Press*, August 7, 1968.

175. Bill Fay, "Belles of the Ball Game, [*sic*]" *Collier's* 124, no. 7 (August 13, 1949): 44.

176. "Max Carey," www.baseball-reference.com (accessed on December 5, 2014). These numbers do not include games played, plate appearances, and at bats, in which Carey came in the top 10 nine, nine, and eight times, respectively, and led the league once in games played and twice each in plate appearances and at bats.

177. Ibid. (accessed on November 27, 2014).

178. Ibid. (accessed on November 27, 2014).

179. The selectors did not have Wins Above Replacement statistics to look at during the years that Carey was being considered for the National Baseball Hall of Fame, but today it is known that the Pirate star finished seven times in the top ten of WAR for National League nonpitchers and four times for all NL players. Ibid. (accessed on January 30, 2015).

180. Ibid. (accessed on November 27, 2014).

181. "Bring Back Spitter?" [Toledo] *Blade*, July 25, 1961.

182. "Max Carey," www.retrosheet.org (accessed on November 27, 2014).

183. Dick Conners, "Carey Steals Show at Induction into Shrine," *The Sporting News*, August 2, 1961, 42.

184. "Carey Thinks 'Hall' Should Give Assist," an article found in Max Carey, Player File, National Baseball Hall of Fame Library, Cooperstown, New York, with a handwritten notation saying that it came from the February 5, 1968, issue of the *Pittsburgh Post-Gazette*, but this author was unable to find the article in the copy of the issue of the *Post-Gazette* that he looked at.

185. "Carey Thinks 'Hall' Should Give Assist."

186. "Max Carey Receives Retroactive Award," *Miami News*, January 27, 1963.

187. Jack Lang, "Max Carey 'Steals' Night," an article found in Max Carey, Player File, National Baseball Hall of Fame Library, Cooperstown, New York, stamped January 16, 1963, with a handwritten notation saying that it came from the *Long Island Press*.

188. Jimmy Burns, "Carey, Wife Honored on 50th Anniversary," *The Sporting News*, February 2, 1963, 13.

189. The 23 were Vic Aldridge, Clyde Barnhart, Fred Brickell, Joe Bush, Adam Comorosky, Joe Cronin, Kiki Cuyler, Johnny Gooch, George Grantham, Carmen Hill, Ray Kremer, Roy Mahaffey, Lee Meadows, Johnny Morrison, Chet Nichols, Hal Rhyne, Earl Smith, Don Songer, Roy Spencer, Pie Traynor, Paul Waner, Glenn Wright, and Emil Yde. However, Bush was given his unconditional release on June 15 of that year; Brickell, Comorosky, Mahaffey, Nichols, and Songer all spent varying amounts of time in the minors and saw limited action with the Pirates; and Johnny Morrison had gone AWOL again, was suspended, and pitched in his last game for the club on July 2.

190. "Standings At Close of Play of September 1, 1938" and "Standings At Close of Play of October 2, 1938," www.retrosheet.org (accessed on December 23, 2014).

191. "Standings At Close of Play of September 25, 1938" and "The 1938 Pittsburgh Pirates Regular Season Game Log," www.retrosheet.org (accessed on November 29, 2014).

192. Besides Adams, Bigbee, and Carey, the men who played at least one game for the 1926 Bucs but who were not part of the 1927 Pirate team were Bud Culloton, Lou Koupal, Stuffy McInnis, Eddie Moore, Walter Mueller, Eddie Murphy, Red Oldham, Johnny Rawlings, and Tom Sheehan.

193. For the best biography of Cronin, see Mark Armour, *Joe Cronin: A Life in Baseball* (Lincoln: University of Nebraska Press, 2010).

194. For more information on Cuyler, see Ronald T. Waldo, *Hazen "Kiki" Cuyler: A Baseball Biography* (Jefferson, NC: McFarland, 2012).

195. Chester L. Smith, "Traynor and Bucs Part After 23 Years," *Pittsburgh Press*, March 2, 1943.

196. For more information on Traynor, see Forr and Proctor.

197. Parker, 262.

198. Ibid., 266–268, 271–278, 280–281, 294–296, and 298.

199. Ibid., 266.

200. See Audrey Glassman, e-mail message to the author, October 2, 2012, and Bud Cul-

loton, Player File, National Baseball Hall of Fame Library, Cooperstown, New York.

201. "Obituaries," *The Sporting News*, January 24, 1983, 54; "Tom Sheehan," www.baseball-reference.com (accessed on November 4, 2014); and "Tom Sheehan," www.retrosheet.org (accessed on November 4, 2014).

202. "Stuffy McInnis Is New Norwich Coach," *Lewiston Evening Journal*, December 30, 1930; John Ahern, "Stuffy McInnis to Coach Harvard's Baseball Team," *Boston Daily Globe*, October 20, 1948; and "Stuffy McInnis Dies at 69—Member of A's Famed Infield," *The Sporting News*, February 24, 1960, 24.

203. The information used in this paragraph was taken from "Vic Aldridge," "Clyde Barnhart," "Fred Brickell," "Joe Bush," "Adams Comorosky," "Johnny Gooch," "George Grantham," "Carmen Hill," "Lou Koupal," "Ray Kremer," "Roy Mahaffey," "Lee Meadows," "Eddie Moore," "Johnny Morrison," "Chet Nichols," "Hal Rhyne," "Earl Smith," "Don Songer," "Roy Spencer," "Glenn Wright," and "Emil Yde," www.baseball-reference.com (accessed on December 5, 2014).

204. "Glenn Wright to Be Mended for Brooklyn," *Schenectady Gazette*, November 19, 1931; "Wright's Injury Another Hazard for Buccaneers," *Pittsburgh Press*, June 29, 1927; Ralph Davis, "Cup to Inspire Tech Gridders," *Pittsburgh Press*, March 13, 1929, though Davis has the wrong year for Wright's beaning; Ralph Davis, "Wright May Be Made Gardener," *Pittsburgh Press*, May 8, 1929; "Glenn Wright Is Total Loss to Brooklyn Club," *Pittsburgh Press*, May 14, 1929; "Glenn Wright Out for Rest of Year," *Milwaukee Journal*, July 24, 1929; "Glenn Wright's Arm Adds to Carey's Woes," *New London Day*, April 20, 1932; "Dodgers Seek Replacements at Short and in Pitching," *Pittsburgh Post Gazette*, January 30, 1933; and Wright, interview.

205. Some men, such as Glenn Wright, also coached in the minors, but because of the difficulty in finding information on minor league coaching, no attempt has been made to compile a list of these men.

206. "Joe Bush," "Johnny Gooch," "Lee Meadows," "Hal Rhyne," "Earl Smith," "Emil Yde," and "Eddie Moore," www.baseball-reference.com (accessed December 11, 2014).

207. "Pirates [sic] Acquire Glenn Wright," *Daytona Beach Morning Journal*, November 8, 1947, and "Now a Scout, Glenn Wright Has Fond Baseball Memories," *Milwaukee Journal*, September 26, 1960.

208. "Johnny Gooch," www.retrosheet.org (accessed on November 29, 2014); "Bucs Release Gooch, Rehire Him as Scout," *Pittsburgh Press*, October 17, 1939; and "Gooch to Manage Pirate Farm Team," *Pittsburgh Press*, December 13, 1940.

209. "Ex-Buc Manager Ens Dies; He 'Learned by Listening,'" *The Sporting News*, January 25, 1950, 25; "Jewel Ens," www.retrosheet.org (accessed on November 29, 2014); and "Jewel Ens," www.baseball-reference.com (accessed on November 29, 2014).

210. "Jewel Ens," www.baseball-reference.com (accessed on November 29, 2014).

211. Wollen, "Pirates Release Onslow," and "Onslow Lands Senator Berth," *Pittsburgh Press*, November 24, 1926.

212. "Jack Onslow," www.baseball-reference.com (accessed on November 4, 2014).

213. "Bucs Release Chick Fraser," *Pittsburgh Press*, December 2, 1930, and Norman Macht, "Do You Remember? Chick Fraser," *Phillies Report*, September 12, 1991, 10–11.

214. Cf. "Bill Hinchman," www.baseball-reference.com (accessed on November 4, 2014), and "Hinchman, Long-Time Scout for Pittsburgh, Dies at 79," an unidentified obituary found in Bill Hinchman, Player File, National Baseball Hall of Fame Library, Cooperstown, New York.

215. Being out of Organized Baseball does not necessarily mean not having anything to do with the sport again. For example, Lee Roy Mahaffey pitched for several teams in the semiprofessional textile leagues in South Carolina after leaving Organized Baseball. Thomas K. Perry, *Textile League Baseball: South Carolina's Mill Teams, 1880–1955* (Jefferson, NC: McFarland, 1993), 113.

216. "Letter from Larry J. O'Neill," April 27, 1973, Vic Aldridge, Player File, National Baseball Hall of Fame Library, Cooperstown, New York; "Obituaries," *The Sporting News*, May 5, 1973, 30; and undocumented newspaper clippings found in Vic Aldridge, Player File, National Baseball Hall of Fame Library, Cooperstown, New York.

217. "Bernard A. Culloton Dies at 79; Ex-Motor Vehicle Aide in Albany," *New York Times*, November 11, 1976.

218. 1940 United States Federal Census.

219. Bill Lee, *The Baseball Necrology: The Post-Baseball Lives and Deaths of Over 7,600 Major League Players and Others* (Jefferson, NC: McFarland, 2003), 21.

220. 1940 United States Federal Census.

221. Certificate of Death, Kansas State Board of Health, Division of Vital Statistics, Fred Brickell, Player File, National Baseball Hall of Fame Library, Cooperstown, New York.
222. Ron Anderson, "Bullet Joe Bush," SABR Baseball Biography Project, http://sabr.org/bioproject (accessed on November 29, 2014).
223. "Adam Comorosky, Ex-Pirate, Dies," *Pittsburgh Press*, March 4, 1951.
224. Bill Nowlin, "Johnny Gooch," SABR Baseball Biography Project, http://sabr.org/bioproject (accessed on November 29, 2014).
225. "George F. Grantham," *The Sporting News*, March 24, 1954, 16.
226. 1940 United States Federal Census.
227. "Obituaries," *The Sporting News*, January 29, 1990, 40.
228. Certificate of Death, State of California—Department of Public Health, Lou Koupal, Player File, National Baseball Hall of Fame Library, Cooperstown, New York.
229. Gregory H. Wolf, "Ray Kremer," SABR Baseball Biography Project, http://sabr.org/bioproject (accessed on November 29, 2014).
230. 1940 United States Federal Census.
231. State of South Carolina, Board of Health, Certificate of Death, Roy Mahaffey, Player File, National Baseball Hall of Fame Library, Cooperstown, New York.
232. 1940 United States Federal Census, and Lee, 270. Lee calls Meadows a "collector."
233. 1940 United States Federal Census.
234. Ibid.; "J. Eddie Murphy Dies; Former Major Leaguer," *Scranton Tribune*, February 22, 1969; and Lee, 289.
235. Lee, 295.
236. 1940 United States Federal Census.
237. Certificate of Death, State of California–Department of Public Health, Red Oldham, Player File, National Baseball Hall of Fame Library, Cooperstown, New York.
238. Bill Nowlin, "Hal Rhyne," SABR Baseball Biography Project, http://sabr.org/bioproject (accessed on November 29, 2014).
239. I. C. Brenner, "Johnny Rawlings Now Sells Insurance in Los Angeles," *Omaha World-Herald*, August 5, 1932.
240. 1940 United States Federal Census.
241. "John Rawlings," www.aagpbl.org (accessed on November 29, 2014).
242. Lee, 329.
243. "Don Songer, 63, Dies," *Kansas City Times*, October 4, 1962. According to the *Kansas City, Missouri, City Directory, 1934*, the correct name of Songer's restaurant was Billy-Don Chicken Shack. *Kansas City, Missouri, City Directory, 1934* (Kansas City, Missouri: Gate City Directory Co., Publishers, 1934), 1405.
244. Forr and Proctor, 184–191, 204–209.
245. Ibid., 183–184.
246. James Forr, "Pie Traynor," SABR Baseball Biography Project, http://sabr.org/bioproject (accessed on November 29, 2014).
247. Ibid (accessed on November 29, 2014).
248. 1940 United States Federal Census.
249. Certificate of Death, State Board of Health, Bureau of Vital Statistics, Florida, Emil Yde, Player File, National Baseball Hall of Fame Library, Cooperstown, New York, and Lee, 438.
250. "Rites to Honor Baseball Scout," *Idaho Evening Times*, May 8, 1940, and "Death Takes Chic Fraser, Old Big League Hurler, Yank Scout," *Idaho Evening Times*, May 8, 1940.
251. The rest of the members who died during the '60s were Stuffy McInnis (1960), Jack Onslow (1960), Red Oldham (1961), Fred Brickell (1961), Lou Koupal (1961), Don Songer (1962), Lee Meadows (1963), Bill Hinchman (1963), Earl Smith (1963), Ray Kremer (1965), Paul Waner (1965), Johnny Morrison (1966), Emil Yde (1968), Eddie Murphy (1969), and Roy Mahaffey (1969).
252. Besides Carey, Hal Rhyne (1971), Walter Mueller (1971), Pie Traynor (1972), Johnny Rawlings (1972), Roy Spencer (1973), Vic Aldridge (1973), Joe Bush (1974), Johnny Gooch (1975), Eddie Moore (1976), and Bud Culloton (1976) all died during the 1970s.
253. Clyde Barnhart in 1980, Chet Nichols and Tom Sheehan in 1982, and Glenn Wright and Joe Cronin in 1984.
254. Wright, interview.
255. Ibid.
256. Ibid.

Chapter 6

1. The statistics used in this table, with the exception of Projected Won-Lost Record, which came from Gillette and Palmer, 170, were taken from "1926 National League Team Statistics and Standings," www.baseball-reference.com (accessed on November 5, 2014). The conversions were done by the author.
2. "Kiki Cuyler," www.baseball-reference.com (accessed on December 15, 2014).

3. The statistics used in this paragraph were taken from "Paul Waner," www.baseball-reference.com (accessed on November 5, 2014).

4. The statistics used in this paragraph were taken from "Ray Kremer" and "1926 National League Pitching Leaders," www.baseball-reference.com (accessed on November 5, 2014).

5. Technically, Barnhart and Brickell finished tied for the third for double plays by a left fielder with one apiece, but 11 other men were tied with them.

6. The statistics used in this paragraph were taken from "1926 National League Fielding Leaders," www.baseball-reference.com (accessed on November 5, 2014).

7. F. C. Lane, "Our All America [sic] Baseball Club of 1926," *Baseball Magazine* 38, no. 1 (December 1926): 312–314.

8. www.baseballchronology.com/Baseball/Awards/TSN-AllStars.asp (accessed on November 5, 2014).

9. The statistics used in this table were taken from "The 1926 St. Louis Cardinals," "The 1926 Cincinnati Reds," and "The 1926 Pittsburgh Pirates," www.retrosheet.org (accessed on November 5, 2014).

10. The statistics used in this table were taken from Gillette and Palmer, 170. Wins attributed to stolen bases were not calculated for 1926 because caught-stealing statistics were not recorded for the National League that season.

11. "The 1925 Pittsburgh Pirates Regular Season Game Log," "The 1925 Pittsburgh Pirates World Series," and "The 1926 Pittsburgh Pirates Regular Season Game Log," www.retrosheet.org (accessed on November 5, 2014).

12. "Pittsburgh Pirates Team History & Encyclopedia," www.baseball-reference.com (accessed on November 5, 2014).

13. Stuart Miller, "Next to the Manager, but a Bit Ahead," *New York Times*, August 19, 2012.

14. Ibid.

15. Bob Bloss, *Baseball Managers: Stats, Stories, and Strategies* (Philadelphia: Temple University Press, 1999), 259.

16. Miller, "Next to the Manager, but a Bit Ahead."

17. Ibid.

18. Eddie Frierson, "Christy Mathewson," SABR Baseball Biography Project, http://sabr.org/bioproject (accessed on November 27, 2014), and Harry Keck, "Sporting Chit-Chat," *Pittsburgh Gazette Times*, July 8, 1919.

19. "Jennings with Giants," [Montreal] *Gazette*, October 30, 1920, and C. Paul Rogers III, "Hughie Jennings," SABR Baseball Biography Project, http://sabr.org/bioproject (accessed on November 27, 2014). Although Rogers calls Jennings McGraw's "number one coach," at the time that Jennings was employed by the Giants, he was referred to as the assistant manager, as seen in "Jennings with Giants."

20. F. H. D., "From the Press Box," *Nashua Telegraph*, December 21, 1926.

21. "Connie Mack's Son to be A's Next Manager," *Daytona Beach Morning Journal*, May 12, 1943.

22. Clyde Barnhart, interviewed by Eugene Converse Murdock, Hagerstown, Maryland, August 4, 1979, Cleveland Public Library, Cleveland, Ohio.

23. Charles J. Doyle, "Wright, Barnhart Hurt as Buc Regulars Win," *Pittsburgh Gazette Times*, March 24, 1926.

24. Ibid.

25. The statistics used in this paragraph were taken from "Clyde Barnhart," www.retrosheet.org (accessed on November 5, 2014).

26. "1926 Pittsburgh Pirates," www.baseball-reference.com (accessed on November 9, 2014).

27. This percentage includes Johnny Morrison, who had been suspended prior to August 7 and was in Kentucky when the affair started.

28. The information used in this table came from a variety of sources including, among others, Eugene Murdock's interviews with Clyde Barnhart, Carmen Hill, Eddie Moore, and Glenn Wright; player files from the National Baseball Hall of Fame Library; the United States Federal Census records; draft registration cards; death certificates; book-length biographies of and/or biographical articles about some of the players; issues of *Baseball Magazine* and *The Sporting News*; the player pages at www.baseball-reference.com; Strauss and Howe, *Generations: The History of America's Future, 1584 to 2069*; and Strauss and Howe, *The Fourth Turning: An American Prophecy*, but the percentages were calculated by the author.

29. As stated in note 163 of Chapter Two, the percentage of men being exposed to higher education would be larger if it could be conclusively proven that Lee Meadows had attended a postsecondary institution prior to 1926.

30. As stated in note 164 of Chapter Two, this percentage would be larger if it could be conclusively proven that Earl Smith had attended high school.

31. Wright, interview.

32. Welsh, "Clarke Denies Statements of Discharged Pirates."

33. The information used in this table came from a variety of sources including, among others, Eugene Murdock's interviews with Clyde Barnhart, Carmen Hill, Eddie Moore, and Glenn Wright; e-mail exchanges and/or telephone conversations with personnel at academic institutions, relatives of some of the players, and residents of the localities where some of the players had lived; player files from the National Baseball Hall of Fame Library; the United States Federal Census records; book-length biographies of and/or biographical articles about some of the players; issues of *Baseball Magazine*, *The Sporting News* and the major Pittsburgh newspapers; and the player pages at www.baseball-reference.com.

34. The information used in this table came from a variety of sources including, among others, Eugene Murdock's interviews with Clyde Barnhart, Carmen Hill, Eddie Moore, and Glenn Wright; e-mail exchanges and/or telephone conversations with relatives of some of the players and residents of the localities where some of the players had lived; player files from the National Baseball Hall of Fame Library; the United States Federal Census records; draft cards; death certificates; book-length biographies of and/or biographical articles about some of the players; issues of *Baseball Magazine*, *The Sporting News*, and the major Pittsburgh newspapers; and the player pages at www.baseball-reference.com.

35. The information used in this table came from a variety of sources including, among others, Eugene Murdock's interviews with Clyde Barnhart, Carmen Hill, Eddie Moore, and Glenn Wright; e-mail exchanges and/or telephone conversations with relatives of some of the players and residents of the localities where some of the players had lived; player files from the National Baseball Hall of Fame Library; the United States Federal Census records; draft cards; book-length biographies of and/or biographical articles about some of the players; and issues of *Baseball Magazine*, *The Sporting News*, and the major Pittsburgh newspapers.

36. McKennan, interview.

37. Finoli and Ranier, *The Pittsburgh Pirates Encyclopedia*, 261.

38. Edward F. Balinger, "Pirate Motorists Reach California and Begin Outing," *Pittsburgh Post*, November 25, 1924.

39. Doyle, "Max Carey Seen as Victim Rather Than Instigator of Rebellion; Penalty Severe."

40. Like McKechnie, Adams and Carey both "came up for cups of coffee" before their true rookie seasons. Adams played in one game in 1906 and four games in 1907, while Carey played in two games in 1910, but Adams' true rookie season was 1909 and Carey's was 1911.

41. Long, "Sporting Gossip and Comment," August 16, 1926.

42. Lewis.

43. Welsh, "Clarke Demands Disciplinary Action Following Expulsion Request."

44. Welsh, "Clarke Denies Statements of Discharged Pirates."

45. Kurtz.

46. "Pirate 3 Told They're Fired, Stay Fired."

47. John Kieran, "Sports of the *Times*," *New York Times*, May 15, 1937.

48. "The 1926 PIT N Regular Season Batting Log for George Grantham," www.retrosheet.org (accessed on February 21, 2015).

49. "The 1926 PIT N Regular Season Pitching Log for Emil Yde," www.retrosheet.org (accessed on February 21, 2015).

50. *N. W. Ayer & Son's American Newspaper Annual and Directory*, 947, 949.

51. McInnis & Associates, "The Basics of Selling Newspaper Advertising," www.ads-online.com/newbasiccourse/products/chaptereight10.html (accessed on November 5, 2014).

52. James Grossman, "The 'Proper Study of History': What the Public Thinks About Historical Thinking," *Perspectives on History* 52, no. 7 (October 2014): 8.

Bibliography

Interviews

Interviews conducted by Angelo J. Louisa:
Margaret Donahoe Burroughs, Fred Clarke's granddaughter. The author was assisted by Pamela A. Louisa. Pittsburgh, Pennsylvania. June 8, 2008.
Daniel Donahoe, Fred Clarke's grandson. By e-mail. Responses sent to the author on September 29, 2007.
Nancy Purviance, Jack Onslow's niece. By telephone. October 13, 2014.
Beverly Reiter, co-owner of the Little Pirate Ranch after the deaths of Fred Clarke and his wife. By telephone. December 5, 2006.
Beverly and Scott Reiter, owners of the Little Pirate Ranch after the deaths of Fred Clarke and his wife. The author was assisted by David Cicotello. Winfield, Kansas. August 15, 2007.
Interviews conducted by Eugene Converse Murdock, Cleveland Public Library, Cleveland, Ohio:
Clyde Barnhart. Hagerstown, Maryland. August 4, 1979.
Charlie Grimm. Scottsdale, Arizona. June 14, 1978.
Carmen Hill. Indianapolis, Indiana. February 21, 1975.
Eddie Moore. Ironton, Ohio. June 13, 1975.
Glenn Wright. Fresno, California. June 23, 1978.
Interviews conducted by members of the Oral History Research Committee of the Society for American Baseball Research:
Charlie Grimm. Interviewed by Walter Langford. Scottsdale, Arizona. June 14, 1982.
Art McKennan. Interviewed by Rob Roberts. Pittsburgh, Pennsylvania. July 14, 1994.
Jimmy Zinn. Interviewed by Mark Bernstein. Memphis, Tennessee. October 7, 1989.

Personal Communications

Jean Alicz, telephone conversation with the author, July 2, 2014.
Kerri Bobish, e-mail messages to the author, October 10 and October 16, 2014.
Terri Bone, e-mail message to the author, May 27, 2014.
Robert L. Bromfield, e-mail message to the author, November 6, 2013.
Margaret Donahoe Burroughs, e-mail message to the author, January 28, 2008.
Gabriel Chadwick, e-mail message to the author, January 6, 2015.
Gabriel Chadwick, telephone conversation with the author, December 18, 2014.
Ralph Christian, e-mail message to the author, September 22, 2001.
S. Kelly Cragg, e-mail message to the author, October 23, 2013.
Carol Donache, e-mail message to the author, December 18, 2014.
T. S. Flynn, telephone conversation with the author, July 14, 2014.
Jenny Gibson, e-mail message to the author, November 20, 2014.
Audrey Glassman, e-mail message to the author, October 2, 2012.
Nancy Snell Griffith, e-mail message to the author, October 16, 2013.
Kevin Hartley, e-mail messages to the author, September 27, October 2, and October 8, 2012.
Dee Ann Horstman, e-mail messages to the author, October 8, October 22, October 23, and October 24, 2014.
Dee Ann Horstman, telephone conversation with the author, October 8, 2014.
Kyle Jones, e-mail message to the author, May 7, 2014.

Patrice Kane, e-mail message to the author, September 28, 2012.

Kathleen Kist, telephone conversation with the author, December 17, 2014.

Susan MacDonald, telephone conversations with the author, July 8 and July 9, 2014.

David Mathis, telephone conversation with the author, July 2, 2014.

Patricia Miller, e-mail message to the author, May 5, 2014.

Anne Elise Morris, e-mail messages to the author, May 14 and May 15, 2014.

Anne Elise Morris, telephone conversation with the author, May 14, 2014.

Carole Nagle, telephone conversation with the author, July 14, 2014.

Marisa Novotney, e-mail messages to the author, July 14 and July 15, 2014.

Kip P. Nygren, e-mail message to the author, April 14, 2014.

David L. Porter, e-mail message to the author, February 1, 2011.

Diane M. Rebar, e-mail message to the author, May 27, 2014.

Liz Robbins, e-mail messages to the author, December 10 and December 15, 2014.

Lauren Ellis Romer, telephone conversations with the author, July 2, 2014.

John Roush, Jr., telephone conversation with the author, December 17, 2014.

Bill Santin, e-mail message to the author, August 30, 2012.

Melissa Scott, telephone conversation with the author, May 5, 2014.

John H. Shafer, e-mail messages to the author, April 14 and April 15, 2014.

Dana Snider, e-mail message to Jenny Gibson, November 19, 2014.

Lindsey Stanton, telephone conversations with the author, May 22, June 6, and June 9, 2014.

Steve Steinberg, e-mail message to the author, February 22, 2013.

Tom Tomlinson, e-mail messages to the author, May 11, May 12, May 13, and May 14, 2014.

Unnamed Employee, Scottdale Public Library, Scottdale, Pennsylvania, telephone conversation with the author, May 5, 2014.

Doug Upshaw, e-mail message to the author, November 12, 2014.

Brian J. Williams, e-mail messages to the author, October 6 and October 7, 2014.

Rodney Williams, e-mail message to the author, May 16, 2014.

Roy L. Wilson, e-mail message to the author, May 16, 2014.

Gregory Wolf, e-mail message to the author, October 21, 2013.

Archival Materials

Madison County Recorder. Madison County Court House. Winterset, Iowa.

Player Files. National Baseball Hall of Fame Library. Cooperstown, New York:
Adams, Babe
Aldridge, Vic
Barnhart, Clyde
Bigbee, Carson
Brickell, Fred
Bush, Joe
Carey, Max
Clarke, Fred
Comorosky, Adam
Cronin, Joe
Crowder, Alvin
Culloton, Bud
Cuyler, Kiki
Dreyfuss, Barney
Ens, Jewel
Fraser, Chick
Gooch, Johnny
Grantham, George
Hill, Carmen
Hinchman, Bill
Hock, Ed
Koupal, Lou
Kremer, Ray
Mahaffey, Roy
McInnis, Stuffy
McKechnie, Bill [cataloged as McKechnie, Deacon Bill]
McNamara, Tom
Meadows, Lee
Molesworth, Carlton
Moore, Eddie
Morrison, Johnny
Morrison, Phil
Mueller, Walter
Murphy, Eddie
Nichols, Chet [cataloged as Nichols, Chet, 1897–1982, to distinguish him from his son]
Oldham, Red
Onslow, Jack
Pierson, William
Rawlings, Johnny
Rhyne, Hal

Sheehan, Tom
Smith, Earl [cataloged as Smith, Earl Sutton, to distinguish him from another Earl Smith]
Songer, Don
Spencer, Roy
Traynor, Pie
Voyles, Phil
Waner, Paul
Wright, Glenn
Yde, Emil
Register of Deeds Office. Cowley County Court House. Winfield, Kansas.
United States Patent and Trademark Office. Alexandria, Virginia:
F. C. Clarke, Diamond Cover, U.S. Patent 983,857, filed June 7, 1909, issued February 7, 1911.
F. C. Clarke, Sliding Pad for Base Ball Players, etc., U.S. Patent 1,044,494, filed May 24, 1911, issued November 19, 1912.

United States Federal Census Records

1860, 1870, 1880, 1900, 1910, 1920, 1930, 1940

Pittsburgh Newspapers

Pittsburgh Chronicle Telegraph
Pittsburgh Gazette Times
Pittsburgh Post
Pittsburgh Post-Gazette
Pittsburgh Press
Pittsburgh Sun

The Sporting News

1921–1927, and select articles from various other issues

Books

Acocella, Nick, and Donald Dewey. *"The All-Stars" All-Star Baseball Book.* New York: Avon Books, 1986.
Armour, Mark. *Joe Cronin: A Life in Baseball.* Lincoln: University of Nebraska Press, 2010.
Barrow, Edward Grant, with James M. Kahn. *My Fifty Years in Baseball.* New York: Coward-McCann, 1951.
Bartell, Dick, with Norman L. Macht. *Rowdy Richard: A Firsthand Account of the National League Baseball Wars of the 1930s and the Men Who Fought Them.* Berkeley: North Atlantic Books, 1987.
The Baseball Encyclopedia: The Complete and Official Record of Major League Baseball. Toronto: Macmillan, 1969.
Baseball Guide. St. Louis: The Sporting News, 2004.
Benner, Rick, comp. *College Baseball: Essential Facts About All Division I Teams.* Jefferson, NC: McFarland, 2007.
Bloss, Bob. *Baseball Managers: Stats, Stories, and Strategies.* Philadelphia: Temple University Press, 1999.
Bowling, Lewis. *Granville County, North Carolina: Looking Back.* Charleston, SC: The History Press, 2007.
Bredemeier, Herbert George. *Concordia College, Fort Wayne, Indiana, 1839–1957.* Fort Wayne: Fort Wayne Public Library, 1978.
Browning, Reed. *Baseball's Greatest Season, 1924.* Amherst: University of Massachusetts Press, 2003.
Cicotello, David, and Angelo J. Louisa, eds. *Forbes Field: Essays and Memories of the Pirates' Historic Ballpark, 1909–1971.* Jefferson, NC: McFarland, 2007.
Clark, Jerry E., and Martha Ellen Webb. *Alexander the Great: The Story of Grover Cleveland Alexander.* Omaha: Making History, 1993.
Connor, Anthony J. *Voices from Cooperstown: Baseball's Hall of Famers Tell It Like It Was.* New York: Macmillan, 1982.
Connors, Jimmy. *The Outsider: A Memoir.* New York: HarperCollins, 2013.
Deane, Bill. *Award Voting: A History of the Most Valuable Player, Rookie of the Year, and Cy Young Awards.* Kansas City: Society for American Baseball Research, 1988.
DeValeria, Dennis, and Jeanne Burke DeValeria. *Honus Wagner: A Biography.* New York: Henry Holt, 1995.
Doutrich, Paul E. *The Cardinals and the Yankees, 1926: A Classic Season and St. Louis in Seven.* Jefferson, NC: McFarland, 2011.
Eckhouse, Morris, and Carl Mastrocola. *This Date in Pittsburgh Pirates History.* New York: Stein and Day, 1980.
Finoli, David. *The Pittsburgh Pirates.* Charleston, SC: Arcadia, 2006.
Finoli, David, and Bill Ranier. *The Pittsburgh*

Pirates Encyclopedia. Champaign, IL: Sports Publishing, 2003.

_____. *When Cobb Met Wagner: The Seven-Game World Series of 1909*. Jefferson, NC: McFarland, 2011.

Forr, James, and David Proctor. *Pie Traynor: A Baseball Biography*. Jefferson, NC: McFarland, 2010.

Frisch, Frank, as told to J. Roy Stockton. *Frank Frisch: The Fordham Flash*. Garden City, NY: Doubleday, 1962.

Frommer, Harvey. *Baseball's Greatest Managers*. New York: Franklin Watts, 1985.

Fuller, Todd. *60 Feet, 6 Inches and Other Distances from Home: The (Baseball) Life of Mose YellowHorse*. Duluth: How Cow! Press, 2002.

Gillette, Gary, and Pete Palmer, eds. *The ESPN Baseball Encyclopedia*, 5th ed. New York: Sterling Publishing, 2008.

Gorman, Bob. *In Your Face—In Your Heart*. n.p.: Baldwin Books, 2007.

Grimm, Charlie, with Ed Prell. *Jolly Cholly's Story: Grimm's Baseball Tales*. Notre Dame, IN: Diamond Communications, 1983. Originally published under the title of *Jolly Cholly's Story: Baseball, I Love You!* Chicago: Henry Regnery, 1968.

Hageman, William. *Honus: The Life and Times of a Baseball Hero*. Champaign, IL: Sagamore, 1996.

Hartley, Bob. *Winfield's Golden Era of Sports: How Five Decades of Champions, Heroes and Dynasties Shaped One of the Richest Athletic Traditions in Kansas*. Westminster, CO: Sniktau Publications, 2009.

Hill, Carmen P. *The Battles of Bunker Hill: The Life and Baseball Times of Carmen P. Hill*. Includes an interview with Hill conducted by Paul Green. Iola, WI: Krause Publications, 1985.

Hirshberg, Al. *From Sandlots to League President: The Story of Joe Cronin*. New York: Julian Messner, 1962.

Hittner, Arthur D. *Honus Wagner: The Life of Baseball's "Flying Dutchman."* Jefferson, NC: McFarland, 1996.

Hollingsworth, Harry. *The Best and Worst Baseball Teams of All Time*. New York: S.P.I. Books, 1994.

Hornsby, Rogers. *My Kind of Baseball*. Edited by J. Roy Stockton. New York: David McKay Company, 1953.

Hornsby, Rogers, and Bill Surface. *My War with Baseball*. New York: Coward-McCann, 1962.

Hynd, Noel. *The Giants of the Polo Grounds: The Glorious Times of Baseball's New York Giants*. New York: Doubleday, 1988.

James, Bill. *The New Bill James Historical Baseball Abstract*, updated ed. New York: Free Press, 2003.

James, Bill, and Rob Neyer. *The Neyer/James Guide to Pitchers: An Historical Compendium of Pitching, Pitchers, and Pitches*. New York: Simon & Schuster, 2004.

James, Bill, John Dewan, Neil Munro, and Don Zminda, eds. *STATS All-Time Baseball Sourcebook*. Skokie, IL: STATS, 1998.

Johnson, Lloyd, and Miles Wolff, eds. *Encyclopedia of Minor League Baseball*, 3d ed. Durham, NC: Baseball America, 2007.

Kansas City, Missouri, City Directory, 1934. Kansas City: Gate City Directory, 1934.

Kavanagh, Jack. *Ol' Pete: The Grover Cleveland Alexander Story*. South Bend, IN: Diamond Communications, 1996.

Kavanagh, Jack, and Norman Macht. *Uncle Robbie*. Cleveland: Society for American Baseball Research, 1999.

Kelley, Brent. *The Case for Those Overlooked by the Baseball Hall of Fame*. Jefferson, NC: McFarland, 1992.

Koehler, Michael D. *America's Greatest Coaches*. Champaign, IL: Leisure Press, 1990.

Langford, Walter M. *Legends of Baseball: An Oral History of the Game's Golden Age*. South Bend, IN: Diamond Communications, 1987.

Lee, Bill. *The Baseball Necrology: The Post-Baseball Lives and Deaths of Over 7,600 Major League Players and Others*. Jefferson, NC: McFarland, 2003.

Levitt, Daniel R. *Ed Barrow: The Bulldog Who Built the Yankees' First Dynasty*. Lincoln: University of Nebraska Press, 2008.

Lieb, Frederick G. *The Pittsburgh Pirates*. New York: G. P. Putnam's Sons, 1948. Reprint, Carbondale: Southern Illinois University Press, 2003.

Louisa, Angelo J., and David Cicotello, eds. *Mysteries from Baseball's Past: Investigations of Nine Unsettled Questions*. Jefferson, NC: McFarland, 2010.

Maranville, Walter "Rabbit." *Run, Rabbit, Run: The Hilarious and Mostly True Tales of Rabbit Maranville*. Edited by John Holway. Cleveland: Society for American Baseball Research, 1991.

Montgomery, Carol McKechnie, with Jerry Hanks. *"The Deacon's" Daughter: "Daddy's Girl" Relives Her Life with Hall of Fame

Baseball Manager Bill McKechnie. West Conshohocken, PA: Infinity, 2011.

Murdock, Eugene. *Baseball Between the Wars: Memories of the Game by the Men Who Played It*. Westport, CT: Meckler, 1992.

_____. *Baseball Players and Their Times: Oral Histories of the Game, 1920–1940*. Westport, CT: Meckler, 1991.

N. W. Ayer & Son's American Newspaper Annual and Directory. Philadelphia: N. W. Ayer & Son, 1927.

Papenfuse, Edward C., Alan F. Day, David W. Jordan, and Gregory A. Stiverson. *A Biographical Dictionary of the Maryland Legislature, 1635–1789*, Volume 1. Baltimore: Johns Hopkins University Press, 1979.

Parker, Clifton Blue. *Big and Little Poison: Paul and Lloyd Waner, Baseball Brothers*. Jefferson, NC: McFarland, 2003.

Perry, Thomas K. *Textile League Baseball: South Carolina's Mill Teams, 1880–1955*. Jefferson, NC: McFarland, 1993.

Pietrusza, David, Matthew Silverman, and Michael Gershman, eds. *Baseball: The Biographical Encyclopedia*. Kingston, NY: Total Sports, 2000.

Pope, Edwin. *Baseball's Greatest Managers*. Garden City, NY: Doubleday, 1960.

Porter, David L., ed. *Biographical Dictionary of American Sports: Baseball*. Westport, CT: Greenwood Press, Inc., 1987.

Reach's Official Base Ball Guide for 1894. Philadelphia: A. J. Reach, 1894.

Reichler, Joseph L. *The Baseball Trade Register*. New York: Macmillan, 1984.

_____. *The Great All-Time Baseball Record Book*. New York: Macmillan, 1981.

Ritter, Lawrence S. *The Glory of Their Times: The Story of the Early Days of Baseball Told by the Men Who Played It*, new enlarged ed. New York: Vintage, 1984.

Skipper, John C. *Wicked Curve: The Life and Troubled Times of Grover Cleveland Alexander*. Jefferson, NC: McFarland, 2006.

Smizik, Bob. *The Pittsburgh Pirates: An Illustrated History*. Edited by Gerald Astor. New York: Walker, 1990.

Snelling, Dennis. *The Pacific Coast League: A Statistical History, 1903–1957*. Jefferson, NC: McFarland, 1995.

Spatz, Lyle, and Steve Steinberg. *1921: The Yankees, the Giants, and the Battle for Baseball Supremacy in New York*. Lincoln: University of Nebraska Press, 2010.

Stadler, Mike. *The Psychology of Baseball: Inside the Mental Game of the Major League Player*. New York: Gotham Books, 2007.

Stinson, Mitchell Conrad. *Deacon Bill McKechnie: A Baseball Biography*. Jefferson, NC: McFarland, 2012.

Strauss, William, and Neil Howe. *The Fourth Turning: An American Prophecy*. New York: Broadway Books, 1997.

_____. *Generations: The History of America's Future, 1584 to 2069*. New York: William Morrow, 1991.

Strickler, David L. *Child of Moriah: A Biography of John D. "Bonesetter" Reese, 1855–1931*. n.p.: D. L. Strickler, 1984.

Sumner, Benjamin Barrett. *Minor League Baseball Standings: All North American Leagues, Through 1999*. Jefferson, NC: McFarland, 2000.

Thorn, John, and John B. Holway. *The Pitcher*. New York: Prentice Hall, 1987.

Thorn, John, Pete Palmer, and Michael Gershman, eds. *Total Baseball*, 7th ed. Kingston, NY: Total Sports, 2001.

Veeck, Bill, with Ed Linn. *Veeck—As in Wreck: The Autobiography of Bill Veeck*. Chicago: University of Chicago Press, 2001. Originally published under the same title, New York: G. P. Putnam's Sons, 1962.

Waldo, Ronald T. *The Battling Bucs of 1925: How the Pittsburgh Pirates Pulled Off the Greatest Comeback in World Series History*. Jefferson, NC: McFarland, 2012.

_____. *Fred Clarke: A Biography of the Baseball Hall of Fame Player-Manager*. Jefferson, NC: McFarland, 2011.

_____. *Hazen "Kiki" Cuyler: A Baseball Biography*. Jefferson, NC: McFarland, 2012.

Wilcox, Sally. *Winfield and the Walnut Valley*. Arkansas City, KS: Gilliland's, 1975.

Wilde, Oscar. *The Importance of Being Earnest and Related Writings*. Edited by Joseph Bristow. London: Routledge, 1992.

Articles from Periodicals and Websites, Other Than the Pittsburgh Newspapers and The Sporting News

Adams, Franklin J. "The Passing Review of Major League Players." *Baseball Magazine* 38, no. 2 (January 1927): 353–354, 372.

Ahern, John. "Stuffy McInnis to Coach Har-

vard's Baseball Team." *Boston Daily Globe,* October 20, 1948.
"All-Time Pirate Line Ups [sic]." http://home.mindspring.com/~gearhard/pilineup.html.
"American and National League Pennant Races Will Get Under Way Next Tuesday." *Los Angeles Times,* April 12, 1925.
Anderson, David. "Bonesetter Reese." SABR Baseball Biography Project. http://sabr.org/bioproject.
Anderson, Ron. "Bullet Joe Bush." SABR Baseball Biography Project. http://sabr.org/bioproject.
Armour, Mark. "Joe Cronin." SABR Baseball Biography Project. http://sabr.org/bioproject.
"'Babe' Adams Succeeded as Manager by Bender." *New York World,* June 5, 1927.
Bennett, John. "Max Carey." SABR Baseball Biography Project. http://sabr.org/bioproject.
"Bernard A. Culloton Dies at 79; Ex-Motor Vehicle Aide in Albany." *New York Times,* November 11, 1976.
Bernstein, Sam. "Barney Dreyfuss." SABR Baseball Biography Project. http://sabr.org/bioproject.
"Big League Ball Teams Open Fire." *Los Angeles Times,* April 14, 1925.
"Big Leagues Ready for Pennant Races." *New York Times,* April 13, 1924.
"Bigbee with Seattle." *Milwaukee Journal,* April 7, 1927.
Blau, Clifford. "Leg Men: Career Pinch-Runners in Major League Baseball." *The Baseball Research Journal* 38, no. 1 (Summer 2009): 70–81.
_____. "Roster Limits." www.dmbforum.yuku.com/topic/7848.
Bloodgood, Clifford. "Baseball Stars in Minor Settings." *Baseball Magazine* 33, no. 4 (September 1924): 465, 474.
_____. "Baseball Stars in Minor Settings." *Baseball Magazine* 37, no. 3 (August 1926): 417, 423–424.
_____. "Players You Ought to Know." *Baseball Magazine* 33, no. 3 (August 1924): 415, 430.
_____. "Players You Ought to Know." *Baseball Magazine* 33, no. 6 (November 1924): 558, 566–567.
_____. "Players You Ought to Know." *Baseball Magazine* 35, no. 5 (October 1925): 508, 516.
_____. "Players You Ought to Know." *Baseball Magazine* 36, no. 2 (January 1926): 368, 372.
_____. "Players You Ought to Know." *Baseball Magazine* 36, no. 5 (April 1926): 511, 518.
_____. "Players You Ought to Know." *Baseball Magazine* 38, no. 3 (February 1927): 417, 423.
_____. "Players You Ought to Know." *Baseball Magazine* 38, no. 5 (April 1927): 513, 516.
Bond, Gregory. "'Too Much Dirty Work': Race, Manliness, and Baseball in Gilded Age Nebraska." *Nebraska History* 85 (Winter 2004): 172–185.
Bradbury, J. C. "How Do Players Age?" *Baseball Prospectus,* January 11, 2010. www.baseballprospectus.com/article.php?articleid=9933.
Brenner, I. C. "Johnny Rawlings Now Sells Insurance in Los Angeles." *Omaha World-Herald,* August 5, 1932.
"Bring Back Spitter?" [Toledo, Ohio] *Blade,* July 25, 1961.
Burr, Harold C. "Pirate Outfielder's Comeback Has All Earmarks of a Baseball Drama." *Brooklyn Daily Eagle,* July 31, 1932.
Burton, Lewis. "Too Many Jugs Fanned 'Jughandle' Morrison." *New York Journal-American,* January 14, 1944.
Bush, Joe. "Pittsburg [sic] Boss Talks to Bushers." *Los Angeles Times,* July 30, 1923.
Carleton, Russell A. "Baseball Therapy: That Peak Age Thing, Part I." *Baseball Prospectus,* February 15, 2010. www.baseballprospectus.com/article.php?articleid=10058.
"Catcher Walter Schmidt May Rejoin Pittsburgh Pirates." *Washington Post,* July 9, 1922.
Cava, Pete, and Paul Sandin. "The First Babe." *Sports Collectors Digest,* April 7, 1995.
Cicotello, David. "Wilbur Cooper." SABR Baseball Biography Project. http://sabr.org/bioproject.
"Clarke in Baseball Post." *New York Times,* January 5, 1937.
"Clarke May Come Back." *Los Angeles Times,* December 29, 1922.
Connery, Don. "Hey, Mr. Banjo!" *Sports Illustrated,* September 19, 1955. www.si.com/vault/1955/09/19/604983/hey-mr-banjo.
"Connie Mack's Son to be A's Next Manager." *Daytona Beach Morning Journal,* May 12, 1943.
Cory, Dan. "The Greatest Outfielders." *Baseball Magazine* 29, no. 2 (July 1922): 360, 375.
"Crown Wagner Diamond's King." *Chicago Daily Tribune,* February 25, 1917.
D., F. H. "From the Press Box." *Nashua Telegraph,* December 21, 1926.

Daley, Arthur. "Sports of the *Times.*" *New York Times*, May 30, 1950.

———. "Sports of *The Times.*" *New York Times*, February 8, 1962.

Daniel, Daniel M. "How Fred Clarke Taught the Pirates Confidence." *Baseball Magazine* 36, no. 4 (March 1926): 443–444.

Davis, Aaron, and C. Paul Rogers III. "Stuffy McInnis." SABR Baseball Biography Project. http://sabr.org/bioproject.

"The Dean of Major League Ball Players." From an interview with Babe Adams. *Baseball Magazine* 36, no. 6 (May 1926): 535–536.

"Death Takes Chic Fraser, Old Big League Hurler, Yank Scout." *Idaho Evening Times*, May 8, 1940.

"Do the Pirates of 1925 Outrank the Pirates of 1909?" From an interview with Fred Clarke. *Baseball Magazine* 36, no. 1 (December 1925): 303, 331.

"Does Pitching Favor the American League Batter?" From an interview with Victor Aldridge. *Baseball Magazine* 39, no. 2 (July 1927): 343–344.

"Don Songer, 63, Dies." *Kansas City Times*, October 4, 1962.

"Earl Smith, Ex-Baseball Player, Dies." *Arkansas Democrat*, June 10, 1963.

"Earl Smith's Case Again Continued." *Boston Globe*, August 26, 1925.

"Editorial Comment." *Baseball Magazine* 37, no. 6 (November 1926): 534, 568.

"Editorial Comment." *Baseball Magazine* 38, no. 2 (January 1927): 342.

"F. Clarke Still Likes to Play." *Atlanta Constitution*, September 8, 1922.

Fay, Bill. "Belles of the Ball Game [sic]." *Collier's* 124, no. 7 (August 13, 1949): 44.

Flynn, T. S. "A Pitcher Saved Peoria Baseball." www.pjstar.com.

"Forbes Field a Lake." *Chicago Daily Tribune*, October 15, 1925.

Forr, James. "Pie Traynor." SABR Baseball Biography Project. http://sabr.org/bioproject.

"The Frame Work [sic] of a Winning Team." From an interview with Walter Schmidt. *Baseball Magazine* 28, no. 4 (March 1922): 735–736, 768.

"Fred Clarke Advocates Shift to the Outfield for Sisler." *New York Times*, March 20, 1924.

"Fred Clarke, Ex-Pirate Boss, May Buy Philly Nationals." *Chicago Daily Tribune*, November 6, 1924.

"Fred Clarke Is Among Us." *Los Angeles Times*, June 14, 1919.

"Fred Clarke Now a Scattergunner." *Los Angeles Times*, June 23, 1919.

"Fred Clarke Seeks Baseball Come-Back [sic]." *Washington Post*, October 30, 1924.

"Fred Clarke Stays as Sandlot Leagues' Head." *Chicago Daily Tribune*, February 27, 1955.

"Fred Clarke: The Baseball Capitalist." *New York Herald*, March 5, 1911, Magazine Section, 7.

"Fred Clarke to Coach." *New York Times*, February 26, 1922.

"Fred Clarke to Head New Baseball Veterans' Group." *Chicago Daily Tribune*, December 17, 1944.

Frierson, Eddie. "Christy Mathewson." SABR Baseball Biography Project. http://sabr.org/bioproject.

Gallagher, Jack. "Pittsburgh's Pennant Chances Hinge on Glenn Wright's Return, Claims Stuffy McInnis." *Los Angeles Times*, September 5, 1926.

———. "Scared of the Pirates." *Los Angeles Times*, July 5, 1925.

Getty, Frank. "Sale of Pirates Would Put Cuyler Back in Buc Lineup." [St. Petersburg, FL] *Evening Independent*, October 14, 1927.

Geyer, Orel R. "The Rise of 'Phenom' Adams." *Baseball Magazine* 4, no. 4 (February 1910): 67–69.

"Giants and Robins Named in Scandal." *New York Times*, January 4, 1927.

"Giants Are 8 to 5 Favorites in Wall Street to Win Flag; Senators and Athletics, 2 to 1." *New York Times*, April 13, 1926.

"Glenn Wright Out for Rest of Year." *Milwaukee Journal*, July 24, 1929.

"Glenn Wright to Be Mended for Brooklyn." *Schenectady Gazette*, November 19, 1931.

"Glenn Wright's Arm Adds to Carey's Woes." *New London Day*, April 20, 1932.

Goewey, Ed A. "The Old Fan Says." *Leslie's Illustrated Weekly Newspaper*, August 6, 1914, 134.

Goins, Jase. "Earl 'Oil' Smith." *Grassroots* (April 2014): 24–25.

Gould, James M. "Baseball's Greatest Infield." *Baseball Magazine* 36, no. 4 (March 1926): 447–448.

———. "A Forecast of the Coming Pennant Race." *Baseball Magazine* 38, no. 6 (May 1927): 535–536, 571–572.

———. "A Forecast of the Coming World's Series." *Baseball Magazine* 37, no. 4 (September 1926): 453–454.

———. "The New Managers and Their

Prospects." *Baseball Magazine* 38, no. 5 (April 1927): 497–498, 519.

———. "Sensational Changes in the Managerial Ranks." *Baseball Magazine* 38, no. 2 (January 1927): 349–350.

———. "The Unsolved Mysteries of 1926." *Baseball Magazine* 37, no. 6 (November 1926): 545–546.

———. "Who Will Win the Big League Pennants in 1926?" *Baseball Magazine* 36, no. 6 (May 1926): 531–533, 564–565.

Graham, Frank. "Graham's Corner." *New York Journal-American*, February 1, 1961.

Griffith, Nancy Snell. "Roy Mahaffey." SABR Baseball Biography Project. http://sabr.org/bioproject.

Grossman, James. "The 'Proper Study of History': What the Public Thinks About Historical Thinking." *Perspectives on History* 52, no. 7 (October 2014): 7–8.

Haas, Rodney. "No Fooling: Cubs, Pirates Played in Kingman April 1, 1924." *Kingman Daily Miner*, March 31, 2013. http://kdminer.com.

Hanna, W. B. "Strong Points and Weaknesses of Baseball's Four Most Prominent Clubs." *Baseball Magazine* 35, no. 6 (November 1925): 535–536.

———. "The Twenty-five Greatest Players." *Baseball Magazine* 33, no. 1 (June 1924): 299–300.

Henderson, Libby. "Charles Benjamin Adams: A Humble, Honorable Hero." www.babeadams.com.

Henry, Bill. "Coast League Confab Opens." *Los Angeles Times*, November 12, 1923.

Hoffman, John C. "Onslow's 64th Victory." *Baseball Digest*, February 1950, 17.

"How Lee Meadows Rose Above All Handicaps to Become a Star Pitcher." Comprising an interview with Lee Meadows. *Baseball Magazine* 36, no. 1 (December 1925): 310, 325.

"How the Baseball Scouts Work." *Reading Eagle*, January 27, 1914.

"In the Press Box with Baxter." *Washington Post*, April 15, 1925.

"J. Eddie Murphy Dies; Former Major Leaguer." *Scranton Tribune*, February 22, 1969.

"Jennings with Giants." [Montreal] *Gazette*, October 30, 1920.

"Johnny Evers Urges Aggressive Ball." *Boston Daily Globe*, February 25, 1917.

Kieran, John. "Sports of the *Times*." *New York Times*, May 15, 1937.

Kling, Dwayne. "Joe Devine." In *Can He Play? A Look at Baseball Scouts and Their Profession*, edited by Jim Sandoval and Bill Nowlin. Phoenix: Society for American Baseball Research, 2011, 41–42.

———. "Joe Devine." SABR Baseball Biography Project. http://sabr.org/bioproject.

Kofoed, J. C. "Are the Giants a Great Ball Club [sic]?" *Baseball Magazine* 28, no. 5 (April 1922): 789–790, 808–809.

Lamb, Bill. "Carlton Molesworth." SABR Baseball Biography Project. http://sabr.org/bioproject.

———. "Jewel Ens." SABR Baseball Biography Project. http://sabr.org/bioproject.

Lane. F. C. "The All America [sic] Baseball Club of 1925." *Baseball Magazine* 36, no. 1 (December 1925): 305–308, 331–332, 334.

———. "The All-America Baseball Club of 1921." *Baseball Magazine* 28, no. 1 (December 1921): 584–587, 618–620, 622.

———. "The All-America Baseball Club of 1923." *Baseball Magazine* 32, no. 1 (December 1923): 307–309, 328–330.

———. "The All-America Baseball Club of 1922." *Baseball Magazine* 30, no. 1 (December 1922): 307–310, 329–330.

———. "Babe Adams' All but Miraculous Control." *Baseball Magazine* 35, no. 6 (November 1925): 545–546.

———. "Bill McKechnie, the Pirate Chief." *Baseball Magazine* 32, no. 5 (April 1924): 487.

———. "Does Max Carey Compare with Tris Speaker?" *Baseball Magazine* 29, no. 4 (September 1922): 447–449, 476, 480.

———. "He Waited Twelve Years for His Big Chance." *Baseball Magazine* 39, no. 6 (November 1927): 543–544.

———. "How Max Carey Became a Baseball Star." *Baseball Magazine* 33, no. 5 (October 1924): 483–484, 519–520.

———. "How Sickness Marred the Brilliant Career of Carson Bigbee." *Baseball Magazine* 37, no. 5 (October 1926): 507, 516.

———. "The Keystone Star of the Pittsburgh Club." *Baseball Magazine* 35, no. 5 (October 1925): 494, 516.

———. "The Man Who Gave Pittsburgh Its Batting Punch." *Baseball Magazine* 33, no. 6 (November 1924): 536, 564.

———. "The New York Yankees Against the World." *Baseball Magazine* 37, no. 6 (November 1926): 531–532, 566.

———. "Our All America [sic] Baseball Club of 1926." *Baseball Magazine* 38, no. 1 (December 1926): 311–314.

_____. "'Pie' Traynor, a Coming Baseball Star." *Baseball Magazine* 31, no. 2 (July 1923): 349–350.

_____. "Turning Points in the Major League Pennant Race of 1926." *Baseball Magazine* 38, no. 2 (January 1927): 351–352, 377.

_____. "Who Will Win the Big League Pennants in 1927?" *Baseball Magazine* 38, no. 6 (May 1927): 531–533, 568–570.

_____. "Who Will Win the World's Championship?" *Baseball Magazine* 35, no. 6 (November 1925): 531–532, 568–569.

_____. "Why Max Carey Is the Most Efficient Outfielder in Baseball." *Baseball Magazine* 36, no. 7 (June 1926): 291–292, 326–328.

_____. "Why Max Carey Should Be a Big Drawing Card." *Baseball Magazine* 33, no. 3 (August 1924): 405–406, 432.

_____. "Wrecking Baseball's Greatest Infield." *Baseball Magazine* 34, no. 4 (March 1925): 453, 469.

Langosch, Jenifer. "Dreyfuss A Baseball Pioneer." http://m.pirates.mlb.com.

"League Teams Set for Season's Start." *New York Times*, April 15, 1923.

Levitt, Dan. "Ed Barrow." SABR Baseball Biography Project. http://sabr.org/bioproject.

Lewis, H. Perry. "'Smile! Smile! No Matter How Things Break,' Clarke's Motto." [Philadelphia] *Public Ledger*, May 23, 1915.

Leyden, Dick. "Rabbit Maranville." SABR Baseball Biography Project. http://sabr.org/bioproject.

Lichtman, Mitchel. "How Do Baseball Players Age? (Part I)." *The Hardball Times*, December 21, 2009. www.hardballtimes.com.

_____. "How Do Baseball Players Age? (Part II)." *The Hardball Times*, December 29, 2009. www.hardballtimes.com.

Lieb, Frederick G. "Baseball's Star Rookies." *Baseball Magazine* 33, no. 3 (August 1924): 393–395, 426.

_____. "Fred Clarke." *Baseball Magazine* 4, no. 4 (February 1910): 47–50.

_____. "The Reserve Strength of the Major Leagues." *Baseball Magazine* 33, no. 5 (October 1924): 489–490.

_____. "The Sad Story of the Failing Veterans." *Baseball Magazine* 33, no. 4 (September 1924): 445–446.

Louisa, Angelo. "Fred Clarke." SABR Baseball Biography Project. http://sabr.org/bioproject.

_____. "Fred Clarke: It All Began in Iowa." The Field of Dreams Chapter of the Society for American Baseball Research. http://chapters.sabr.org/fieldofdreams.

Macht, Norman. "Do You Remember? Chick Fraser." *Phillies Report*, September 12, 1991, 10–11.

"Major League Moguls Air Views on Eve of Opening." *Los Angeles Times*, April 16, 1923.

"Major Leagues Open Title Races Tuesday." *New York Times*, April 12, 1925.

"Major Races Open Tuesday." *Los Angeles Times*, April 11, 1926.

Mann, Arthur. "The Dead Ball and the New Game." *Baseball Magazine* 37, no. 3 (August 1926): 407–408.

Mason, Ward. "Ray Kremer, Pittsburgh's Veteran Ace." *Baseball Magazine* 43, no. 4 (September 1929): 449, 474.

"Max Carey Receives Retroactive Award." *Miami News*, January 27, 1963.

"Max Carey Wants Job in Baseball." *Milwaukee Journal*, February 28, 1940.

Maxwell, Robert W. "Few Changes Made in Pirate Line-Up [sic]." *Washington Post*, March 24, 1922.

McGraw, John. "Close Races Predicted." *Los Angeles Times*, April 12, 1925.

"McGraw Selects All-National Team." *Atlanta Constitution*, November 8, 1922.

"McGraw the Mussolini of Managers." From an interview with William Southworth. *Baseball Magazine* 39, no. 6 (November 1927): 533–534, 569.

Miller, Clarence W. "Fred Clarke—Ball Player [sic], Ranchman—Kansan." *Kansas Magazine* (November 1909): 46–53.

Miller, Stuart. "Next to the Manager, but a Bit Ahead." *New York Times*, August 19, 2012.

"Now a Scout, Glenn Wright Has Fond Baseball Memories." *Milwaukee Journal*, September 26, 1960.

Nowlin, Bill. "Hal Rhyne." SABR Baseball Biography Project. http://sabr.org/bioproject.

_____. "Johnny Gooch." SABR Baseball Biography Project. http://sabr.org/bioproject.

"Oakland Caseys Head South." *Los Angeles Times*, February 20, 1924.

"Oakland K. of C. Baseballers Win State Championship." *Los Angeles Times*, February 23, 1924.

"'Oil' Smith, the Pirates Colorful Catcher." Comprising an interview with Earl Smith. *Baseball Magazine* 39, no. 1 (June 1927): 311–312.

"Once Grocery Clerk." *Washington Post*, July 30, 1911.

"Outlook Is Bright for St. Louis Clubs." *New York Times*, April 11, 1922.

Phelon, W. A. "Can The Runners-Up Pull Through?" *Baseball Magazine* 33, no. 5 (October 1924): 507–509, 521.

———. "How the Pennant Tide Ebbed and Flowed Through 1922." *Baseball Magazine* 29, no. 6 (November 1922): 557–559, 563, 573–576.

———. "Making Things Hum for the Annual Spring Training." *Baseball Magazine* 34, no. 5 (April 1925): 507–508, 518–521.

———. "The New York Clubs Against the Field." *Baseball Magazine* 33, no. 4 (September 1924): 455–456, 478, 480.

———. "When the Pace of the Pennant Race Quickens." *Baseball Magazine* 31, no. 3 (August 1923): 413–415, 425.

———. "Who Will Win the Big League Pennants?" *Baseball Magazine* 28, no. 6 (May 1922): 819–822, 851–852.

———. "Who Will Win the Big League Pennants?" *Baseball Magazine* 32, no. 6 (May 1924): 531–533, 571.

———. "Who Will Win the Big League Pennants in 1925. [sic]" *Baseball Magazine* 34, no. 6 (May 1925): 531–534, 571–573.

———. "Who Will Win the Big League Pennants of 1923?" *Baseball Magazine* 30, no. 6 (May 1923): 531–533, 563–564.

———. "Who Will Win the World's Series of 1924?" *Baseball Magazine* 33, no. 6 (November 1924): 547–549.

Phelps, Frank V. "Fred Clifford Clarke." In *Baseball's First Stars*, edited by Frederick Ivor-Campbell, Robert L. Tiemann, and Mark Rucker. Cleveland: Society for American Baseball Research, 1996, 29–30.

"Pirates [sic] Acquire Glenn Wright." *Daytona Beach Morning Journal*, November 8, 1947.

"Pirates Are Favored to Capture Pennant." *New York Times*, August 22, 1926.

"Pirates' Boss Says Team Won, Not He." *Chicago Daily Tribune*, October 18, 1925.

"Pirates Clinch Flag; Beat the Phils, 2–1." *New York Times*, September 24, 1925.

"Pirates Get Walt Schmidt." *Los Angeles Times*, September 12, 1915.

"Pirates Have Upset the Dope: Clarke Will Help In National League Race." *Washington Post*, July 5, 1925.

"Pirates Recover and Beat Robins." *New York Times*, August 29, 1921.

"Pirates Smear Fading Giants." *Boston Globe*, August 25, 1925.

"Pitcher Aldridge, Who Was Well Named 'Victor.'" From an interview with Victor Aldridge. *Baseball Magazine* 36, no. 1 (December 1925): 304.

"A Pitcher Who Wins with a Losing Club." Comprising an interview with Harold Carlson. *Baseball Magazine* 39, no. 1 (June 1927): 296, 323–324.

"Pittsburg [sic] Has a Stronger Club than Washington." From an interview with George Kelly. *Baseball Magazine* 35, no. 6 (November 1925): 533, 566.

"Pittsburg [sic] Pirates' Wives Must Stay Home When Team Travels." *Boston Daily Globe*, May 13, 1923.

"Pittsburgh Scout Tells Why Baseball Material Is Scarce." *Ludington* [Michigan] *Daily News*, October 8, 1922.

"Playing Sunfield Detrimental to Batting; Hooper, Red Sox, One of Most Adept on Job." *Washington Post*, November 5, 1916.

Redeh, Dick. "Where Two Managerial Systems Clash." *Baseball Magazine* 38, no. 5 (April 1927): 495–496.

"Rites to Honor Baseball Scout." *Idaho Evening Times*, May 8, 1940.

Rogers III, C. Paul. "Hughie Jennings." SABR Baseball Biography Project. http://sabr.org/bioproject.

Ryder, Jack. "Reds Seen as Keen Factor in National League Race." *Washington Post*, April 2, 1925.

"Sam Dreyfuss Dead; A Baseball Notable." *New York Times*, February 23, 1931.

Sanborn, I. E. "Comiskey Predicts Rough Going for Major Leagues." *Chicago Daily Tribune*, December 13, 1919.

Sanborn, Irving E. "The Decline of Curve Ball [sic] Pitching." *Baseball Magazine* 32, no. 5 (April 1924): 483–485.

———. "The Recent Eclipse of the Player-Manager." *Baseball Magazine* 38, no. 3 (February 1927): 391–393.

Sawyer, Ford. "The Champion Pinch-Pitcher." *Baseball Magazine* 32, no. 4 (March 1924): 459, 463.

———. "Players You Ought to Know." *Baseball Magazine* 29, no. 4 (September 1922): 463, 472–473.

———. "Players You Ought to Know." *Baseball Magazine* 29, no. 5 (October 1922): 511, 522.

———. "Players You Ought to Know." *Baseball Magazine* 29, no. 6 (November 1922): 556.

———. "Players You Ought to Know." *Baseball Magazine* 30, no. 5 (April 1923): 498, 519, 520.

———. "Players You Ought to Know." *Baseball Magazine* 31, no. 2 (July 1923): 358, 372, 373.
———. "Players You Ought to Know." *Baseball Magazine* 32, no. 2 (January 1924): 368, 377.
———. "Players You Ought to Know." *Baseball Magazine* 32, no. 6 (May 1924): 556, 575.
"Six Countries to Compete in Semi-Pro [sic] Meet." *Chicago Daily Tribune*, January 30, 1939.
Smiley, Richard. "Reb Russell." SABR Baseball Biography Project. http://sabr.org/bioproject.
Smith, Chester L. "Barney Dreyfuss Unearths a Player Gold Mine." *Baseball Magazine* 34, no. 5 (April 1925): 489, 516, 518.
———. "First-Basing That Fairly Glitters." *Baseball Magazine* 33, no. 4 (September 1924): 448, 473.
———. "Rookies Who Strengthened the World's Champions." *Baseball Magazine* 37, no. 4 (September 1926): 444.
———. "Will Pittsburgh Stand Pat?" *Baseball Magazine* 36, no. 5 (April 1926): 507, 517.
Smith, Frank. "Indians 'Doped' to Nose Out Yanks." *Chicago Daily Tribune*, April 13, 1924.
"Smith's Accuser Again Absent." *Boston Globe*, August 27, 1925.
"Speaker Makes His 3,000th Safe Drive." *Cleveland Plain Dealer*, May 18, 1925.
"Sports Briefs." *Owosso* (MI) *Argus-Press*, December 22, 1948.
"Springfield Signs Adams." *New York World*, July 31, 1927.
Stevens, Brian. "Babe Adams." SABR Baseball Biography Project. http://sabr.org/bioproject.
Strecker, Trey. "George Gibson." SABR Baseball Biography Project. http://sabr.org/bioproject.
"Stuffy McInnis Is New Norwich Coach." *Lewiston Evening Journal*, December 30, 1930.
"Sun Glasses." *Sporting Life*, February 10, 1912, 14.
"The Supreme Importance of Balance in Baseball." From an interview with Max Carey. *Baseball Magazine* 35, no. 4 (September 1925): 435–436.
"Talk: Vic Aldridge." http://en.wikipedia.org/wiki/Talk%3AVic_Aldridge.
Tangotiger. "When Do Pitchers Peak?" *The Book: Playing the Percentages in Baseball*, April 8, 2010. www.insidethebook.com.
Untitled Article. *Mohave County Miner*, May 22, 1915. http://www.newspapers.com.
Vaughn, Irving. "Baseball Only Incidental in Aldridge's Life." *Chicago Daily Tribune*, October 18, 1925.
———. "Pirates Hard Band to Dope; Morale of Men Great Big?" *Chicago Daily Tribune*, March 28, 1922.
———. "Three Cornered [sic] Fights Loom in Major League Flag Wars." *Chicago Daily Tribune*, April 11, 1926.
"Veterans Are Hopeful." *Reading Eagle*, August 30, 1926.
Vidmer, Richards. "Major Leagues Open Season This Week." *New York Times*, April 11, 1926.
"Walter Schmidt Plays with Pittsburgh Club." *Washington Post*, August 8, 1922.
"Walter Schmidt to Join Pittsburgh Nine." *Los Angeles Times*, April 14, 1920.
Walters, Steve. "It Ain't Necessarily So." *The Wages of Wins Journal*. www.wagesofwins.com.
Wancho, Joseph. "Paul Waner." SABR Baseball Biography Project. http://sabr.org/bioproject.
Ward, John J. "The Best Curve Ball [sic] Since Mordecai Brown." *Baseball Magazine* 31, no. 4 (September 1923): 450.
———. "George Grantham, Baseball's Speediest Rookie." *Baseball Magazine* 31, no. 5 (October 1923): 501.
———. "Has Pittsburgh Found a Worthy Successor to Hans Wagner?" *Baseball Magazine* 35, no. 6 (November 1925): 538, 568.
———. "The Hero of the 1925 World's Series." *Baseball Magazine* 36, no. 1 (December 1925): 297, 335.
———. "John Gooch of the Ex-World's Champions." *Baseball Magazine* 38, no. 2 (January 1927): 358, 378.
———. "The Pitcher With the Deceiving Delivery." *Baseball Magazine* 34, no. 6 (May 1925): 558, 568.
———. "The Third Member of the Pirates Great Outfield." *Baseball Magazine* 35, no. 6 (November 1925): 547.
Welch, Judy. "Cowley County's Fred Clarke Brought Fame, Glory to Pittsburgh Pirates." *Arkansas City* (KS) *Traveler*, November 8, 1976.
"The Western League." *Kansas City Star*, June 20, 1893.
"What One Ball Player Owes to Another." From an interview with Max Carey. *Baseball Magazine* 31, no. 1 (June 1923): 307–308, 323.
"Will He Quit?" *Chicago Daily Tribune*, September 4, 1925.

Wolf, Gregory H. "Ray Kremer." SABR Baseball Biography Project. http://sabr.org/bioproject.
"A Word on the Proper Batting Stance." From an interview with Hazen Cuyler. *Baseball Magazine* 35, no. 6 (November 1925): 542.
"Yanks Get Holiday to Join Mardi Gras." *New York Times*, March 5, 1924.

Musical Compositions

Steinman, Jim. "Two Out of Three Ain't Bad." *Bat Out of Hell*. Epic Records/CBS Inc., 1977.

Unpublished Materials

Christian, Ralph J. "Edward Grant Barrow: The Des Moines Years." Paper presented at the Society for American Baseball Research National Convention, Scottsdale, Arizona, 1999.
"The Clarke Family." Biographical information compiled from data that belonged to William Howard Scarff, Fred Clarke's brother-in-law. Given to the author by Margaret Donahoe Burroughs.
"The Clarke Family Tree." Constructed and given to the author by Margaret Donahoe Burroughs.
Pletchette, John. "Fred Clifford Clarke, Major League Baseball Hall of Famer." Timeline compiled for the 150th anniversary of the founding of Winterset, Iowa. Madison County Historical Society, Winterset, Iowa.

Websites Consulted

www.aagpbl.org
www.ads-on-line.com/newbasiccourse/products/chaptereight10.html
www.ancestry.com
www.baseball-almanac.com
www.baseballchronology.com/Baseball/Awards/TSN-AllStars.asp
www.baseballguru.com/bburgess/analysisbburgess20.html
www.baseballindex.org
www.baseballlibrary.com/ballplayers
www.baseball-reference.com
www.measuringworth.com
www.pagenweb.org/~luzerne/patk/swoy1.htm
www.retrosheet.org
www.tarentumboro.com/index.php/documents?task=document.viewdoc&id=20
www.tenmilelake.org/history/adams.htm
www.thebaseballpage.com
www.winfieldcountryclub.com

Index

Numbers in ***bold italics*** indicate pages with photographs.

AAGPBL *see* All-American Girls Professional Baseball League
Abrams, Al 247
Ada, Oklahoma 245
Adams, Babe *see* Adams, Charles Benjamin "Babe"
Adams, Blanche 197
Adams, Charles Benjamin "Babe" ***10***, ***149***, ***221***; call to Davis on August 21, 1926 159; personal information 203, 206, 218, 220, 221, 235; as a player 13, 14, 18, 35, 42, 50, 64, 80, 96, 101, 107, 135, 150, 152, 154–156, 160, 161, 163, 164, 170, 193–194, 201, 202, 222, 250–251, 255–256, 258, 263n19, 276n6, 281–282n165, 294n157, 294n158, 295n192, 299n40; role in the ABC Affair 9–10, 138–145, 147–154, 156–157, 162, 163–165, 168–169, 189, 193–194, 220–228, 261n3; tell-all article 10, 88–90, 93, 121, 128–129, 176–180, 182–188, 189, 196–197, 261n1
Adams, Samuel 235
AL *see* American League
Alamac Hotel, New York, New York 140, 142
Aldridge, Christopher 168, 171, 172, 235
Aldridge, Victor, III 46, 48, 50, 54, 56, 78–79, 80, 83, 84, 93–94, 96, 103, 106, 113, 114–115, 119, 121–122, 126, 130–132, 134–135, 161, 168, 171–172, ***171***, 204, 215, 218, 228, 235, 250–251, 255–256, 258, 276n6, 295n189, 297n252
Alexander, Aimee 116
Alexander, Grover Cleveland 116–118, 168, 211, 282n173
All-American Girls Professional Baseball League 197, 199, 205
Allegheny County, Pennsylvania 162, 205; officials 112
Allegheny Steel Club 51, 112
All-Star Game *see* Major League All-Star Game
Alston, Walt 214
Amateur Baseball Congress 198
American Association (major league) 266n121

American Association (minor league) 92, 95, 99, 103, 116, 170, 171, 267n34
American Heating Company 205
American Historical Association 231
American League 15, 67, 82, 84, 92, 108, 123, 145, 156, 158, 162, 190, 201, 214, 262n5, 266n121; All-Star team 190
Amherst College 202
Anson, Cap 60
Archie, Missouri 245
Associated Press 104
Aston, George "Chauff" 88
Astros *see* Houston Astros
Athletics *see* Philadelphia Athletics
Atlanta Crackers 92, 201
Atlantic City, New Jersey 66, 95

Babe, Loren 214
Babe Adams Highway 197
Baker, Frank "Home Run" 11, 99
Baker Bowl 115
Balinger, Edward F. 36, 44, 56, 66, 87, 94, 95, 100, 105, 107, 118, 134, 167, 174, 244, 273n164, 277n39, 282n173, 283n186
Baltimore Orioles (American League) 266n121
Baltimore Orioles (International League) 118
Bancroft, Dave 39, 136–137, 195, 265n85
Barbare, Walter 13
Barlow, Kentucky 241
Barnhart, Cecil 235
Barnhart, Clyde Lee "Pooch" 36, 50, 79, 80, 83, 96, 101–102, 109, 110, 111, 116, 161, 187, 204, 206, 210, 215–216, ***215***, 234–235, 250–251, 259, 263n18, 263n19, 276n6, 295n189, 297n253, 298n5
Barnhart, Nora 216
Barons *see* Birmingham Barons
Barrow, Edward Grant 60, 270n85
Barry, John "Jack" 11, 99
Bartell, Dick 261n3
Baseball Magazine: Major League All-America Club 80; Major League All-America Team

313

211; National League All-Star Club 80; National League All-Star Team 211
Baseball Writers' Association of America 197, 199, 200, 294n157; Most Valuable Player Award 200
batting orders 78, 109, 110, 111, 114, 124, 125, 161, 165, 172, 216
BBWAA *see* Baseball Writers' Association of America
Beantown *see* Boston, Massachusetts
Belton, South Carolina 240
Bender, Albert "Chief" 11, 99
Bennett, John 198, 236–237
Berger, Ralph 264n42
Berger, Wally 191
Berra, Yogi 214
Bezdek, Hugo 15, 262n7
Biederman, Lester J. 83
Big Apple *see* New York, New York
Bigbee, Callie 219, 236
Bigbee, Carson Lee "Skeeter" *10, 138,* 225; call to Davis on August 21, 1926 159; as a manager 197; personal information 197, 203, 206, 218–219, 221, 235–236; as a player 23, 38–39, 50, 83, 96, 109, 110, 111, 114, 116, 149–150, 152, 160, 161, 170, 197, 201, 202, 221, 222, 226, 250–251, 259, 260, 263n18, 263n19, 276n6, 295n192; role in the ABC Affair 9–10, 137–145, 147–154, 156–157, 162, 163–165, 168–169, 189, 193, 220, 222–228, 261n2, 261n3; tell-all article 10, 88–90, 93, 121, 128–129, 176–180, 182–188, 189, 196–197, 261n1
Bigbee, Claiborne 219, 236
Billy-Don Chicken Shack, Kansas City, Missouri 205, 297n243
Birmingham Barons 92, 107, 108
Bisons *see* Buffalo Bisons
Black Sox Scandal *see* Chicago White Sox
Bloomfield, Iowa 242
Bloss, Bob 214
Bluege, Ossie 82
Bosox *see* Boston Red Sox
Boston, Massachusetts 55, 115, 117, 140, 147, 174
Boston Bees *see* Boston Braves
Boston Braves 9, 13, 15, 21–23, 25, 28, 30, 33, 50, 55, 77, 104, 105, 110, 113, 115, 119, 124, 128, 135–136, 142, 145, 158, 161, 168, 173, 174–175, 176, 185, 190–191, 203, 209, 212, 213, 226
Boston Red Sox 47, 201, 203
Bottomley, Jim 47
Boudreau, Lou 214
Boyle, Havey J. 89, 127, 145–147, 170, 182, 224
Bradenton, Florida 192
Brainerd, Minnesota 236
Brainerd High School 236
Braves *see* Boston Braves; Milwaukee Braves
Brickell, Albert 236
Brickell, Fred *see* Brickell, George Frederick
Brickell, George Frederick 135, 145, 172, 204, 236, 250–251, 259, 260, 285n65, 295n189, 297n251, 298n5
Bridgeport, Connecticut 175
Bristol-Myers 198
Brooklyn, New York 42, 139, 145, 165
Brooklyn Dodgers 10, 15, 17, 18, 19, 21, 22, 23, 25, 27, 28, 30, 31, 32, 33, 36, 37, 41, 42, 49, 52–53, 55, 77, 90, 92, 105, 106, 110, 113, 114, 115, 116, 117, 119, 120, 124, 126, 131, 134, 140, 142, 145, 158, 159, 160, 161, 164, 173, 176, 197, 198, 203, 209, 212, 213, 224
Brooklyn Robins *see* Brooklyn Dodgers
Brooklyn Tip-Tops 267–268n36
Brooks School, North Andover, Massachusetts 202
Brower, Eddie 93, 95
Brown, Harry 267n26
Brown, Joe 93, 95, 99, 100
Brown, Mordecai "Three Finger" 14
Browns *see* St. Louis Browns
Brunswick Hotel, Boston, Massachusetts 139
Bryant & Stratton's Chicago Business College 247
Buck Valley, Pennsylvania 235
Buffalo, New York 118, 121
Buffalo Bisons 92, 99, 118, 160
Bureau of Recreation, Philadelphia, Pennsylvania 204
Burlington Bees 286n129
Burroughs, Margaret Donahoe 63
Bush, Bullet Joe *see* Bush, Leslie Ambrose "Bullet Joe"
Bush, Donie *see* Bush, Owen "Donie"
Bush, Joe *see* Bush, Leslie Ambrose "Bullet Joe"
Bush, John 236
Bush, Leslie Ambrose "Bullet Joe" 123, 124, 126, 136, 145, 161, 171, 173–174, 203, 204, 236, 250–251, 255–256, 258, 295n189, 297n252
Bush, Owen "Donie" 195, 196

Cain, Cullen 151
Cale, Indiana 235
Camnitz, Howie 155–156, 288n173
Cardinals *see* St. Louis Cardinals
Carey, Max "Scoops" (Carnarius, Maximilian George) *11,* 200; call to Davis on August 21, 1926 159; as a coach 197–198; personal information 198–199, 206, 218, 221, 236–237, 297n252; as a player 13–14, 16, 18, 19, 23, 36, 50, 52, 70, 78, 79, 80, 83, 96, 99–100, 107, 109, 110, 111, 112, 114, 125, 150, 154–155, 157–160, 161, 163, 164, 166, 170, 193–194, 199–201, 210, 215, 220–222, 226, 250–251, 259, 260, 263n19, 276n6, 295n176, 295n179, 295n192, 299n40; role in the ABC Affair 9–10, 11, 137–145, 147–154, 156–157, 162, 163–166, 168–169, 189, 193–194, 219, 220–228, 261n3; tell-all article 10, 88–90, 93, 121, 128–129, 176–180, 182–188, 189, 196–197, 219, 261n1

Carey Day 158
Carlson, Hal 211, 263n18
Carnarius, Frank 236–237
Caroline County, Maryland 59
Carthage, Illinois 59
Catalina Island, California 35
Cava, Pete 197
Center Township, Arkansas 243
Central Normal College 235
Central Township, Saint Louis County, Missouri 241
Chamberlain, South Dakota 240
Chance, Frank 58
Chattanooga Lookouts 201, 203
Cherokee Outlet 60, 271n87
Cherokee Strip *see* Cherokee Outlet
Chicago, Illinois 42, 73, 103, 132, 247, 248
Chicago Cubs 15, 21, 22, 23, 25, 27, 28, 30, 33, 35, 36, 38, 42, 46, 48, 49, 50, 51, 53–54, 56–57, 66, 75, 77, 79, 104, 110, 113, 116, 117, 118, 119, 124, 132, 158, 161, 167, 168, 169, 171, 174, 176, 201, 209, 212, 282n173
Chicago White Sox 35, 92, 185, 203, 214
Chicago White Stockings 60
Chicks *see* Grand Rapids Chicks; Milwaukee Chicks
Cincinnati Reds 15, 17, 18, 21, 22, 23, 25, 26–31, 33, 38, 41, 43, 47, 55, 75, 77, 97, 104, 105, 106, 107, 109, 110, 111, 113, 115, 117–119, 120, 123, 124, 131, 135–136, 158, 161, 162, 165, 168–169, 171, 173, 174, 175, 176, 185, 190, 191–192, 203, 207–209, 210, 211–212, 226, 227, 228, 282n173
Clarke, Annette 140, 145
Clarke, Fred Clifford **61, 85, 196**; as an advisor 65–66, 67; as a manager 9, 15, 46, 56, 57–58, 61–64, 155–156, 220–221, 226, 262n8, 288n169; personal information 58–60, 64–65, 66–67, 70–71, 72–73, 90–91, 102, 123, 195–196, 198, 203, 206, 217–219, 220, 224, 246, 269n74, 270n82, 272n110, 273n155; as a player 9, 15, 46, 57, 58, 60–62, 64, 67, 226, 270n85, 270n86, 271n93, 271n94, 271n95; return to the Pirates 11–12, 57, 67–70, 73, 80–81, 84, 85–86, 87, 90, 93, 103, 106, 111, 115, 116, 118, 121, 124, 126, 131, 134–135, 160, 162, 164, 167, 172, 175, 198, 211, 213–215, 222, 224, 226, 283n186; role in the ABC Affair 9–10, 137–149, 151–152, 154–155, 157, 159–160, 163, 164, 182, 189, 193–195, 217–225, 226–229, 230–231; as a sportswriter 66; tell-all article 10–11, 88–90, 128–130, 178–181, 182–185, 186–187, 189, 219
Clarke, Joshua (Fred Clifford Clarke's brother) 102
Clarke, Joshua (Fred Clifford Clarke's paternal grandfather) 59
Clarke, Joshua (Fred Clifford Clarke's paternal great-great grandfather) 58
Clarke, Joshua (Fred Clifford Clarke's paternal great-great-great grandfather) 58

Clarke, Lucy 58, 59
Clarke, Sarah 59
Clarke, William Dickinson 58, 59, 246, 269n78, 270n82
Cleveland Indians 34, 35, 190, 214
Coast League *see* Pacific Coast League
Cobb, Ty 46, 57, 156, 200
Collins, Eddie 11, 99
Colonels *see* Louisville Colonels
Colonials *see* Kingston Colonials
Columbia *see* Columbia Comers
Columbia, Missouri 245
Columbia, South Carolina 121, 283n186
Columbia Comers 95, 99, 145, 160, 287n129
Columbia University 238
Columbus 115, 163
Columbus College 240
Commercial Clothing Store, Kingman, Arizona 204
Comorosky, Adam Anthony 161, 172, 204, 206, 237, 250–251, 259, 260, 295n189
Comorosky, Anthony 237
Comorosky, Helen 237
Concordia Seminary 237
Connery, Don 264n44
Connors, Jimmy 128
Constans, Leslie 154
Cook, John "Doc" 93, 99, 102
Cooper, Wilbur 13–14, 18, 46, 48, 49–50, 53, 56, 57, 75, 79, 170, 263n19, 267n12
Cooperstown, New York *see* National Baseball Hall of Fame
Corry, Pennsylvania 239
Corry High School 239
Coveleski, Stanley 82
Craft Club 86
Crafton, Pennsylvania 86
Crawford, Sam 156
Critz, Hughie 210
Cronin, Jeremiah 238
Cronin, Joseph Edward 51, 88, 93, 95, 96, 112, 135, 172, 201, 206, 238, 250–251, 258, 259, 295n189, 297n253
Crosetti, Frank 88
Crowder, Alvin 93, 95, 96, 101, 107–108, 135, 211
Cubs *see* Chicago Cubs
Culloton, Anna 238
Culloton, Bernard 238
Culloton, Bernard Aloysius "Bud" 51, 96, 118, 202, 204, 238, 252–253, 255–256, 258, 276n6, 295n192, 297n252
Cumberland Valley State Normal School 235
Cutler, John, Sr. 59
Cutler, Lucy *see* Clarke, Lucy
Cutshaw, George 263n18
Cuyler, George 238
Cuyler, Hazen Shirley "Kiki" 18, 50, 52, **52**, 70, 78, 79, 80, 83, 93, 96, 100, 101, 102, 109, 110, 111, 114, 119, 125, 137, 144, 145, 161, 172, 174, 179–180, 196, 201, 206, 210, 211, 218,

238–239, 250–251, 259, 260, 263n18, 263n19, 276n6, 295n189
Cuyler, Kiki *see* Cuyler, Hazen Shirley "Kiki"

Daley, Arthur 183
Daley, George 105
Dalhart, Texas 100
Daniel, Daniel M. 69, 81, 85, 86
Danville, Indiana 235
Davis, Ralph 14, 16, 36, 37, 39–40, 42, 43, 50, 57, 65, 68, 70, 80, 81, 87, 89, 90, 93, 100, 103, 106, 107, 112, 121, 122, 127, 128, 134–135, 137, 139, 142, 144, 149, 150, 153, 154, 156–157, 159, 164, 175, 178, 180, 181, 182, 186, 188, 193, 196, 198, 211, 228–230, 261n1, 273n144, 277n38, 288n177
Deadball Era 83
Deanefield, Kentucky 241
Dempsey, Jack 178
Denham, Mary Elizabeth 197
Derby City *see* Louisville, Kentucky
Des Moines, Iowa 59, 246, 270n82
Des Moines Colts 60
Des Moines Demons 80, 97
Des Moines Hawkeyes 60
Des Moines Mascots 270n85
Des Moines Stars 270n85
Detroit Tigers 15, 41, 155, 156, 191, 195, 203
DeValeria, Dennis 155
DeValeria, Jeanne Burke 155
Devine, Joe 88, 91, 293n140
Dickenson public schools 246
Dickey, Bill 190
Dickinson, Sarah Ann Elizabeth *see* Clarke, Sarah
DiMaggio, Joe 88, 190
Dodgers *see* Brooklyn Dodgers
Donahoe, Muriel 144, 246
Doyle, Charles F. "Chilly" 38, 50, 107, 132, 134, 166–167, 171, 189, 216, 287n158
Doyle, Chilly *see* Doyle, Charles F. "Chilly"
Dressen, Charlie 191
Dreyfuss, Barney *14, 117*; and the ABC Affair 146, 147, 152, 163–165, 178, 183, 185–186, 197, 225–227; with the Louisville Colonels 14–15, 60–61, 271n92; as the owner of the Pittsburgh Pirates 13–14, 15–16, 18, 19, 35, 38, 40, 42–43, 44–45, 46–50, 53–54, 55, 56–57, 62, 64, 65, 66–68, 69–70, 80–81, 84, 86, 88–90, 91, 93, 95, 108, 115–116, 128–130, 153–154, 175, 181–182, 187–190, 193–195, 196, 198, 211, 213–214, 224, 293n140; personal information 14
Dreyfuss, Florence 83, 115
Dreyfuss, Samuel "Sam" 69–70, 102–103, 115, 123, 134, 144, 145, 148, 151–152, 154, 160–161, 163, 164, 165, 185, 193, 198
Dugdale, Daniel E. 92

East Central State Normal School 245
East End Republican Club 67

East Farmingdale, New York 242
East Liberty American Legion, Pittsburgh, Pennsylvania 108
East Liberty neighborhood, Pittsburgh, Pennsylvania 67
Eastern League 118
Ebbets Field 141
Edwards, Foster 174
Elk County, Pennsylvania 187
Emporia, Kansas 236
Ens, Anton 246
Ens, Jewel 51, 73, 88, 92, 102, 106, 145, 198, 201, 203, 206, 246
Eugene, Oregon 236

fall classic *see* World Series
Farr, Thomas 145, 286–287n129
Federal League 15, 267n36
Finoli, David 18, 48, 261n3
Flagstaff, Arizona 239
Fletcher, Art 195
Flint, Michigan 100
Florida International League 202
Florida State Dog Racing Commission 199
The Flying Dutchman *see* Wagner, Honus
Fogarty, Jack 88
Fohl, Lee 195
Folsom Prison 205
Forbes Field 66, 70, 88, 112, 131, 148, 158, 159
Fordham University 238; School of Law 202
Forr, James 34, 94, 95, 205
Fort Wayne Daisies 199
Foster, John B. 103
Foxx, Jimmie 190
Framingham, Massachusetts 245
Francona, Terry 214
Fraser, Alexander 247
Fraser, Charles Carrolton "Chick" 68, 73, 86, 88, 92, 135, 145, 203, 206, 247–248, 293n140
Frisch, Frankie 27, 47
Frock, Sam 155
Frommer, Harvey 192
Fuller, Todd 264n42
Fullerton, Hugh 104

Galena, Kansas 239
Gallagher, Jack 80
Gallagher and Sheen 36
General Motors 204
Getty, Frank 196
Giants *see* New York Giants; San Francisco Giants
Gibson, George 13, 15–16, 35, 36–37, 38, 39, 40, 42, 43, 44, 50, 65, 170, 195, 226, 262n8
Glazner, Charles "Whitey" 49, 263n18
Glorious Generation 72
Gloucester, Massachusetts 240
Gloucester High School 240
Goldroad, Arizona 239
Gooch, George 239

Gooch, John Beverly 50, 96, 101, 109, 110, 111, 114, 116, 120, 125, 161, 172, 179–180, 201, 203, 204, 210, 239, 250–251, 258, 263n18, 265n81, 276n6, 295n189, 297n252
Gooch Lamp Company 204
Gooch Manufacturing Company 204
Goslin, Goose see Goslin, Leon "Goose"
Goslin, Leon "Goose" 82, 84
Gould, James M. 104–105
Grand Rapids Chicks 205
Grand Ridge, Illinois 243
Grand Ridge High School 243
Grantham, Anna 239
Grantham, B.F. 239
Grantham, George Farley 46, *48*, 49, 51, 56, 79, 84, 85, 96, 100, 107, 109, 110, 111, 114, 125, 140, 144, 161, 172, 179–180, 181, 203, 204, 206, 218, 228, 239, 250–251, 258, 267n19, 274n175, 276n6, 295n189
Grantham, Ruby 140
Grays see Williamsport Grays
Great Lakes, Illinois 245; Naval Station 245
Grimm, Charlie 14, 17, 18, *21*, 35–37, 41, 46, 47–48, 49, 50, 53, 56–57, 65, 75, 79, 166, 263n19, 264n44, 266n100
Groh, Heinie 47
Grossman, James 207, 231
Grumman Aircraft Engineering Corporation, Bethpage, New York 205
Gull River, Minnesota 236

Haas, George "Mule" 88, 92, 93, 274n177
Haller, Frank 293n140
Hamilton, Earl 263n18
Hancock, New York 242
Hanlon, Ned 58
Hanna, W.B. 67, 82
Harder, Mel 214
Harrah, Toby 34
Harrah, Oklahoma 245
Harris, Bucky see Harris, Stanley "Bucky"
Harris, Joe 82
Harris, Stanley "Bucky" 82, 83, 84
Harrisville, Michigan 238
Hartford Bees 203
Harvard University 202
Hawkeyes see Des Moines Hawkeyes
Henderson, Libby 197, 235, 294n150
Hendricks, Jack 47
Hershman, Oliver S. 154
Heydler, John A. 55, 81, 108, 112, 151–153, *153*, 158, 159, 160, 182, 184, 185, 186, 219, 287n155
Hill, Carmen Proctor 171–172, 173, 204, 206, 234, 239, 250–251, 255–256, 258, 291n37, 295n189
Hill, Henry 239
Hinchman, William White 73, 86, 88, 92, 195, 201, 203, 248, 293n140, 297n251
Hingham, Massachusetts 59
Historic Overview Committee 197, 294n158

Hock, Eddie 93, 95
Hoffman, John C. 183
Hollingsworth, Harry 175, 291n65
Holy Name Catholic Church 65
Horner Military School 241
Hornsby, Rogers 200, 215, 218
Hot Springs, Arkansas 103, 243, 244, 273n164; spring training 65–66
Houston Astros 213
Howe, Neil 71–72, 234, 273n161
Huggins, Miller 67
Hughes, Bill 267n26
Hynd, Noel 41

Indian Springs, Indiana 235
Indianapolis, Indiana 204
Indianapolis Indians 95, 103, 171
Indians see Cleveland Indians
Internal Revenue Service 204
International League 92, 99, 145; Hall of Fame 203
International News Service 104, 106
Iowa Sports Hall of Fame 195
Isaminger, James C. 16
Izzies see Wichita Izzies

Jackson, Travis 47
James, Bill 36
Jennings, Hugh 13, 41, 215, 298n19
Johnson, Byron "Ban" 84
Johnson, Lloyd 270–271n86
Johnson, Walter 82, 83, 85
Johnstown Johnnies 197
Jones School 244, 273n164
Judge, Joe 82

Kansas Baseball Hall of Fame 195
Kansas City, Missouri 87, 205, 244
Kansas City Blues 92, 95, 102, 116, 135, 267n34, 271n86, 276n6
Kansas Sports Hall of Fame 195
Kelly, George 47
Kieran, John 227–228
Killefer, Wade 195
Killefer, William J. 56–57, 195, 215
King, Joe 271n106, 272n113
Kingman, Arizona 204, 239
Kingston, New York 139, 140, 204, 238
Kingston, Pennsylvania 237
Kingston Colonials 140
Kissinger, George 93, 95
Knight, Dr. Harry 134, 172
Koehler, Michael D. 192
Korean War 197
Koupal, Louis Ladislaus 51, 99, 100, 118, 135, 160, 172, 204, 239–240, 252–253, 255–256, 258, 267n34, 276n6, 295n192, 297n251
Koupal, Matthias 240
Kremer, Nicholas 240
Kremer, Ray see Kremer, Remy Peter "Ray"
Kremer, Remy Peter "Ray" 50, 52, 70, 78–79,

83, 84, 85, 88, 96, 103, 112, 113, 114–115, 119, 120, 125, 161, 170, 171–172, 173, 174, 203, 204, 210–211, *210*, 215, 228, 240, 250–251, 255–256, 258, 263n18, 263n19, 276n6, 295n189, 297n251
Ku Klux Klan 65, 272n110
Kunz, Earl 267n26

Lackawanna County, Pennsylvania 205
Land, Grover 51, 267n36
Landis, Kenesaw Mountain 67, 112, 150–151, 153, 160, 164
Lane, F.C. 38, 39, 41, 47
Langford, Walter M. 91
La Russa, Tony 214
Lassies *see* Muskegon Lassies
Lazzeri, Tony 92
Lebanon, Oregon 236
Leever, Sam 155
Leifield, Lefty 155, 288n169
Lewis, H. Perry 62–64
Lewis, Walter J. 55, 269n64
Lexington, Tennessee 95
Lieb, Frederick G. 36, 46, 49, 104, 153–154, 261n3
Lindsay Township, California 243
Little Pirate Ranch 10, 59, 64–65, 93, 102, 221
Little Rock, Arkansas 99, 103
Locke, William 154
Lockheed Corporation 205
Long, James J. 137, 143, 158, 161, 166, 181–182, 286n110
Los Angeles, California 66, 95, 100, 242, 243
Los Angeles Angels 197
Los Angeles Sports Center 205
Lost Generation 72, 73
Louisville, Kentucky 60, 103
Louisville Colonels (American Association) 92, 103
Louisville Colonels (National League) 14, 57, 60, 61, 62, 95, 226
Louisville directors 271n92

Maass, A.A. 67
Macht, Norman 261n3
Mack, Connie 56, 92
Mack, Earle 215
Maddon, Joe 214
Maddox, Nick 155, 288n169
Madison, Wisconsin 245
Madison County, Iowa 59
Mahaffey, Buice 240
Mahaffey, Lee Roy 145, 160, 172, 201, 204, 240, 252–253, 255–256, 258, 295n189, 296n215, 297n251
Mahaffey, Roy *see* Mahaffey, Lee Roy
Major League All-Star Game 190, 200
Mamaux, Al 195
Manhattanites *see* New York Giants
Maranville, Rabbit *see* Maranville, Walter James Vincent "Rabbit"
Maranville, Walter James Vincent "Rabbit" 13,
14, 16, 18, 34–37, *34*, 39–40, 41–42, 46, 47, 49, 50, 51, 53, 56–57, 75, 79, 262n1, 263n19, 264n44, 264n48
Marberry, Frederick "Firpo" 82
Martin, Billy 88, 214
Martinez, Dave 214
Maryland Correctional Institution 204
Mascots *see* Des Moines Mascots
Mathewson, Christy 214
Mays, Carl 47
McCarey, Caleb "Socko" 88
McCarthy, Joe 116–117
McCloskey, John 95
McDonald, Romauld "Romey" 93–94
McGraw, Bob 116
McGraw, John 27, 31, 35, 39, 41, 43, 44, 46, 58, 67, 73, 75, 80, 81, 84, 85, 86, 104, 114, 120, 183, 209, 214–215, 265n85, 266n121, 298n19
McHugh, Roy 199
McInnis, John Phalen "Stuffy" 55–56, 57, 79, 84–85, 97, 99, 101, 107, 109, 110, 111, 138, 161, 166, 172, 175, 176, 181–182, *181*, 202, 210, 240, 250–251, 258, 276n6, 276n24, 295n192, 297n251
McInnis, Stephen 240
McInnis, Stuffy *see* McInnis, John Phalen "Stuffy"
McInnis & Associates 229
McKechnie, Archibald 72, 246
McKechnie, Deacon *see* McKechnie, William Boyd
McKechnie, Wilkinsburg Will *see* McKechnie, William Boyd
McKechnie, William Boyd *85*, *188*; as coach 214; as manager 11, 16, 35, 38, 40, 42–43, 50, 51, 52, 53, 54, 56–57, 66–67, 68, 69–70, 81, 84–85, 86, 87, 93, 94, 102–103, 105–106, 109, 110–111, 112, 114, 115, 116, 121, 123, 124–125, 126, 128, 131, 132–133, 134, 135, 145, 160, 161, 162, 165, 167, 172, 174, 190–192, 195, 213, 216, 222, 223, 226, 284n27; personal information 72–73, 192, 203, 206, 223, 246; as a player 195, 222, 299n40; role in ABC Affair 9–10, 136, 137, 139–140, 141, 142–143, 145–149, 151–152, 154, 157, 163, 164, 193, 194, 196, 221, 222–225, 226, 227, 228, 261n1; tell-all article 11, 88–90, 121, 177–180, 182–185, 186–190
McKennan, Art 34, 220
McNamara, Tom 293n140
McWeeny, Doug 116
Meadows, Henry Lee "Specs" 49, 50, 52, 78–79, 80, 97, 112, 113, 114–115, 118, 119, 161, 171–172, 173, 179–180, 203, 204, 210, 241, 250–251, 255–256, 258, 263n18, 263n19, 273n163, 276n6, 291n37, 295n189, 297n232, 297n251, 298n29
Meadows, John 241
Meadows, Lee *see* Meadows, Henry Lee "Specs"
Memphis Chickasaws 203
Meusel, Emil "Irish" 137

Miami Sun Sox 202
Midwest City High School 248
Milholland, Harry C. 154
Miller, Clarence W. 270n82
Miller, Stuart 213–214
Mills, Brad 213
Milwaukee, Wisconsin 60
Milwaukee Braves 202
Milwaukee Brewers 60
Milwaukee Chicks 199
Mission High School 238
Missionary Generation 72, 73
Mississippi Valley League 286n129
Missouri General Assembly 197
Mokan, Johnny 36
Molesworth, Carlton 195, 293n140
Monitor *see* Daley, George
Montgomery, Carol McKechnie 73
Moore, Eddie *see* Moore, Graham Edward
Moore, Graham Edward 42, 50, 52, 78, 79, 83, 84, 97, 101, *102*, 107, 109, 110, 111–112, 113, 114, 116, 119, 121, 125, 126–130, *130*, 131, 132, 134–135, 144, 177, 178, 203, 210, 215, 216, 218, 234, 241, 250–251, 258, 259, 276n6, 284n27, 295n192, 297n252
Moose Temple 109
Moran, Pat 43
Morris, Annie Elise 73
Morrison, Arreatus 241
Morrison, John Dewey "Jughandle" 14, *17*, 18, 36, 48, 50, 52, 70, 78–79, 94, 97, 103–104, 106, 112, 115, 119, 120, 126, 132–133, *133*, 134–135, 143, 160, 161, 172, 174, 215, 218, 241, 250–251, 255–256, 258, 264n48, 276n6, 295n189, 297n251, 298n27
Morrison, Phil 93, 94, 95, 101, 133, 216, 264n48, 277n33
Motor City *see* Detroit, Michigan
Mount Moriah, Missouri 197, 235
Mount Moriah High School 235
Mount Union College *see* University of Mount Union
Mueller, Charles 241
Mueller, Walter John Edward 160, 164, 172, 202, 204, 241–242, 250–251, 259, 260, 295n192, 297n252
Murdock, Eugene Converse 42, 101, 128, 129–130, 206, 216, 234
Murphy, Charles, Sr. 242
Murphy, Eddie *see* Murphy, John Edward
Murphy, John Edward 145, 161, 166, 173, 202, 204, 242, 250–251, 259, 260, 295n192, 297n251
Muskegon Lassies 197

Nashville, Tennessee 204, 239
National Baseball Congress 195
National Baseball Hall of Fame 57, 59, 61, 192, 195, 197, 199–200, 201, 203, 226, 234, 237, 295n179
National League 9, 11, 14–15, 17, 18, 19, 21, 22, 23, 25, 28, 30, 31, 33, 37, 38, 39, 41, 44, 46, 47, 48, 49, 52, 55, 60, 62, 67, 75, 77, 78–79, 80, 87, 92, 93, 99, 103, 104, 106, 108, 110, 112, 113, 119, 124, 127, 150, 151, 153, 154, 158, 161, 162, 165, 166, 168, 173, 175, 176, 178, 179, 188, 190, 191, 199, 200, 201, 207, 209, 210–211, 213, 222, 228–229, 252–253, 255–256, 260, 266n121, 288n169, 295n179; standings 110, 113, 119, 124, 161, 176
National League Award 80, 210, 211
Neale, Earl "Greasy" 195
Nebraska State League 270n86
New England League 202
New Haven, Connecticut 145, 149
New Haven Profs 112, 118, 135, 145, 160
New York, New York 16, 35, 40, 42, 49, 66, 69, 103, 116, 117, 121, 140, 150, 151, 172, 200, 238
New York Giants 11, 15, 16–17, 19, 21, 22, 23–33, 37, 40, 41–42, 43, 44, 47, 53, 55, 66, 70, 73, 75, 76, 77, 81, 82, 83, 103–105, 110, 112, 113, 114, 115, 119, 120, 121, 124, 126, 158, 161, 170–171, 173–174, 176, 201, 209, 212, 214, 266n121, 298n19
New York-Pennsylvania League 160
New York State Department of Taxation and Finance 204
New York State School of Agriculture on Long Island 242
New York Yankees 47, 60, 66, 67, 88, 92, 162, 201, 203, 228
Newark, New Jersey 145
newspaper circulation statistics 229, 285n61
Nichols, Chester Raymond, Sr. 118, 120, 126, 135, 160, 205, 206, 242, 252–253, 255–256, 258, 295n189, 297n253
Nichols, Joseph 242
Nicholson, Fred 13
Niehaus, Al 46, 49, 50–51, 54, 55, 56, 79, 93, 97
NL *see* National League
Norfolk, Virginia 244
Norfolk County, England 59
Northern Arizona Normal School 239
Northwestern League (Midwest) 60
Northwestern League (Northwest) 92
Norwich, England 59
Norwich University 202

Oakland, California 240
Oakland Oaks 94, 101
O'Conner, L.J. 106
October classic *see* World Series
O'Farrell, Bob *210*
Oklahoma City, Oklahoma 248
Oklahoma City Indians 95, 98, 267n34, 276n6
Oldham, John Cyrus "Red" 79–80, 84, 88, 97, 101, 135, 202, 205, 242, 250–251, 255–256, 258, 274n177, 295n192, 297n251
Oldham, Lewis 242
Oldham, Red *see* Oldham, John Cyrus "Red"
Onslow, Eddie 234, 247
Onslow, Jack *see* Onslow, John James

Onslow, James 73, 247
Onslow, John James 51, 73, 88, 92, 106, 112, 120, 139–140, 145, 182–184, 203, 223, 247, 261n1, 274n170, 274n171, 297n251
Orioles *see* Baltimore Orioles
Owensboro, Kentucky 132, 133, 241
Oxford, North Carolina 241

Pacific Coast League 67, 91, 92, 94, 197
Parker, Clifton Blue 202
Parks Department of Allegheny County 205
Paso Robles, California 91, 243; spring training 54, 66, 91, 93, 95, 99, 100
Patesville, Kentucky 241
PCL *see* Pacific Coast League
Peckinpaugh, Roger 82, 83
Peerless Quartet 36
Peet, William 282–283n181
Pellville, Kentucky 241
Penn Avenue, Pittsburgh, Pennsylvania 109
Penn State University 15, 262n7
Peoria Tractors 203
Pepper, George Wharton 108
Phelon, W.A. 38, 40, 41, 53
Phelps, Frank 270n82
Philadelphia, Pennsylvania 16, 86, 117, 145, 182, 204, 248
Philadelphia Athletics 11, 82, 86, 92, 99, 215, 262n5
Philadelphia Phillies 15, 21, 22, 25, 27, 28, 30, 33, 36, 49, 67, 77, 104, 110, 113, 115, 119, 124, 135, 142, 154, 158, 161, 173, 176, 202, 203, 209, 212
Phillies *see* Philadelphia Phillies
Phillippe, Deacon 155
Pierson, Bill 93, 95
Pinchot, Gifford 108
Pirate Boosters' Club 162
Pittsburgh Athletic Company 90, 194
Pittsburgh Umpires' Association 188, 226
Plank, Eddie 11, 99
Polo Grounds 21, 41, 44, 66, 75, 113, 115
Ponder, Elmer 38
Pope, Edwin 273n155
Prince, Bob 227
Proctor, David 34, 94, 95
Profs *see* New Haven Profs
Prussia 237
Purviance, Nancy 247, 274n170

Queen Anne's County, Maryland 59

Ranier, Bill 18, 48, 261n3
Rash, Dr. O.W. 133
Rawlings, John William 49, 50, 97, 120, 125, 128, 161, 179–180, 182, 202, 205, 242, 250–251, 258, 263n18, 274n175, 276n6, 295n192, 297n252
Rawlings, William 242
Red Sox *see* Boston Red Sox
Redbirds *see* St. Louis Cardinals

Redland Field 118
Reds *see* Cincinnati Reds
Reese, John D. "Bonesetter" 113, 120, 161, 167
Reiser, Pete 214
Retroactive Award 200–201
Rhyne, Ferol 140, 145
Rhyne, Harold J. "Hal" 91–92, 93, 95, 97, 101, 109, *109*, 110, 111–112, 114, 119, 120, 125, 126, 128, 136, 140, 145, 161, 165, 172, 174, 179–180, 203, 205, 215, 243, 250–251, 258, 259, 295n189, 297n252
Rhyne, Henry 243
Rice, Edgar "Sam" 82, 83, 84
Richmond Colts 51
Rickey, Branch 70
Rigler, Charles "Cy" 55
Rising Sun, Maryland 242
Ritchey, Claude 64
Ritter, Lawrence S. 37
Robertson, Davis ("Dave"; "Davey") 38, 43
Robins *see* Brooklyn Robins
Robinson, Wilbert 19, 52–53, 198, 209
Rochester, New York 134
Rochester Tribe 145, 173
Rockford Peaches 205
Rohwer, Claude 267n26
Rowswell, A.K. "Rosey" 187
Royalton, Minnesota 239
Ruel, Muddy 82
Ruether, Walter "Dutch" 82, 84

Sacred Heart High School 238
Saffordville, Kansas 236
St. Catherine Hotel, Catalina Island, California 35
St. Ignatius College *see* University of San Francisco
St. Louis, Missouri 36, 95, 99, 104, 105, 106, 120, 160, 164, 237, 246
St. Louis Browns 35
St. Louis Cardinals 10, 15, 21–22, 23, 25, 28, 30, 33, 47, 53, 75, 77, 95, 103, 104–106, 107, 109, 110, 113, 117–119, 124, 158, 161–162, 165, 168–169, 171, 173, 174, 175, 176, 190, 201, 203, 207–209, 210, 211–212, 215, 218, 226, 228, 281–282n165, 282n173
St. Mary's Hospital 65
Salem Witches 202
Sallies *see* Springfield Sallies
San Francisco, California 238, 240
San Francisco Giants 202
San Francisco Seals 38, 91, 92
San Jose, California 243
San Jose High School 243
Sandin, Paul 197
Savannah Modocs 60
Schmidt, Walter 13–14, 16, 18, 37, 38–39, *39*, 43, 50, 51, 53, 54, 56, 262n4, 263n19, 265n80, 265n81
Scio College 247
Scio School 247, 274n170

Scottdale, Pennsylvania 247
Scranton, North Carolina 244
Scripps-Howard Newspapers 154
Seals *see* San Francisco Seals
Seattle Giants 92
Seattle Indians 197
Segura, Pancho 128
Selee, Frank 58
Senators *see* Washington Senators
Sheehan, Jeremiah 243
Sheehan, Thomas Clancy 55–56, 57, 97, 107, 116, 202, 206, 216, 234, 243, 250–251, 255–256, 258, 276n6, 281–282n165, 295n192, 297n253
Sheridan, Arkansas 243
Shippensburg, Pennsylvania 235
Sidney, New York 242
Silent Generation 72
Simon, Mike 262n8
Slater Dyer Works, Inc. 205
Smith, Bob 136
Smith, Chester L. "Chet" 47–48, 51–52, 136, 144, 158, 162, 189, 194, 287n158
Smith, Earl Sutton 50, 51, 55, **55**, 79, 80, 83, 88, 97, 109, 110, 111, 114, 121–122, 125, 135, 136–137, 161, 172, 180, 203, 211, 234, 243–244, 250–251, 258, 273n164, 276n6, 295n189, 297n251, 299n30
Smith, Frank 40
Smith, Jordan 243
Smith, Julia Belle (Bell) 243
Smith, Sean 47
Smyrna, Tennessee 239
Snyder, Frank 120–121
Society for American Baseball Research 230
Somerville, Massachusetts 245
Somerville High School 234, 245
Songer, Donald C. 51, 57, 98, 99, 112, 114, 125, 135, 136, 161, 167, 172, 205, 215, 228, 244, 250–251, 255–256, 258, 267n34, 276n6, 295n189, 297n243, 297n251
Songer, Frank 244
Songer, Pearl 244
South Atlantic League 95, 145, 160
Southern Association 92, 107, 201
Southworth, Billy 13
Spatz, Lyle 37
Spencer, Roy Hampton 51, 98, 101, 109, 110, 111, 244, 250–251, 258, 276n6, 295n189, 297n252
Spencer, William 244
Spoehr, Luther W. 197, 237
The Sporting News' Major League All-Star Team 80, 211
Sportsman's Park 105, 118
spring training 35, 54, 67, 199; Pittsburgh Pirates 54, 65–66, 91, 93–95, 99–100, 102–103, 105, 107, 121, 127, 135, 145, 160, 195, 202, 216, 264n48, 277n38, 277n39; *see also* Hot Springs, Arkansas; Paso Robles, California
Springfield Midgets 197

Springfield Sallies 197
Sprowston, England 59
Stallings, George 58
Stars *see* Des Moines Stars
Steinberg, Steve 37
Stengel, Casey 195
Stinson, Mitchell Conrad 87, 117
Strauss, William 71–72, 234, 273n161
Strunk, Amos 11, 99
Studio Wrestling 205
Sturgeon Point, Michigan 238
Suhr, Gus 88
Sumner, Benjamin Barrett 270n86
Sun Sox *see* Miami Sun Sox
Sweet Home, Oregon 236
Swoyersville, Pennsylvania 204, 237

TAB *see* total advanced bases
Tabor, South Dakota 240
Talbot County, Maryland 59
Tarentum, Pennsylvania 112
Tauscher, Walter 161
Teapot Dome scandal 178
Tener, John K. 108
Tenney, Fred 62
Terre Haute, Indiana 103, 168, 172, 236
Thompson, Lafayette Fresco "Tommy" 88, 92, 93, 274n177
Tierney, James "Cotton" 23, 35–36, 49, 263n18, 264n48
Tigers *see* Detroit Tigers
Tipton, Indiana 235
Toledo Mud Hens 170
Torre, Joe 214
total advanced bases 200
training camp *see* spring training
Traynor, Arthur 93–95, 101
Traynor, Harold Joseph "Pie" 18, 34, 36, 46–48, 50, 52, 70, 78, **78**, 79, 80, 83, 88, 94, 98, 101, 107, 109, 110, 111, 114, 116, 119, 125, 148, 158, 161, 162, 172, 179–180, 201–202, 203, 205, **205**, 211, 221, 228, 234, 245, 250–251, 259, 263n18, 263n19, 276n6, 295n189, 297n252
Traynor, James 245
Traynor, Pie *see* Traynor, Harold Joseph "Pie"
Tribe *see* Rochester Tribe
Tyson, Al 112

United Services Organizations Inc. 205
United States Military Academy 239
United States Post Office Department 204
University of Illinois 245
University of Kansas 67
University of Missouri 245
University of Mount Union 247
University of Oregon 197, 219, 236
University of San Francisco 240
University of Southern California School of Law 242
University of Wisconsin 245

Upper Providence Township, Pennsylvania 242
Urbana-Champaign, Illinois 245

Vance, Dazzy 94
Vaughan, Irving 42, 103–104
Veach, Bobby 84
Veeck, William L., Jr. 35, 214
Veeck, William L., Sr. 35, 56–57, 112, 282n173
Veterans Committee 199, 294n158
Vidmer, Richards 104
Villanova, Pennsylvania 242
Villanova University 242
Virginia League 51
Volstead Act 40
Voyles, Phil 93, 95, 160–161

Waddell, Rube 64, 271n106
Wagner, Honus 15, 42–43, 64, 65, 108, 155–156
Waldo, Ronald 56–57, 81
Wall Street, New York, New York 105
Wallace, Bobby 191
Wallace University School 239
Walnut, Kansas 244
Walsh, Davis J. 104
Waner, Lloyd 88, 145
Waner, Ora 245
Waner, Paul Glee 88, 91–92, *91*, 93, 95, 98, 102, 109, 111, 114, 125, 145, 161, 170–171, 172, 173–174, 179–180, 201–202, 210, 211, 228, 234, 245, 250–251, 259, 260, 295n189, 297n251
Washington Senators 82–86, 108, 123, 127, 201, 203, 213
Waterloo, Oregon 236
Waterloo White Hawks 203
Watters, Sam *see* Watters, S.E. "Sam"
Watters, S.E. "Sam" 88, 116, 139–141, 145, 151, 189
Welsh, Regis M. 105–106, 107, 121, 130, 137, 138, 149, 182–183, 186, 287n158
Wentz, Lewis 196
Wertz, Johnny 136
West Penn Hospital, Pittsburgh, Pennsylvania 167
West Point, New York 239
Western Association 60, 270–271n86
Western League 95, 97, 98, 135, 145, 267n34, 270n86
Weyhing, Gus 60
Wheat, Zach 41
White Mills, Pennsylvania 242
White Sox *see* Chicago White Sox
White Stockings *see* Chicago White Stockings
Whitted, George "Possum" 35–36, 38, 40, 43, 49, 263n18
Whitted, Possum *see* Whitted, George "Possum"
Wichita, Kansas 93, 102, 204, 236
Wichita High School 236
Wichita Izzies 135, 145
WIIC-TV 205

Wilde, Oscar 177–178
Wilkinsburg, Pennsylvania 42, 73, 188, 190, 192, 246
Wilkinsburg High School 73, 246
William Penn Hotel, Pittsburgh, Pennsylvania 151
Williams, Ted 190
Williamsport Grays 160–161
Willis, Vic 155–156, 288n169, 288n173
Winfield, Kansas 10, 58, 59, 65, 93, 195, 221, 246
Winfield Country Club 65
Winfield Rotary Club 65
Winterset, Iowa 59, 246
witches *see* Salem witches
Wolff, Miles 270–271n86
Wollen, L.H. 94–95, 100, 107, 113, 119, 121–122, 125, 128, 131, 132, 134, 136, 144, 154–157, 159, 168, 174, 188, 193–194, 196, 198, 211, 228, 229, 230
Wollen, Lou *see* Wollen, L.H.
Woonsocket, Rhode Island 242
Works Progress Administration (Work Projects Administration) 204
World Series 9, 11, 15, 17, 27, 41, 44, 56, 58, 62, 64, 66, 80, 82–86, 87–92, 99, 106, 108, 109–110, 112, 114, 127, 128, 135, 139, 145, 149, 150, 155–156, 162, 177, 178, 190, 191, 192, 200, 201, 203, 213, 214, 218, 221, 226, 228–229, 288n173, 291n65
World War I 116
World War II 197, 205
Wright, Alberta 174
Wright, Forest (Forrest) Glenn 34, 36, 37, 40, 46–47, 48, 49, 50, 52, 70, 78, 79, 80, 83, 84, 91, 93, 98, 107, 109, 110, 111, 114, 119, 121–122, 125, 126, 136, 143–144, 161, 165–167, *166*, 169–170, 172, 174, 179–180, 187, 203, 206, 215, 218, 228, 234, 245, 250–251, 259, 263n18, 263n19, 267n19, 276n6, 295n189, 296n205, 297n253
Wright, Glenn *see* Wright, Forest (Forrest) Glenn
Wright, Robert 174, 245
Wrigley Field 131
Wyoming Seminary Prep School 237

Yankees *see* New York Yankees
Yde, Emil Ogden 50, 52, 57, 79, 98, 104, 121–122, 125, 126–127, *127*, 128, 132, 133–134, 135, 161, 172, 173, 175, 179–180, 203, 206, 218, 221, 228, 245, 250–251, 255–256, 258, 263n18, 276n6, 295n189, 297n251
Yde, Peter 245
YellowHorse, Mose 35, 36–37, 49, 264n42, 267n26
Youngstown, Ohio 113, 120, 167
Youngstown General Tires 160

Zimmer, Don 214
Zinn, Jimmy 37, 42, 43, 263n18
Zion, Maryland 242

www.ingramcontent.com/pod-product-compliance
Ingram Content Group UK Ltd.
Pitfield, Milton Keynes, MK11 3LW, UK
UKHW041923140426
5217IPUK00014B/289